Contributions to Economics

The series *Contributions to Economics* provides an outlet for innovative research in all areas of economics. Books published in the series are primarily monographs and multiple author works that present new research results on a clearly defined topic, but contributed volumes and conference proceedings are also considered. All books are published in print and ebook and disseminated and promoted globally. The series and the volumes published in it are indexed by Scopus and ISI (selected volumes).

Roberto Cellini • Tiziana Cuccia •
Francesco Drago • Marco Romano •
Gianpiero Torrisi
Editors

Cultural, Social, and Political Participation in the Internet Era

Measuring and Fostering Engagement, Lawfulness and Inclusion in the Networked Society

Springer

Editors
Roberto Cellini
Department of Economics and Business
University of Catania
Catania, Italy

Francesco Drago
European University Institute
Florence, Italy

Gianpiero Torrisi
Department of Economics and Business
University of Catania
Catania, Italy

Tiziana Cuccia
Department of Economics and Business
University of Catania
Catania, Italy

Marco Romano
Department of Economics and Business
University of Catania
Catania, Italy

ISSN 1431-1933 ISSN 2197-7178 (electronic)
Contributions to Economics
ISBN 978-3-032-33071-0 ISBN 978-3-032-33072-7 (eBook)
https://doi.org/10.1007/978-3-032-33072-7

This work was supported by NextGenerationEU (E63C22002120006).

This Springer imprint is published by the registered company Springer Nature Switzerland AG
The registered company address is: Gewerbestrasse 11, 6330 Cham, Switzerland

Preface

This volume collects a selection of research contributions developed within Spoke 8 "Social Sustainability", one of the thematic research strands of the GRInS (Growing Resilient, Inclusive and Sustainable) project, a large interdisciplinary initiative funded by the European Union under the Italian National Recovery and Resilience Plan (PNRR). GRInS represents a comprehensive effort to build an integrated analytical framework and a harmonised data infrastructure aimed at understanding the determinants, constraints, and territorial patterns of sustainable growth in Italy, in alignment with the broader objectives of European cohesion and resilience policies.

The overarching goal of the GRInS project was the creation of an integrated platform of harmonised data, designed to support the analysis of sustainable growth dynamics across Italian territories. This platform—labelled AMELIA—was conceived both as a repository of statistical information and as an analytical tool capable of linking economic, social, institutional, cultural, and environmental dimensions of development. By doing so, GRInS seeks to provide public institutions, private stakeholders, and civil society actors with a robust knowledge base to analyse past trajectories, identify territorial disparities and best practices, and design future-oriented strategies and policies fostering balanced and inclusive development.

The research activities of GRInS were organised into eight thematic Spokes, each addressing a specific dimension of sustainable growth. Within this architecture, Spoke 8 "Social Sustainability" focused on the social foundations of development, exploring issues such as cohesion, inclusion, and participation. These concepts are widely invoked in both academic and policy discourses, yet often lack shared definitions and standardised measurement tools. The contribution of Spoke 8 therefore lies in providing and analysing data, and in advancing conceptual clarity, empirical measurement, and policy-relevant evidence on the social dimensions of sustainability.

Research within Spoke 8 was articulated into four interrelated Work-packages. The first Work-package addressed the definition and measurement of social cohesion, social inclusion, and social sustainability, proposing analytical frameworks and indicators capable of capturing their multidimensional and territorial nature. The second Work-package focused on cultural, social, and political participation, with particular attention to participation dynamics in the digital era and their implications for inequality, opportunities, and democratic engagement. The third Work-package examined lawfulness and the fight against organised crime, analysing how legality mechanisms, institutional integrity, and crime-prevention policies affect firms, local governments, and social cohesion. The fourth Work-package concentrated on skilling and reskilling strategies, with specific attention to entrepreneurial and micro-entrepreneurial education as instruments for social inclusion, particularly for vulnerable individuals and groups.

Many outputs of the GRInS project, along with the AMELIA platform, are available on the official website www.grins.it in the form of deliverables with a predominantly operational and policy-oriented focus. The present volume, by contrast, collects contributions with a more explicitly scientific orientation, while maintaining constant attention to their practical and policy implications. The chapters included here were originally presented and discussed at a workshop held in Catania in September 2026, which hosted approximately 60 papers. From these, 21 contributions were selected for publication in this volume, with the aim of offering a representative overview of the main research lines, methods, and perspectives that characterised Spoke 8.

The volume is organised into three parts, corresponding to three core dimensions of social sustainability: participation, lawfulness, and entrepreneurship as a driver of inclusion.

Part I of this volume, "Social and Cultural Participation in the Digital Era", focuses on social and cultural participation, addressing its relevance for democratic life and examining how participation opportunities are shaped by socio-economic conditions, territorial contexts, and digital technologies.

Giuseppe Pignataro's chapter, "From Acts to Chances: Measuring Participation and Inequality of Opportunity", introduces a conceptual shift from participation as a set of observed behaviours to participation as a capability unequally distributed across individuals. The chapter proposes an Inclusive Participation Index, combined with an ex-ante opportunity perspective that allows participation gaps to be interpreted as inequality of opportunity. By explicitly addressing normative assumptions through transparent normalisation and weighting rules, the proposed framework enables meaningful comparisons across groups and contexts. Simulation results illustrate how digital participation may either mitigate or reinforce existing inequalities, depending on institutional and social conditions.

The measurement of multidimensional inequalities is further developed by Cinzia Di Nuzzo, Venera Tomaselli, and Gianpiero Torrisi in "Measuring Inequalities in Well-Being: A Three-Way Approach", with applications to Italy and the European Union. Using a three-way multidimensional Gini index, the chapter integrates social, cultural, digital, economic, and demographic indicators to analyse territorial disparities over time. The empirical applications document persistent regional inequalities in Italy, most notably the North–South divide, as well as centre–periphery dynamics across European regions. The results highlight the relevance of multidimensional approaches for monitoring social sustainability and informing regional policy.

Paola Bordandini and Luca Bortolotti contribute "A New Map of Social Capital in Italy: An Emerging Trade-Off between Prosperity and Civic Engagement?", which updates classic territorial analyses of social capital. Using provincial data for the period 2008–2022, the chapter documents significant transformations in Italy's civic landscape, including the weakening of traditionally "civic" regions and the emergence of new territorial patterns. The analysis reveals an inverted-U relationship between economic development and civic engagement, suggesting a potential tension between rising prosperity and the social foundations of collective action.

The relationship between participation, social capital, and organised civic action is further explored by Marialuisa Villani and Stella Volturo in "From Social Participation to the Civic Gift: The Geography of Blood Donation in Italy". Interpreting blood donation as a form of organised altruism and a "civic gift", the chapter highlights the role of nonprofit organisations and institutional infrastructures in sustaining trust, reciprocity, and social cohesion. Empirical evidence from national and regional data sources reveals marked territorial differences in donation patterns, reflecting uneven civic infrastructures and associational capacities.

Empirical evidence on cultural participation is provided by Roberto Cellini, Tiziana Cuccia, and Alessandro de Cristofaro in "Cultural Participation in Italy: A Preliminary Analysis of New Survey Evidence". Using data from a new 2025 survey of 10,000 adults, the chapter analyses participation across six cultural activities and a composite indicator of out-of-home participation. Education emerges as the strongest predictor of cultural participation, followed by income, employment status, age, and city size. The chapter also examines post-pandemic dynamics and the complex relationship between digital engagement and in-person participation.

The role of age and digitalisation is further addressed by Flavia Coda Moscarola, Simone Seregni, and Roberto Zanola in "Cultural Engagement of Older Adults in the Digital Age: Barriers and Opportunities". Focusing on individuals aged 60 and above, the study documents low and uneven participation in cultural activities, especially those requiring physical attendance. While digital technologies may expand access, online participation largely complements rather than substitutes traditional forms and remains concentrated among individuals with higher education and digital skills. As a result, digitalisation risks reinforcing existing inequalities in cultural access.

In their contribution, Felice Russo, Debora Assisi, and Abbey Walusimbi investigate educational poverty among students in the Italian school system using multidimensional poverty measures. They analyse INVALSI data on achievements in Italian, Mathematics, and English to assess the incidence, breadth, severity, and inequality of educational deprivation. The study also explores differences across regions, gender, migration background, and socio-economic status, highlighting relevant policy implications.

The first part also includes Giuliana Amore's chapter, "Data Cooperatives and Digital Neomutualism", which examines the legal and institutional framework of data cooperatives under the European Data Governance Act. Situating data cooperatives at the intersection of third-sector regulation, data protection, and digital platform governance, the chapter highlights both the innovative potential and regulatory gaps of this emerging model. Data cooperatives are interpreted as a possible institutional vehicle for inclusive and participatory data governance in the digital economy.

Part II, "Lawfulness, Firms' Performance and Social Cohesion", addresses lawfulness and institutional integrity as key components of social sustainability, focusing on firms, local governments, and the management of assets affected by organised crime.

Angela Maria Greco, Mariastella Messina, and Davide Rizzotti analyse institutional integrity mechanisms in "Does Fraud Risk Affect Legality Ratings? Evidence from Italian Listed Firms". Focusing on the Italian legality rating introduced under Law No. 190/2012, the authors examine whether this tool captures risks of financial reporting manipulation. The results suggest that legality ratings are weakly related to fraud risk, indicating that they primarily reflect formal compliance rather than substantive financial integrity. The chapter highlights the need to enhance legality frameworks with quantitative indicators capable of capturing concrete misconduct.

The link between institutional vulnerability and organised crime is explored by Eleonora Cardillo, Angela Maria Greco, and Mariastella Messina in "The Effects of Financial and Non-Financial Indicators on Mafia-Related Dissolution". Analysing Italian municipalities with more than 15,000 inhabitants, the study identifies structural financial weaknesses, staff composition, and socio-economic conditions as significant determinants of mafia-related dissolution. The findings contribute to the understanding of preventive policies aimed at strengthening institutional resilience and protecting democratic governance.

Firm-level responses to organised crime infiltration are examined by Giovanni Scirè and Enzo Bivona in "Exploring the Impact of Soft Preventive Judicial Measures on Business Resilience and Performance". Using a multi-case analysis of firms subject to judicial administration or control, the chapter evaluates the effects of "soft" preventive measures introduced by the Italian Anti-Mafia Code. The results indicate that these measures generally preserve operational continuity and production levels, although profitability and liquidity remain fragile and post-intervention vulnerabilities persist. The chapter highlights the importance of complementary managerial and institutional support to ensure long-term resilience.

The social reuse of assets confiscated from organised crime is analysed by Pierpaolo Parrotta, Marco Stimolo, Alessandro Stringhi, Marianna Marino, and Giovanni Immordino in "From Seizure to Social Value". Drawing on survey evidence from social cooperatives, the chapter documents challenges related to asset conditions, financial sustainability, and administrative complexity. At the same time, it highlights adaptive strategies based on partnerships, community engagement, and revenue diversification. The analysis underscores the role of institutional coordination and financial support in enhancing the social value of confiscated assets.

Part III, "Entrepreneurship and Social Inclusion", focuses on entrepreneurship as a tool for social inclusion, addressing gender, youth, migrant entrepreneurship, and territorial development.

Veronica Scuotto, Theofilos Tzanidis, and Enrico di Taranto open this section with "Entrepreneurial Education and Non-WEIRD Countries: Might AI Make a Difference?". The chapter proposes the AI-EENI framework for entrepreneurial education in non-WEIRD contexts, combining AI-enabled forecasting with secondary data sources to design context-sensitive educational interventions. The framework demonstrates the potential of AI to support inclusive and scalable entrepreneurial education in resource-constrained settings.

Gender and generational dimensions are analysed by Francesca Colella, Laura Falci, and Carola Continenza in "Sustainability, Gender and Generation". Drawing on Delphi evidence, the chapter frames young women's entrepreneurship as embedded in a complex ecosystem of structural, cultural, and institutional constraints. Empowerment, mentoring, and sustainability-oriented training emerge as key drivers of inclusive growth.

Emilio Chiodo, Carola Continenza, Maria Laura Fornaci, Maria Saide Liperi, and Rita Salvatore, in "Good Practices in Socialisation to Sustainable Entrepreneurship among Young Women", present a theoretical and methodological framework used to identify "good practices" for socialising young women into sustainable entrepreneurship. Referring to relational sociology and adopting the capability approach, the study defines good practices as situated learning opportunities able to activate transformative processes.

Corporate governance and gender equality are addressed by Simona Catuogno and Roberto Tizzano in "Gender Equality in Governance and Social Topics of Italian Sustainability Reports". Using content analysis of sustainability reports during the transition to the European Sustainability Reporting Standards, the chapter documents improvements in gender-related disclosure and comparability. However, evidence on the effective implementation of gender equality policies remains limited, highlighting ongoing challenges in integrating gender considerations into ESG practices.

Youth exclusion and the NEET phenomenon are analysed by Angelo Bonfanti, Rossella Canestrino, Vania Vigolo, Giovanna Bagnato, and Francesco Bonetti in "Entrepreneurship Education in Action", which focuses on the La Paranza cooperative in Naples. The case study highlights experiential learning, place-based approaches, and stakeholder networks as key drivers of inclusion and employability. Veronica De Crescenzo, Giorgio Mion, Pierpaolo Magliocca, and Irene Gottoli examine funding instruments in "Policies for Contrasting and Preventing the NEET Phenomenon", discussing both traditional grants and innovative tools such as Social Impact Bonds. The analysis highlights the complexity and long-term nature of preventive interventions.

Migrant entrepreneurship is analysed through complementary approaches. Mohamed Rida Kheit, Massimo Mucciardi, Andrea Nucita, and Mariachiara Fichera provide quantitative evidence from Sicily in "Foreign Entrepreneurship in the District of Municipalities of Catania and Messina", documenting business characteristics, financial constraints, and the role of family networks. Andrea Biagiotti, Alessandro Irrera Assanti, Giuliana Russo, and Tiziana Tarsia adopt a qualitative perspective in "Practices and Social Relations in Foreign Entrepreneurship", highlighting entrepreneurial trajectories, social embeddedness, and persistent barriers. Finally, Giulia Contu, Carla Massidda, Marco Ortu, and Silvio Tunis offer a national perspective in "Mapping Migrant Entrepreneurship and Integration in Italy", linking entrepreneurial intensity to social and occupational integration outcomes across provinces.

Taken together, the contributions collected in this volume provide a comprehensive and empirically grounded analysis of social sustainability. By integrating measurement, empirical evidence, legal analysis, and policy-oriented research, the volume reflects the interdisciplinary and applied approach that characterises the whole GRInS project. While not offering definitive solutions, the chapters contribute analytical tools, empirical insights, and evidence-based policy perspectives that can support more inclusive, cohesive, and sustainable development trajectories.

Catania, Italy — Roberto Cellini
Catania, Italy — Tiziana Cuccia
Florence, Italy — Francesco Drago
Catania, Italy — Marco Romano
Catania, Italy — Gianpiero Torrisi

Contents

Contributors

Giuliana Amore Department of Economics and Business, University of Catania, Catania, Italy

Debora Assisi Department of Economic Sciences, University of Salento, Lecce, Italy

Giovanna Bagnato Department of Management, University of Verona, Verona, Italy

Andrea Biagiotti Department of Cognitive, Psychological and Educational Sciences and Cultural Studies, University of Messina, Messina, Italy

Enzo Bivona Department of Political Science and International Relations, University of Palermo, Palermo, Italy

Francesco Bonetti Department of Business and Quantitative Studies, Parthenope University of Naples, Naples, Italy

Angelo Bonfanti Department of Management, University of Verona, Verona, Italy

Paola Bordandini Department of Political and Social Sciences, University of Bologna, Bologna, Italy

Luca Bortolotti Department of Human and Social Sciences, E-Campus University, Rome, Italy

Rossella Canestrino Department of Business and Quantitative Studies, Parthenope University of Naples, Naples, Italy

Eleonora Cardillo Department of Economics and Business, University of Catania, Catania, Italy

Simona Catuogno Department of Economics and Statistics, University of Naples Federico II, Naples, Italy

Roberto Cellini Department of Economics and Business, University of Catania, Catania, Italy

Emilio Chiodo Department of Bioscience and Technology for Food, Agriculture and Environment, University of Teramo, Teramo, Italy

Francesca Colella Department of Humanities, University of L'Aquila, L'Aquila, Italy

Carola Continenza Department of Education Sciences, Roma Tre University, Rome, Italy

Giulia Contu Department of Economics and Business Administration, University of Cagliari, Cagliari, Italy

Tiziana Cuccia Department of Economics and Business, University of Catania, Catania, Italy

Veronica De Crescenzo Department of Management, University of Verona, Verona, Italy

Alessandro de Cristofaro Department of Economics and Business, University of Catania, Catania, Italy

Cinzia Di Nuzzo Department of Economics and Business, University of Catania, Catania, Italy

Enrico di Taranto Department of Economics, Management and Institutions, University of Naples Federico II, Naples, Italy

Laura Falci Department of Humanities, University of L'Aquila, L'Aquila, Italy

Mariachiara Fichera Comunità di Sant'Egidio – Sicilia OdV ETS, Messina, Italy

Maria Laura Fornaci Fondazione Giacomo Brodolini, Rome, Italy

Irene Gottoli Department of Human Sciences, University of Verona, Verona, Italy

Angela Maria Greco Department of Economics and Business, University of Catania, Catania, Italy

Giovanni Immordino Department of Economics and Statistics, University of Naples Federico II, Naples, Italy

Alessandro Irrera Assanti Department of Cognitive, Psychological and Educational Sciences and Cultural Studies, University of Messina, Messina, Italy

Mohamed Rida Kheit Comunità di Sant'Egidio – Sicilia OdV ETS, Messina, Italy

Maria Saide Liperi Fondazione Giacomo Brodolini, Rome, Italy

Pierpaolo Magliocca Department of Social Sciences, University of Foggia, Foggia, Italy

Marianna Marino Laboratory for the Analysis of Complex Economic Systems, IMT Lucca Institute for Advanced Studies, Lucca, Italy

Carla Massidda Department of Economics and Business Administration, University of Cagliari, Cagliari, Italy

Mariastella Messina Department of Economics and Business, University of Catania, Catania, Italy

Giorgio Mion Department of Management, University of Verona, Verona, Italy

Flavia Coda Moscarola Department of Law and Political, Economic and Social Sciences (DiGSPES), University of Eastern Piedmont, Alessandria, Italy
CeRP–Collegio Carlo Alberto, Turin, Italy

Massimo Mucciardi Department of Cognitive, Psychological and Educational Sciences and Cultural Studies, University of Messina, Messina, Italy

Andrea Nucita Department of Cognitive, Psychological and Educational Sciences and Cultural Studies, University of Messina, Messina, Italy
Comunità di Sant'Egidio – Sicilia OdV ETS, Messina, Italy

Marco Ortu Department of Economics and Business Administration, University of Cagliari, Cagliari, Italy

Pierpaolo Parrotta Department of Economics and Statistics, University of Siena, Siena, Italy

Giuseppe Pignataro Department of Economics, University of Bologna, Bologna, Italy

Davide Rizzotti Department of Economics and Business, University of Catania, Catania, Italy

Felice Russo Department of Economic Sciences, University of Salento, Lecce, Italy

Giuliana Russo Comunità di Sant'Egidio – Sicilia OdV ETS, Messina, Italy

Rita Salvatore Department of Political Science, University of Teramo, Teramo, Italy

Giovanni Scirè Department of Political Science and International Relations, University of Palermo, Palermo, Italy

Veronica Scuotto Department of Economics, Management and Institutions, University of Naples Federico II, Naples, Italy

Simone Seregni Fondazione Fitzcarraldo ETS, Turin, Italy

Marco Stimolo Department of Economics and Statistics, University of Siena, Siena, Italy

Alessandro Stringhi Department of Business Administration, Prague University of Economics and Business, Prague, Czech Republic

Tiziana Tarsia Department of Cognitive, Psychological and Educational Sciences and Cultural Studies, University of Messina, Messina, Italy

Roberto Tizzano Department of Economics and Statistics, University of Naples Federico II, Naples, Italy

Venera Tomaselli Department of Economics and Business, University of Catania, Catania, Italy

Gianpiero Torrisi Department of Economics and Business, University of Catania, Catania, Italy

Silvio Tunis Department of Economics and Business Administration, University of Cagliari, Cagliari, Italy

Theofilos Tzanidis Business School, University of the West of Scotland, Paisley Campus, Paisley, UK

Vania Vigolo Department of Management, University of Verona, Verona, Italy

Marialuisa Villani Department of Political and Social Sciences, University of Bologna, Bologna, Italy

Stella Volturo Department of Sociology and Business Law, University of Bologna, Bologna, Italy

Abbey Walusimbi Department of Economic Sciences, University of Salento, Lecce, Italy

Roberto Zanola Department of Law and Political, Economic and Social Sciences (DiGSPES), University of Eastern Piedmont, Alessandria, Italy

Part I
Social and Cultural Participation in the Digital Era

From Acts to Chances: Measuring Participation and Inequality of Opportunity

Giuseppe Pignataro

Abstract Participation is a form of social presence and a resource for democratic voice, but it is also a capability that is unequally distributed. This chapter develops an accessible measurement framework that makes participation gaps legible as inequality of opportunity. The first element is an Inclusive Participation Index (IPI)—a bounded composite coefficient that aggregates a small set of offline and digital participation acts through explicit normalization and weighting rules, so that normative choices are visible and contestable. The second element is an *ex-ante* opportunity lens: individuals are grouped into circumstance types, and opportunity inequality is read from the dispersion of type-specific participation chances. For continuous outcomes, we report a variance-based opportunity share; for binary participation, we use a dissimilarity index with a transparent minimal-reallocation interpretation and an opportunity-adjusted participation rate. Because circumstances are multidimensional, Shapley attribution allocates opportunity inequality across circumstance domains without privileging any particular ordering. A final numerical section illustrates, by simulation, how digital participation can either reinforce or partly compensate for offline opportunity gaps.

1 Introduction

Participation is the ordinary way in which citizens become publicly present. It includes joining associations, volunteering, attending neighborhood meetings, voting, donating, helping to organize collective initiatives, and, increasingly, using digital platforms to mobilize information and support. Through these practices, people acquire voice, communities accumulate social capital, and political systems learn which needs are urgent and which remain unseen (Putnam, 2000; Putnam et al., 1993; Verba et al., 1995). Participation therefore matters both intrinsically, as

G. Pignataro (✉)
Department of Economics, University of Bologna, Bologna, Italy
e-mail: giuseppe.pignataro@unibo.it

R. Cellini et al. (eds.), *Cultural, Social, and Political Participation in the Internet Era*, Contributions to Economics, https://doi.org/10.1007/978-3-032-33072-7_1

a form of belonging, and instrumentally, because it shapes representation and the production of trust.

Yet participation is systematically stratified. The resource and civic-skills account of Verba et al. (1995) implies that time, money, and competencies are not evenly distributed, and neither are the organizational gateways that turn a willingness to act into actual engagement. Cross-country evidence connects socioeconomic inequality, trust, and engagement in ways that suggest cumulative dynamics: groups with fewer resources and thinner networks tend to participate less, and lower participation can translate into weaker political influence and weaker access to social capital (Lancee & Van de Werfhorst, 2012; Solt, 2008; Uslaner & Brown, 2005). Community composition and heterogeneity add another layer. Social distance and the availability of bridging ties can shape engagement and cohesion (Alesina & La Ferrara, 2000; Putnam, 2007). Describing average participation is therefore not enough; one must also ask how participation chances are distributed.

Digitalization has changed the technology of engagement without resolving this distributional question. Online channels can reduce some classic barriers—information costs, geographic distance, coordination frictions—and they can offer lighter forms of engagement for people with constrained time budgets. At the same time, access and digital skills remain unequally distributed, and platform architectures can create new forms of unequal visibility and agenda setting (Boulianne, 2015; Hargittai, 2002; Norris, 2001). The digital sphere may therefore operate as a complement to offline civic life, as a partial substitute for those facing offline barriers, or as an amplifier of preexisting opportunity gaps. Without a clear measurement framework, these possibilities are easy to confuse.

This chapter interprets participation gaps through the lens of equality of opportunity (Roemer, 1998; Roemer & Trannoy, 2016). The normative idea is to distinguish participation differences that track predetermined circumstances—family background, place, cohort, gender, migration background—from differences that plausibly reflect idiosyncratic preferences or choices. Operationally, the chapter follows the *ex-ante* approach: individuals are grouped into circumstance types and opportunity inequality is read from the dispersion of type-specific participation outcomes (Checchi & Peragine, 2010; Ferreira & Gignoux, 2011; Van de Gaer, 1993). The aim is deliberately diagnostic rather than causal. The framework does not try to estimate mechanisms; it provides a transparent language to describe whether participation chances are evenly distributed and, if not, where the unevenness is concentrated.

The toolkit has three elements. First, it introduces an Inclusive Participation Index (IPI) that aggregates offline and online acts through explicit scaling and weighting rules, so that normative choices about what counts as participation remain visible and contestable. Second, it proposes opportunity measures that remain interpretable in the participation domain: a variance-based opportunity share for continuous outcomes, and a dissimilarity index for binary outcomes with a direct minimal-reallocation meaning and a natural link to opportunity-adjusted participation rates (Paes de Barros et al., 2009; Shorrocks, 1980). Third, because circumstances overlap, Shapley-value attribution decomposes opportunity inequality across circumstance domains without privileging an arbitrary ordering (Bonacini et al., 2026; Pignataro, 2010, 2012; Pignataro & Costa, 2023; Shapley, 1953).

The remainder of the chapter is organized as follows. Section 2 positions the framework in the literatures on equality of opportunity, participation and social capital, and the digital transformation of civic life. Section 3 clarifies the conceptual distinction between participation acts and participation chances. Section 4 develops the IPI as a transparent outcome for the digital era. Section 5 introduces opportunity-inequality measures for participation and discusses how to read them economically, including a diagnostic for whether online participation compensates offline gaps. Section 6 presents Shapley attribution for circumstance domains. Section 7 proposes a minimal reporting discipline. Section 8 closes with a numerical illustration and a simple simulation that checks the internal logic of the indices.

2 Related Literature

The framework developed here brings together three conversations that have largely progressed in parallel: the measurement of equality of opportunity, the study of participation and social capital, and the analysis of digital inequality and online engagement. The purpose is not encyclopedic coverage. It is to clarify what the opportunity lens adds to participation studies and, conversely, what participation contributes to the opportunity agenda.

On the opportunity side, the starting point is the ethical distinction between circumstances and responsibility (Roemer, 1998; Roemer & Trannoy, 2016). Empirically, effort is rarely observed in a way that is both rich and normatively uncontroversial. A widely used operational response is the *ex-ante* approach: define circumstance types and measure unfair inequality as the dispersion of type-specific outcome distributions (often summarized by differences in type means) (Ferreira & Gignoux, 2011; Van de Gaer, 1993). This approach has been implemented for incomes and for a range of non-income outcomes, including education and health (Checchi & Peragine, 2010; Paes de Barros et al., 2009). Two methodological implications are important for any participation application. First, measured opportunity inequality is typically a lower bound, because circumstances are never fully observed and omitted circumstances are absorbed into the residual (Ferreira & Gignoux, 2011). Second, circumstances are multidimensional. Family background, place, gender, and cohort overlap, and naïve sequential decompositions allocate overlaps in an order-dependent way. This is why Shapley-value attribution has become a standard tool to allocate the opportunity component across circumstance domains in an order-independent manner (Pignataro, 2010, 2012; Shapley, 1953). Recent methodological contributions reinforce that decompositions are not merely technical: they structure how policy questions are posed and interpreted (Bonacini et al., 2026; Pignataro & Costa, 2023).

On the participation side, classic work treats engagement as a foundation of democratic life and as a generator of social capital. The resource-and-skills perspective of Verba et al. (1995) stresses that civic participation depends on time, money, competencies, and mobilization opportunities, all of which are unequally distributed. The social-capital tradition emphasizes networks, norms, and civic traditions as inputs into institutional performance and community cooperation (Putnam, 2000; Putnam et al., 1993). A common theme is that participation is relational: people participate because they are invited, because they are embedded in networks, or because participation is socially recognized. This relational aspect matters for opportunity because it creates spillovers and persistence. If disadvantaged types are underrepresented in civic networks, they may face additional barriers that are not reducible to preferences: lower information, weaker mobilization, and thinner bridges to organizations. Community heterogeneity can further interact with circumstances by changing the costs of engagement and the availability of bridging ties (Alesina & La Ferrara, 2000; Putnam, 2007). A related empirical literature links income inequality and participation (Lancee & Van de Werfhorst, 2012; Solt, 2008) and connects inequality to trust and civic engagement (Uslaner & Brown, 2005). These contributions are mainly empirical and do not typically frame their results as inequality of opportunity, but they motivate a normative question that the opportunity lens makes explicit: when participation is stratified, is it stratified along morally arbitrary lines?

Digitalization modifies the technology of participation and, potentially, the distribution of participation chances. Optimistic accounts emphasize that online channels can reduce information and coordination costs, making engagement feasible despite time and mobility constraints. Skeptical accounts emphasize that access, skills, and platform literacy are unequally distributed. The digital divide captures the access barrier, while the second-level digital divide stresses inequalities in effective use (Hargittai, 2002; Norris, 2001). Meta-analytic evidence suggests that social media use is associated with participation, but the relationship is heterogeneous and context dependent (Boulianne, 2015). Comparative work suggests that digital inequalities can map into civic inequalities rather than dissolving them (Jhu, 2020). For an opportunity-based measurement agenda, the key point is that digital tools should be treated not as an afterthought but as a potential change in the constraint set. The same platform can lower participation costs for one type and raise them for another, depending on access, skills, and social environment.

Finally, the chapter relates to the general debate on composite indicators. Participation is multidimensional, and no single act, not even voting, captures the repertoire of contemporary civic and social engagement. Composite indices are therefore attractive, but they can obscure normative choices through technicalities. The response here is not to deny the normativity of aggregation; it is to make it explicit. The IPI is constructed through monotone transformations to a common unit interval and through documented weights, so that readers can dispute the weighting scheme without disputing the underlying items. This emphasis on transparent accounting is aligned with the decomposition tradition in inequality analysis (Shorrocks, 1980). The guiding principle is legibility: measurement cannot be value-free, but it can be auditable and communicable.

3 From Participation Acts to Participation Chances

Participation is typically observed as an act: one joins, attends, signs, posts. Yet for an opportunity-based evaluation, the more relevant object is a chance: the probability that a person in a given circumstance position can realistically take part in civic and social life. A simple way to connect acts to chances is to view participation as a choice under constraints. An individual participates when perceived benefits exceed perceived costs:

$$\text{participate} \quad \Longleftrightarrow \quad B\,(E, C) \geq K\,(E, C)\,,$$

where E denotes effort and choices, and C denotes circumstances. This representation is intentionally general. It allows costs to include time, money, information, and psychological barriers; it allows benefits to include intrinsic motivations, social recognition, and expected influence.

Seen as a choice under constraints, participation gaps do not necessarily reflect weaker civic preferences. They can reflect systematically different constraint sets. A demanding job schedule, caregiving duties, or long commutes raise the time cost of participation; limited civic skills or information raise the cognitive cost of navigating organizations and institutions; discrimination and social distance raise the psychological cost of entering civic spaces; weak local infrastructures make some forms of engagement physically unavailable. Digital participation adds its own constraints: devices, connectivity, and platform literacy. Many of these constraints are strongly patterned by family background and place, which is why participation is a natural candidate for an opportunity-based assessment.

An opportunity perspective is also justified by the social nature of participation. Participation generates externalities: it produces information for organizations and policymakers, it builds trust, and it enlarges the stock of bridging ties that sustain cooperation. When disadvantaged types participate less, the resulting voice deficit can persist even if individual preferences remain unchanged, because organizations and institutions respond to the voices that are present. Opportunity inequality in participation is therefore not only a distributive concern; it is also a diagnostic of how open the public sphere is to different social experiences.

The equality-of-opportunity distinction does not deny agency. It asks a different question: how much of the participation set is structured by circumstances that precede agency? Digital skills are a useful example of the ambiguity. Skills can be acquired, which suggests an effort component. But access to devices, early exposure, learning environments, and the presence of mentors are systematically patterned by family and place, which suggests a circumstance component. The chapter adopts the standard empirical stance: define a set of circumstances that are plausibly predetermined and ethically salient, construct types from them, and treat systematic between-type differences in participation outcomes as inequality of opportunity (Ferreira & Gignoux, 2011; Roemer & Trannoy, 2016).

Formally, let Y denote a participation outcome. It may be continuous (the IPI) or binary (any participation). Let $T \in \{1, \ldots, G\}$ denote the circumstance type, with population shares $\pi_g = \Pr(T = g)$. The set of type means $\mu_g = \mathbb{E}[Y \mid T = g]$ is the opportunity profile of participation: it describes the expected participation outcome that a person can anticipate given their circumstances. Under the *ex-ante* approach, opportunity inequality is the dispersion of this profile across types. The rest of the chapter is an exercise in making this dispersion measurable, interpretable, and communicable.

4 An Inclusive Participation Index (IPI) for the Digital Era

A participation measure must confront a practical fact: participation comes in many forms, and these forms are not perfect substitutes. Being active in a neighborhood association is not the same as posting political content online. Yet both can be part of civic life, and both can contribute to voice and social capital. A composite outcome is therefore justified, provided it is transparent.

A composite index is useful here for the same reason that composite measures are used in other multidimensional domains: participation is a portfolio, and exclusion can occur through different missing links. Some individuals may vote but never join associations; others may volunteer locally but avoid formal politics; some may be active online while being absent from offline organizations. A single indicator risks mistaking substitution across channels for exclusion. A well-designed index should therefore reward breadth across a limited set of meaningful acts while remaining interpretable enough to be audited and debated in public.

Suppose we observe K participation indicators $X_1, \ldots, X_K$ that jointly cover offline and online acts. The indicators may be binary (did the person sign a petition), ordinal (how often did the person volunteer), or counts (how many associations). We map each indicator to a score on the unit interval,

$$S_k = f_k(X_k) \in [0, 1], \qquad k = 1, \ldots, K,$$

where the mapping $f_k(\cdot)$ is monotone and explicitly documented. For binary indicators, the natural map is $S_k = X_k$. For ordinal frequency measures, a simple and auditable map assigns equally spaced values between 0 and 1. For counts, a transparent cap-and-rescale rule can prevent a small number of extreme observations from mechanically dominating the index.

The Inclusive Participation Index is then a convex aggregation of the normalized scores:

$$\text{IPI} = \sum_{k=1}^{K} w_k S_k,$$

with weights $w_k \geq 0$ and $\sum_{k=1}^{K} w_k = 1$. This construction guarantees that the index remains bounded in $[0, 1]$ and that each component has a clear marginal meaning: increasing participation in a given act cannot reduce the index. The point of spelling out the construction is not to claim that weights are neutral. They are not. The point is to ensure that the normative choices embedded in weights and scaling are visible.

In practice, two principles help keep the index informative without becoming arbitrary. The first is parsimony: include only a small set of items that capture distinct participation channels, rather than many near-duplicates that mechanically increase the score for some lifestyles. The second is robustness: report the index together with its components and show that the opportunity conclusions are not sensitive to small changes in weights. If an opportunity ranking disappears when weights are perturbed within a reasonable range, the measurement problem should be made explicit rather than hidden behind a single headline number.

A useful way to expose the role of digitalization is to structure the index into two blocks: an offline block and an online block. Let

$$\text{IPI}^{\text{off}} = \sum_{k \in \mathcal{K}_{\text{off}}} w_k^{\text{off}} S_k, \qquad \text{IPI}^{\text{on}} = \sum_{k \in \mathcal{K}_{\text{on}}} w_k^{\text{on}} S_k,$$

where the two sets of indicators form a partition of the K items. The overall index can then be written as

$$\text{IPI} = \alpha \ \text{IPI}^{\text{off}} + (1 - \alpha) \ \text{IPI}^{\text{on}},$$

for some $\alpha \in [0, 1]$ that captures the relative normative importance assigned to offline and online participation. This is not a technical detail. It is a substantive choice about what is being measured. A defensible baseline is to allocate equal weight to offline and online blocks and then equal weight within each block, unless there is a clear normative reason to do otherwise.

The economic reason to preserve the offline–online split is that these domains often differ in fixed costs and gatekeeping. Offline participation typically requires proximity to organizations, time in specific schedules, and physical accessibility. Online participation may require devices and skills, but can be performed at lower marginal time costs and with different forms of gatekeeping. Keeping the domains visible makes it possible to ask whether the digital sphere is broadening the participation set of disadvantaged types or simply adding an extra layer of engagement for the types that already face low offline barriers.

Economically, the advantage of a bounded and block-structured outcome is interpretability. The IPI can be read as an index of participation capability: a summary of how many participation channels are effectively used, weighted by an explicit view of their importance. Because the index is bounded, it remains stable in the presence of outliers and can be compared across contexts without being mechanically driven by scale differences. Because the blocks are visible, one can ask an economic question that is otherwise hard to phrase: Does online engagement widen the participation set of disadvantaged types, or does it mainly add an extra layer of engagement for those who already participate offline?

This chapter does not impose a definitive list of items. Instead, it insists on a protocol for credibility. The item set must be stated; the normalization $f_k(\cdot)$ must be documented; weights must be reported; and a minimal sensitivity analysis must show whether conclusions about opportunity inequality survive reasonable alternative choices. The point is to make the participation measure a public object: not merely a number, but a number with an intelligible construction.

5 Measuring Inequality of Opportunity in Participation

Opportunity measurement starts from the opportunity profile $\{\mu_g\}$ and asks how dispersed it is. The *ex-ante* approach interprets between-type dispersion as the circumstantial component of inequality. For participation, this interpretation has a natural reading: types differ in constraints, in access to civic infrastructures, in exposure to civic skills, and in digital access and literacy. The measures below are designed to keep these readings transparent.

5.1 *Continuous Outcomes: Opportunity Shares*

When the participation outcome is continuous, as in the IPI, a simple and interpretable statistic is the variance-based opportunity share. By the standard law of total variance,

$$\mathrm{Var}(Y) = \mathrm{Var}\left(\mathbb{E}\left[Y \mid T\right]\right) + \mathbb{E}\left[\mathrm{Var}\left(Y \mid T\right)\right].$$

The first term is between-type dispersion: the inequality in expected participation that is associated with circumstances. The second term is within-type dispersion: heterogeneity among individuals who share the same observed circumstances. The opportunity share is

$$\theta = \frac{\mathrm{Var}\left(\mathbb{E}\left[Y \mid T\right]\right)}{\mathrm{Var}(Y)} \in [0, 1].$$

A value near zero means that types have similar expected participation outcomes; a value near one means that types almost fully determine participation outcomes.

Interpreting the opportunity share benefits from thinking in counterfactual terms. If types had identical expected participation outcomes, the between-type term would vanish, and the remaining dispersion would be within-type heterogeneity. A positive opportunity share means that equalizing the mean participation outcome across observed types would mechanically compress the overall distribution. The statistic therefore translates the ethical question "how much do circumstances matter?" into an accounting statement about dispersion. In participation contexts, even moderate values can be politically meaningful because participation is connected to voice: a small circumstantial component in participation can still generate large representational distortions if the same types are persistently absent from civic arenas.

Two cautions are essential, and they are methodological rather than rhetorical. First, θ depends on the circumstances used to construct types. Adding relevant circumstances tends to increase the between-type component, so empirical estimates of θ should be read as lower bounds on opportunity inequality (Ferreira & Gignoux, 2011). Second, θ is not a causal decomposition. It does not identify mechanisms. It identifies a patterned component of inequality: participation differences that track circumstances. In policy discussions, that patterned component is precisely the one that raises fairness concerns and motivates institutional diagnostics.

Variance is not the only possible inequality concept. Decomposable inequality indices in the sense of Shorrocks (1980) can also be used, and they can be chosen to reflect stronger sensitivity to the bottom of the distribution if one believes that exclusion at low participation levels is normatively central. The opportunity logic remains the same: the between-type component captures the circumstantial share of inequality.

5.2 *Binary Outcomes: Dissimilarity and Opportunity-Adjusted Participation*

Participation is often also studied on the extensive margin: whether people participate at all. Let $Y \in \{0, 1\}$ indicate a binary participation outcome, such as any civic participation or any digital participation. Let $p_g = \Pr(Y = 1 \mid T = g)$ and $\overline{p} = \Pr(Y = 1)$ denote type-specific and overall participation rates. A widely used opportunity measure for binary outcomes is the dissimilarity index (Paes de Barros et al., 2009),

$$D = \frac{1}{2\overline{p}} \sum_{g=1}^{G} \pi_g \mid p_g - \overline{p} \mid .$$

The index takes values between 0 and 1. It is zero when all types have the same participation rate. It increases when participation becomes concentrated in a subset of types.

Two features make D particularly suitable for communicating opportunity gaps. First, it is scale-consistent: the absolute gaps $\mid p_g - \overline{p} \mid$ are aggregated with type weights, and the normalization by $\overline{p}$ expresses the result relative to the total mass of realized participation. Second, its extreme cases are intuitive. If all types participate at the same rate, the index is zero. If participation is almost entirely confined to a small set of types while others are effectively excluded, the index approaches one. In between, D increases when participation becomes more unevenly distributed across circumstance types, even if the overall participation rate remains unchanged.

The economic attraction of D is that it speaks the language of reallocations. It answers a question that policymakers can understand: how much of participation would need to be shifted from high-participation types to low-participation types for chances to be equalized? The related Human Opportunity Index intuition is that inclusive participation is not just a high $\overline{p}$, but a high $\overline{p}$ combined with a low dissimilarity across types. An opportunity-adjusted participation rate can therefore be written as $\overline{p}\,(1 - D)$ (Paes de Barros et al., 2009).

Proposition 1 (Dissimilarity as minimal reallocation). *For binary Y, the quantity* $\frac{1}{2}\sum_{g=1}^{G} \pi_g \mid p_g - \overline{p} \mid$ *equals the minimal amount of participation probability mass that must be transferred from high-rate types to low-rate types to make all type rates equal to* $\overline{p}$. *Dividing by* $\overline{p}$ *expresses this minimal transfer as a fraction of total realized participation probability mass, yielding D.*

Proof. See Appendix 10.1.

The proposition does not introduce a new statistic; it clarifies why D is a natural opportunity metric for the extensive margin. Because D is defined in terms of the opportunity profile $\{p_g\}$, it isolates the part of nonparticipation that is systematically linked to circumstances. This distinction matters in practice. A policy that raises the overall participation rate $\overline{p}$ can leave opportunity inequality unchanged, or even worsen it, if the gains accrue mainly to already advantaged types. Conversely, a policy can be opportunity-improving even with modest effects on $\overline{p}$ if it disproportionately expands participation chances for low-rate types. Reporting $\overline{p}$ and D together therefore separates the level of participation from its inclusiveness, and it keeps the focus on the distribution of chances rather than on the distribution of acts.

The same logic helps interpret the opportunity-adjusted participation rate $\overline{p}\,(1 - D)$. It is not a measure of average participation; it is a measure of average participation discounted by the degree to which participation is unequally accessible across circumstance types. In contexts where participation is politically consequential, this adjusted rate provides a compact way to say that a society can be both active and unequal, or moderately active and comparatively inclusive. The appropriate normative emphasis depends on the purpose of the analysis, but the accounting remains transparent.

5.3 When Digital Participation Compensates or Reinforces Offline Gaps

The block structure allows a diagnostic that is specific to the digital era. Let $Y^{\text{off}} = \text{IPI}^{\text{off}}$ and $Y^{\text{on}} = \text{IPI}^{\text{on}}$, and define the type-mean profiles

$$m^{\text{off}}(T) = \mathbb{E}\left[Y^{\text{off}} \mid T\right], \qquad m^{\text{on}}(T) = \mathbb{E}\left[Y^{\text{on}} \mid T\right].$$

The covariance between these two profiles tells us whether types that are disadvantaged offline are also disadvantaged online. To make this idea comparable across contexts, it is useful to normalize the covariance into an alignment coefficient.

The alignment coefficient is simply the correlation between the offline and online type means. It is computed over types (weighted by type shares), not over individuals. This matters because the object of interest is the opportunity profile: whether circumstances that disadvantage a type offline also disadvantage it online. A value close to one corresponds to near-perfect alignment of offline and online opportunity gaps across types; a value close to minus one corresponds to a near-perfect compensatory pattern; a value close to zero indicates that the two profiles are largely orthogonal.

Proposition 2 (A bounded alignment coefficient for offline and online opportunity profiles). *Assume* $\text{Var}(m^{\text{off}}(T)) > 0$ *and* $\text{Var}(m^{\text{on}}(T)) > 0$ *and define* $\rho_T = \frac{\text{Cov}(m^{\text{off}}(T), m^{\text{on}}(T))}{\sqrt{\text{Var}(m^{\text{off}}(T))\ \text{Var}(m^{\text{on}}(T))}}$. *Then* $-1 \leq \rho_T \leq 1$. *Moreover, for the block index* $Y = \alpha Y^{\text{off}} + (1-\alpha)Y^{\text{on}}$, $\text{Var}\left(\mathbb{E}\left[Y \mid T\right]\right) = \alpha^2 \text{Var}\left(m^{\text{off}}(T)\right) + (1-\alpha)^2 \text{Var}\left(m^{\text{on}}(T)\right) + 2\alpha\left(1-\alpha\right)\rho_T \sqrt{\text{Var}\left(m^{\text{off}}(T)\right)\ \text{Var}\left(m^{\text{on}}(T)\right)}$.

Proof. See Appendix 10.2.

The economic content of Proposition 2 is that the between-type dispersion of the composite index has three ingredients: the offline opportunity dispersion, the online opportunity dispersion, and a cross-domain term that depends on the alignment coefficient. The weights are governed by α, which captures the normative importance assigned to offline versus online participation. If ρ_T is positive and large, offline and online opportunity gaps tend to line up: types that face low participation chances offline also face low chances online. In that case, the cross-domain term is positive, and the composite opportunity inequality is amplified. If ρ_T is negative, the digital sphere partly compensates: types that are disadvantaged offline tend to have relatively higher online chances, and the cross-domain term reduces the overall between-type dispersion of the composite index. When ρ_T is near zero, the two domains contribute largely independently.

Note that a negative ρ_T does not mean that the digital sphere is universally inclusive; it means that the ranking of types differs across domains in a way that reduces overall dispersion in the composite outcome. Likewise, a positive ρ_T does not identify the mechanism of reinforcement; it signals that the same circumstance types are disadvantaged on both margins, which is consistent with correlated barriers such as unequal civic skills, weak mobilization networks, and digital access and literacy gaps. The main value of ρ_T is diagnostic: it turns a qualitative question—compensation or reinforcement—into a bounded and comparable statistic that can be reported alongside the opportunity shares of each domain.

6 Attributing Opportunity Inequality to Circumstance Domains

Opportunity inequality in participation is rarely driven by a single circumstance. Family background, place, gender, and cohort overlap. If one simply adds domains sequentially to a model or partition, the attributed contributions depend on order: the first domain in the sequence captures all shared explanatory power. This order dependence is not innocuous. In a policy discussion, it can be mistaken for evidence of priority.

Shapley attribution provides an order-independent alternative. Group circumstances into M domains, indexed by $N = \{1, \ldots, M\}$. For any subset $S \subseteq N$, compute the chosen opportunity-inequality measure $\theta(S)$ using types defined only by the domains in S. The Shapley contribution of domain m is then

$$\phi_m = \sum_{S \subseteq N \setminus \{m\}} \frac{|S|!\,(M - |S| - 1)!}{M!} \left(\theta\left(S \cup \{m\}\right) - \theta(S)\right).$$

A simple two-domain example illustrates the intuition. Suppose we have only family background and place. If we attribute opportunity inequality by adding domains sequentially, the domain added first absorbs all overlap: adding family first captures both the direct family association and any shared variation between family and place, while adding place second captures only what is left. Reversing the order reverses the attribution. Shapley attribution averages these marginal contributions over all possible orders, so that overlap is split symmetrically. The result is not a causal share, but it is a disciplined descriptive share that avoids building an arbitrary priority into the accounting.

The formula averages the marginal contribution of domain m across all possible orderings in which domains could be added. It satisfies an efficiency property: the contributions add up to the total explained component, so that $\sum_{m=1}^{M} \phi_m = \theta(N) - \theta(\varnothing)$ (Shapley, 1953). In applied opportunity work this matters because it turns a multidimensional set of circumstances into an interpretable narrative: how much of opportunity inequality is associated with family background, how much with place, how much with cohort, and how much with gender, net of overlaps that would otherwise be arbitrarily allocated.

The contribution of Shapley attribution is not that it produces causal shares. It produces fair shares in a precise sense: it treats all domains symmetrically and allocates overlap in a way that does not depend on the analyst's ordering. This is why Shapley methods have become standard for decomposing opportunity inequality across circumstance domains (Pignataro, 2010, 2012). The output can be used descriptively to guide the next question. If place dominates, one looks at local civic infrastructures and digital access; if family background dominates, one looks at the transmission of civic skills and cultural participation; if cohort dominates, one asks how participation technologies and norms shift across generations.

7 A Minimal Reporting Discipline

Opportunity measures are meant to inform public debate. They lose their meaning when their construction is opaque. A practical virtue of the IPI and the associated opportunity metrics is that they can be reported in a way that is compact but auditable.

A credible report starts from the outcome. The list of participation items, the normalization rules $f_k(\cdot)$, and the weights w_k must be stated. The second step is to state the circumstances used to define types and the way types are constructed. Because small cells can distort between-type comparisons, it is good practice to report the effective size of types and, where needed, the coarsening rules used to keep types meaningful.

The third step is to show the opportunity profile itself. Type means μ_g are not ancillary; they are the object that the opportunity lens interprets. Reporting the dispersion of μ_g through a single statistic without showing at least the main type gaps can make the analysis feel abstract. A compact table or figure that ranks types by μ_g often communicates more than a long list of indices.

Finally, the opportunity measures should be paired with a minimal sensitivity analysis. Because the IPI is a composite index, readers should see whether the qualitative conclusions are robust to reasonable alternative weights and to mild alternative normalizations. Because opportunity measurement depends on circumstances, readers should see whether adding a salient circumstance domain changes θ materially. The purpose is not to chase robustness for its own sake; it is to show that the results are not artifacts of arbitrary coding decisions.

8 Numerical Illustration and a Small Simulation

The framework above is nonempirical, but it should not remain abstract. This section uses numbers and a simple simulation to check the internal logic of the measures. The goal is verification of the accounting, not the production of empirical claims.

8.1 A Hand-Calculable Opportunity Profile

Consider two circumstance types of equal size. Suppose the average IPI is 0.55 for type A and 0.45 for type B. The opportunity profile gap is 0.10 on a $[0, 1]$ scale, and the between-type variance of type means is $0.5(0.55 - 0.50)^2 + 0.5(0.45 - 0.50)^2 = 0.0025$. If the overall variance of the IPI is 0.02, the opportunity share is $\theta = 0.0025/0.02 = 0.125$. Interpreted literally, one-eighth of participation inequality, as measured by dispersion in the IPI, is statistically associated with the circumstances used to define the two types.

Now consider a binary participation outcome with $p_A = 0.50$, $p_B = 0.20$, and therefore $\overline{p} = 0.35$. The dissimilarity index is

$$D = \frac{1}{2 \cdot 0.35} \left(0.5\,|0.50 - 0.35| + 0.5\,|0.20 - 0.35|\right) = \frac{0.15}{0.70} \approx 0.214.$$

The opportunity-adjusted participation rate is $\overline{p}\,(1 - D) \approx 0.275$. In this toy example, participation is not only low for one type; it is unevenly distributed across types in a way that can be summarized as a reallocation share.

8.2 Simulation: Reinforcement Versus Compensation in the Digital Era

A central question of the chapter is whether digital participation compensates for offline gaps or reinforces them. Proposition 2 provides a compact diagnostic through the alignment coefficient ρ_T. To see how it behaves, consider four types of equal size and define an offline score and an online score on $[0, 1]$. For each type, we draw 5000 individuals and generate noisy participation around type means, truncating to keep outcomes in $[0, 1]$. We then compute ρ_T and the opportunity share θ for the composite IPI with $\alpha = 0.5$. This baseline gives equal weight to the offline and online blocks and equal weights within each block purely for transparency; in empirical applications, these weights could instead be calibrated through expert elicitation or public preference surveys.

For transparency, the table reports the between-type variances of the offline and online opportunity profiles, denoted $B_{\text{off}} = \text{Var}(m^{\text{off}}(T))$ and $B_{\text{on}} = \text{Var}(m^{\text{on}}(T))$. It also reports the implied between-type variance of the composite, $B_{\text{total}} = \text{Var}\left(\mathbb{E}\left[Y \mid T\right]\right)$, together with the corresponding opportunity share θ.

Table 1 reports the resulting statistics under three scenarios. In the reinforcement scenario, online type means increase with offline type means, and ρ_T is close to 1. In the compensation scenario, online type means decrease with offline type means, and ρ_T is strongly negative. In the neutral scenario, online type means vary across types but are essentially uncorrelated with offline type means, so ρ_T is close to 0.

Table 1 A simple simulation illustrating the offline–online alignment coefficient and the opportunity share (four types, 20,000 individuals, $\alpha = 0.5$)

Scenario	B_{off}	B_{on}	ρ_T	B_{total}	θ
Reinforcement	0.049	0.049	1.000	0.049	0.877
Neutral	0.049	0.012	0.000	0.015	0.685
Compensation	0.049	0.028	−0.988	0.001	0.117

Table 1 is only an accounting check, but it makes the logic vivid. When offline and online participation chances are aligned, the composite opportunity inequality is high. When online participation tends to be higher for types that are disadvantaged offline, the overall between-type dispersion of the composite index can shrink dramatically, even if offline gaps remain large. The neutral scenario sits between the two extremes: online participation adds its own inequality, but it does not systematically reinforce or offset offline inequality.

This is exactly the kind of diagnostic that is otherwise hard to extract from a single composite measure. A society can have rising digital participation and still have widening opportunity gaps in voice if the same types are advantaged on both margins. Conversely, digital channels can contribute to inclusion if they create credible low-cost entry points into civic life for types facing strong offline barriers. The indices above do not settle this empirical question, but they structure it into transparent components.

9 Conclusion

Participation is often discussed as a matter of civic virtue or individual motivation. The opportunity lens shifts the emphasis. It asks whether the chances to participate are themselves fairly distributed, or whether participation is structured by predetermined circumstances in a way that produces unequal voice. In the digital era, this shift is especially useful because new channels can coexist with old barriers. The relevant question is not whether online engagement exists, but whether it alters the opportunity structure of participation.

This chapter has developed a measurement framework that is deliberately transparent. The IPI provides a bounded outcome that can include both offline and online acts without hiding the normative choices embedded in aggregation. The *ex-ante* opportunity perspective then reads participation gaps as between-type differences in expected participation outcomes. For continuous outcomes, a variance-based opportunity share summarizes the circumstantial component of dispersion. For binary outcomes, a dissimilarity index translates uneven chances into a minimal-reallocation interpretation that can be communicated beyond specialist audiences. Shapley attribution, finally, offers a disciplined way to allocate opportunity inequality across circumstance domains when those domains overlap.

The framework does not pretend to be a causal model, and it cannot resolve the normative boundary between circumstances and effort. Its ambition is more modest and, in practice, more useful: to provide an auditable language in which participation inequalities can be described as opportunity inequalities, and to separate the level of participation from its inclusiveness. If participation is a cornerstone of democratic life, then measuring who is effectively able to participate is not a technical exercise. It is part of the diagnosis of how open, or how closed, a society is to the voices of its members.

Appendix

Proofs

This appendix collects the proofs of the propositions stated in the main text. The proofs are written to keep the accounting behind the indices transparent.

Proof of Proposition 1

Proof. The object of interest is the opportunity profile on the extensive margin: the type-specific participation rates $p_g = \Pr(Y = 1 \mid T = g)$. The equal-opportunity benchmark is that all types share the same participation rate, equal to the overall rate $\overline{p} = \sum_{g=1}^{G} \pi_g p_g$, where $\pi_g = \Pr(T = g)$ are type shares.

The proof is an accounting exercise. Think of each type's participation rate as a mass of participation probability. A reallocation that equalizes chances must reduce the mass of the high-rate types and increase the mass of the low-rate types, leaving the overall mass $\overline{p}$ unchanged.

Define the deviation of type g from the benchmark as

$$\Delta_g = p_g - \overline{p}.$$

Types with $\Delta_g > 0$ have an excess of participation probability relative to the benchmark; types with $\Delta_g < 0$ have a deficit. Because $\overline{p}$ is the type-weighted average, the deviations add up to zero:

$$\sum_{g=1}^{G} \pi_g \Delta_g = \sum_{g=1}^{G} \pi_g p_g - \overline{p} = 0.$$

Hence, the total excess equals the total deficit in absolute value:

$$\sum_{g:\Delta_g>0} \pi_g \Delta_g = - \sum_{g:\Delta_g<0} \pi_g \Delta_g = \sum_{g:\Delta_g<0} \pi_g \left|\Delta_g\right|.$$

Consider any reallocation that achieves equalized rates $p_g{}' = \overline{p}$ for all g. For each type with $\Delta_g > 0$, the rate must be reduced by exactly Δ_g. Therefore, the total mass that must leave the set of high-rate types is at least the aggregate excess,

$$\sum_{g:\Delta_g>0} \pi_g \Delta_g.$$

This lower bound is attainable. One can take exactly $\pi_g \Delta_g$ from each high-rate type and distribute it across low-rate types so that each low-rate type receives exactly $\pi_g |\Delta_g|$. Feasibility follows from the equality of aggregate excess and aggregate deficit shown above. This constructs an equalizing reallocation whose total transferred mass is precisely the aggregate excess. Therefore, the minimal mass that must be transferred to equalize participation chances equals the aggregate excess.

Finally, express this minimal transfer in a symmetric way. Using the identity between excess and deficit,

$$\sum_{g:\Delta_g>0} \pi_g \Delta_g = \frac{1}{2} \sum_{g=1}^{G} \pi_g \left|\Delta_g\right| = \frac{1}{2} \sum_{g=1}^{G} \pi_g \left|p_g - \overline{p}\right|.$$

This proves the first claim in Proposition 1. Dividing by the total realized participation mass $\overline{p}$ expresses the minimal transfer as a share of realized participation probability, yielding

$$D = \frac{1}{2\overline{p}} \sum_{g=1}^{G} \pi_g \left|p_g - \overline{p}\right|,$$

which is the dissimilarity index D.

Proof of Proposition 2

Proof. The proof has two parts. The first shows that the alignment coefficient is bounded between -1 and 1. The second derives the between-type variance expression for the composite index.

Write $m^{\text{off}}(T) = \mathbb{E}\left[Y^{\text{off}} \mid T\right]$ and $m^{\text{on}}(T) = \mathbb{E}\left[Y^{\text{on}} \mid T\right]$. These are random variables over the distribution of types: they take value $m^{\text{off}}(g)$ when $T = g$, with probability π_g, and similarly for m^{on}.

Define centered versions

$$\tilde{m}^{\text{off}}(T) = m^{\text{off}}(T) - \mathbb{E}\left[m^{\text{off}}(T)\right], \qquad \tilde{m}^{\text{on}}(T) = m^{\text{on}}(T) - \mathbb{E}\left[m^{\text{on}}(T)\right].$$

By definition,

$$\text{Cov}\left(m^{\text{off}}(T), m^{\text{on}}(T)\right) = \mathbb{E}\left[\tilde{m}^{\text{off}}(T)\, \tilde{m}^{\text{on}}(T)\right].$$

Apply the Cauchy–Schwarz inequality to the random variables $\tilde{m}^{\text{off}}(T)$ and $\tilde{m}^{\text{on}}(T)$:

$$\left|\mathbb{E}\left[\tilde{m}^{\text{off}}(T)\,\tilde{m}^{\text{on}}(T)\right]\right| \le \sqrt{\mathbb{E}\left[\left(\tilde{m}^{\text{off}}(T)\right)^2\right]}\sqrt{\mathbb{E}\left[(\tilde{m}^{\text{on}}(T))^2\right]}.$$

The right-hand side is the product of standard deviations,

$$\sqrt{\mathbb{E}\left[\left(\tilde{m}^{\text{off}}(T)\right)^2\right]} = \sqrt{\text{Var}\left(m^{\text{off}}(T)\right)}, \qquad \sqrt{\mathbb{E}\left[(\tilde{m}^{\text{on}}(T))^2\right]} = \sqrt{\text{Var}\,(m^{\text{on}}(T))}.$$

Therefore

$$\left|\text{Cov}\left(m^{\text{off}}(T), m^{\text{on}}(T)\right)\right| \le \sqrt{\text{Var}\left(m^{\text{off}}(T)\right)\ \text{Var}\,(m^{\text{on}}(T))}.$$

Dividing both sides by the positive denominator in the definition of ρ_T yields $|\rho_T| \le 1$.

For the variance identity, start from the block index $Y = \alpha Y^{\text{off}} + (1-\alpha)Y^{\text{on}}$. Taking conditional expectations given T gives

$$\mathbb{E}\,[Y \mid T] = \alpha\ \mathbb{E}\left[Y^{\text{off}} \mid T\right] + (1-\alpha)\ \mathbb{E}\left[Y^{\text{on}} \mid T\right] = \alpha\ m^{\text{off}}(T) + (1-\alpha)\ m^{\text{on}}(T).$$

Compute the variance across types using the variance formula for a linear combination:

$$\begin{aligned}\text{Var}\,(\mathbb{E}\,[Y \mid T]) &= \text{Var}\left(\alpha\ m^{\text{off}}(T) + (1-\alpha)\ m^{\text{on}}(T)\right)\\ &= \alpha^2\text{Var}\left(m^{\text{off}}(T)\right) + (1-\alpha)^2\text{Var}\,(m^{\text{on}}(T)) + 2\alpha\,(1-\alpha)\,\text{Cov}\left(m^{\text{off}}(T), m^{\text{on}}(T)\right).\end{aligned}$$

Finally, rewrite the covariance term through ρ_T:

$$\text{Cov}\left(m^{\text{off}}(T), m^{\text{on}}(T)\right) = \rho_T\sqrt{\text{Var}\left(m^{\text{off}}(T)\right)\ \text{Var}\,(m^{\text{on}}(T))}.$$

Substituting this into the previous display yields the final result.

References

Alesina, A., & La Ferrara, E. (2000). Participation in heterogeneous communities. *Quarterly Journal of Economics, 115*(3), 847–904. https://doi.org/10.1162/003355300554935

Bonacini, L., Costa, M., & Pignataro, G. (2026). Inequality of opportunity and variance decomposition: A methodological insight. *Social Indicators Research, 181*, 72. https://doi.org/10.1007/s11205-026-03810-2

Boulianne, S. (2015). Social media use and participation: A meta-analysis of current research. *Information, Communication & Society, 18*(5), 524–538. https://doi.org/10.1080/1369118X.2015.1008542

Checchi, D., & Peragine, V. (2010). Inequality of opportunity in Italy. *Journal of Economic Inequality, 8*(4), 429–450. https://doi.org/10.1007/s10888-009-9118-3

Ferreira, F. H. G., & Gignoux, J. (2011). The measurement of inequality of opportunity: Theory and an application to Latin America. *Review of Income and Wealth, 57*(4), 622–657. https://doi.org/10.1111/j.1475-4991.2011.00467.x

Hargittai, E. (2002). Second-level digital divide: Differences in people's online skills. *First Monday, 7*(4). https://doi.org/10.5210/fm.v7i4.942

Jhu, Y.-J. (2020). Online civic engagement among young adults in Korea: A comparison with America and Finland. *Journal of Social Science Research, 46*(1), 1–17. https://doi.org/10.1080/01488376.2018.1468224

Lancee, B., & Van de Werfhorst, H. G. (2012). Income inequality and participation: A comparison of 24 European countries. *Social Science Research, 41*(5), 1166–1178. https://doi.org/10.1016/j.ssresearch.2012.04.005

Norris, P. (2001). *Digital divide: Civic engagement, information poverty, and the internet worldwide*. Cambridge University Press.

Paes de Barros, R., Ferreira, F. H. G., Vega, J. M., & Saavedra, J. (2009). *Measuring inequality of opportunities in Latin America and the Caribbean*. World Bank. https://doi.org/10.1596/978-0-8213-7721-9

Pignataro, G. (2010). Measuring equality of opportunity by Shapley value. *Economics Bulletin, 30*(1), 786–798.

Pignataro, G. (2012). Equality of opportunity: Policy and measurement paradigms. *Journal of Economic Surveys, 26*(5), 800–834. https://doi.org/10.1111/j.1467-6419.2011.00679.x

Pignataro, G., & Costa, M. (2023). The foster–Greer–Thorbecke index and the inequality factors: An analysis through the Gini index decomposition. *Journal of Economic Inequality, 21*(2), 483–497. https://doi.org/10.1007/s10888-022-09557-3

Putnam, R. D. (2000). *Bowling alone: The collapse and revival of American community*. Simon & Schuster.

Putnam, R. D. (2007). E pluribus Unum: Diversity and community in the twenty-first century. *Scandinavian Political Studies, 30*(2), 137–174. https://doi.org/10.1111/j.1467-9477.2007.00176.x

Putnam, R. D., Leonardi, R., & Nanetti, R. Y. (1993). *Making democracy work: Civic traditions in modern Italy*. Princeton University Press.

Roemer, J. E. (1998). *Equality of opportunity*. Harvard University Press.

Roemer, J. E., & Trannoy, A. (2016). Equality of opportunity: Theory and measurement. *Journal of Economic Literature, 54*(4), 1288–1332. https://doi.org/10.1257/jel.20151206

Shapley, L. S. (1953). A value for *n*-person games. In H. W. Kuhn & A. W. Tucker (Eds.), *Contributions to the theory of games II* (Annals of mathematics studies) (Vol. 28, pp. 307–317). Princeton University Press.

Shorrocks, A. F. (1980). The class of additively decomposable inequality measures. *Econometrica, 48*(3), 613–625. https://doi.org/10.2307/1913126

Solt, F. (2008). Economic inequality and democratic political engagement. *American Journal of Political Science, 52*(1), 48–60. https://doi.org/10.1111/j.1540-5907.2007.00298.x

Uslaner, E. M., & Brown, M. (2005). Inequality, trust, and civic engagement. *American Politics Research, 33*(6), 868–894. https://doi.org/10.1177/1532673X04271903

Van de Gaer, D. (1993). *Equality of opportunity and investment in human capital*. Ph.D. dissertation, Katholieke Universiteit Leuven.

Verba, S., Schlozman, K. L., & Brady, H. E. (1995). *Voice and equality: Civic voluntarism in American politics*. Harvard University Press.

Measuring Inequalities in Well-Being: A Three-Way Approach with Applications to Italy and the European Union

Cinzia Di Nuzzo, Venera Tomaselli, and Gianpiero Torrisi

Abstract This chapter discusses two applications of the three-way multidimensional inequality Gini Index to measure territorial disparities in well-being across regions, accounting for multiple dimensions and temporal dynamics. The inequality index integrates information on social, cultural, digital, economic, and demographic indicators. The empirical analysis illustrates the methodology through two complementary applications. First, disparities in cultural participation and digitalisation across Italian regions from 2011 to 2022 are examined, highlighting the evolution of social sustainability at the national level. Second, EU NUTS2 regions for the period 2013–2019 are analysed, capturing broader structural inequalities in socio-economic and demographic outcomes across European countries. Results show persistent spatial inequalities, with notable—though consistent—variation depending on the dimensions considered. The Italian case highlights the North–South divide and the impact of region-specific events, while the EU analysis reveals a centre-periphery pattern driven by social and demographic factors beyond income disparities. Overall, the three-way multidimensional inequality Gini index provides a flexible and policy-relevant framework for understanding and monitoring multidimensional regional inequalities over time.

1 Introduction

Understanding and measuring territorial disparities in well-being has become an increasingly central issue for both researchers and policymakers. In recent decades, the growing awareness that economic development cannot be fully captured by traditional macroeconomic indicators has stimulated a large body of literature devoted to the measurement of multidimensional well-being and inequality. In particular, relying solely on income-based measures such as GDP per capita provides only a partial representation of social conditions and often fails to capture

C. Di Nuzzo · V. Tomaselli · G. Torrisi (✉)
Department of Economics and Business, University of Catania, Catania, Italy
e-mail: cinzia.dinuzzo@unict.it; venera.tomaselli@unict.it; gianpiero.torrisi@unict.it

R. Cellini et al. (eds.), *Cultural, Social, and Political Participation in the Internet Era*, Contributions to Economics, https://doi.org/10.1007/978-3-032-33072-7_2

important aspects of human development, social participation, and quality of life (Atkinson, 2015).

This limitation is particularly relevant when regional disparities are analysed. Regions may display similar levels of economic performance while substantially differ in terms of social opportunities, access to services, cultural participation, or demographic conditions. For this reason, several international institutions and research initiatives have promoted the development of multidimensional frameworks able to integrate different aspects of well-being into synthetic indicators (OECD, 2008). These approaches aim to provide a broader and more informative representation of socio-economic conditions, allowing policymakers to identify structural imbalances that may not emerge from mainstream economic indicators.

Within this perspective, the analysis of territorial inequality has progressively moved towards multidimensional frameworks that jointly consider economic, social, and demographic dimensions (Crescenzi et al., 2016).

Recent studies also emphasise that access to cultural resources and digital technologies represents an increasingly important component of social inclusion and collective well-being. Cultural participation contributes to the accumulation of social capital, fosters civic engagement, and promotes individual capabilities (Bertacchini et al., 2021). At the same time, the diffusion of digital technologies has profoundly transformed the way individuals access information, interact with cultural institutions, and participate in social life (Cellini & Cuccia, 2025), especially during the recent COVID-19 crisis (Cellini et al., 2024). The emergence of digital platforms and online services has created new forms of cultural consumption and communication, but it has also introduced new forms of inequality associated with the so-called digital divide (van Dijk, 2020).

In response to these developments, several methodological contributions have been proposed to construct multidimensional indicators capable of summarising complex socio-economic phenomena. Synthetic indicators represent one of the most widely used tools in this context. By aggregating multiple variables into a single synthetic measure, these indicators allow researchers to compare territorial units, monitor temporal trends, and evaluate the effectiveness of public policies (Nardo et al., 2005). However, the construction of synthetic indicators raises several methodological challenges related to the selection of variables, the normalisation of values, and, most importantly, the determination of aggregation weights (Decancq & Lugo, 2013).

Another important limitation of many existing multidimensional inequality measures concerns their cross-sectional nature. Most traditional approaches are designed for datasets observed at a single point in time and therefore do not fully exploit the information contained in longitudinal data structures. In empirical applications involving repeated observations over time, ignoring temporal dynamics may lead to an incomplete understanding of the evolution of territorial disparities.

Furthermore, regional datasets often display hierarchical or nested structures. For instance, European statistical data are typically organised according to a multilevel territorial hierarchy involving the European Union (EU), national economies, and regional units such as NUTS2 regions. Standard inequality measures are generally not designed to explicitly account for these hierarchical structures, thereby limiting their ability to analyse inequality patterns across different territorial levels.

To address these methodological challenges, recent research has explored the use of tensor-based approaches and multidimensional data decomposition techniques for the construction of synthetic indicators. In particular, tensor decomposition models allow researchers to analyse complex datasets characterised by multiple dimensions, such as units, variables, and time periods while simultaneously extracting latent structures from the data (Kolda & Bader, 2009). These methods provide a flexible framework for constructing synthetic indicators that incorporate both multidimensional and longitudinal information.

Building upon these methodological developments, the present study applies a multidimensional inequality framework based on tensor decomposition techniques to investigate territorial disparities in cultural participation and digitalisation across Italian regions. The analysis relies on the three-way Multidimensional Inequality Gini Index (3wMDIGI) (Di Nuzzo et al., 2025), which extends traditional inequality measurement by explicitly incorporating three dimensions simultaneously: statistical units, variables, and time.

Unlike conventional composite indicators based on predefined weighting schemes, the adopted approach derives aggregation weights endogenously from the data through Candecomp/Parafac decomposition. This data-driven strategy allows the multidimensional structure of the dataset to emerge directly from observed statistical relationships, reducing the degree of arbitrariness typically associated with weighting procedures in composite indicator construction. Moreover, the tensor-based framework enables the joint analysis of cross-sectional and temporal variability, thereby capturing the dynamic evolution of regional disparities.

The empirical application focuses on Italy, a particularly relevant case study due to the persistence of strong territorial imbalances that characterise its socio-economic structure.

In this context, cultural participation and digitalisation, in addition to being linked to mainstream measures of inequality according to very recent contributions (Cellini & Cuccia, 2026), are interpreted as complementary dimensions of social sustainability. Cultural activities such as reading, visiting museums, or attending cultural events contribute to social cohesion and individual well-being, while digital technologies increasingly represent essential channels for accessing cultural resources, information, and public services. The interaction between these two domains has intensified over the last decade, particularly following the rapid diffusion of broadband infrastructure and digital platforms.

The contribution of this chapter is threefold. First, it provides an empirical application of a tensor-based multidimensional inequality measure to a regional dataset characterised by both temporal and multidimensional complexity. Second, it proposes an integrated framework for analysing cultural participation and digitalisation jointly, thereby extending the empirical literature on regional well-being beyond purely economic indicators. Third, the study offers new empirical evidence on the evolution of territorial disparities in Italy during the period 2011–2022, including the structural changes associated with the expansion of digital technologies and the asymmetric effects of the COVID-19 pandemic.

2 Methodology

The methodological framework builds upon the three-way Multidimensional Inequality Gini Index (3wMDIGI) (Di Nuzzo et al., 2025), and the R code can be found on https://github.com/CinziaDiNuzzo/3wMDIGI. The approach extends traditional multidimensional inequality measures by explicitly incorporating three sources of variability: statistical units, observed dimensions, and time occasions.

Given a three-way array $\mathbf{X} = \{x_{ijh}\}$, a rank-one CANDECOMP/PARAFAC (CP) decomposition is applied to extract latent structure $\mathbf{X}_h = \mathbf{A}\, c_h \mathbf{B}^\top + \mathbf{E}_h$, from which data-driven weights w_{jh} are obtained.

Normalised indicators are aggregated into multidimensional scores via a generalised mean:

$$s_{ih} = \left(\sum_{j=1}^{J} w_{jh} (x^*_{ijh})^\beta \right)^{1/\beta},$$

where β controls substitutability. Inequality is then measured through a Gini-type index:

$$I_h(\mathbf{X}) = 1 - \frac{\sum_{i=1}^{N} \left[\left(\frac{r_{ih}}{N}\right)^\delta - \left(\frac{r_{ih}-1}{N}\right)^\delta \right] s_{ih}}{\left(\sum_{j=1}^{J} w_{jh} \mu^\beta_{jh}\right)^{1/\beta}},$$

with δ governing inequality aversion. For a global measure, let $\tilde{x}_{ij}$ be temporally aggregated indicators and ω_j global weights. The overall index is

$$I(\mathbf{X}) = 1 - \frac{\sum_{i=1}^{N} \left[\left(\frac{\tau_i}{N}\right)^\delta - \left(\frac{\tau_i-1}{N}\right)^\delta \right] \left(\sum_{j=1}^{J} \omega_j \tilde{x}^\beta_{ij}\right)^{1/\beta}}{\left(\sum_{j=1}^{J} \omega_j \mu(\tilde{\mathbf{x}}_j)^\beta\right)^{1/\beta}},$$

where τ_i denotes the ranking based on aggregated scores.[1]

[1] The parameters β and δ are chosen within the admissible ranges $\beta < 1$ and $1 \leq \delta \leq 2$, ensuring consistency with the Unfair Rearrangement (UR) principle (Decancq and Lugo, 2012). A sensitivity analysis over $\beta \in (0, 1)$ and $\delta \in [1, 2]$ (Di Nuzzo et al., 2025) shows that results are qualitatively robust: Rankings and relative inequality patterns remain stable, while absolute levels vary with substitutability (β) and inequality aversion (δ). This supports the overall stability of the measure.

This framework integrates dimensional, temporal, and cross-sectional heterogeneity, allowing inequality to be assessed jointly across variables and time, with data-driven weights derived endogenously via tensor decomposition. For further methodological details, see Di Nuzzo et al. (2025).

3 Disparities in Cultural Participation and Digitalisation Across Italian Regions

This section presents the empirical application of the three-way Multidimensional Inequality Gini Index (3wMDIGI) (Di Nuzzo et al., 2025) to the Italian regional context. The primary objective is to evaluate territorial disparities in social sustainability by jointly analysing cultural participation and digitalisation dynamics across the 20 Italian administrative regions over the period 2011–2022. The application represents the first empirical implementation of the proposed methodology on an integrated socio-cultural and technological dataset, allowing the multidimensional framework to reveal latent inequality structures that remain hidden within traditional approaches.

Italy provides a particularly suitable empirical setting for testing the methodological contribution introduced in this study. The country is historically characterised by persistent spatial heterogeneity affecting economic development, infrastructure availability, institutional quality, and access to cultural opportunities.

The empirical analysis relies on harmonised regional indicators obtained through the AMELIA platform https://grins.it/progetto/piattaforma-amelia, developed within the framework of the GRINS (Growing Resilient, Inclusive and Sustainable) project financed under the Italian National Recovery and Resilience Plan (PNRR). The platform provides longitudinal datasets designed to monitor resilience, inclusiveness, and sustainability across Italian territories, ensuring methodological consistency across regions and time periods. The availability of a structured and validated statistical infrastructure represents a key advantage, as multidimensional inequality measures require high comparability across observational units.

The statistical units of analysis correspond to the $N = 20$ Italian regions observed over $H = 12$ yearly occasions. The resulting dataset forms a balanced panel structure suitable for tensor representation. Let x_{ijt} denote the observed value of indicator j for region i at time t, with $i = 1, \ldots, 20$; $j = 1, \ldots, 20$; $t = 1, \ldots, 12$. The data are organised into a third-order tensor: $\mathbf{X} \in \mathbb{R}^{20\times 20\times 12}$, where the three modes correspond to regions, indicators, and time, respectively. This representation preserves the multidimensional nature of inequality and constitutes the analytical foundation for the Candecomp/Parafac decomposition described in Sect. 2.

The selection of variables follows both theoretical and empirical criteria. From a theoretical perspective, indicators are chosen to capture two complementary dimensions of social sustainability: access to digital environments and participation in cultural life. From an empirical standpoint, variables displaying sufficient variability across regions are preferred, since inequality measures require heterogeneity to meaningfully identify disparities.

The dataset includes 20 indicators equally divided into two macro-dimensions.

The first dimension captures digitalisation processes and describes both access to digital infrastructure and intensity of online engagement. Indicators include regular Internet usage, households with Internet access, individuals using the Internet in the last 3 months, broadband connectivity, frequency of Internet use, weekly and daily online access, online banking adoption, participation in e-commerce activities, and interaction with public authorities through digital services. Together, these variables measure digital inclusion not only as technological availability but also as effective participation in the digital society.

The second dimension measures cultural participation through indicators reflecting engagement in traditional cultural activities. These include book reading, newspaper readership, cinema attendance, visits to museums and exhibitions, participation in sports activities, visits to archaeological sites, theatre attendance, concert participation, library usage, and broader engagement with cultural sites. The inclusion of multiple indicators allows cultural participation to be interpreted as a multidimensional behavioural phenomenon rather than a single activity.

The joint consideration of these dimensions reflects an important conceptual assumption underlying the empirical application. Cultural participation and digitalisation are increasingly interconnected processes. Digital technologies facilitate access to cultural information, enable online participation, and expand opportunities for engagement beyond geographical constraints. Conversely, participation in cultural activities is often associated with educational attainment and digital competencies, suggesting mutually reinforcing mechanisms between cultural and technological inclusion (OECD, 2019; van Dijk, 2020).

Within this framework, the objective of the Italian application is not merely descriptive but rather aims to evaluate whether multidimensional inequality dynamics change when cultural and digital dimensions are analysed simultaneously and when their relative importance emerges endogenously from the data. Traditional composite indices typically impose equal or arbitrarily chosen weights, potentially masking the true drivers of territorial disparities. The 3wMDIGI approach instead derives weights through Candecomp/Parafac tensor decomposition, allowing the statistical structure of the dataset itself to determine the contribution of each indicator.

Before decomposition, all variables are normalised to ensure comparability across indicators measured on different scales. The normalisation procedure transforms each variable into a unit-free measure, preserving relative differences across regions and time while preventing scale dominance effects. This step is essential because tensor factorisation relies on variance structures that could otherwise be distorted by heterogeneous measurement units.

The Candecomp/Parafac model decomposes the tensor $\mathcal{X}$ into a sum of rank-one components, $x_{ijt} \approx \sum_{r=1}^{R} a_{ir} b_{jr} c_{tr}$, where vectors **a**, **b**, and **c** represent latent regional, variable, and temporal loadings, respectively. Unlike traditional dimensionality reduction methods, Candecomp/Parafac preserves interpretability across all modes simultaneously, allowing the identification of patterns linking regions, indicators, and time dynamics.

The resulting variable loadings play a crucial methodological role because they provide endogenous weights used in constructing the multidimensional indicator underlying the 3wMDIGI framework. Consequently, inequality measurement becomes directly connected to the latent statistical structure of the data rather than external normative assumptions.

The empirical strategy, therefore, proceeds in three sequential stages. First, tensor decomposition identifies latent structures governing multidimensional participation patterns. Second, Candecomp/Parafac-derived weights are used to construct regional multidimensional scores capturing combined cultural and digital engagement. Third, the three-way multidimensional Gini index measures inequality dynamics across regions and over time.

This integrated framework allows the Italian application to address a central research question: whether technological diffusion has reduced territorial disparities in social participation or whether structural inequalities persist despite digital expansion. By explicitly modelling temporal evolution, the methodology also enables the identification of structural breaks associated with external shocks, most notably the COVID-19 pandemic.

The following subsections analyse the digitalisation dimension, the cultural participation dimension, and their joint interaction, highlighting how each contributes to the overall multidimensional inequality structure revealed by the 3wMDIGI framework.

3.1 Digitalisation Dynamics and Multidimensional Inequality

The first stage of the empirical application focuses on the digitalisation dimension analysed independently of cultural participation. This step is crucial from a methodological perspective because it allows us to isolate the contribution of digital variables to regional heterogeneity before integrating the two domains within the three-way multidimensional framework.

The tensor associated with digitalisation includes $N = 20$ regions, $J = 10$ variables, and $H = 12$ time occasions, generating a three-way structure that preserves spatial, dimensional, and temporal information simultaneously. Applying Candecomp/Parafac decomposition to this tensor produces latent components describing the joint evolution of digital behaviour across Italian regions.

Unlike traditional composite indicators, the weights are not imposed ex ante but emerge endogenously from the tensor structure. This represents one of the main innovations of the proposed methodology: The relevance of each indicator is statistically determined by its contribution to multidimensional variability.

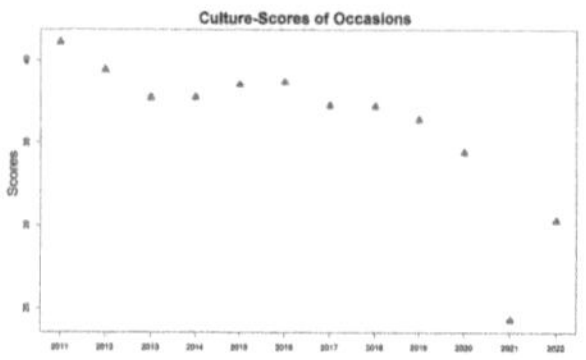

(a) Temporal Candecomp/-Parafac scores for cultural participation indicators.

(b) Regional Candecomp/-Parafac scores for cultural participation across Italian regions.

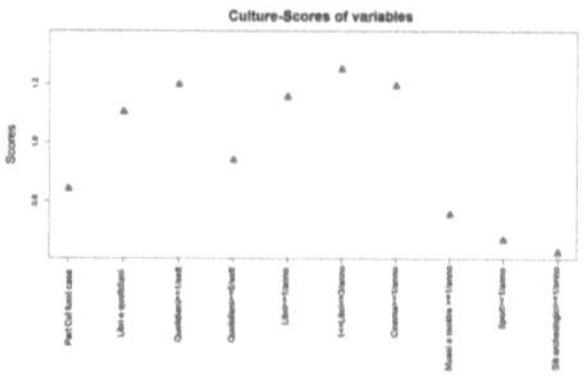

(c) Variable loadings for cultural participation indicators.

Fig. 1 (**a**) Temporal loadings from Candecomp/Parafac decomposition for digitalisation indicators (2011–2022). (**b**) Regional loadings from Candecomp/Parafac decomposition for digitalisation indicators. (**c**) Variable loadings for digitalisation indicators derived from Candecomp/Parafac decomposition

Figure 1a reports the temporal scores obtained from the Candecomp/Parafac decomposition applied to the digitalisation tensor. The trajectory shows a clear and almost monotonic upward trend across the entire observation period.

From a statistical perspective, this pattern indicates that digitalisation represents a structural growth process rather than a cyclical phenomenon. The increase becomes particularly pronounced after 2015, corresponding to the expansion of broadband infrastructure and increasing diffusion of mobile Internet technologies in Italy.

The absence of strong downward fluctuations suggests that digital adoption behaves as a cumulative process: Once technologies are adopted, regions rarely revert to previous levels of digital engagement. This property is consistent with diffusion-of-innovation models and confirms the stability of the latent temporal component extracted by Candecomp/Parafac.

The acceleration observed during 2020–2021 reflects the COVID-19 shock, which dramatically increased reliance on online services for work, education, and communication. Importantly, the tensor approach captures this change as a structural shift rather than an isolated outlier.

Figure 1b presents regional loadings associated with the digital component. The spatial configuration reveals a pronounced territorial gradient aligned with the historical Italian North–South divide.

Within the multidimensional framework, these differences represent variations in latent digital capability rather than simple differences in single indicators. The Candecomp/Parafac model aggregates correlated behaviours into a unified structural dimension, revealing deeper territorial patterns.

Figure 1c reports the variable loadings, which determine the endogenous weighting scheme used later in the 3wMDIGI construction.

A key empirical result emerges clearly: Indicators related to *intensive digital usage* receive higher weights than basic access indicators. Variables such as daily Internet usage, online banking, and interaction with public authorities contribute more strongly to the latent component than simple Internet availability measures.

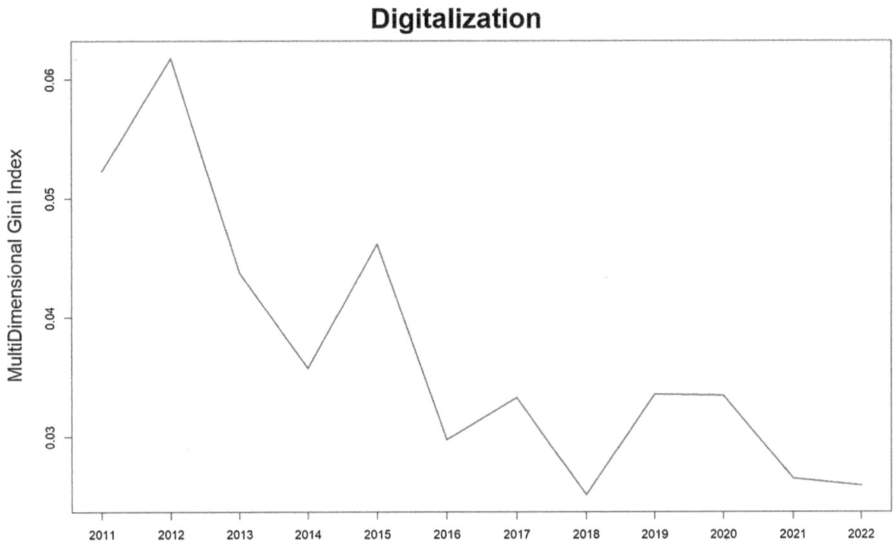

Fig. 2 Multidimensional Gini index for digitalisation across Italian regions

This finding has important methodological implications. It shows that regional inequality in Italy is no longer primarily driven by access to infrastructure, but by differences in digital skills and behavioural adoption. In statistical terms, variability across regions is maximised by usage intensity rather than connectivity presence.

The result supports the interpretation of a transition from a first-level digital divide (access) to a second-level divide (usage and capabilities) (van Dijk, 2020).

Using Candecomp/Parafac weights, regional scores are aggregated into the digital multidimensional index: $s_{it}^{(D)} = \left(\sum_{j=1}^{10} w_j \tilde{x}_{ijt}^{\beta}\right)^{1/\beta}$, where $\beta = 0.1$ limits substitutability across dimensions, ensuring that weaknesses in specific digital behaviours cannot be fully compensated by strengths in others.

This aggregation rule preserves multidimensional heterogeneity and represents a core innovation of the 3wMDIGI framework.

Figure 2 shows the evolution of digital inequality measured through the multidimensional Gini index.

The trajectory reveals a gradual decline in inequality during most of the analysed period, indicating partial convergence among regions. This convergence is mainly driven by diffusion effects: Lagging regions progressively adopt digital technologies, reducing extreme disparities.

However, the decline slows after 2019, suggesting the emergence of structural limits to convergence. While access gaps narrow, differences in advanced digital usage persist.

The pandemic period generates only a moderate increase in inequality compared with the cultural dimension analysed later. This confirms that digitalisation acted as a resilience factor during the crisis.

3.1.1 Interpretation Within the 3wMDIGI Framework

From the perspective of the proposed methodology, digitalisation provides an ideal testing ground for the three-way inequality approach.

First, the tensor decomposition successfully separates temporal growth from regional heterogeneity, demonstrating the capacity of Candecomp/Parafac to identify latent structural components.

Second, endogenous weights reveal which behaviours statistically drive inequality, avoiding arbitrary aggregation assumptions common in composite indicators (Nardo et al., 2005).

Third, the multidimensional Gini index captures convergence dynamics while preserving information on distributional asymmetries.

Overall, the digitalisation analysis shows that technological diffusion contributes to reducing territorial inequality but does not eliminate structural disparities. Regions differ increasingly in how digital tools are integrated into everyday life, rather than in simple access conditions.

This result highlights the analytical advantage of the 3wMDIGI methodology: By combining tensor decomposition with inequality measurement, it becomes possible to distinguish between growth processes and distributive outcomes within complex multidimensional systems.

3.2 Cultural Participation

After analysing digitalisation dynamics, the empirical application proceeds with the second macro-dimension of the multidimensional framework: cultural participation. While digitalisation captures technological inclusion and access to informational infrastructures, cultural participation reflects behavioural and social engagement patterns that evolve through slower institutional and socio-economic processes.

Within the proposed three-way multidimensional inequality framework (3wMDIGI), cultural participation plays a complementary analytical role. Unlike digital variables, which are primarily driven by technological diffusion, cultural indicators capture long-term social structures associated with education, accessibility, cultural capital, and territorial organisation. Analysing this dimension separately allows the identification of structural disparities that may remain hidden when only technological indicators are considered.

The selected variables describe both individual cultural consumption and participation in collective cultural experiences: book reading, newspaper readership, cinema attendance, museums and exhibitions attendance, sports participation, archaeological site visits, theatre attendance, concert attendance, library usage, and cultural sites engagement.

Together, these indicators provide a multidimensional representation of cultural engagement, capturing both passive and active forms of participation (Sen, 1999; OECD, 2019).

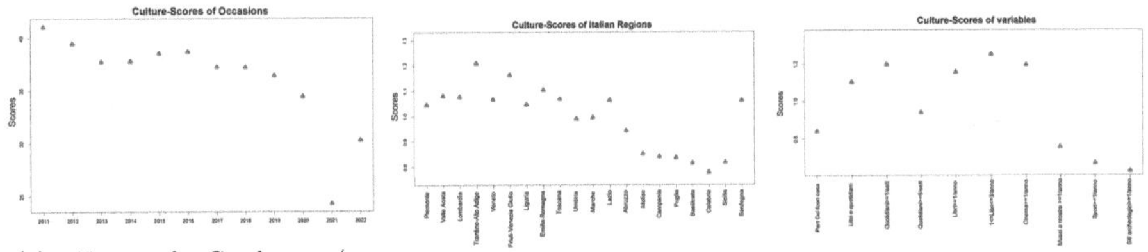

(a) Temporal Candecomp/-Parafac scores for cultural participation indicators.

(b) Regional Candecomp/-Parafac scores for cultural participation across Italian regions.

(c) Variable loadings for cultural participation indicators.

Fig. 3 (**a**) Temporal Candecomp/Parafac scores for cultural participation indicators. (**b**) Regional Candecomp/Parafac scores for cultural participation across Italian regions. (**c**) Variable loadings for cultural participation indicators

The first analytical step consists of applying the Candecomp/Parafac decomposition to the cultural participation tensor. The resulting temporal loadings are reported in Fig. 3a.

Unlike digitalisation, which exhibited a nearly monotonic growth trajectory, cultural participation displays a markedly irregular temporal pattern. The scores remain relatively stable during the early years of the observation period but show visible fluctuations linked to macroeconomic and social shocks.

This behaviour reflects a fundamental structural difference between technological adoption and cultural engagement. Cultural participation depends heavily on discretionary household expenditure and physical accessibility to cultural institutions. Consequently, participation tends to decline during periods of economic uncertainty and recover gradually afterward.

A pronounced structural break emerges around 2020, corresponding to the COVID-19 pandemic. Restrictions on mobility and closures of cultural venues produced a sharp contraction in participation opportunities. This shock appears clearly in the temporal scores, confirming the sensitivity of cultural activities to external disruptions (OECD, 2021; ISTAT, 2022).

Importantly, the post-pandemic recovery does not immediately restore previous levels, suggesting that cultural participation follows slower adjustment dynamics compared with digital adoption.

Regional Candecomp/Parafac loadings are presented in Fig. 3b.

The spatial distribution reveals strong territorial heterogeneity. Northern and Central regions systematically obtain higher scores, reflecting stronger engagement in cultural activities such as museum attendance, reading, and participation in organised events.

Conversely, several Southern regions display lower loadings despite possessing significant cultural heritage assets. This apparent paradox highlights a key empirical insight: The availability of cultural resources does not automatically translate into effective participation.

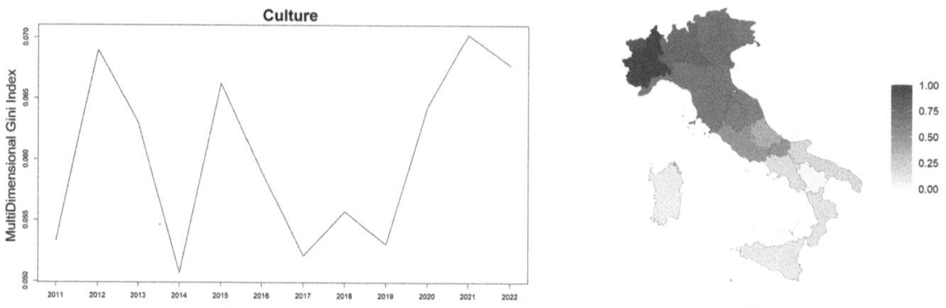

(a) Multidimensional Gini index for cultural participation.

(b) Synthetic cultural participation index across Italian regions.

Fig. 4 (**a**) Multidimensional Gini index for cultural participation. (**b**) Synthetic cultural participation index across Italian regions

Participation requires enabling socio-economic conditions, including transportation accessibility, income availability, and educational background (Bertacchini et al., 2021; SVIMEZ, 2022).

From the perspective of the 3wMDIGI methodology, these regional scores demonstrate that cultural inequality originates primarily from structural socio-economic differences rather than temporary fluctuations. The variable loadings derived from the Candecomp/Parafac decomposition are reported in Fig. 3c.

The results show that experiential cultural activities receive the highest weights within the latent component. These variables contribute most strongly to regional differentiation.

In contrast, passive activities such as newspaper reading or basic book consumption display lower weights, indicating more homogeneous diffusion across regions.

This distinction is methodologically relevant. The endogenous weighting mechanism of the Candecomp/Parafac decomposition reveals which dimensions truly generate inequality rather than assuming equal importance across indicators. The results suggest that territorial disparities arise primarily from activities requiring physical participation and institutional accessibility.

Using Candecomp-/Parafac-derived weights, the cultural participation index is constructed, and the multidimensional Gini coefficient is computed for each year. The evolution of cultural inequality is shown in Fig. 4a.

The trajectory differs substantially from digital inequality dynamics. Rather than a steady decline, cultural inequality follows a volatile pattern characterised by alternating phases of stability and disruption. Three phases can be identified: (1) relative stability during the early period, (2) gradual deterioration associated with economic uncertainty, and (3) a sharp pandemic shock followed by partial recovery. The pandemic period produced the largest increase in inequality, reflecting heterogeneous regional capacity to maintain cultural engagement under restrictions. Regions with stronger institutional ecosystems adapted more effectively through hybrid or digitally mediated cultural activities.

Figure 4b reports the synthetic cultural participation index across regions. The spatial configuration confirms persistent polarisation between Northern–Central and Southern Italy. Regions characterised by strong urban systems and institutional density systematically achieve higher participation levels. Importantly, disparities cannot be explained solely by income differences. Accessibility, institutional presence, and educational structures jointly determine participation opportunities. Cultural inequality, therefore, reflects multidimensional territorial development rather than purely economic performance.

From the perspective of the proposed methodology, cultural participation provides a crucial counterbalance to digitalisation dynamics. Whereas digital inequality tends to decrease through technological diffusion, cultural inequality remains structurally persistent because it depends on long-term social processes. The analysis demonstrates that multidimensional inequality cannot be fully understood through technological indicators alone. Cultural participation captures deeper forms of social integration that evolve slowly and remain sensitive to external shocks. The cultural dimension, therefore, validates the necessity of the three-way framework: Only by jointly modelling regions, variables, and time is it possible to distinguish between rapidly converging technological inequalities and persistent social disparities embedded in territorial structures.

3.3 Joint Analysis of Cultural Participation and Digitalisation

While the previous analyses examined digitalisation and cultural participation independently, the combined tensor allows for identifying latent structures that cannot emerge from separate analyses. The multidimensional approach, therefore, reveals whether regional disparities originate from single domains or from their interaction.

The joint tensor is defined as $\mathbf{X} \in \mathbb{R}^{20\times 20\times 12}$, where the three modes correspond to Italian regions, indicators, and time occasions, respectively. The Candecomp/Parafac decomposition extracts a latent component summarising the common evolution of cultural and digital participation patterns across the country.

Unlike traditional composite indicators, the weights used in the aggregation are not imposed ex ante but emerge endogenously from the tensor structure. This characteristic constitutes one of the main methodological innovations of the 3wMDIGI framework, allowing inequality measurement to reflect the empirical organisation of the data.

Figure 5a reports the temporal scores extracted from the joint decomposition. Compared with the cultural-only analysis, the trajectory appears considerably smoother and characterised by a persistent upward trend. This result highlights a fundamental methodological insight: Digitalisation introduces a structural growth component that stabilises multidimensional participation dynamics over time. Cultural participation alone displayed cyclical fluctuations, whereas the inclusion of digital indicators produces a clearer long-run trajectory. The upward movement

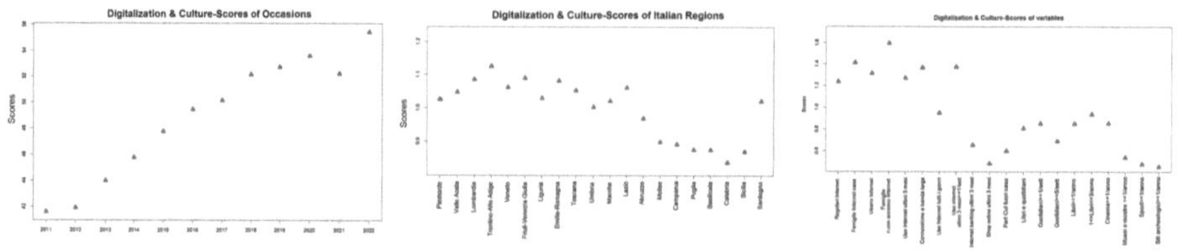

(a) Temporal loadings obtained from the Candecomp/Parafac decomposition of cultural participation and digitalisation indicators.

(b) Regional loadings from the joint Candecomp/Parafac decomposition.

(c) Variable loadings for cultural and digital indicators in the joint Candecomp/Parafac model.

Fig. 5 (**a**) Temporal loadings obtained from the Candecomp/Parafac decomposition of cultural participation and digitalisation indicators. (**b**) Regional loadings from the joint Candecomp/Parafac decomposition. (**c**) Variable loadings for cultural and digital indicators in the joint Candecomp/Parafac model

observed after the mid-2010s reflects the progressive consolidation of digital engagement within everyday social behaviour. The visible discontinuity around 2020 corresponds to the COVID-19 shock, which altered participation modes rather than simply reducing activity levels.

From the perspective of the proposed methodology, this confirms that temporal inequality cannot be correctly interpreted without accounting for multidimensional substitution effects. Physical cultural participation declined sharply, but digital engagement expanded simultaneously, preventing a permanent increase in multidimensional deprivation. Figure 5b presents regional scores derived from the integrated tensor. The spatial configuration remains aligned with the traditional North–Centre–South divide, but differences appear less polarised compared with the cultural-only configuration. Northern regions maintain the highest scores, reflecting strong performance in both digitalisation and cultural participation. However, several Southern regions move closer to the national average when digital indicators are included. This finding represents one of the most important empirical contributions of the analysis. Digitalisation acts as a partial equalising mechanism by compensating for structural disadvantages in cultural infrastructure. Regions historically characterised by lower cultural participation benefit from improvements in digital connectivity that expand access to cultural content and information. The three-way structure of the model allows this compensatory mechanism to emerge explicitly, something that would remain hidden in traditional two-dimensional inequality measures. Figure 5c provides direct evidence on the relative importance of variables within the multidimensional structure. Digitalisation indicators systematically receive higher loadings than cultural participation variables. This result shows that digital engagement explains a larger share of total variability across Italian regions during the analysed period. In statistical terms, digitalisation represents the dominant latent dimension shaping regional differentiation. Importantly, this dominance does not imply that cultural participation loses relevance. Instead, it indicates that digital infrastructure increasingly acts as an enabling layer through which cultural

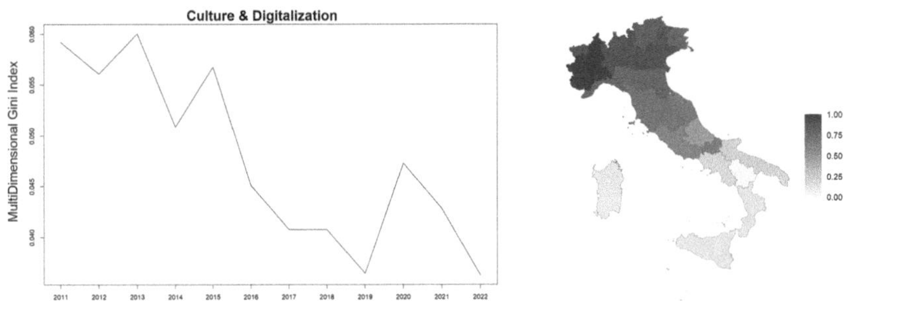

(a) Joint cultural–digital multidimensional index across years.

(b) Joint cultural–digital multidimensional index across Italian regions.

Fig. 6 (**a**) Joint cultural–digital multidimensional index across years. (**b**) Joint cultural–digital multidimensional index across Italian regions

participation is mediated. The endogenous weighting scheme, therefore, reveals information that equal-weight indices cannot provide: The hierarchy of dimensions emerges from the empirical covariance structure rather than subjective assumptions. Using the Candecomp-/Parafac-derived weights, the multidimensional score for region i at time t is computed as $s_{it} = \left(\sum_{j=1}^{20} w_j \tilde{x}_{ijt}^{\beta}\right)^{1/\beta}$, where $\beta = 0.1$ limits substitutability between dimensions and ensures that strong imbalances remain penalised.

Figure 6a illustrates the evolution of the joint indicator. The trajectory combines two dynamics previously identified separately: a structural upward trend driven by digitalisation and short-term fluctuations associated with cultural participation. Regions exhibiting rapid digital growth experience faster improvements even when cultural participation evolves more slowly. This confirms that multidimensional well-being depends increasingly on technological inclusion. Figure 6b reports the evolution of the 3wMDIGI. The index displays a gradual declining trend over the observation period, indicating progressive convergence in multidimensional participation opportunities. Two temporary increases are visible. The first corresponds to mid-decade adjustments associated with uneven diffusion of digital technologies. The second, more pronounced spike occurs during the pandemic period, reflecting asymmetric regional resilience. The key methodological insight is that inequality dynamics emerge from interactions between dimensions rather than isolated changes. Digital expansion reduces inequality in the long run, but shocks affecting culturally dependent activities may temporarily reverse convergence.

The integrated analysis leads to three main conclusions directly linked to the methodological contribution of the 3wMDIGI. First, digitalisation emerges as the primary driver of temporal convergence. Its rapid diffusion generates a structural reduction in multidimensional inequality. Second, cultural participation remains structurally heterogeneous and strongly sensitive to external shocks, reflecting deeper socio-economic and institutional differences among regions. Third, the interaction between dimensions produces compensatory effects. Improvements in digital access partially offset territorial disadvantages in cultural participation, reducing overall inequality without eliminating structural disparities. These findings demonstrate the analytical advantage of the three-way framework. By simultaneously modelling regions, variables, and time, the methodology captures dynamic substitution mechanisms and latent structural hierarchies that cannot be observed through standard inequality measures.

4 Disparities Among EU Regions via the Multidimensional Inequality Gini Index

In order to further illustrate the flexibility and empirical relevance of the proposed three-way multidimensional inequality framework, this section applies the 3wMDIGI framework to the analysis of regional disparities across European Union NUTS2 regions. The European analysis considers a broader set of socio-economic and demographic indicators within a multilevel territorial system.

The European Union represents a particularly suitable context for multidimensional inequality analysis. Despite decades of cohesion policies aimed at reducing regional disparities, substantial differences persist across European territories in terms of economic performance, demographic conditions, and labour market outcomes. Traditional income-based measures capture only part of these disparities, whereas multidimensional approaches allow a more comprehensive assessment of regional well-being.

The dataset is obtained from EUROSTAT and covers the period 2013–2019, including $N = 234$ NUTS2 regions belonging to 24 European countries observed over $H = 7$ time periods. The territorial structure naturally defines a hierarchical system composed of three nested levels: the European Union as a whole, national economies, and regional units. This multilevel configuration makes the dataset particularly appropriate for the application of the three-way MDIGI framework, which explicitly accounts for hierarchical data structures.

The empirical analysis relies on a set of $J = 10$ indicators capturing complementary dimensions of regional well-being. Economic performance is represented by GDP per capita, while human capital is captured through the share of human resources in science and technology (HRST) and participation in education and training. Demographic conditions are measured through population size, fertility rate, mortality rate, infant mortality, and life expectancy. Labour market performance is represented by employment, unemployment, and the share of young people not in employment, education, or training (NEET).

The inclusion of heterogeneous indicators reflects the multidimensional nature of well-being, consistent with the growing literature emphasising that income alone cannot adequately describe social progress (Atkinson, 2015; Decancq & Lugo, 2013). In particular, demographic and labour market variables capture long-term structural conditions influencing regional resilience and social inclusion.

Before constructing the inequality index, all variables are normalised using the min–max transformation, which rescales each indicator into the interval [0, 1], ensuring comparability across heterogeneous variables while preserving relative regional differences. Variables characterised by negative polarity, such as mortality and unemployment rates, are reversed so that higher values consistently represent better outcomes.

Based on the normalised dataset, the three-way multidimensional inequality Gini index is computed following the framework described in Sect. 2. Consistent with the sensitivity analysis presented in Di Nuzzo et al. (2025), the parameters are set to $\delta = 2$ and $\beta = 0.005$. This specification implies limited substitutability among dimensions and increased sensitivity to disparities affecting lower performing regions, thereby emphasising structural inequality rather than average performance differences.

The computation of the three-way Multidimensional Inequality Gini Index provides a dynamic representation of regional disparities across the European Union over the period 2013–2019. The resulting values of the index indicate a moderate but a persistent level of multidimensional inequality, with index values ranging approximately between 0.203 and 0.229 throughout the observation period.

The temporal evolution of the indicator suggests the presence of a gradual convergence process among European regions. Inequality slightly decreases during most of the analysed years, indicating that less developed regions partially reduced their relative disadvantage in multidimensional well-being. This trend is consistent with the objectives of European cohesion policies, which aim to promote balanced territorial development and reduce structural disparities across member states.

Despite this tendency to convergence, the dynamics are not entirely smooth. A temporary increase in inequality emerges around 2018, reflecting heterogeneous regional responses to economic and demographic changes occurring during the late phase of the post-financial crisis recovery. Differences in labour market adjustment, demographic ageing, and productivity growth contributed to uneven regional trajectories, preventing a uniform reduction of disparities.

An important insight emerges from the analysis of the loadings obtained through the Candecomp/Parafac decomposition. Among the considered indicators, life expectancy displays one of the strongest contributions to the multidimensional inequality structure, whereas GDP *per capita* plays a comparatively smaller role. This finding provides empirical support for the argument that well-being inequalities cannot be fully understood through income differences alone. Health-related and demographic dimensions appear to capture deeper structural disparities affecting long-term regional development.

The relatively lower contribution of GDP also highlights a key advantage of multidimensional approaches. Regions with similar income levels may still differ substantially in terms of demographic sustainability, labour market inclusion, or human capital accumulation. Consequently, income-based inequality measures risk, overlooking important dimensions of social vulnerability that influence long-run development prospects.

To further assess this issue, we compare three alternative inequality measures: the proposed 3wMDIGI, a multidimensional index excluding GDP (3wMDIGI-GDP), and the traditional Gini index computed solely on GDP per capita. Although the three indicators display broadly similar temporal patterns, the GDP-based Gini index consistently reports slightly higher inequality levels. This result suggests that income disparities represent only one component of the broader inequality structure, while multidimensional indicators capture compensating effects arising from social and demographic factors.

4.1 Multilevel Interpretation of European Regional Inequality

Beyond aggregate dynamics, the three-way framework allows for computing multilevel inequality scores reflecting contributions at different territorial levels.

Within the theoretical framework of 3wMDIGI in Sect. 2, an interesting representation consists of a multilevel representation of the inequality measures and scores associated with a nested structure of the data (see Di Nuzzo et al., 2025). Specifically, for hierarchical or nested data (e.g., EU $\rightarrow$ countries $\rightarrow$ regions), inequality scores are computed as $\eta_{ih} = \frac{s_{ih}}{\left(\sum_{j=1}^{J} w_{jh}\mu_{jh}^{\beta}\right)^{1/\beta}}$, $\gamma_i = \frac{\left(\sum_{j=1}^{J} \omega_j \tilde{x}_{ij}^{\beta}\right)^{1/\beta}}{\left(\sum_{j=1}^{J} \omega_j \mu(\tilde{\mathbf{x}}_j)^{\beta}\right)^{1/\beta}}$. Therefore, multilevel contributions within and between clusters are $\boldsymbol{\vartheta}_{VU} = \frac{\gamma_{|V*}}{\gamma_{|U*}}$, $\boldsymbol{\vartheta}_{UX} = \frac{\gamma_{|U*}}{\gamma}$, where **X** indicates the first level (EU), **U** the middle level (Countries), and **V** the last level (Regions).

The European Union is modelled as a hierarchical system composed of three nested layers: the supranational level (EU), the national level, and the regional level (NUTS2). This structure makes it possible to distinguish between inequality occurring between countries and inequality arising within countries across regions.

The multilevel decomposition reveals that regional disparities within countries represent a substantial component of overall European inequality. In several member states, differences between metropolitan and peripheral regions contribute more strongly to inequality than differences between national averages. This finding emphasises the importance of place-based policies targeting subnational territories rather than relying exclusively on national redistribution mechanisms.

A clear centre-periphery spatial pattern emerges from the regional inequality scores. Core regions, typically located in Western and Northern Europe and characterised by diversified economic structures and strong human capital endowments, display higher contributions to multidimensional performance. Peripheral regions, including parts of Southern and Eastern Europe, tend to exhibit lower scores associated with weaker labour markets and less favourable demographic conditions.

Importantly, the results indicate that multidimensional inequality is shaped by structural characteristics that evolve slowly over time. Demographic indicators, such as life expectancy and fertility, contribute significantly to persistent disparities, suggesting that regional inequality is linked not only to economic cycles but also to long-term socio-demographic processes.

Overall, the European application demonstrates the analytical potential of the three-way multidimensional inequality framework in complex multilevel contexts. By integrating temporal evolution, multidimensional information, and hierarchical spatial structures, the 3wMDIGI framework provides a comprehensive representation of regional disparities that extends beyond traditional income-based measures. The evidence confirms that understanding territorial inequality within the European Union requires considering the interaction between economic, demographic, and social dimensions rather than focusing on single indicators in isolation.

5 Conclusions

This chapter proposes and empirically illustrates a multidimensional framework for measuring territorial inequality based on the three-way Multidimensional Inequality Gini Index (3wMDIGI) (Di Nuzzo et al., 2025). The proposed approach extends traditional inequality measures by jointly accounting for multiple dimensions of well-being, temporal dynamics, and spatial structures within a unified analytical framework. By integrating tensor decomposition techniques with multidimensional inequality measurement, the methodology provides a flexible tool capable of capturing complex socio-economic phenomena that evolve over time and across territories.

Despite its flexibility, the framework presents some limitations. First, it requires reasonably structured data, as the reliability of the CP decomposition benefits from a sufficient number of observations across units, variables, and time, while sparse or noisy data may affect stability. Second, interpretability may become less immediate in high-dimensional settings, where the meaning of variable scores and associated weights can be harder to assess. Third, the weighting scheme is data-driven and depends on the covariance structure of the dataset, as the CP decomposition extracts latent components based on joint variability across dimensions and time. Finally, results may show some sensitivity to modelling choices, such as normalisation procedures and parameter selection. These aspects should be considered, particularly in applications with high dimensionality, multicollinearity, or limited data availability.

References

Atkinson, A. B. (2015). *Inequality: What can be done?* Harvard University Press.

Bertacchini, E., Dalle Nogare, C., & Scuderi, R. (2021). Cultural participation and well-being: A review of empirical evidence. *Journal of Cultural Economics*.

Cellini, R., & Cuccia, T. (2025). In-person and on-line cultural participation amidst the digital change and the great lockdown: Reflections on regional data from Italy. In *New perspectives in the public and cultural sectors: Festschrift in honor of Ilde Rizzo* (pp. 103–121). Springer.

Cellini, R., & Cuccia, T. (2026). Income distribution and cultural participation: Evidence from Italy. *Journal of Cultural Economics*, 1–28.
Cellini, R., Cuccia, T., & De Cristofaro, A. (2024). The resilience of in-person cultural activities across the Italian regions amid the COVID-19 shock. *Scienze Regionali*, 1–34. Società editrice il Mulino.
Crescenzi, R., Di Cataldo, M., & Giua, M. (2016). EU Cohesion Policy and the socio-economic divide in Italy. *Regional Studies, 50*(10), 1650–1667.
Decancq, K., & Lugo, M. A. (2012). Inequality of wellbeing: A multidimensional approach. *Economica, 79*(316), 721–746.
Decancq, K., & Lugo, M. A. (2013). Weights in multidimensional indices of wellbeing: An overview. *Econometric Reviews, 32*(1), 7–34.
Di Nuzzo C., Tomaselli V., & Torrisi G. (2025). Assessing multilevel spatial inequality in EU regions: A multidimensional approach. *Spatial Economic Analysis*.
ISTAT. (2022). *Cittadini e ICT*. Istituto Nazionale di Statistica.
Kolda, T. G., & Bader, B. W. (2009). Tensor decompositions and applications. *SIAM Review, 51*(3), 455–500.
Nardo, M., Saisana, M., Saltelli, A., Tarantola, S., Hoffman, A., & Giovannini, E. (2005). *Handbook on constructing composite indicators*. OECD Statistics Working Paper.
OECD. (2008). *Handbook on constructing composite indicators: Methodology and user guide*. OECD Publishing.
OECD. (2019). *Measuring the digital transformation: A roadmap for the future*. OECD Publishing.
OECD. (2021). *The digital transformation during COVID-19*. OECD Policy Responses to Coronavirus.
Sen, A. (1999). *Development as freedom*. Oxford University Press.
SVIMEZ. (2022). *Rapporto SVIMEZ sull'economia del Mezzogiorno*. Associazione per lo sviluppo dell'industria nel Mezzogiorno.
van Dijk, J. (2020). *The digital divide*. Polity Press.

A New Map of Social Capital in Italy: An Emerging Trade-Off Between Prosperity and Civic Engagement?

Paola Bordandini and Luca Bortolotti

Abstract This chapter updates the geography of social capital in Italy, building on the territorial analyses of Putnam (1993) and Cartocci (2007). Using comparable provincial data for 2008, 2013, 2018, and 2022, it reconstructs the evolution of civic resources and examines their relationship with economic development. The geography of social capital still reflects Italy's North–South divide but shows new dynamics: the decline of the former "red regions", the strengthening of North-eastern provinces, and weaker social capital in large urban areas. At the same time, the link between GDP per capita and social capital has also weakened. The analysis suggests a curvilinear pattern: civic engagement increases with prosperity up to a threshold, beyond which it declines. This inverted-U relationship points to a potential trade-off between economic development and civic engagement. Overall, the chapter contributes to broader debates on modernisation by showing how rising prosperity may erode the social foundations of collective action.

1 Social Capital as Civic Engagement: A Tradition of Study

Analysing social capital and civic engagement in contemporary Italy means engaging with a long-standing tradition of studies on Italian civic culture, rooted in the classic works of the 1950s and 1960s (Almond & Verba, 1963; Banfield, 1958) and further developed over subsequent decades with increasing attention to Italy's internal diversity. This overview selectively highlights the key contributions that are most relevant to understanding the Italian case.

Over time, scholars moved away from the notion of a unified national political culture and instead advanced the idea of a country characterised by "Italies"—

P. Bordandini (✉)
Department of Political and Social Sciences, University of Bologna, Bologna, Italy
e-mail: paola.bordandini@unibo.it

L. Bortolotti
Department of Human and Social Sciences, E-campus University, Novedrate, Italy
e-mail: luca.bortolotti@uniecampus.it

R. Cellini et al. (eds.), *Cultural, Social, and Political Participation in the Internet Era*, Contributions to Economics, https://doi.org/10.1007/978-3-032-33072-7_3

three, four, or even five—each marked by distinct historical, economic, and social trajectories (Bagnasco, 1977; Caciagli, 1988; Cartocci, 1987; Trigilia, 1986).

This literature provides the background for Putnam et al.'s (1993) seminal work, "Making Democracy Work", and its first territorial mapping of social capital in Italy.

In his 1958 study, Banfield described southern Italy in the 1950s as a society dominated by what he called "amoral familism"—a behaviour that tends to "maximize the material, short-run advantage of the nuclear family" and "assume that all others will do likewise". Banfield's work was widely criticised (e.g. Marselli, 1963; Pizzorno, 1967; Silverman, 1968), yet familism, which can be seen as an extreme form of bonding social capital, has remained a central element in analyses of Italian political culture.

In 1963, the American political scientists Almond and Verba published "The Civic Culture", which compared five political systems—Italy, Mexico, the United States, Germany, and Great Britain—exploring the relationship between political culture and democratic stability. They described Italians as a people who "tend to look upon government and politics as unpredictable and threatening forces, and not as social institutions amenable to their influence". According to Almond and Verba, "the political culture of Italy does not support a stable and effective democratic system" (1963, 403). Although their analysis did not account for Italy's internal diversity, it represents the first systematic attempt to link civic culture to democratic stability. In the wake of "The Civic Culture", a wide range of comparative surveys was launched in different countries—such as the Eurobarometer, the World Values Survey, and the European Social Survey. These studies made it possible to compare citizens' cultural traits and their relationship with political institutions, and they portrayed Italian political culture as characterised by widespread dissatisfaction with the functioning of the political–administrative system and democracy, low confidence in political parties, and generalised social distrust (Bordandini, 2015, 2025).

Alongside these cross-national studies, from the 1960s onwards, a series of regionally focused investigations also developed in Italy, often supported by American research funding. The first of these initiatives was a large programme led by the Istituto Cattaneo in Bologna, aimed at analysing Italy's two major parties at the time—Christian Democracy (DC) and the Italian Communist Party (PCI). Although the aims of these studies were not explicitly centred on political culture, but rather on the functioning of the Italian political system as a whole, an exploration of the country's cultural characteristics proved inevitable and led to fundamental insights (Alberoni et al., 1967; Capecchi et al., 1968).

In the following decades, intra-regional analyses increasingly involved economists, sociologists, and political scientists. Their shared aim was to examine the economic, political, and cultural characteristics of the so-called "red" and "white" territorial subcultures (Caciagli, 1988, 2017; Trigilia, 1986), which had developed in the central and North-Eastern regions of the country—areas later referred to as the "Terza Italia" (Bagnasco, 1977).[1] This area stood apart from both the industrialised North-West—characterised by large enterprises, high levels of social mobilisation, and intense conflict between labour and capital—and from the less industrialised, more fragmented, and migration-prone South.[2] Beyond ideological divisions, the regions of the "Terza Italia" were distinguished by a peculiar civic culture based on strong social integration, low levels of conflict, high political and social participation, and highly legitimate local institutions.

It was on the basis of this line of research that Putnam et al. (1993) developed their concept of social capital and produced the first geography of civic culture in Italy, using territorial data as a proxy for civic engagement. In their view, social capital referred to "features of social organisation, such as trust, norms, and networks, that can improve the efficiency of society by facilitating coordinated actions" (Putnam et al., 1993, 167). Within this framework, social capital was conceived as an ingredient of spontaneous cooperation that sustains collective action. In other words, social capital is a collective and indivisible resource grounded in shared values and a sense of moral obligation towards others (Cartocci, 2007). From this perspective, social capital is not a private asset but a bridging good that fosters both spontaneous and organised cooperation, improving the overall functioning of democratic systems in their economic, social, and political dimensions (Cartocci, 2000).

In empirical terms, the index of social capital proposed by Putnam et al. in "Making Democracy Work" was based on two main dimensions—political participation and social participation—and five indicators specific to the Italian context: preference voting, referendum turnout, newspaper readership, and the density of sporting and cultural associations. These so-called objective territorial indicators captured behaviours closely linked to civic action, at least within the context of the "First Republic".[3]

However, the social, political, and economic transformations that re-shaped Italy during the 1990s and 2000s reduced the validity of these measures, prompting Cartocci (2007) to revise the original indicators in "Mappe del tesoro: Atlante del capitale sociale" in Italia and to propose a more detailed geography of social capital

[1] The red area featured a local political system dominated by the PCI and by its associative network. It included four regions in the Centre and North of Italy: Emilia-Romagna, Tuscany, Marche, and Umbria. The white area, dominated by the Catholic Church and the DC, included three regions of the northeast: Veneto, Friuli-Venezia Giulia, and Trentino-South Tyrol.

[2] The division of Italy into macro-regions has long characterised studies on electoral behaviour and political culture, dating back to the first research conducted by the Istituto Cattaneo in the 1960s. Over time, several classifications have been proposed, but no shared agreement has been reached (see Cartocci, 1987). In this chapter, we adopt the following classification into five Italian macro-regions: North-West (Piedmont, Aosta Valley, Lombardy, and Liguria), North-East or former white zone (Trentino-Alto Adige, Veneto, and Friuli Venezia Giulia), Central-North or former red zone (Emilia-Romagna, Tuscany, Umbria, and Marche), Central-South (Lazio, Abruzzo, Molise, and Sardinia), and South (Campania, Apulia, Basilicata, Calabria, and Sicily).

[3] The expression "First Italian Republic" refers to the political period from 1948 to 1992–94, which ended with the collapse of the traditional party system following major anti-corruption investigations (Mani Pulite, also known as Tangentopoli).

at the sub-regional level. His maps confirmed the historical North–South divide while also revealing growing differentiation within northern regions. More recently, this approach has been revisited and extended in a diachronic perspective, providing updated evidence on the evolution of social capital over time (Bordandini, 2025). Building on this line of research, this chapter first reconstructs the contemporary geography of social capital in Italy at the provincial level. It then explores how this geography relates to economic development, with particular attention to whether the association between social capital and prosperity remains linear or has evolved over time.

2 A New Geography of Social Capital in Italy: 2008–2022

As mentioned above, social capital has been measured both by Putnam et al. (1993) and by Cartocci (2007) through two analytical dimensions: political participation and social participation. In this study, building on the empirical analysis presented in Bordandini (2025), we retain the same dimensions while updating and integrating the indicators used to measure them.

As shown in Table 1, the social capital index for the 4 years considered (2008, 2013, 2018, and 2022) is based on five indicators measured at the provincial level. For the political participation dimension, we use turnout at national and European

Table 1 Indicators of social capital in Italy: a comparison (Bordandini, 2025; Cartocci, 2007 and Putnam et al., 1993)

Putnam et al., 1993	Cartocci, 2007	Bordandini, 2025
Unit of analysis: region Data: 1980s	*Unit of analysis: province Data: early 2000s*	*Unit of analysis: province Data for four time points: 2008, 2013, 2018, and 2022*
POLITICAL PARTICIPATION: 1. Preference voting between 1953 and 1979 2. Turnout at referendums held between 1974 and 1987 SOCIAL PARTICIPATION: 1. Newspaper readership in 1975 2. Density of sports and cultural associations in 1981	POLITICAL PARTICIPATION: 1. Turnout at the 1999 European elections and 2001 National elections 2. Turnout at the 1999, 2000, and 2001 referendums 3. Share of non-sports newspapers sold (2000–2001) SOCIAL PARTICIPATION: 1. Distribution of grassroots sports associations (1999–2002) 2. Share of blood donors and blood donations (2002)	POLITICAL PARTICIPATION: 1. Turnout at National and European elections (2008–2024) 2. Share of non-sports newspapers sold (2008–2022) SOCIAL PARTICIPATION: 1. Distribution of grassroots sports association (2008–2019) 2. Diffusion of non-profit organisations (2011–2021) 3. Share of blood donations (2009–2022)

Source: Author's elaboration based on data from Putnam et al. (1993); Cartocci (2007); Bordandini (2025)

elections and the newspaper readership. These two indicators measure, respectively, visible and invisible political participation, consistently with the previous literature. For the social participation dimension, we include the distribution of grassroots sports associations, the presence of non-profit organisations, and blood donations—three indicators that capture the spread of the values of sport, solidarity, and altruism (for further details, see Bordandini, 2025).

To construct the social capital index, the five indicators were first standardised and then combined into a single aggregate measure. Prior to aggregation, their empirical coherence was assessed in each year by examining the correlation matrix of the five indicators. All pairwise correlations were positive across the four time points, although electoral turnout was not always statistically significant and emerged as the weakest indicator overall (Bordandini & Bortolotti, 2025a). This contrasts sharply with Cartocci's earlier findings, in which turnout displayed the highest coefficients and constituted the core component of the index (Cartocci, 2007: 97).

A Principal Component Analysis (PCA) of the five indicators, carried out before constructing the index, confirmed the existence of a single latent dimension in 2013 and 2018 and a two-dimensional structure in 2008 and 2022, with electoral participation loading more weakly on the main component. To ensure comparability across the four time points, the PCA was constrained to extract a single factor also in 2008 and 2022 (for details, see Bordandini & Bortolotti, 2025a).

Table 2 shows the values of the social capital indices in the different years and Italian regions, as well as the standard deviation between provinces across the four periods. The lowest values were consistently recorded in the southern regions—namely Campania (64–66), Calabria (69–73), Apulia (70–71), and Sicily (70–78). The highest values were found in the North-eastern regions: Trentino-South Tyrol (141–155), Friuli-Venezia Giulia (130–137), and Aosta Valley (139–142). The other northern regions, the former "red regions", and Sardinia showed values slightly above the national average of 100, while the Central-South and southern regions were slightly below the average.

The standard deviation between provinces, as well as the gap between the maximum and minimum values, increased over time. This result suggests a slow but steady transformation in the distribution of social capital across Italy—a pattern that will be further discussed in the following pages.

Figure 1 shows the distribution of social capital across Italian provinces in 2022, divided into quintiles.[4] This territorial distribution of social capital closely resembles those identified by Putnam et al. (1993) and Cartocci (2007), based respectively on data from the 1980s and the early 2000s. At the same time, however, our map reveals important differences from these earlier studies. In brief, the once

[4] The maps show provinces coloured according to quintiles of social capital. Provinces coloured white fall into the first quintile and have the lowest levels of social capital, while those coloured black belong to the fifth quintile and display the highest levels. In Fig. 1, the boundaries and names of the Italian regions are also shown to facilitate interpretation.

Table 2 Indices of social capital by region (national average = 100), standard deviation between provinces, province minimum (min), province maximum (max), difference max−min. Years: 2008, 2013, 2018, and 2022

Region		Social capital index			
		2008	2013	2018	2022
North West	Aosta Valley	139	142	140	136
	Piedmont	104	106	106	104
	Lombardy	104	102	102	102
	Liguria	116	120	121	118
North East (former white area)	Trentino-South Tyrol	141	146	152	155
	Friuli-Venezia Giulia	130	134	138	137
	Veneto	111	111	112	112
Centre-North (former red area)	Emilia-Romagna	114	114	112	113
	Tuscany	108	110	109	110
	Marche	112	115	117	116
	Umbria	108	110	106	105
Centre-South	Lazio	87	88	86	84
	Molise	96	96	92	88
	Abruzzo	94	95	94	97
	Sardinia	109	105	117	121
South	Campania	66	64	65	64
	Apulia	73	70	71	70
	Basilicata	88	89	85	82
	Calabria	73	71	69	69
	Sicily	78	75	70	72
Standard deviation between provinces		20	21	23	24
Province minimum		55	55	50	49
Province maximum		149	153	159	169
Difference max − min		94	98	109	120

cohesive "red regions" of central Italy have lost their traditional primacy, overtaken by the northern special-statute regions. Major urban areas now display lower levels of social capital than their surrounding provinces, while Sardinia performs above the national average. Increasing internal fragmentation also characterises the North-West and parts of central Italy.

Figure 2 compares Bordandini's social capital index (Y) with Putnam's index (X). As Putnam measured social capital at the regional, rather than provincial, level, we aggregate provinces by region to ensure comparability. The fitted line closely follows the bisector, indicating, as expected, a positive correlation between the two indices. Regions falling below the fitted line display lower levels of social capital in 2022 than would be predicted on the basis of Putnam's index, while those above the line perform better than expected. Most regions in the South and Centre-South remain in the lower-left quadrant of the plot, showing low levels of social capital according to both measures. However, Abruzzo and Sardinia stand out: while they

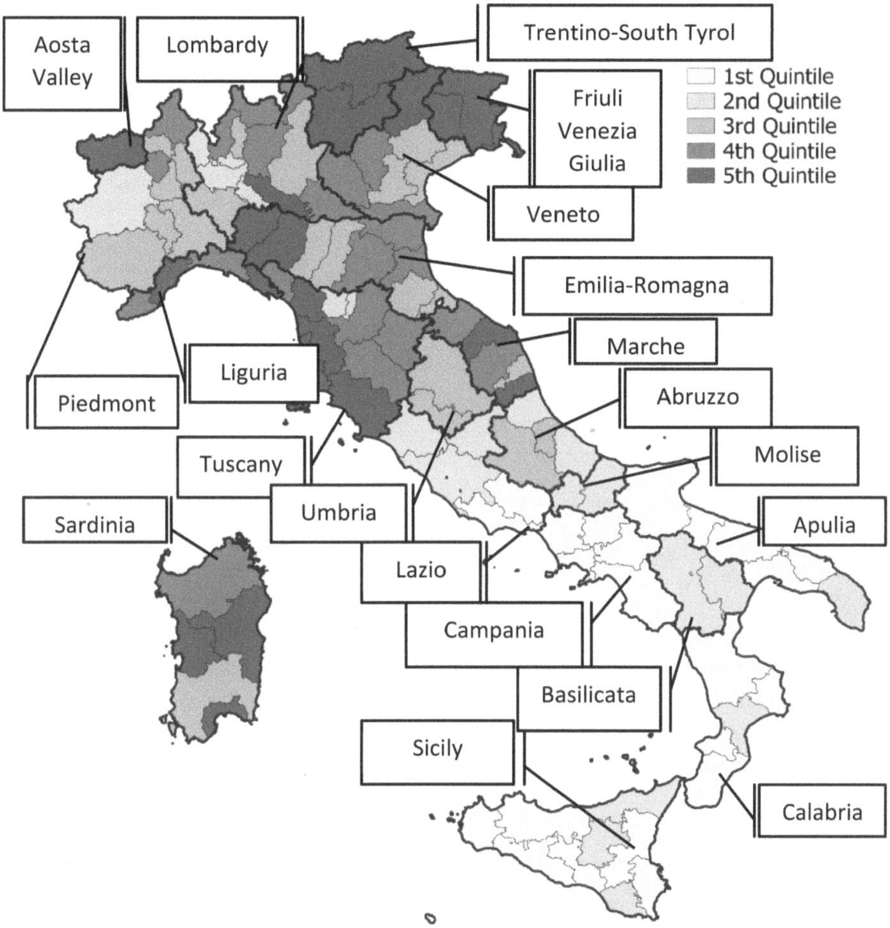

Fig. 1 Geography of social capital in Italian provinces, 2022, divided into five quintiles from those with lowest social capital (1st) to those with highest social capital (5th)

were characterised by medium-low levels of social capital in Putnam's index, they reached medium-high levels in 2022. Finally, among the regions with high levels of social capital in Putnam's classification, many in the Centre and North-West fall below the fitted line, indicating a lower-than-expected performance in 2022.

The availability of a social capital index based on the same indicators at four points in time allows a diachronic comparison over a period characterised by economic, political, and social challenges. Figure 3 maps the changes in the provincial ranking of social capital between 2008 and 2022, respectively, the first and the last year considered. Interestingly, some of the results emerging from this figure recall the differences observed in Fig. 2. Five major cities in the Centre-North

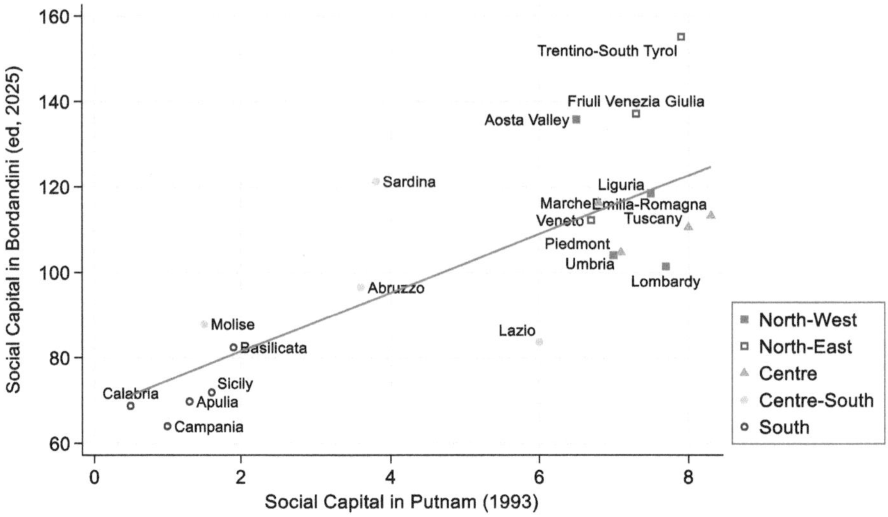

Fig. 2 Social Capital in Putnam et al. (1993) and Bordandini (2025)

(Bologna, Florence, Genoa, Milan, and Venice) have lost more than 20 positions in the ranking (shown in red in Fig. 3). Notable losses in the ranking also occurred in other provinces of the "Terza Italia" and in Sicily. By contrast, the largest gains involved several Sardinian provinces, while other provinces in the "Terza Italia" and in Abruzzo also recorded significant improvements.

Given the changes observed over the last 55 years, it is useful to examine the extent to which these developments are territorially structured. In particular, this allows us to examine whether provinces experiencing increases or decreases in social capital tend to be geographically close to each other. Since social capital can be conceived as a territorial resource, we investigate its spatial distribution through spatial autocorrelation using Moran's I statistic (1950). This test considers a weight matrix based on the inverse distance between all 107 provinces, assessing whether geographically closer provinces display more similar levels of social capital. Although a positive spatial autocorrelation might be expected, it is also important to assess Moran's I trend over time. The analysis reveals a strong and statistically significant positive spatial autocorrelation in all 4 years examined. However, the strength of this spatial clustering shows a decline over time, with Moran's I decreasing from 0.410 in 2008 to 0.366 in 2022, as shown in Fig. 4. The standard error, which remains constant over time, indicates that the results are statistically significant in all years. In other words, provinces with similar levels of social capital tend to cluster geographically, but this relationship has weakened over the last 15 years.

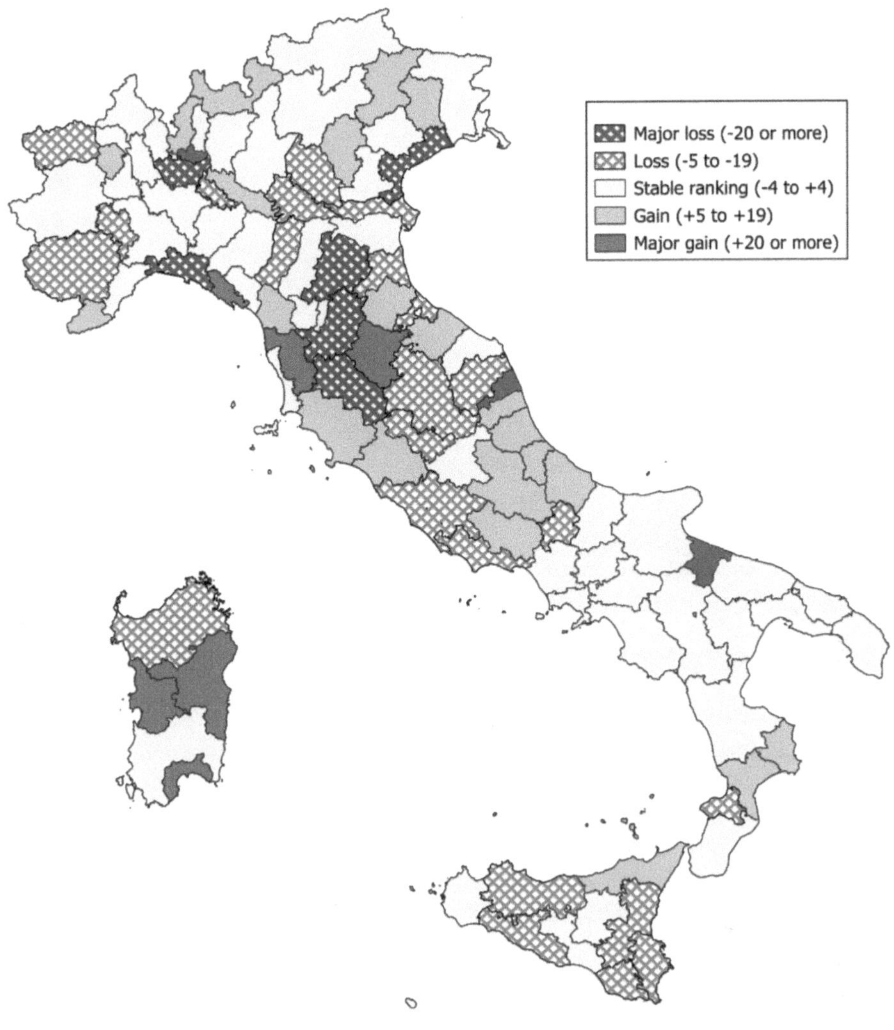

Fig. 3 Main differences in social capital 2008–2022

3 Social Capital and Economic Growth: An Inverted-U Relationship?

Examining changes in social capital over time also provides a useful perspective on its relationship with economic development. Although much of the literature reports a positive association between these two dimensions, the debate remains unsettled. Some studies emphasise the beneficial effects of social capital on economic performance, while others question the direction of causality or suggest that the

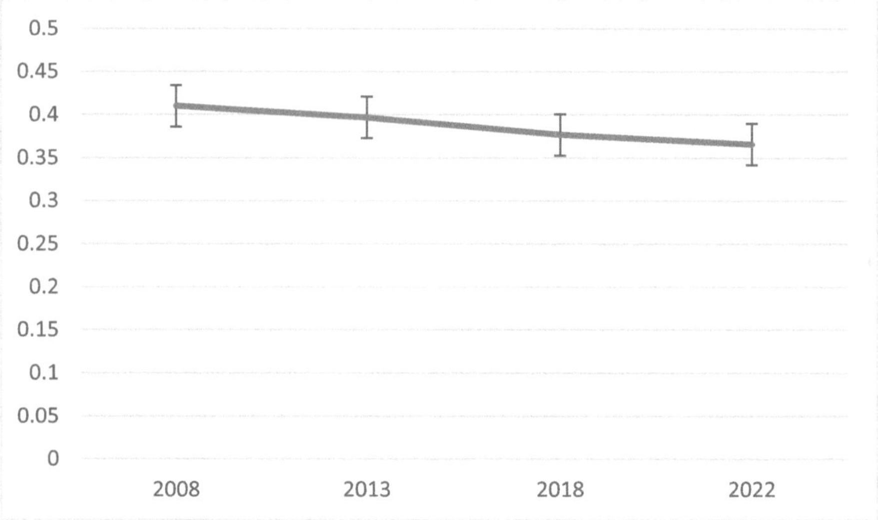

Fig. 4 Spatial autocorrelation of social capital: Moran's I between 2008 and 2022

relationship may be non-linear, context-dependent, or even negative under specific conditions.

A first line of research interprets social capital, or related concepts such as generalised trust, as a resource that fosters investment, innovation, and institutional performance, helping to account for part of the "Solow residual"[5] (Fukuyama, 1995; Hall & Jones, 1996; Helliwell, 2008; Zack & Knack, 2001). Italy has often been central to this debate. Since the Seventies, Giacomo Becattini (1975, 1989) had described the take-off of several industrial districts in Italy (more precisely in regions such as Tuscany, Emilia-Romagna, Marche, and Veneto, i.e. those labelled as "Terza Italia" by Bagnasco, 1977) thanks to the "industrial atmosphere" that intrinsically characterised specific communities sharing tacit knowledge and minimising transaction costs.

However, not all the literature considers social capital as a positive and constructive: other scholars argue that insular and dense networks can constrain entrepreneurial activity and economic development (Alesina & La Ferrara, 2002; Granovetter, 2005). A more nuanced perspective relaxes the assumption of a linear and unidirectional relationship: economic growth can both foster and damage social capital, for example, an excessive marketisation of social and entertainment activities may substitute altruistic motivations with market pricing. Indeed, (some)

[5] According to the neoclassical growth model (Solow, 1956), capital and labour investments determine most of the economic growth, besides these, the remaining, unexplained factors that sustain growth (TFP—Total Factor Productivity) are a broad and somewhat nebulous category that include social, institutional, and organisational factors.

goods provided through the market and (some) goods provided by altruism are substitute goods. In this perspective, an emblematic concept of the social capital—growth nexus is the "defensive growth" theory (Bartolini, 2021; Bartolini & Bonatti, 2008): if general trust is lacking in a society, individuals divert part of their income for supervision costs and other expenditure to protect their assets (defensive expenditure); this transaction has a negative externality which further hamper general trust, inducing other individuals to reduce their social participation in favour of market activities that generates the resources for further defensive expenditures. The defensive growth theory (Bartolini, 2021) also explains how the negative relationship between social capital and growth may exacerbate over time in a vicious circle, eventually outweighing the "positive" channels mentioned above.

The previous empirical measures of social capital in Italy have tested the relationship with economic development through correlations, not exploring the case of non-linearity. Indeed, Putnam et al. (1993: 219) compute an index of economic modernity of Italian regions, comprehensive of per capita income, regional GDP, the shares of the workforce in agricultural and industrial sectors, and the share of value added in agricultural and industrial sectors. This index exhibits a strong correlation with social capital (Pearson's coefficient = 0.81). This nexus has not weakened in the following decades. Cartocci and Vanelli (2008) observe a correlation coefficient between Italian provinces' social capital and GDP per capita at the turn of the century even stronger: 0.82.

Although the correlation indicated by our dataset remains strong and significant, also mirroring the North-South divide, it is substantially lower than the previous ones, and it exhibits a decreasing trend over time, reaching Pearson's coefficient = 0.62 in 2022. This decrease could be linked to the already mentioned decreasing social capital in large cities of the Centre and North, which are also among the richest provinces, and once reinforced the magnitude of the correlation. This weakened correlation (better described in Bordandini & Bortolotti, 2025b: 130–132) encouraged us to estimate the possibility of a non-linear correlation.

A parabolic correlation can be estimated through an OLS regression considering the impact of GDP per capita and squared GDP per capita on social capital. We remind that a parabola trend is represented mathematically by the formula:

$$y = -ax^2 + bx + c$$

An inverted-U parabola has a significantly negative value −a and a significantly positive value b. The turning point x_{TP}, which represents the level of x at which y reaches its maximum, is identified by the formula:

$$x_{TP} = \frac{-b}{2a}$$

Returning to the relationship between social capital and income, with social capital as the dependent variable and GDP per capita as the independent variable, it should be recalled that both variables are expressed as index numbers, with 100

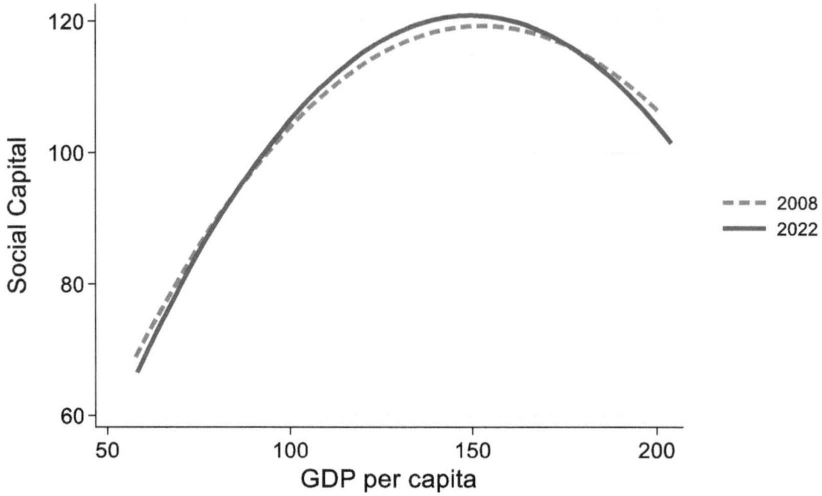

Fig. 5 Fitted values social capital-GDP per capita parabolic relationship in 2008 and 2022

Table 3 Estimated coefficients of GDP and GDP2 in explaining social capital, 2008, 2013, 2018, and 2022, OLS estimation

	2008	2013	2018	2022
GDP/c^2	−0.0056***	−0.0061***	−0.0062***	−0.0065***
GDP/c	1.714***	1.865***	1.864***	1.950***
x_{TP}	152	152	150	149

Note: *, **, *** indicate, respectively, 10%, 5%, and 1% significance level

corresponding to the national average. This point is important for interpreting Fig. 5. As long as the estimated turning point remains above 100 on the income scale, most provinces still lie on the upward-sloping segment of the curve. In other words, for the majority of provinces, higher income levels are still associated with higher levels of social capital, although with a decreasing marginal effect.

The estimates reported in Table 3 confirm the hypothesis of an inverted-U relationship and also indicate that this pattern becomes slightly more pronounced in 2022 than in previous years. At the same time, the estimated turning point remains above 100. This means that only a limited number of provinces have already reached income levels above the turning point. These are mainly large urban provinces in central and northern Italy, including some of the cases showing declining social capital already illustrated in Fig. 3.

Milan is the clearest example. Although it ranks as the wealthiest Italian province in terms of GDP per capita, it displays below-average levels of social capital, and these have declined over the period considered here. A similar pattern can be observed in other metropolitan contexts. Indeed, the inverted-U pattern reported in Table 3 remains robust and statistically significant even after excluding Milan from the analysis. This suggests that, in some highly advanced local economies, economic growth may be associated with lifestyles and forms of social organisation that reduce the time and opportunities available for civic engagement and social participation. This pattern is consistent with the defensive growth hypothesis, although the present analysis does not identify the causal mechanisms involved.

Although the differences in the estimates for 2008, 2013, 2018, and 2022 are slight, these shifts suggest a transformation in the relationship between GDP and social capital towards a curvilinear pattern, as illustrated in Fig. 5. This graph shows the fitted values of the relationship between GDP per capita and social capital in 2008 and 2022 (which was already observed in Bordandini & Bortolotti, 2025b: 123), confirming the inverted-U (concave) parabolic relationship. The two parabolas, the dotted line for 2008 and the straight line for 2022, are very similar: initially there is a positive correlation, but beyond a certain provincial GDP threshold (approximately 50% above the national average), the relationship tends to reverse. This result is robust over time, with very slight differences: the parabolic trend is more pronounced in 2022, with a turning point recorded at a lower level of GDP.

It is too early to determine whether this trade-off will spread to a larger number of northern provinces. In 2022, it remained concentrated in a limited set of large and relatively affluent provinces in central and northern Italy.

In economics, inverted-U curves related to the effects of economic development are famous under the name of the Kuznets curve, named for the influential economist Simon Kuznets, who first proposed a mechanical relationship between income and inequality (1955). According to this hypothesis, economic development initially fuels inequality before reaching a turning point after which the relationship becomes negative. A similarly optimistic scenario was formulated regarding the environmental impact of GDP growth in terms of greenhouse emissions (Grossman & Krueger, 1991).

Here arises a curious paradox: notably, our social capital variable points to a positive social attribute, fundamentally different from inequality or emissions. Consequently, the identification of a turning point and potential trade-off between economic development and this beneficial social resource carries opposite (pessimistic) normative implications. However, Kuznets curve formulations have frequently proven overly simplistic for capturing the complexity of development processes, both regarding inequality (Piketty, 2006) and environmental emissions (Stern, 2004). We believe that this critique could extend to the social capital domain as well. Indeed, social capital data in Italian provinces suggests that the relationship between social capital and economic development is more complex than a simple linear or even consistent curvilinear model, and may change over time. The defensive growth hypothesis remains a plausible explanation for the observed inverted-U patterns, particularly in high-income metropolitan contexts where time scarcity and changing leisure patterns may erode traditional forms of social connection. However, current data only points to a trade-off in a limited number of cases, and assuming a strong causal relationship could fail to account for the institutional, political, and cultural mediators that shape how economic development affects political and social participation.

4 Conclusions

The updated geography of social capital in Italy confirms both persistence and change. The enduring North–South divide remains a defining feature of the country's civic landscape, yet new patterns have emerged. The former "red" regions of central Italy, once the core of civic engagement, have lost their traditional advantage, while several provinces in the North-East display the highest levels of social capital. The decline observed in major metropolitan areas suggests that civic resources are increasingly rooted in medium-sized and smaller communities rather than large urban centres.

From a diachronic perspective, the analysis reveals a slow but steady reconfiguration of Italy's civic map. The weakening of spatial autocorrelation points to a growing fragmentation of civic cohesion, as provinces with similar levels of social capital are now less geographically clustered than in the past. This indicates a more complex, less regionally homogeneous pattern of civic engagement.

The relationship between social capital and economic development, while still positive, appears to have changed in nature. The evidence of an inverted-U relationship suggests that economic growth may yield diminishing—or even negative—returns for civic life once a certain threshold of prosperity is reached. This trade-off, observable mainly in large and affluent provinces, raises questions about the social sustainability of development.

These findings invite further reflection on how economic modernisation, urban lifestyles, and institutional frameworks interact with civic engagement—and on how policy can support both prosperity and the social foundations that make collective life possible.

Acknowledgments We thank the anonymous referee and the editors for their valuable comments. Part of this chapter draws on results presented in the book *Civic Decline or Civic Shift* (Bordandini, 2025). We also acknowledge all those who directly or indirectly contributed to the preparation of that volume. The views and opinions expressed in this chapter are solely those of the authors.

References

Alberoni, F., Capecchi, V., Manoukian, A., Olivetti, F., & Tosi, A. (1967). *L'attivista di partito: Una indagine sui militanti di base nel Pci e nella Dc*. Il Mulino.

Alesina, A., & La Ferrara, E. (2002). Who trusts others? *Journal of Public Economics, 85*(2), 207–234.

Almond, G. A., & Verba, S. (1963). *The civic culture: Political attitudes and democracy in five nations*. Princeton University Press.

Bagnasco, A. (1977). *Tre Italie: la problematica territoriale dello sviluppo italiano*. Il Mulino.

Banfield, E. C. (1958). *The moral basis of a backward society*. The Free Press.

Bartolini, S. (2021). *Ecologia della felicità. Perché vivere meglio aiuta il pianeta*. Aboca Editore.

Bartolini, S., & Bonatti, L. (2008). Endogenous growth, decline in social capital and expansion of market activities. *Journal of Economic Behavior and Organization, 67*(3–4), 917.

Becattini, G. (1975). Lo sviluppo economico della Toscana. Firenze: Irpet. In G. Becattini (Ed.), (1987) *Mercato e forze locali: il distretto industriale*. Bologna.
Becattini, G. (1989). *Il distretto industriale*. Rosenberg & Sellier.
Bordandini, P. (2015). La fiducia in Italia. In *L'Italia e le sue regioni-volume quarto: "Società"* (pp. 79–92). Istituto della Enciclopedia Italiana Fondata da G. Treccani.
Bordandini, P. (Ed.). (2025). *Civic decline or civic shift? Social capital in Italy* (pp. 95–115). Springer Nature Switzerland.
Bordandini, P., & Bortolotti, L. (2025a). A geography of social capital in Italy 2008–2022. In *Civic decline or civic shift? Social capital in Italy* (pp. 95–115). Cham.
Bordandini, P., & Bortolotti, L. (2025b). Social capital, GDP and quality of services. In *Civic decline or civic shift? Social capital in Italy* (pp. 117–140). Cham.
Caciagli, M. (1988). Quante Italie? Persistenza e trasformazione delle culture politiche subnazionali. *Polis, 3*, 429–457.
Caciagli, M. (2017). *Addio alla provincia rossa. Origini, apogeo e declino di una cultura politica*. Carocci.
Capecchi, V., Cioni, P. V., Galli, G., & Sivini, G. (1968). *Il comportamento elettorale in Italia*. Il Mulino.
Cartocci, R. (1987). Otto risposte a un problema: la divisione dell'Italia in zone politicamente omogenee. *Rivista Italiana di Scienza Politica, 17*(1), 3–32.
Cartocci, R. (2000). Chi ha paura dei valori? Capitale sociale e dintorni. *Rivista Italiana di Scienza Politica, 30*(3), 423–474.
Cartocci, R. (2007). *Mappe del tesoro. Atlante del capitale sociale in Italia*. Il Mulino.
Cartocci, R., & Vanelli, V. (2008). Acqua, rifiuti e capitale sociale in Italia. Una geografia della qualità dei servizi pubblici e del senso civico. In *Misure—Materiali di ricerca dell'Istituto Cattaneo*. Il Mulino.
Fukuyama, F. (1995). *Trust: The social virtues and the creation of prosperity*. Free Press.
Granovetter, M. (2005). The impact of social structure on economic outcomes. *Journal of Economic Perspectives, 19*(1), 33–50.
Grossman, G. M., & Krueger, A. B. (1991). Environmental impacts of a North American free trade agreement. *NBER Working Paper* 3914, NBER.
Hall, R. E., & Jones, C. I. (1996). The productivity of nations. *NBER Working Paper* w5812.
Helliwell, J. (2008). *Life satisfaction and quality of development*. Working Paper 14507. National Bureau of Economic Research.
Kuznets, S. (1955). Economic growth and income inequality. *The American Economic Review, 45*(1), 1–28.
Marselli, G. A. (1963). American sociologists and Italian peasant society: With reference to the book of Banfield. *Sociologia Ruralis, 3*(1), 319–338.
Moran, P. A. (1950). Notes on continuous stochastic phenomena. *Biometrika, 37*(1/2), 17–23.
Piketty, T. (2006). The Kuznets curve: Yesterday and tomorrow. In *Understanding poverty* (pp. 63–72).
Pizzorno, A. (1967). Familismo amorale e marginalità storica ovvero perché non c'è niente da fare a Montegrano. *Quaderni di Sociologia, 26*(27), 349–362.
Putnam, R., Leonardi, R., & Nanetti, R. (1993). *Making democracy work: Civic traditions in modern Italy*. Princeton University Press.
Silverman, S. F. (1968). Agricultural organization, social structure, and values in Italy: Amoral familism reconsidered. *American Anthropologist, 70*(1), 1–20.
Solow, R. M. (1956). A contribution to the theory of economic growth author (s): Robert M. Solow source. *The Quarterly Journal of Economics, 70*(1), 65–94.
Stern, D. I. (2004). The rise and fall of the environmental Kuznets curve. *World Development, 32*(8), 1419–1439.
Trigilia, C. (1986). *Grandi partiti e piccole imprese: Comunisti e democristiani nelle regioni*. Il Mulino.
Zack, P. J., & Knack, S. (2001). Trust and growth. *Economic Journal, 111*, 295–321.

From Social Participation to the Civic Gift: The Geography of Blood Donation in Italy

Marialuisa Villani and Stella Volturo

Abstract This chapter examines the relationship between social participation, social capital and blood donation as a form of civic engagement in contemporary Italy. Drawing on the civic tradition of social capital, participation is conceptualised as a socially embedded process shaped by organisational infrastructures, institutional arrangements and territorial contexts. Particular attention is given to non-profit organisations as key intermediaries sustaining networks of cooperation, trust and reciprocity, and contributing to social cohesion and sustainability. Within this framework, blood donation is interpreted as a paradigmatic form of organised altruism and as an empirical expression of a "civic gift". In the Italian context, it represents a link between associative participation and individual civic action, translating organisational infrastructures into repeated practices of giving. Unlike other forms of volunteering, donation involves a tangible contribution to collective well-being, mediated by institutional systems ensuring equitable redistribution. The empirical analysis, based on secondary data from the National and Regional Blood Centres, highlights territorial differences in donation patterns, reflecting uneven civic infrastructures and associational capacity. Focusing on the geography of donation, the chapter shows how participation is structured and unevenly distributed, and argues that civicness is a territorially embedded relational process through which solidarity is organised and reproduced.

1 Introduction

In contemporary societies, social participation represents a crucial dimension for understanding how collective life is organised and sustained. Civic engagement,

---

M. Villani (✉)
Department of Political and Social Sciences, University of Bologna, Bologna, Italy
e-mail: marialuisa.villani@unibo.it

S. Volturo
Department of Sociology and Business Law, University of Bologna, Bologna, Italy
e-mail: stella.volturo2@unibo.it

R. Cellini et al. (eds.), *Cultural, Social, and Political Participation in the Internet Era*, Contributions to Economics, https://doi.org/10.1007/978-3-032-33072-7_4

voluntary action and participation in associative networks contribute to the formation of relational environments in which cooperation, trust and shared norms can develop. These relational structures, commonly described through the concept of social capital, facilitate collective action and provide a basis for forms of solidarity that extend beyond immediate personal interests (Fukuyama, 1995; Putnam, 2000).

In this chapter, social capital is understood primarily in the civic tradition associated with Putnam's work. From this perspective, social capital refers to the networks, norms of reciprocity and trust that facilitate coordination and cooperation for mutual benefit (Putnam, 2000; Putnam et al., 1993). Rather than being interpreted solely as an individual resource, social capital is considered here as a collective property characterised by dense associative networks and widespread civic engagement. This civic dimension of social capital, often described as civicness, highlights the importance of participation in voluntary organisations, associational life and practices of collective action in sustaining cooperative social relations.

The relationship between social capital and social cohesion has long been debated in social science literature. While the concept of cohesion has historically been used to refer to the conditions that enable social order, integration and collective stability, its analytical boundaries remain contested and often intertwined with broader normative and political concerns (European Committee for Social Cohesion, 2004; Pahl, 1991). Social cohesion is frequently invoked in public discourse as an objective that societies should pursue, particularly in contexts characterised by growing inequalities, fragmentation and institutional uncertainty. In this sense, cohesion functions both as an analytical concept and as a normative reference that signals the importance of maintaining inclusive and cooperative social environments.

Within this debate, social capital offers a more operational perspective for analysing how cohesion is produced and reproduced in everyday interactions. Networks of relationships, shared expectations and norms of reciprocity can support cooperation among individuals and groups, facilitating collective initiatives and strengthening the capacity of communities to respond to common challenges (Edwards et al., 2001; Putnam et al., 1993). From this perspective, civic engagement is not only a manifestation of individual participation but also a mechanism for reinforcing social cohesion (Prandini & Villani, 2025).

Participation in associative life plays a particularly important role in this process. Voluntary associations and non-profit organisations represent organisational arenas where individuals can contribute to collective initiatives, develop networks of solidarity and take part in activities aimed at improving community life. These organisations can therefore be interpreted as infrastructures of civic engagement that mediate between individual motivations and broader patterns of social cooperation (Edwards et al., 2001; Sirianni & Friedland, 2001). However, the relationship between participation and social capital is neither automatic nor uniform. The density of associative networks, the institutional context and the socio-economic characteristics of territories all influence the capacity of organisations to generate meaningful forms of social capital.

In this sense, the territorial distribution of non-profit organisations often reflects broader social and institutional ecosystems rather than purely cultural predispositions towards participation. Differences in economic development, governance structures and social infrastructure contribute to shaping opportunities for civic engagement and influence the capacity of communities to organise collective action. These territorial variations highlight the importance of considering participation not only as an individual behaviour but also as a phenomenon embedded within specific social and institutional contexts.

The growing attention to social sustainability further reinforces the relevance of these dynamics. While the environmental and economic dimensions of sustainability have long dominated international debates, the social dimension has progressively gained recognition as a crucial element for understanding the long-term viability of development processes (Boulding, 1966; WCED, 1987). From this perspective, social sustainability refers to the conditions that allow societies to promote equity, participation and collective well-being while maintaining the capacity of communities to cooperate and pursue shared goals. Social capital is often considered a key resource in this framework, since networks of trust and reciprocity can support inclusive social relations and facilitate democratic participation.

Among the various forms of civic engagement that contribute to social sustainability, blood donation represents a particularly meaningful practice. Unlike many other forms of voluntary participation, donation involves a direct and tangible contribution to the well-being of others. It is a form of organised altruism that combines individual motivations with institutional arrangements designed to ensure the equitable distribution of a vital resource. In this sense, blood donation can be interpreted as a concrete expression of what may be defined as a civic gift, a practice through which individuals participate in the production of collective goods and contribute to the reproduction of solidarity within society.

Analysing blood donation from this perspective enables exploration of how civic participation takes shape within specific institutional and territorial contexts. Donation systems rely on organisational infrastructures, regulatory frameworks and voluntary mobilisation that together structure the ways in which individuals contribute to collective welfare.

Building on these considerations, this chapter explores the relationship between social capital, social participation and blood donation as a form of civic engagement. The analysis develops a conceptual framework that links debates on social cohesion and social sustainability with the empirical study of associative participation and non-profit infrastructures. By focusing on blood donation as a case of organised altruism, the chapter aims to show how civic participation can materialise in concrete practices that contribute to collective well-being and to the maintenance of cooperative social relations.

The chapter is organised as follows. The next section discusses the relationship between social capital, social cohesion and social sustainability, outlining the theoretical framework that informs the analysis. The third section examines social participation and the role of non-profit organisations as infrastructures of civic engagement. The fourth section introduces the concept of the civic gift and discusses blood donation as a form of altruistic participation. The empirical section then analyses data on blood donation in Italy, highlighting territorial patterns and regional differences. The final section reflects on the implications of these findings for understanding the relationship between participation, solidarity and social sustainability.

2 Social Capital, Cohesion and Sustainability

The relationship between social capital and social cohesion has long been at the centre of sociological and interdisciplinary debate. Although the two concepts are frequently used together in discussions about collective well-being and democratic stability, they refer to distinct analytical dimensions. Social cohesion generally indicates the capacity of a society to sustain stable and legitimate social bonds among its members, ensuring inclusion, participation and trust across both interpersonal relations and institutional arrangements. In contrast, social capital (Cartocci, 2007; Putnam, 2000), as conceptualised by Putnam as features of social organisation such as trust, norms and networks, focuses more specifically on the relational resources that facilitate coordination and collective action.

Several scholars have emphasised that these two concepts should be understood as closely interconnected but not interchangeable. As Hulse and Stone (2007) argue, dense networks of social relations can reinforce cohesion by enabling individuals to participate in social and civic life, while cohesive social environments provide the institutional and cultural conditions that support their formation. In this sense, social capital contributes to the strengthening of social cohesion by fostering trust, cooperation and shared expectations within communities. At the same time, cohesive societies are more capable of ensuring that individuals, including those in vulnerable positions, are able to participate meaningfully in social life and benefit from collective resources (Oxoby, 2009; Sen, 1985, 1992).

Distinguishing between the two concepts is analytically important because it allows us to move from a general reflection on the conditions that hold societies together to a more precise examination of the mechanisms through which cooperation is produced and reproduced in everyday life. Social cohesion describes the broader social environment within which individuals interact, encompassing both the legitimacy of institutions and the inclusiveness of social relations. Social capital, by contrast, highlights the relational processes through which individuals build networks, develop trust and engage in forms of reciprocal exchange.

From this perspective, social capital can be interpreted as one of the relational mechanisms through which cohesive social environments are constructed and maintained. Networks of trust and cooperation not only facilitate collective initiatives but also contribute to the development of shared civic norms that sustain participation and collective engagement. Where such relational infrastructures are dense and widely accessible, individuals are more likely to participate in associative life and to contribute to collective goods.

The distinction between social capital and social cohesion, therefore, helps clarify how cooperation operates across different levels of social life. While social cohesion captures the overall capacity of societies to maintain inclusive and legitimate social relations, social capital focuses on the concrete relational dynamics through which these relations are produced. In this sense, social capital should not be interpreted as a simple indicator of cohesion, but rather as one of the processes through which cohesion may be strengthened, particularly in contexts where participation and shared civic norms are present (Hulse & Stone, 2007; Klein, 2013; Oxoby, 2009).

In this perspective, the notion of social sustainability offers a broader analytical lens through which the interplay between social capital and social cohesion can be interpreted in relation to the long-term stability and well-being of societies.

In the last decades, the notion of social sustainability has gained autonomy as a theoretical and policy framework, deeply intertwined with the civic dimension of social life, or civicness. Civicness refers to the set of prosocial norms, trust relations, and civic engagement practices that sustain cooperation and legitimacy within a democratic community (Colantonio, 2011; Vallance et al., 2011). As several scholars highlight (Dempsey et al., 2011; Pieper et al., 2019), social sustainability encompasses equity and inclusion, participatory democracy and the subjective dimension of well-being. Social sustainability is therefore not only about the fair distribution of resources and opportunities, but about the shared culture of trust, participation and cooperation that people enact in their everyday lives.

Within this framework, civicness acts as an interface between social capital and sustainability. It is through civic behaviours—volunteering, associational membership, participation in local initiatives and practices of giving—that the abstract potential of social capital translates into concrete practices. The geography of these practices reveals the uneven distribution of civic infrastructures across territories: some territories exhibit dense networks of cooperation, while others remain characterised by social fragility and low institutional trust. Mapping these differences means understanding the spatial logic of social cohesion.

If civic participation is to be analysed empirically, it is useful to distinguish between its organised and its embedded forms. On the one hand, participation takes shape through formal settings such as associations, voluntary organisations and non-profit networks, where cooperation becomes durable and publicly recognisable. On the other hand, it is also expressed through less visible but socially meaningful practices of giving, helping and contributing to collective well-being. This distinction helps clarify why the study of civicness cannot stop at attitudes alone: it requires attention both to the organisational environments that support participation and to the concrete practices through which solidarity is enacted in everyday social life (Cartocci, 2007; Putnam, 2000).

3 The Geography of Social Participation: The Non-Profit Sector

A first empirical lens through which to observe the geography of participation in Italy is the non-profit sector. Non-profit organisations provide both a social arena where civic participation takes shape and a vehicle through which civic values and practices are promoted and sustained across communities. They represent social laboratories where civic culture, reciprocity and interpersonal trust are continuously produced and maintained (Cartocci, 2007; Putnam, 2000; Putnam et al., 1993). Through volunteering, associative life and community services, the non-profit world strengthens the moral infrastructure of society, facilitating the development of both bonding and bridging forms of social capital (Anheier & Toepler, 2023).

Between 2011 and 2021, the number of non-profit entities in Italy grew from approximately 301,000 to over 360,000, a 19.6% increase (ISTAT, 2024). When measured per capita, the density rose from 50 to 61 organisations per 10,000 inhabitants. This expansion, however, follows a markedly territorial pattern. The North-East remains at the top—with provinces such as Trento, Bolzano and Aosta consistently exceeding 110 organisations per 10,000 residents—while the South, though growing, still lags behind. Yet, even within high-civicness regions, some anomalies persist: for example, Monza-Brianza shows relatively low associative density despite favourable socio-economic conditions.

These territorial contrasts mirror the historical roots of Italian civic traditions. Regions with strong cooperative and municipal histories, such as Emilia-Romagna or Trentino-Alto Adige, display a long-standing culture of collective action and trust in institutions. Conversely, areas with weaker local governance or higher dependence on state transfers often exhibit more fragile associative systems. Nonetheless, the gradual growth of the non-profit sector in Southern Italy—particularly in metropolitan areas like Naples and Catania—highlights an important trend towards civic activation and the diffusion of participatory norms.

Yet the use of non-profit density as an indicator of civic participation requires some caution. It captures the organised and formally visible side of collective action, but it cannot fully account for the more informal forms of help, cooperation and mutual support that also sustain local social life. In some territorial contexts, especially where resources are limited or relations with institutions are fragile, participation may take place through loose networks, episodic initiatives or neighbourhood-based practices rather than through stable organisations (Einolf et al., 2016; Eliasoph, 2013). For this reason, lower organisational density should not automatically be interpreted as an absence of civic engagement. Rather, it may also reflect different modes through which participation is structured, practiced and publicly recognised in local settings. However, territorial data capture forms of cooperation that leave observable traces, while informal and embedded practices remain less visible and are not analysable by territorial data.

Furthermore, the civic importance of the non-profit sector depends not only on the number of organisations in a given area but also on the quality of the relationships they can establish. Formal membership does not always align with a strong sense of belonging, nor does the mere existence of an organisation necessarily foster inclusive forms of social capital (Claridge, 2020; Hustinx & Lammertyn, 2003; Yuval-Davis, 2006). Some associations act primarily as bonding spaces among socially similar actors, while others are more capable of building bridging ties across different groups and institutions. The territorial distribution of non-profit organisations should therefore be read not as a simple map of civic virtue, but as an indicator of local organisational infrastructures whose social effects vary according to their inclusiveness, relational intensity and capacity to connect citizens, communities and public institutions.

These considerations also help explain why non-profit density is unevenly distributed across Italy. The emergence and consolidation of non-profit organisations cannot be reduced to civic traditions but also depend on contextual conditions such as demographic concentration, administrative capacity, availability of skills and previous associative experiences. In this sense, some territories possess a stronger organisational carrying capacity, that is, a greater ability to generate and sustain new collective initiatives over time (Segre & Zamaro, 2016). The recent expansion of the sector in parts of Southern Italy can thus be interpreted not merely as a delayed cultural alignment with the centre-north, but as the result of changing local ecosystems in which new resources, institutional arrangements and associative networks have made organised participation more feasible (Memo, 2023; Memo & Moro, 2023).

Against this background, the non-profit sector remains a relevant benchmark of organised participation. It shows where civic engagement becomes institutionally stabilised and where local infrastructures are available to transform individual dispositions towards solidarity into durable collective practices.

For this reason, it also constitutes an important bridge towards the next step of the analysis: forms of participation, such as blood donation, in which altruism becomes observable through repeated, concrete and socially consequential acts.

4 The Civic Gift: Blood Donation as a Practice of Altruistic Participation

Blood donation represents a particularly significant example of civic participation in contemporary societies. Unlike many other forms of voluntary engagement, it involves the provision of a biological resource that becomes immediately available for the benefit of unknown others. For this reason, blood donation has often been interpreted as a paradigmatic form of altruistic participation and as a concrete manifestation of civic solidarity.

Practices of giving have long been recognised as central mechanisms for the construction and maintenance of social relationships. In his seminal essay on the gift, Mauss (1924) showed how systems of exchange based on giving, receiving and reciprocating contribute to the creation of bonds between individuals and groups. Although blood donation differs from the traditional forms of exchange described by Mauss, it nevertheless preserves an important relational dimension. The act of giving blood does not produce a direct return to the donor, yet it contributes to sustaining a collective system of mutual support within society.

The absence of direct reciprocity makes blood donation particularly interesting from the point of view of social theory. In modern societies, the donor does not know the recipient of the blood and does not expect a direct compensation. Instead, donation takes place within an institutional framework that guarantees the redistribution of blood products according to medical needs. This transformation of the logic of the gift reflects the evolution of solidarity in complex societies, where relations of reciprocity are often mediated by institutions and organised welfare systems.

Titmuss (1970) famously analysed blood donation as an example of altruism embedded in welfare institutions. In his comparative study of blood donation systems, he argued that voluntary and unpaid donation represents an important mechanism for reinforcing social solidarity and civic responsibility. According to Titmuss, systems based on voluntary donors tend to strengthen collective responsibility for the well-being of others, while systems based on market incentives risk undermining the moral foundations of solidarity.

In this perspective, blood donation can be interpreted as a form of civic gift. The donor voluntarily provides a resource that becomes part of a collective pool available to the entire community. This act contributes to the functioning of public health systems and ensures the availability of blood for medical treatments and emergency interventions. The gift is therefore directed not towards a specific individual but towards society as a whole.

At the same time, blood donation cannot be understood solely in terms of pure altruism (Cartocci, 2007). Sociological analyses of giving have shown that even apparently disinterested acts are embedded in systems of symbolic recognition and social meaning (Caillé, 1994). Donors often derive forms of moral satisfaction, social recognition and personal fulfilment from their participation. These symbolic dimensions do not diminish the altruistic value of donation; rather, they help explain why individuals continue to participate in such practices over time.

The connection between blood donation and civic participation can also be examined through the concept of social capital. Several scholars have emphasised that practices of voluntary engagement contribute to strengthening networks of trust, cooperation and solidarity within societies (Putnam, 2000; Putnam et al., 1993). Blood donation represents a particular expression of this dynamic because it embodies a form of solidarity directed towards unknown others and mediated by collective institutions.

In this sense, donation may be interpreted as an expression of bridging social capital (Putnam, 2000). Unlike forms of solidarity limited to family or close personal relationships, donation extends cooperation beyond immediate social circles. By giving blood, individuals contribute to the well-being of members of the wider community with whom they have no direct relationship.

However, the existence of donation practices does not depend solely on individual altruistic dispositions. The diffusion of donation is also strongly influenced by the presence of organisational infrastructures capable of mobilising and sustaining participation. In many countries, voluntary associations play a crucial role in recruiting donors, organising donation campaigns and promoting a culture of solidarity within local communities (Cartocci, 2007; Cartocci & Vanelli, 2015).

These organisations operate at the intersection between civic participation and institutional systems of healthcare. They help translate individual willingness to donate into stable patterns of participation and contribute to building networks of trust between citizens and public institutions. Through their activities, blood donation becomes embedded in a broader civic culture that values solidarity and collective responsibility.

Blood donation can therefore be interpreted as a practice through which altruistic participation takes concrete form. It illustrates how individual motivations, social norms and organisational infrastructures interact in the production of collective goods. By transforming personal generosity into a shared resource, donation contributes to reinforcing both social cohesion and civic engagement in contemporary societies.

4.1 Blood Donation in Italy

In the Italian context, blood donation represents a relevant empirical site for observing how civic participation becomes territorially embedded. The organisation of the national transfusion system relies on the interaction between public institutions, health infrastructures, donor associations and individual citizens. Since the establishment of the National Blood Centre and the National Blood Register in 2007, coordination at the national level has strengthened, while Regional Blood Centres continue to play a central role in managing blood collection. Alongside these institutional structures, donor associations such as AVIS, FRATRES, FIDAS and the Italian Red Cross contribute significantly by promoting donation and maintaining links between institutions and local communities. Although the decision to donate remains individual, these organisations act as intermediaries that mobilise citizens and sustain participation through local networks (Bassi et al., 2024; Guglielmetti Mugion et al., 2021; Saturni, 2013).

Qualitative interviews with key informants, including officials from the National Blood Centre and representatives of donor associations, highlight how blood donation is embedded within broader networks of civic participation. In contexts where institutional centres cannot guarantee full service provision, donor associations ensure continuity of collection activities. According to recent data from the National Blood Centre, blood units collected through External Collection Units (UDR), many operating with donor associations, account for approximately 40% of the national total. This confirms that blood donation is rooted in local infrastructures that translate social participation into concrete practices of solidarity.

Blood donation has been widely used as a behavioural indicator of civicness, as it captures voluntary contributions to the common good and allows participation to be observed through concrete practices (Cartocci, 2007; Putnam, 2000). For this reason, the empirical analysis focuses on the number of blood units donated rather than on the number of donors. While donors represent a relatively stable stock, collected units constitute a flow variable that better reflects both the availability of blood and the intensity of participation over time (Cartocci, 2007).

The data used in this chapter were assembled from secondary sources collected by the National Blood Centre and the Regional Blood Centres. Regional and provincial series were harmonised to reconstruct patterns of donation across Italy. While regional data provide a general overview, the provincial scale makes it possible to identify local configurations of participation that remain hidden at higher levels of aggregation.

The empirical evidence summarised in Table 1 illustrates the evolution and territorial distribution of blood donation in Italy. At the national level, the total number of blood units collected remained relatively stable between 2009 and 2022, fluctuating between approximately 2.55 and 2.64 million units. When standardised per 10,000 inhabitants aged 18–65, the indicator increased from 438 donations in 2009 to 459 in 2013, before stabilising around 454 in the following years. The most striking element emerging from the data, however, is the strong territorial variability. Provincial values range from very high levels, exceeding 900 donations per 10,000 inhabitants in the most active areas, to extremely low levels in the least performing provinces.

Regional averages also reveal significant differences across the Italian territory. Several regions of the north and north-east maintain relatively high levels of donation, including Veneto, Friuli-Venezia Giulia and Emilia-Romagna, areas historically characterised by dense associational networks and established traditions of civic participation. At the same time, the data highlight important changes over time. In several regions of the centre-south and in the islands, blood donation has grown substantially, reducing the gap that earlier studies had identified between northern and southern Italy.

Sardinia represents one of the most notable examples of this transformation. Over the period considered, the region experienced a marked increase in the number of blood units donated per 10,000 inhabitants, reaching some of the highest levels recorded in the country.[1] This trajectory suggests that blood donation can expand significantly even in contexts that were previously considered peripheral within the Italian geography of civic participation.

A closer look at the provincial level further illustrates how local social and organisational environments shape donation practices. Provinces such as Ragusa consistently rank among the areas with the highest levels of blood donation.

[1] Within our research, we also examined recreational and sports participation as an indicator of broader civic engagement, finding that over the same period. Sardinia experienced an increase in the number of sports associations (Villani et al., 2025).

Table 1 Units of blood[a] donated at national and regional levels

		2009	2013	2019	2022
Total units of blood donated		2,551,734	2,638,332	2,564,843	2,571,997
Units of blood donated per 10,000 of population 18–65 years of age		438	459	454	454
Highest provincial value per 10,000 of population 18–65 years of age		780	841	941	963
Lowest provincial value per 10,000 of population 18–65 years of age		143	210	0[b]	0
AREA	*REGION*	Mean per 10,000 of population 18–65 years of age			
NW	Valle d'Aosta	490	484	463	444
	Piemonte	506	502	476	458
	Lombardia	477	481	462	457
	Liguria	393	415	446	522
NE	Trentino-Alto Adige	460	445	454	448
	Friuli-Venezia Giulia	553	509	503	475
	Veneto	538	559	558	536
Centre-N	Emilia-Romagna	580	525	488	492
	Toscana	457	475	447	434
	Marche	406	466	519	512
	Umbria	458	492	447	432
Centre-S	Lazio	311	343	315	309
	Molise	446	478	508	405
	Abruzzo	362	404	413	446
	Sardegna	431	633	629	666
South	Campania	277	286	302	306
	Puglia	355	381	399	406
	Basilicata	372	472	415	429
	Calabria	330	371	367	374
	Sicilia	371	424	441	471

[a]A unit of donated blood is a bag containing approximately 450 mL (±10%) of whole blood collected from a healthy donor

[b]Several blood collection centres in Calabria and Campania have closed since 2018. Therefore, some zero values do not indicate an absence of donations, but rather that blood collected in one province may be processed and recorded by a centre located in another province.

Previous research has linked this pattern to the presence of particularly strong local donor associations, dense relational networks and a civic culture in which blood donation is widely recognised as a socially valued practice and a form of active citizenship (Cartocci, 2007; Nicodemi, 2019). In these contexts, participation appears to be sustained by the interaction between families, schools, voluntary organisations and health institutions, which together create local infrastructures capable of transforming individual willingness to donate into stable and repeated forms of civic engagement.

At the lower end of the distribution, provinces such as Cosenza, Messina and Frosinone[2] consistently appear among those with the lowest levels of blood donation per 10,000 inhabitants across the years considered. However, these cases also highlight the need for caution in interpreting territorial disparities at face value.

These patterns suggest that the geography of blood donation should not be interpreted as a fixed map of civic virtue but rather as the outcome of evolving interactions between institutional arrangements, associational infrastructures and local civic cultures. Provincial-level data make these dynamics particularly visible. While regional averages provide a general overview of participation, the provincial scale reveals local configurations in which organisational capacity, social networks and community norms interact in shaping donation practices. The territorial variability observed in Table 1 therefore reflects not only demographic or structural differences but also the uneven distribution of civic infrastructures capable of transforming individual altruism into sustained forms of collective participation.

5 Comments and Conclusions

This chapter has adopted a funnel-shaped analytical perspective to examine civicness in contemporary Italy, moving from the broad terrain of social participation to the organisational field of the non-profit sector and, finally, to blood donation as a specific practice of civic engagement. This progression makes it possible to connect different analytical levels that are often treated separately: the cultural and relational dimension of social capital, the organisational infrastructures through which participation becomes publicly visible, and the concrete practices through which solidarity is enacted in everyday life. In this sense, the chapter contributes to the literature that interprets civic participation not simply as an individual disposition, but as a socially embedded process shaped by institutions, associations and territorial contexts (Edwards et al., 2001; Putnam, 2000; Putnam et al., 1993).

[2] Qualitative information collected during the data reconstruction process suggests that, in some cases, recorded values may reflect organisational arrangements rather than actual levels of participation. For example, in the province of Frosinone, part of the blood donations is managed and registered by AVIS Rome rather than by local collection centres. This results in a partial misallocation of data at the provincial level, which may lead to an underestimation of local donation levels.

From a theoretical perspective, the chapter confirms the usefulness of the social capital perspective for understanding the civic value of participation. As classical and contemporary studies have shown, networks of association can foster trust, reciprocity and cooperation, strengthening the social fabric and supporting democratic life (Fukuyama, 1995; Putnam, 2000; Sirianni & Friedland, 2001). In particular, non-profit organisations may act both as environments of bonding social capital, reinforcing solidarity among actors who share similar values, and as environments of bridging social capital, connecting different groups and widening the horizons of mutual recognition and solidarity (Anheier & Toepler, 2023; Putnam, 2000). However, the chapter also suggests that this relationship should not be understood in automatic or deterministic terms. The presence of non-profit organisations does not in itself guarantee inclusive, cohesive or democratic forms of participation. Rather, their civic implications depend on the kinds of relations, meanings and opportunities for involvement that they are able to generate in practice.

This point is particularly important when interpreting the territorial distribution of non-profit organisations. The non-profit sector represents a crucial field of organised collective action, but it is also a heterogeneous and internally differentiated ecosystem, marked by different legal forms, organisational cultures, fields of intervention and relations with public and market actors (Della Queva et al., 2023; DiMaggio & Anheier, 1990). Its role in welfare and local development may be cooperative, supplementary, innovative, but at times also ambivalent or conflictual, especially when tensions emerge between civic aims, managerial logics and institutional constraints (Volturo & De Luigi, 2025). For this reason, the chapter invites us to read the geography of the non-profit sector not as a direct map of civic virtue, but as the spatial expression of differentiated organisational infrastructures whose social effects depend on broader relational and institutional conditions.

The empirical analysis of the Italian case reinforces this argument. The longitudinal and territorial evidence points to persistent inequalities in the distribution of non-profit organisations, with historically higher densities in many areas of the centre-north and lower ones in several southern provinces. Yet the provincial scale also reveals a more articulated pattern than a simple macro-regional dualism. Internal regional differences, local exceptions and recent growth dynamics complicate the image of a country divided into two homogeneous civic blocs. This finding is consistent with research showing that the emergence and consolidation of non-profit initiatives depend not only on cultural traditions of participation, but also on territorial soft carrying capacity, that is, on the local availability of competencies, organisational infrastructures, institutional support and socio-economic conditions favourable to collective action (Memo, 2023; Memo & Moro, 2023; Segre & Zamaro, 2016). In this perspective, territorial disparities should be interpreted as the outcome of historically sedimented yet evolving configurations in which civic cultures interact with demographic, economic and institutional factors.

Blood donation, in this framework, represents a particularly meaningful empirical field. As discussed in the chapter, it is not merely a morally charged act of individual generosity, but a socially organised form of participation that requires trust, continuity, civic recognition and institutional mediation. Donating blood means contributing to a collective good that is both highly concrete and deeply relational: the well-being, and at times the survival, of unknown others. For this reason, blood donation can be read as a powerful expression of what the chapter defines as “civic gift”. At the same time, its diffusion across territories cannot be reduced to the sum of individual altruistic motivations. It depends on the existence of associative and institutional environments able to recruit, socialise, retain and symbolically value donors. In this sense, the geography of donation reflects not only personal moral orientations, but also the strength of local civic infrastructures and the capacity of organisations to transform dispositions towards solidarity into repeated and publicly meaningful practices.

The chapter thus proposes broader theoretical implications. Civicness should not be seen solely as a cultural trait or just as an effect of organisational presence. Instead, it is better understood as a territorially embedded relational process through which values, networks, institutions and practices are interconnected. Social capital, participation in non-profit activities and blood donation are related, but their connection is context-dependent. For this reason, territorial analysis is important: it enables us to see how civic participation is organised, maintained and unevenly distributed across different locations. In this light, the Italian case does not present a fixed map of civic virtue but rather a varied and evolving mosaic in which solidarity takes organised form under diverse local conditions. Ultimately, the chapter highlights that social sustainability relies not only on norms and values but also on the organisational and territorial structures that turn those values into concrete action. The non-profit sector plays a key role in this process, though in ways that are never entirely straightforward or without tension. Blood donation clearly demonstrates this, as it involves the moral, relational and institutional aspects of civic life in a single act. The civic gift, therefore, should be understood not simply as a “natural” expression of altruism, but as the result of social processes through which communities build trust, coordinate efforts and uphold shared commitments to the common good.

Acknowledgments We thank the National Blood Centre, the Regional Blood Centres and donor associations, in particular FIDAS and AVIS, for their collaboration and support in this research. We thank an anonymous referee and the editors for their valuable comments. The views and opinions expressed are solely those of the authors.

References

Anheier, H. K., & Toepler, S. (2023). *Nonprofit organizations: Theory, management, policy* (3rd ed.). Routledge.

Bassi, A., Fabbri, A., & Briola, G. (2024). *Il dono di sé, dono per gli altri. Tra civismo e solidarietà: indagine sui giovani donatori AVIS*. FrancoAngeli.

Boulding, K. (1966). The economics of the coming spaceship earth. In H. Jarrett (Ed.), *Environmental quality in a growing economy* (pp. 3–14). John Hopkins University Press.

Caillé, A. (1994). *Don, intérêt et désintéressement*. La Découverte.

Cartocci, R. (2007). *Mappe del tesoro: Atlante del capitale sociale in Italia*. Il Mulino.

Cartocci, R., & Vanelli, V. (2015). Una mappa del capitale sociale e della cultura civica in Italia. In *L'Italia e le sue regioni. L'età repubblicana—Società* (Vol. 4, pp. 17–36). Istituto dell'Enciclopedia Italiana Treccani.

Claridge, T. (2020). *Identity and belonging: An aspect of the relational dimension of social capital*. Social Capital Research. https://doi.org/10.5281/zenodo.8053300

Colantonio, A. (2011). Social sustainability: Exploring the linkages between research, policy and practice. In Jaeger et al. (Eds.), *European research on sustainable development* (Vol. 1). Springer.

Della Queva, S., Nicosia, M., & Stoppiello, S. (2023). Il settore non profit nelle aree interne del Mezzogiorno: Una prima analisi descrittiva. *Autonomie Locali e Servizi Sociali, 3*, 367–386.

Dempsey, N., Bramley, G., Power, S., & Brown, C. (2011). The social dimension of sustainable development: Defining urban social sustainability. *Sustainable Development, 19*, 289–300.

DiMaggio, P., & Anheier, H. K. (1990). A sociological conceptualization of nonprofit organizations and sectors. *Annual Review of Sociology, 16*, 137–159.

Edwards, B., Foley, M. W., & Diani, M. (Eds.). (2001). *Beyond Tocqueville: Civil society and the social capital debate in comparative perspective*. University Press of New England.

Einolf, C., Prouteau, L., Nezhina, T., & Ibrayeva, A. (2016). Informal, unorganized volunteering. In D. H. Smith et al. (Eds.), *The Palgrave handbook of volunteering, civic participation, and nonprofit associations* (pp. 223–239). Palgrave Macmillan.

Eliasoph, N. (2013). *The politics of volunteering*. Polity Press.

European Committee for Social Cohesion (CDCS). (2004). *A new strategy for social cohesion. Revised strategy for social cohesion approved by the committee of ministers of the council of Europe on 31 March 2004*.

Fukuyama, F. (1995). *Trust: The social virtues and the creation of prosperity*. Free Press.

Guglielmetti Mugion, R., Pasca, M. G., Di Di Pietro, L., & Renzi, M. F. (2021). Promoting the propensity for blood donation through the understanding of its determinants. *BMC Health Services Research, 21*(1), 127.

Hulse, K., & Stone, W. (2007). Social cohesion, social capital and social exclusion: A cross-cultural comparison. *Policy Studies, 28*(2), 109–128.

Hustinx, L., & Lammertyn, F. (2003). Collective and reflexive styles of volunteering. *VOLUNTAS: International Journal of Voluntary and Nonprofit Organizations, 14*(2), 167–187.

ISTAT. (2024). *Struttura e profili del settore non profit*. https://www.istat.it/wp-content/uploads/2024/10/REPORT_Istituzioni-non-profit_2022.pdf

Klein, C. (2013). Social capital or social cohesion: What matters for subjective well-being? *Social Indicators Research, 110*(3), 891–911.

Mauss, M. (1924). *Essai sur le don: Forme et raison de l'échange dans les sociétés archaïques*. Année Sociologique.

Memo, G. (2023). *Terzo settore e Mezzogiorno*. Rubbettino.

Memo, G., & Moro, G. (2023). Introduzione. *Autonomie locali e servizi sociali, 3*, 341–346.

Nicodemi, G. (2019). *La donazione di sangue a Faenza e Ragusa*. Rapporto di ricerca.

Oxoby, R. (2009). Understanding social inclusion, social cohesion, and social capital. *International Journal of Social Economics, 36*(12), 1133–1152.

Pahl, R. E. (1991). The search for social cohesion. *European Journal of Sociology, 32*(2), 345–360.

Pieper, R., Karvonen, S., & Vaarama, M. (2019). The SOLA model. *Social Indicators Research, 146*, 553–580.

Prandini, R., & Villani, M. (2025). Cohesion and social capital. In P. Bordandini (Ed.), *Civic decline or civic shift?* Cham: Palgrave Macmillan. https://doi.org/10.1007/978-3-032-14753-0_9

Putnam, R. D. (2000). *Bowling alone: The collapse and revival of American community*. Simon & Schuster.

Putnam, R. D., Leonardi, R., & Nanetti, R. (1993). *Making democracy work: Civic traditions in modern Italy*. Princeton University Press.

Saturni, V. (2013). Il ruolo delle associazioni nel sistema sangue italiano. *Rivista di Sociologia, 50*(2), 301–316.

Segre, E., & Zamaro, N. (2016). Su alcune determinanti della diffusione delle istituzioni nonprofit. In G. P. Barbetta et al. (Eds.), *Le istituzioni nonprofit in Italia: Dieci anni dopo*. Il Mulino.

Sen, A. (1985). *Commodities and capabilities*. North-Holland.

Sen, A. (1992). *Inequality re-examined*. Harvard University Press.

Sirianni, C., & Friedland, L. (2001). *Civic innovation in America*. University of California Press.

Titmuss, R. M. (1970). *The gift relationship: From human blood to social policy*. Allen & Unwin.

Vallance, S., Perkins, H. C., & Dixon, J. E. (2011). What is social sustainability? *Geoforum, 42*(3), 342–348.

Villani, M., Trifuoggi, M., & Prandini, R. (2025). Recreational and cultural participation. In P. Bordandini (Ed.), *Civic decline or civic shift?* Palgrave Macmillan. https://doi.org/10.1007/978-3-032-14753-0_4

Volturo, S., & De Luigi, N. (2025). Social participation and non-profit organisations. In P. Bordandini (Ed.), *Civic decline or civic shift?* Palgrave Macmillan. https://doi.org/10.1007/978-3-032-14753-0_3

WCED. (1987). *Our common future*. Oxford University Press.

Yuval-Davis, N. (2006). Belonging and the politics of belonging. *Patterns of Prejudice, 40*(3), 197–214. https://doi.org/10.1080/00313220600769331

Cultural Participation in Italy: A Preliminary Analysis of New Survey Evidence

Roberto Cellini, Tiziana Cuccia, and Alessandro de Cristofaro

Abstract This chapter provides a preliminary analysis of the determinants of in-person cultural participation in Italy, using data from a new 2025 survey of 10,000 adults. The study examines attendance across six cultural activities, providing pieces of evidence coming from descriptive statistics, correlation patterns, and logistic regression results. Participation is widespread yet highly unequal, with education emerging as the strongest predictor, followed by a rich set of co-determinants including age, employment status, income, and city size. Economic cost and lack of free time are the most frequently reported barriers. Post-pandemic participation has largely normalised, while digital engagement shows associations with in-person cultural behaviour varying across different activities. The findings inform policies aimed at reducing structural constraints and promoting broader cultural access.

1 Introduction

This chapter presents a preliminary analysis of the determinants of cultural participation outside the home in Italy, based on an original 2025 survey of a representative sample of 10,000 individuals aged 18–80. The survey—carried out within the GRInS Project (see www.grins.it) funded by the European Union under the Italian National Recovery and Resilience Plan—captures a broad set of behaviours relevant to cultural life, with a focus on attendance at in-person cultural activities. Alongside detailed information on participation in cinema, theatre, classical and popular music concerts, museum and exhibition visits, and visits to heritage sites, the questionnaire includes extensive modules on socio-demographic characteristics, digital habits, perceptions of digital tools, use of online cultural resources, and self-reported social and political attitudes.

The analysis in this chapter deliberately concentrates on in-person participation, providing an initial descriptive and econometric assessment of individual

R. Cellini (✉) · T. Cuccia · A. de Cristofaro
Department of Economics and Business, University of Catania, Catania, Italy
e-mail: cellini@unict.it; Tiziana.cuccia@unict.it; alessandro.decristofaro@phd.unict.it

R. Cellini et al. (eds.), *Cultural, Social, and Political Participation in the Internet Era*, Contributions to Economics, https://doi.org/10.1007/978-3-032-33072-7_5

behavioural patterns and their determinants. The survey's timing—a few years after the lifting of COVID-19 restrictions—allows us to examine whether the substantial shifts observed during lockdown, including the rapid expansion of online cultural offerings and the temporary suspension of in-person activities, have left persistent effects or whether behaviours have largely reverted to pre-pandemic patterns.

Descriptive evidence shows that in-person participation has largely normalised, converging towards pre-2020 patterns, while digital practices continue to spread and online cultural consumption gains relevance. Within in-person activities, cinema is the most widely enjoyed form of cultural consumption, followed by museums and exhibitions and visits to heritage sites, whereas performing arts register lower participation rates. A composite indicator of out-of-home cultural participation—constructed following the Italian National Statistics Institute (ISTAT) criterion—indicates that about two-thirds of respondents engaged in at least two cultural activities during the reference period, whereas roughly one-third of Italian adults can be classified as culturally inactive by this criterion.

The survey also measures perceived barriers to participation in detail. Nearly half of the respondents identify economic cost as the main limitation, while about one-third report a lack of free time. Supply-side and preference-matching constraints—such as insufficient quantity or variety of events, or a lack of shared interests—are less frequent but remain significant.

The correlation evidence is consistent with a clustered nature of participation: cultural activities are positively associated with each other, and participation in one domain tends to accompany engagement in others. Age and employment status, as well as education and internet usage, display strong simple correlations with many cultural activities. Regression models estimated for each cultural activity provide a systematic assessment of these determinants. Education stands out as the most consistent explanatory factor across all activities. Income effects are significant, though less pronounced for cinema and classical music. Age is negatively associated with most activities. Gender differences are modest and largely activity-specific. Internet usage is most relevant for pop concert attendance, pointing to a specific link between digitally intensive behaviours and certain forms of cultural consumption. Employment status and city size further shape participation, with individuals residing in larger cities enjoying greater access to cultural opportunities.

Overall, the chapter offers an updated portrait of post-pandemic in-person cultural participation in Italy and confirms patterns well-known in available literature, while providing new evidence on the socio-economic and demographic factors structuring engagement, derived from microdata. These results lay the groundwork for subsequent studies that will leverage the survey's rich information on online behaviours and attitudes towards digitalisation to assess how the growing prevalence of digital tools may reshape cultural consumption in the years ahead.

2 Background and Related Literature

Economic analyses of cultural participation conceptualise attendance as a choice shaped by individual preferences, constraints, and accumulated experience. Seminal contributions emphasise that cultural consumption is a normal good whose demand increases with income and is reinforced through learning and habit formation (Stigler & Becker, 1977). Within this framework, education plays a dual role—enhancing the returns to cultural experiences and raising permanent income—and consistently emerges as a primary determinant of in-person cultural participation (Lévy-Garboua & Montmarquette, 2003; Seaman, 2006). Intergenerational transmission mechanisms further contribute to participation patterns: exposure to cultural practices within the family lowers entry costs and shapes tastes, and parental background—in particular maternal schooling—is a well-documented predictor of adult participation (Bourdieu, 1984).

A second set of findings concerns individual characteristics and socio-demographic regularities. Cultural participation declines with age or follows an inverted-U life-cycle pattern, with lower attendance at mature and older ages. Gender differences are modest and largely activity-specific, with women somewhat over-represented in theatre and museum attendance in many Western contexts (Seaman, 2006; Heilbrun & Gray, 2001), and EU-wide evidence points to small but persistent female advantages (Eurostat, 2024; Falk & Katz-Gerro, 2016).

Large-scale Italian surveys, including those conducted by ISTAT, document widespread but uneven participation across socio-economic groups, with cinema consistently attracting the largest audience and performing arts the smallest. Participation also tends to cluster across activities, leading to widespread use of composite indicators—such as the ISTAT criterion—to summarise multi-domain engagement.

The literature also highlights how barriers shape engagement. Price and time constraints are the most frequently reported obstacles, whereas supply-side issues—such as limited quantity or variety of events—and preference-matching problems play secondary yet meaningful roles. These categories align with recent contributions that interpret access as a multidimensional construct encompassing opportunity, participation, and reception barriers (Feder, 2023). Related evidence indicates that online cultural provision does not fully overcome cost barriers or attract new audiences, especially in highbrow domains (De la Vega et al., 2020), suggesting that digital access and in-person participation are not simple substitutes.

Spatial and contextual factors add another layer of explanation. Urban residence and proximity to cultural venues increase attendance probabilities, while supply constraints depress them (Brook, 2016). In the Italian case, differences between macro-regions tend to diminish once individual characteristics are controlled for, implying that territorial disparities reflect underlying socio-economic endowments more than geography per se (Cellini & Cuccia, 2025).

Finally, two broader themes, though not central to the present analysis, help nevertheless situate cultural participation within current research. First, the trade-off between online and in-person participation represents an open question: quasi-experimental evidence for Germany suggests positive complementarities between broadband access and live attendance (Bauernschuster et al., 2014), whereas UK-based studies report negligible or context-specific effects (Geraci et al., 2022). Micro-level studies for Italy and other countries generally point to partial complementarity, with temporary substitution clear for the lockdown periods, and specific activities (Ateca-Amestoy & Castiglione, 2023; Bakhshi et al., 2023; Cellini & Cuccia, 2025; Feder et al., 2022). Second, the relationship between cultural participation, social capital, and inequality: participation correlates with civic engagement and trust, yet it is stratified by socio-economic background. Territorial and longitudinal evidence for Italy indicates that higher income inequality reduces participation net of individual characteristics (Cellini & Cuccia, 2026), in line with findings for other contexts (OECD, 2022; Tubadji et al., 2022).

These insights motivate the empirical analysis presented in the following sections, which examines how individual characteristics, economic resources, digital habits, and contextual conditions shape in-person participation in Italy, based on newly collected microdata.

3 Empirical Analysis

This section provides an empirical analysis of the determinants of cultural participation in Italy, focussing on the individual determinants and drawing on the original survey dataset collected in 2025. The dataset comprises 10,000 respondents, representative of the Italian adult population aged 18–80, and covers a broad range of behaviours related to cultural activities as well as a set of individual socio-demographic characteristics.[1]

In the analysis presented below, the dependent variables capture participation over the previous 12 months, as reported by respondents, across 6 cultural activities: cinema, theatre, classical music concerts, pop concerts, museums and exhibitions, and architectural monuments or heritage sites. All dependent variables are binary, taking the value 1 if the respondent participated in the given activity and 0 otherwise. In addition, a composite indicator—Cultural Participation Outside the Home (*CPOH*)—is constructed to identify individuals who engaged in at least two of these activities (with a minimum frequency threshold of four for cinema attendance). This criterion corresponds to the definition adopted by ISTAT (2022) for identifying culturally active individuals; *CPOH* takes the value 1 if the respondent can be classified as culturally active.

The set of explanatory variables includes education level (four categories: primary or lower secondary, upper secondary, bachelor's degree, and post-graduate

[1] In line with the guidelines and requirements applying to EU-funded GRInS project, the data are freely available through the Amelia Data Bank, which can be accessed on the GRInS Project website (www.grins.it)

degree), household monthly income (five brackets, ranging from up to €1000 to more than €4000), gender, age group (six categories from 18–24 to 65 or more), employment status (employed, unemployed, student, retired, and other), daily internet usage (five categories from less than 1 h to 10 or more hours), and city size (large city above 100,000 inhabitants, medium city between 20,000 and 100,000, and small town or rural area below 20,000). Summary statistics for the independent variables are reported in Table 1.

3.1 Descriptive Analysis

Figure 1 presents the distribution of cultural participation outside the home in 2025 among the respondents.

When examining specific cultural activities, cinema emerges as the most popular form of cultural consumption, with 66% of respondents reporting at least one visit during the reference period. This is followed by museums and exhibitions (60%), and visits to architectural monuments or heritage sites (53%). Performing arts show lower participation rates: pop concerts attract roughly 40% of respondents, while theatre and classical concerts engage approximately 39% and 20% of the sample, respectively. The composite indicator of cultural participation (*CPOH*) reveals that 64% of the sample engaged in at least two of the considered activities.

These patterns are consistent with previous findings in the literature on cultural participation (Falk & Katz-Gerro, 2016; Suarez-Fernandez et al., 2020), indicating that more accessible and mainstream activities (such as cinema) tend to attract broader audiences than highbrow cultural forms such as classical music and theatre. Visual arts activities (museums and heritage sites) also exhibit higher participation than performing arts.

Understanding the factors that limit cultural engagement requires moving beyond consumption patterns to examine the barriers individuals face when seeking to participate in cultural activities. Recent research (Feder, 2023) has conceptualised access to cultural consumption as a multidimensional construct, distinguishing between barriers related to opportunity (geographical availability of cultural supply), participation (economic and time constraints), and reception (cultural background and educational capital).

Figure 2 presents respondents' self-reported barriers to cultural consumption.

The most frequently cited obstacle is the high cost of cultural activities, reported by 47% of respondents. This is followed by lack of free time (32%), indicating that participation barriers—those linked to the individual resources required to engage in cultural consumption—represent the primary constraints for Italian cultural consumers. Barriers related to opportunity and reception are less prevalent but remain significant: 23% of respondents report that few people share their cultural interests, 17% find available event typologies unappealing, 14% cite limited event availability, and only 9% point to low quality of offerings.

Table 1 Summary statistics for socio-economic variables

	Obs	Mean	Min	Max
Educational level				
Primary or lower secondary education	10,000	.082	0	1
Upper secondary education	10,000	.546	0	1
Bachelor's degree	10,000	.275	0	1
Post-graduate degree	10,000	.097	0	1
Household monthly income				
Up to 1000 €	8331	.085	0	1
1001–1500€	8331	.170	0	1
1501–2500€	8331	.313	0	1
2501–4000€	8331	.307	0	1
More than 4000€	8331	.125	0	1
Gender				
Male	10,000	.492	0	1
Female	10,000	.507	0	1
Other	10,000	.001	0	1
Age				
18–24	10,000	.091	0	1
25–34	10,000	.125	0	1
35–44	10,000	.139	0	1
45–54	10,000	.176	0	1
55–64	10,000	.179	0	1
65 or more	10,000	.290	0	1
Employment status				
Employed	10,000	.507	0	1
Unemployed	10,000	.066	0	1
Student	10,000	.067	0	1
Retired	10,000	.209	0	1
Other	10,000	.151	0	1
Daily internet usage				
Less than1 h	10,000	.007	0	1
1–3 h	10,000	.287	0	1
3–6 h	10,000	.414	0	1
6–10 h	10,000	.178	0	1
10 or more h	10,000	.114	0	1
City size				
Large city (>100,000)	10,000	.358	0	1
Medium city (20,000–100,000)	10,000	.317	0	1
Small town/rural (<20,000)	10,000	.325	0	1

Source: Our elaboration on original survey

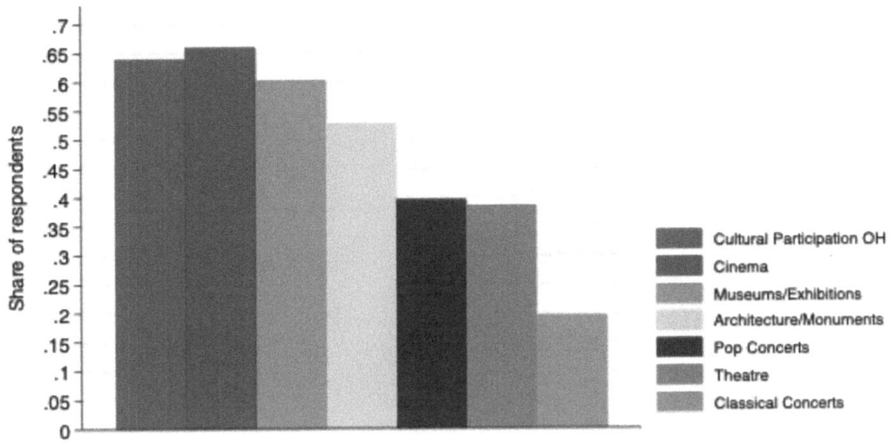

Fig. 1 Cultural participation outside the home. Note: 10,000 observations. Source: Original survey

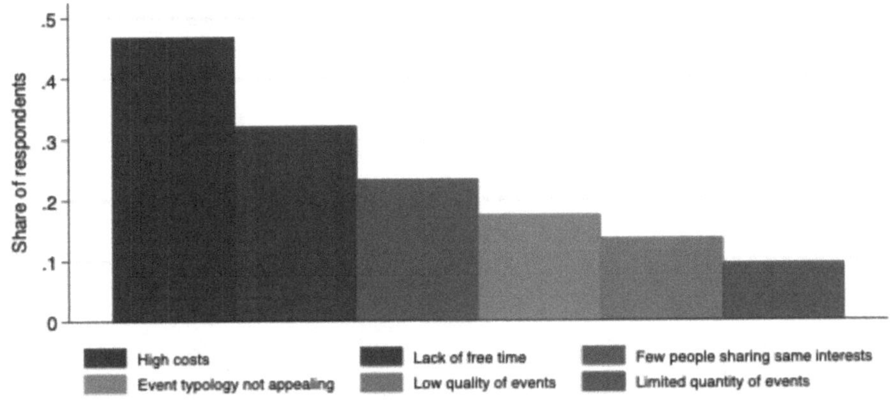

Fig. 2 Barriers to cultural participation: factors limiting cultural consumption. Note: 10,000 observations. Question: "*Are there any factors that limit your cultural consumption?*" Source: Original survey

These patterns reveal a hierarchy of constraints that shape cultural participation in Italy. Economic affordability emerges as the foremost limiting factor, followed by time scarcity. Supply-side dimensions (quantity and variety of events) and social aspects (shared interests, appealing content) play secondary but meaningful roles.[2]

[2] De la Vega et al. (2020) discuss the evidence that online cultural participation is not effective in overcoming cost barriers. A discussion on social barriers to cultural participation in Italy is also offered by Panarese and Azzarita (2021).

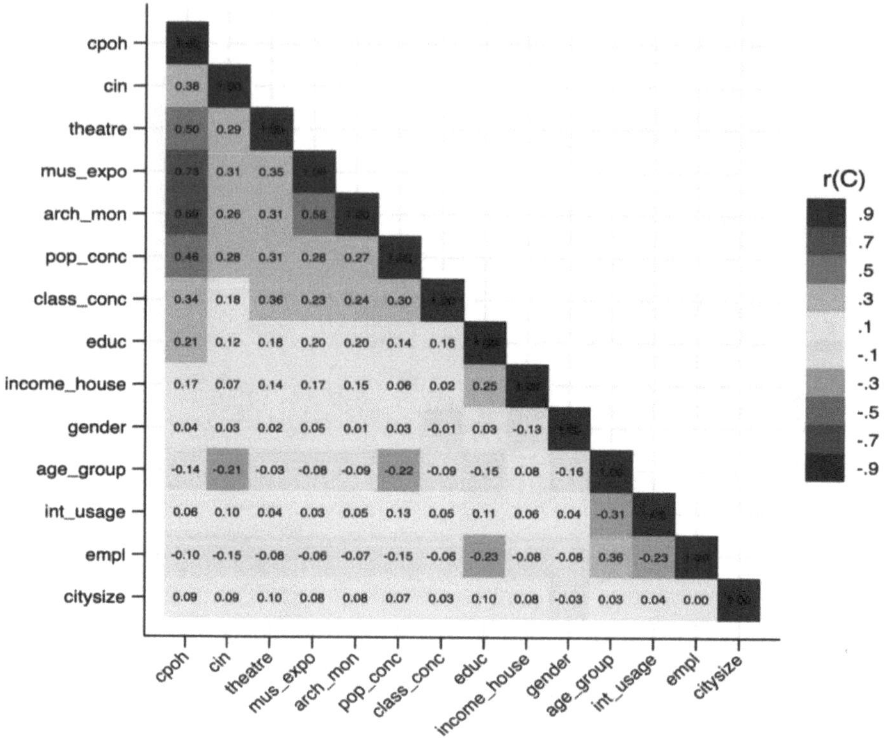

Fig. 3 Correlation matrix

The relatively low prevalence of quality-related concerns suggests that accessibility issues are more critical than the perceived value of available cultural offerings.

Before turning to the results of a multiple regression analysis, it is worth examining the correlation structure among the variables under scrutiny. Figure 3 presents the correlation matrix as a heatmap, which allows for an immediate visual assessment of the pairwise relationships between cultural participation outcomes and socio-demographic predictors.

Among the cultural activity variables, all pairwise correlations are positive, confirming that cultural participation tends to cluster within individuals—those who engage in one form of cultural activity are more likely to participate in others as well. Within this general pattern of positive association, however, some meaningful variation emerges. At one end of the spectrum, museum visits and archaeological or monumental heritage sites display the strongest mutual correlation ($r = 0.58$), suggesting the existence of a highbrow participation cluster. At the other end, the weakest association is found between cinema attendance and classical music concerts ($r = 0.18$), a pairing that reflects the considerable distance—in terms of accessibility, cost, and cultural capital requirements—between the arguably most popular and the most exclusive of the activities considered.

Turning to the socio-demographic explanatory factors, age and employment status emerge as the variables with the broadest and most consistent pattern of linear associations across the matrix. Age exhibits negative correlations with virtually all cultural participation outcomes, with the strongest associations observed for cinema attendance ($r = -0.21$) and pop music concerts ($r = -0.22$). This pattern suggests that younger individuals are disproportionately represented among participants in more accessible and lowbrow cultural forms. Notably, age is also negatively correlated with education ($r = -0.15$) and with internet usage ($r = -0.31$), indicating that younger cohorts in the sample tend to be both more educated and more digitally engaged—two characteristics that, as the regression results will confirm, are positively associated with cultural participation.

Employment status (specifically, being employed) exhibits negative correlations with cultural participation, particularly for pop music concerts and cinema (r around -0.15 in both cases). Being employed is also positively correlated with age ($r = 0.36$) and negatively correlated with education ($r = -0.23$), indicating that employed individuals in the sample tend to be older and less educated on average. This constellation of characteristics suggests a self-reinforcing configuration: occupational status, age, and lower educational attainment act as interrelated channels through which participation is shaped, reflecting both differences in motivations and constraints on time availability. The correlation matrix thus points to a compound mechanism of exclusion that the regression analysis will help to disentangle.

4 Logistic Regression Results

We estimate separate logit models for each cultural activity (*CPOH*, cinema, theatre, museums/expositions, archaeological sites/monuments, pop concerts, classical concerts), revealing how education, income, age, gender, employment status, and city size differentially shape participation across the cultural spectrum—from highbrow activities like theatre and classical music to more popular forms like cinema and pop concerts (Table 2).

The results of the logistic regression analysis are reported in Table 2 as Average Marginal Effects to facilitate interpretation and cross-model comparison, allowing us to identify factors that act as universal drivers of cultural participation versus activity-specific determinants. Together, they reveal a set of consistent and theoretically meaningful patterns across the seven cultural participation outcomes considered.

Education emerges as the strongest and most consistent explanatory factor of cultural participation across all activities. Relative to individuals with primary or lower secondary education, those holding a bachelor's or post-graduate degree are about 25% points more likely to participate according to the composite index *CPOH*, with the largest effects observed for museums and exhibitions, and archaeological or monumental heritage sites. Even upper secondary education is associated with substantially higher participation probabilities across all outcomes. The only

Table 2 Average marginal effects on probability of cultural participation

Variable	CPOH	Cinema	Theatre	Mus/Exp	Arch/Mon	Pop music	Class music
Education (ref: Primary/lower secondary)							
Upper secondary	0.124***	0.050***	0.085***	0.111***	0.120***	0.089***	0.046***
Bachelor's degree	0.258***	0.106***	0.226***	0.245***	0.245***	0.160***	0.161***
Post-graduate degree	0.259***	0.080***	0.208***	0.241***	0.267***	0.142***	0.175***
Household income (ref: €4000+)							
Up to €1000	−0.185***	−0.060**	−0.156***	−0.190***	−0.160**	−0.057**	0.035*
€1001–1500	−0.155***	−0.021	−0.130***	−0.169***	−0.147**	−0.049**	0.021
€1501–2500	−0.105***	−0.020	−0.114***	−0.092***	−0.105***	−0.074***	−0.026*
€2501–4000	−0.046***	0.025	−0.053***	−0.046**	−0.044**	−0.025	−0.022
Gender (ref: Male)							
Female	0.039***	0.014	0.029***	0.065***	0.019*	0.000	−0.014
Age group (ref: 18–24)							
25–34	−0.074***	−0.090***	−0.089***	−0.051**	−0.002	−0.053**	−0.103***
35–44	−0.147***	−0.178***	−0.038	−0.100***	−0.057**	−0.175***	−0.147***
45–54	−0.129***	−0.172***	−0.034	−0.095***	−0.055**	−0.156***	−0.132***
55–64	−0.113***	−0.221***	−0.006	−0.055**	−0.031	−0.204***	−0.132***
65 or more	−0.172***	−0.247***	−0.021	−0.076***	−0.124***	−0.285***	−0.148***
Internet usage (ref: 1–3 h)							
Less than 1 h	−0.089	−0.117*	0.015	−0.214***	0.031	−0.128**	−0.087**
3–6 h	0.018	0.051***	0.013	0.017	0.052***	0.029**	0.009
6–10 h	0.002	0.025	−0.009	−0.006	0.023	0.062***	0.030**
10+ h	−0.013	0.022	0.033*	−0.037*	0.005	0.061***	0.005

Employment status (ref: Employed)							
Unemployed	−0.064***	−0.073***	−0.046**	−0.069***	−0.044*	−0.048**	−0.051***
Student	0.063**	−0.008	0.001	0.059**	0.039	−0.048*	−0.068***
Retired	−0.033*	−0.100***	−0.064***	−0.031	0.033	−0.076***	−0.012
Other	−0.078***	−0.085***	−0.052***	−0.088***	−0.065***	−0.034**	−0.044***
City size (ref: Large city > 100,000)							
Medium city (20–100 k)	−0.076***	−0.063***	−0.060***	−0.071***	−0.060***	−0.068***	−0.005
Small town/rural (<20 k)	−0.075***	−0.087***	−0.082***	−0.060***	−0.076***	−0.074***	−0.021**

Note: 8331 observations. *p < 0.10, **p < 0.05, ***p < 0.01. Source: Our elaboration on original survey data partial exception is cinema, where the education gradient, while still positive and significant, is considerably smaller in magnitude, confirming cinema as the activity least dependent on formal educational attainment and, correspondingly, the most broadly accessible across social strata. These findings are consistent with a well-established body of literature linking education to cultural participation (Bourdieu, 1984; Lévy-Garboua & Montmarquette, 1996), and suggest that formal education remains the single most powerful lever of cultural participation in the Italian context.

Household income displays a complementary but distinct pattern. Lower income brackets are consistently associated with reduced probabilities of cultural participation relative to the highest income group (€4000+), with the largest penalties observed for the lowest earners across most activities. A particularly telling result concerns cinema: with the exception of the lowest income bracket (up to €1000 per month), income differences are largely non-significant for cinema attendance. This finding reinforces the descriptive evidence discussed earlier, consistent with cinema as the most economically accessible among the cultural activities considered, where cost barriers are comparatively low. For classical music concerts, income effects are similarly weak and largely non-significant, though this result should be interpreted with caution, given the relatively small number of respondents attending classical music events.

Older age is a consistently negative predictor of participation, with the youngest cohort (18–24) displaying the highest participation probabilities across virtually all activities—with the notable exception of theatre, where the age gradient is considerably flatter and several marginal effects for older groups are not statistically significant. The age penalty is particularly evident for cinema (−24.7% points for the 65+ group) and pop music concerts (−28.5%), confirming that younger individuals are disproportionately represented among participants in more accessible and popular cultural forms. The relative resilience of theatre participation across age groups may reflect the consolidation of this taste among older, highly educated cohorts for whom live performance represents an established cultural habit.

Gender effects are modest but present in specific domains. Female respondents display a higher probability of attending theatre (+2.9% points) and, most notably, in museum and exhibition visits (+6.5%), while no significant gender differences are observed for cinema, pop music concerts, or classical music. The composite indicator *CPOH* also shows a small but significant female advantage (+3.9%). These results are consistent with existing evidence on gendered cultural preferences (see, e.g., Katz-Gerro, 1999, and Katz-Gerro & Sullivan, 2023).

Internet usage exhibits a noteworthy pattern, most clearly interpretable in the case of pop music concerts. Individuals reporting six or more hours of daily internet use show the strongest positive and significant association with pop concert attendance, whereas no comparable pattern emerges for the other cultural activities. This finding may reflect the extent to which participation in popular music events is embedded within digital social practices—not only through online discovery of events and ticket purchasing, but also, and perhaps more fundamentally, through the role of digital environments in shaping musical tastes, given that music consumption increasingly occurs online, often almost exclusively so. In this respect, online listening habits contribute directly to the formation of preferences and may therefore increase the propensity to attend live events. Heavy internet users are likely to be active participants in online communities and social media, for whom attending a pop concert carries expressive and reputational value that extends beyond the enjoyment of the performance itself. The opportunity to share the experience publicly may thus serve as an additional—and in some cases primary—incentive to participate, suggesting that for this type of activity, cultural demand and digital social behaviour are tightly intertwined.

Employment status reveals an articulated pattern across labour-market categories. Unemployed individuals display consistently negative and significant marginal effects across all cultural activities, a result straightforwardly interpretable in terms of income constraints. Students, by contrast, show positive and significant effects for the composite indicator *CPOH* and for museum visits, suggesting that when financial barriers are partially offset—likely through student discounts, subsidised access, or simply greater availability of discretionary time—younger individuals are more likely to engage actively with cultural life. Retired respondents show reduced participation primarily for cinema (−10%) and theatre (−6.4%), potentially reflecting a combination of physical constraints, reduced social stimulation, and likely lower exposure to the digital channels through which cultural events are increasingly promoted and discovered.

Finally, city size emerges as a clear structural determinant of participation. Residents of medium-sized cities and small towns or rural areas are significantly less likely to participate in most cultural activities relative to inhabitants of large cities, with marginal effects ranging from approximately −6 to −9% points. This result is consistent with a supply-side interpretation: larger urban centres offer a denser and more diversified cultural infrastructure, lowering the effective cost—in terms of both money and effort—of accessing cultural events and venues (Feder, 2023).

5 Conclusions

This chapter has presented a preliminary examination of the determinants of cultural participation in presence in Italy, based on a large and newly collected survey conducted in 2025. The survey was designed not only to investigate patterns of cultural consumption in the digital era, but also to assess whether the disruption caused by the COVID-19 pandemic—which temporarily halted in-person cultural participation—has produced lasting changes in participation behaviours and modes of cultural consumption. The descriptive, correlational, and econometric evidence confirms a set of robust and well-established pieces of evidence: cultural participation is widespread yet unevenly distributed across socio-economic groups; education emerges as the most powerful predictor of engagement; income constraints continue to limit access to many activities; and age plays a role, with younger individuals consistently more involved in the most accessible and popular cultural forms. At the same time, participation tends to cluster across activities, suggesting that individuals who engage in one form of cultural consumption are also more likely to be active in others, reflecting not only specific tastes but also broader dispositions and capabilities.

The analysis also highlights the continued relevance of structural barriers. Financial and time-related constraints remain the most frequently reported obstacles, underscoring that economic affordability and work–life conditions continue to shape cultural access in meaningful ways. Supply-related limitations—including the density, variety, and appeal of cultural offerings—matter as well, particularly for individuals living outside large urban centres. These findings point to a persistent geography of cultural opportunities that policymakers should take seriously.

Although this chapter has focused exclusively on in-person cultural participation, the results concerning digital engagement suggest avenues for future research. Heavy internet users show a distinctive pattern only in relation to pop concerts, yet the broader diffusion of online cultural practices may reshape participation trajectories in the years ahead. The survey's rich information on digital behaviours will allow for more advanced analyses in future work.

From a policy perspective, the findings resonate with the European Union's emphasis on cultural participation as a lever for promoting social cohesion, inclusion, and sustainable development (European Commission, 2018; European Council, 2017, 2022). Enhancing access to culture—through education, support for lower-income households, territorial rebalancing of cultural infrastructures, and the removal of economic and time-related barriers—can contribute not only to individual well-being but also to broader societal goals. In this sense, the results presented here reinforce the idea that cultural policy is most effective when integrated with social, educational, and regional development strategies. Strengthening cultural participation is therefore not only a cultural objective but also a key component of a more cohesive and equitable society.

References

Ateca-Amestoy, V., & Castiglione, C. (2023). Live and digital engagement with the visual arts. *Journal of Cultural Economics, 47*, 643–692. https://doi.org/10.1007/s10824-022-09466-3

Bakhshi, H., Di Novo, S., & Fazio, G. (2023). The great lockdown and cultural consumption in the UK. *Journal of Cultural Economics, 47*, 555–587. https://doi.org/10.1007/s10824-022-09463-6

Bauernschuster, S., Falck, O., & Woessmann, L. (2014). Surfing alone? The internet and social capital: Quasi-experimental evidence from an unforeseeable technological mistake. *Journal of Public Economics, 117*, 73–89. https://doi.org/10.1016/j.jpubeco.2014.05.007

Bourdieu, P. (1984). *A social critique of the judgement of taste*. Harvard University Press.

Brook, O. (2016). Spatial equity and cultural participation: How access influences attendance at museums and galleries in London. *Cultural Trends, 25*, 21–34. https://doi.org/10.1080/09548963.2015.1134098

Cellini, R., & Cuccia, T. (2025). In-person and online cultural participation amidst the great lockdown: Regional evidence from Italy. In C. Guccio, I. Mazza, & G. Pignataro (Eds.), *New perspectives in the public and cultural sector. Festschrift in honor of Ilde Rizzo* (pp. 103–121). Springer. https://doi.org/10.1007/978-3-031-81892-9_6

Cellini, R., & Cuccia, T. (2026). Income distribution and cultural participation: Evidence from Italy. *Journal of Cultural Economics, 50*, 1. https://doi.org/10.1007/s10824-025-09572-y

De la Vega, P., Suárez-Fernández, S., Boto-García, D., & Prieto-Rodríguez, J. (2020). Playing a play: Online and live performing arts consumers' profiles and the role of supply constraints. *Journal of Cultural Economics, 44*, 425–450. https://doi.org/10.1007/s10824-019-09367-y

European Commission. (2018). *A new European agenda for culture*. European Commission.

European Council. (2017). *European council conclusions*. European Council.

European Council. (2022). *Council resolution on the EU workplan for culture 2023–26*. European Council.

EUROSTAT. (2024). *Culture statistics – cultural participation*. https://ec.europa.eu/eurostat/statistics-explained/index.php?title=Culture_statistics_-_cultural_participation. Accessed on 31 Mar 2026.

Falk, M., & Katz-Gerro, T. (2016). Cultural participation in Europe: Can we identify common determinants? *Journal of Cultural Economics, 40*, 127–162. https://doi.org/10.1007/s10824-015-9242-9

Feder, T. (2023). Access to arts consumption: The stratification of aesthetic life-chances. *Journal of Consumer Culture, 23*, 672–691. https://doi.org/10.1177/14695405221133269

Feder, T., McAndrew, S., O'Brien, D., & Taylor, M. (2022). Cultural consumption and Covid-19: Evidence from the taking part and COVID-19 cultural participation monitor surveys. *Leisure Studies, 42*, 38–55. https://doi.org/10.1080/02614367.2022.2088831

Geraci, A., Nardotto, M., Reggiani, T., & Sabatini, F. (2022). Broadband internet and social capital. *Journal of Public Economics, 206*, 104578. https://doi.org/10.1016/j.jpubeco.2021.104578

Heilbrun, J., & Gray, C. M. (2001). *The economics of art and culture*. Cambridge University Press.

ISTAT. (2022). *Tempo libero e partecipazione culturale. Tra vecchie e nuove pratiche*. Istat.

Katz-Gerro, T. (1999). Cultural consumption and social stratification: Leisure activities and musical tastes. *Sociological Perspectives, 42*, 627–646. https://doi.org/10.2307/1389577

Katz-Gerro, T., & Sullivan, O. (2023). Cultural stratification in the UK: Persistent gender and class differences in cultural voraciousness. *Journal of Consumer Culture, 23*, 391–408. https://doi.org/10.1177/14695405221100388

Lévy-Garboua, L., & Montmarquette, C. (1996). A microeconometric study of theatre demand. *Journal of Cultural Economics, 20*(1), 25–50. https://doi.org/10.1007/BF00148269

Lévy-Garboua, L., & Montmarquette, C. (2003). Demand. In R. Towse (Ed.), *A handbook of cultural economics* (pp. 201–213). Edward Elgar.

OECD. (2022). *The culture fix: Creative people, places and industries*. OECD.

Panarese, P., & Azzarita, V. (2021). Nuove pratiche, antichi divari? La partecipazione culturale online in Italia tra opportunità di coinvolgimento e rischi di esclusione. *Studi Culturali, 3*, 369–392. https://doi.org/10.1405/102364

Seaman, B. (2006). Empirical studies of demand for the performing arts. In V. Ginsburgh & D. Throsby (Eds.), *Handbook of the economics of art and culture* (pp. 416–472). Elsevier. https://doi.org/10.1016/S1574-0676(06)01014-3

Stigler, G., & Becker, G. (1977). De gustibus non est disputandum. *American Economic Review, 67*, 76–90.

Suarez-Fernandez, S., Prieto-Rodriguez, J., & Perez-Villadoniga, M. J. (2020). The changing role of education as we move from popular to highbrow culture. *Journal of Cultural Economics, 44*, 189–212. https://doi.org/10.1007/s10824-019-09355-2

Tubadji, A., Gheasi, M., Crociata, A., & Odoardi, I. (2022). Cultural capital and income inequality across Italian regions. *Regional Studies, 56*, 459–475. https://doi.org/10.1080/00343404.2021.1950913

Cultural Engagement of Older Adults in the Digital Age: Barriers and Opportunities

Flavia Coda Moscarola, Simone Seregni, and Roberto Zanola

Abstract This chapter analyses cultural participation among older adults in Italy, focusing on the interplay between onsite and online engagement. Using original survey data from a representative sample of individuals aged 60 and above, the study documents low and highly uneven participation in cultural activities, particularly those requiring physical attendance. While digital technologies have the potential to expand access, their diffusion remains limited and strongly associated with education and digital skills. The evidence suggests that online cultural consumption largely complements, rather than substitutes, traditional participation, but is concentrated among already active individuals. As a result, digitalisation risks reinforcing existing inequalities in cultural access. The findings highlight the role of cultural capital, health conditions and digital literacy, and point to the need for policies that address both traditional barriers and the digital divide in ageing societies.

1 Introduction

Last December, ISTAT released preliminary results from the 2024 population census. The figures confirm the progressive ageing of the Italian population: the average age has reached 46.9 years, 3 months higher than in 2023, while the

F. Coda Moscarola (✉)
Department of Law and Political, Economic and Social Sciences (DiGSPES), University of Eastern Piedmont, Alessandria, Italy

CeRP-Collegio Carlo Alberto, Torino, Italy
e-mail: flavia.codamoscarola@uniupo.it

S. Seregni
Fondazione Fitzcarraldo ETS, Turin, Italy
e-mail: simone.seregni@fitzcarraldo.it

R. Zanola
Department of Law and Political, Economic and Social Sciences (DiGSPES), University of Eastern Piedmont, Alessandria, Italy
e-mail: roberto.zanola@uniupo.it

R. Cellini et al. (eds.), *Cultural, Social, and Political Participation in the Internet Era*, Contributions to Economics, https://doi.org/10.1007/978-3-032-33072-7_6

share of individuals aged 65 and over has increased from 24.3% to 24.7% (ISTAT, 2025). These trends are part of a broader demographic transformation affecting most advanced economies. Declining fertility and rising life expectancy have led to what is often described as a "demographic winter", a structural shift in which older cohorts represent an increasingly large proportion of the population. According to the United Nations (2023), the number of people aged 65 and above worldwide is expected to more than double between 2021 and 2050, while in several Western countries older individuals will soon outnumber younger cohorts.

Population ageing is therefore not only a demographic phenomenon but also a major social and economic challenge. For a long time, older individuals were primarily considered as recipients of welfare support due to declining health conditions or reduced economic activity. More recent perspectives, however, emphasise the active role that older adults can play in contemporary societies and highlight the importance of promoting their social inclusion and participation (Super, 2020; Vlandas et al., 2021). In this perspective, ageing is increasingly interpreted not simply as a phase of dependency but as a stage of life characterised by new forms of engagement and contribution, with important implications for social innovation and economic activity (Lipp & Peine, 2022).

Within this broader debate, several studies highlight that participation in cultural activities is associated with improvements in both psychological and physical well-being (Francourt & Finn, 2019; Tymoszuk et al., 2020; Huang et al., 2025). Cultural engagement can foster social interaction, cognitive stimulation and emotional enrichment, contributing to a better quality of life among older adults (Creech et al., 2013; Goulding, 2018; Noice et al., 2013; Ferraro et al., 2019) and happiness (Brown et al., 2015; Wheatley & Bickerton, 2017; Murtin & Zanobetti, 2024).

At the same time, participation in cultural activities is shaped by important structural factors. Cultural consumption requires time, resources and, often, a certain degree of cultural competence. According to Becker's (1965) theory of time allocation, individuals must allocate limited time across different activities, and cultural engagement competes with other forms of leisure and household responsibilities. Moreover, the literature on cultural demand emphasises the role of accumulated cultural capital and learning processes (Bourdieu, 1986; Stigler & Becker, 1977; Lévy-Garboua & Montmarquette, 1996), which contribute to explaining why cultural participation tends to remain stratified across social groups (Katz-Gerro, 1999; Feder, 2023).

More recently, the rapid diffusion of digital technologies has introduced an additional dimension to the analysis of cultural participation. Online platforms have significantly expanded the ways in which individuals can access cultural content, reducing some traditional barriers to participation, particularly for individuals with mobility limitations or living far from cultural venues (Radermecker, 2021; Ateca-Amestoy & Castiglione, 2023). However, digitalisation may also generate new inequalities in access. The so-called digital divide remains particularly pronounced among older generations, reflecting differences in education, digital skills and access to technological infrastructure (Mihelj et al., 2019; Beaunoyer et al., 2020).

Understanding how these dynamics interact is therefore crucial for studying cultural engagement in ageing societies. This chapter contributes to this debate by analysing cultural participation among older adults in Italy, with particular attention to the relationship between onsite and online modes of engagement. Based on original survey data collected in January 2025 from a representative sample of Italian residents aged 60 and above, the analysis investigates patterns of cultural consumption across several artistic domains.

Previous studies based on the same dataset have already examined some relevant aspects of cultural participation among older Italians. Coda Moscarola et al. (2025b) analyse the relationship between cultural participation and well-being, showing that engagement in cultural activities is mainly associated with the social dimensions of well-being, while the link with broader evaluative measures is weaker. The results also indicate that cultural expertise does not systematically reinforce these effects, suggesting that the benefits of participation are largely connected to the relational and experiential nature of cultural activities. A second study, Coda Moscarola et al. (2025a), focuses instead on the relationship between onsite and online cultural participation. Performing bivariate models for four cultural domains, museums, theatre, classical music and other concerts, the analysis highlights elements of complementarity between the two modes of consumption and reveals differences in participation patterns across age groups and gender.

Using the same dataset and analytical framework, the chapter aims to shed light on the mechanisms that shape cultural engagement in later life with the objective of capturing how different forms of participation interact within a broader pattern of cultural engagement.

The remainder of the chapter is organised as follows. The next section describes the survey design and the characteristics of the dataset used in the analysis. This is followed by a descriptive analysis of cultural participation among older Italians. The subsequent sections explore barriers to participation and the role of digital technologies, before presenting the econometric analysis of multi-domain cultural consumption. The final section discusses the main findings and their implications for cultural and social policy.

2 Data

To examine how older adults engage with cultural activities and how digital opportunities relate to traditional participation, this chapter relies on original survey data. The empirical analysis relies on data collected through a CATI (Computer-Assisted Telephone Interviewing) survey conducted in January 2025. Telephone interviews were chosen to minimise potential selection biases that could arise from alternative data collection methods, such as mobile applications or online questionnaires, which tend to overrepresent individuals who are more familiar with digital technologies. In total, 957 interviews were completed with a representative random sample of Italian residents aged 60 and above. The sampling design followed a cell quota approach aimed at reproducing the actual population distribution across a set of key socio-demographic characteristics. Quotas were defined according to gender and age group, macro-area of residence, municipality size, altimetric zone and level of education. Population benchmarks for these variables were obtained from administrative statistics provided by the Italian National Institute of Statistics (ISTAT).

Table 1 compares the distribution of the survey sample with the corresponding population benchmarks provided by ISTAT. For each control variable, the relative frequencies observed in the sample are contrasted with the official population shares. Differences are evaluated using a z-test for proportions. The results show that none of the differences are statistically significant, indicating that the sample closely reproduces the demographic structure of the Italian population aged 60 and above.

3 Patterns of Cultural Participation Among Older Italians: A Descriptive Overview

3.1 The Cultural Consumptions of the Elderly

Among Italians aged 60 and over, television continues to occupy a central place among cultural media. A large majority of respondents (81%) reported that they regularly watch television and would not easily give it up, while only a very small share of the sample (2.8%) declared having no interest in it.

Reading also remains a widespread but low-intensity practice. Overall, 70.8% of respondents reported having read at least one book, newspaper or magazine during the 12 months preceding the survey. By contrast, digital formats such as e-books or audiobooks are still relatively uncommon among older adults and are used by only 19.6% of the sample. On average, respondents reported reading 4.39 printed books during the previous year (standard deviation 6.76), with a median expenditure of €50 on new books. The use of digital books is much more limited: the average number of e-books read is only 0.53 (standard deviation 3.75), and the median expenditure amounts to €10. Considering both traditional and digital formats together, 73.1% of respondents reported reading at least one of these materials during the year preceding the interview. The detailed statistics on reading habits by mode of consumption are reported in Table 2.

The involvement in onsite cultural activities is relatively limited. As shown in Fig. 1, the overall participation rate is low for all the cultural activities listed. Respondents attended on average fewer than one of the activities listed in the questionnaire during the 12 months preceding the survey. Most individuals (59.6%) reported not having taken part in any onsite cultural event over the reference period, while about one quarter of respondents (25%) explicitly declared having no interest in such activities.

Table 1 Comparison between sample quotas and the demographic structure of the Italian population

		Sample			ISTAT		
Variable	Modalities	Obs.	Mean	SD	Mean	SD	P(|Z| > |z|)
Gender and age class	Man 60–69	195	0.204	0.403	0.205	0.404	0.900
	Man 70–80	154	0.161	0.367	0.163	0.369	0.878
	Man over 80	81	0.085	0.278	0.083	0.276	0.844
	Woman 60–69	207	0.216	0.412	0.222	0.415	0.689
	Woman 70–80	185	0.193	0.395	0.191	0.393	0.885
	Woman over 80	135	0.141	0.348	0.136	0.343	0.634
Macro area of residence	North-West Italy	259	0.271	0.444	0.273	0.446	0.847
	North-East Italy	191	0.200	0.400	0.198	0.399	0.912
	Central Italy	195	0.204	0.403	0.203	0.402	0.949
	South Italy	212	0.222	0.415	0.218	0.413	0.788
	Island	100	0.104	0.306	0.108	0.310	0.758
Size class of municipality of residence	<10. 000 citizens	302	0.316	0.465	0.315	0.465	0.970
	10.000–30.000 citizens	226	0.236	0.425	0.240	0.427	0.781
	30.000–100.000 citizens	209	0.218	0.413	0.213	0.409	0.684
	Over 100.000 citizens	220	0.230	0.421	0.232	0.422	0.877
Altimetric zone of residence	Inner or coastal mountains	124	0.130	0.336	0.130	0.336	0.969
	Inner hills	229	0.239	0.427	0.236	0.425	0.811
	Coastal hills	148	0.155	0.362	0.154	0.361	0.956
	Plain	456	0.476	0.499	0.480	0.500	0.828
Education level	None, ISCED 1, ISCED 2	657	0.687	0.464	0.675	0.468	0.437
	ISCED 3	214	0.224	0.417	0.233	0.423	0.493
	ISCED 6–8	86	0.090	0.286	0.092	0.289	0.798

Note: Population benchmarks are drawn from ISTAT administrative statistics: population by sex and age (ISTAT, 2024a), municipality size and altimetric classification (ISTAT, 2024b) and educational attainment (ISTAT, 2020)

These figures suggest that participation in cultural activities requiring physical attendance remains rather uneven among older Italians. While a large share of respondents does not engage in onsite cultural events, a smaller group attends several activities during the year, which explains the relatively high dispersion of the distribution. This pattern indicates that cultural participation among the elderly tends to be concentrated within a limited segment of the population rather than being evenly spread across individuals.

Table 2 Reading habits among older Italians (aged 60 and over)

	Obs.	Mean	Std. dev.
Books	957	0.567	0.496
Newspapers	957	0.449	0.498
Magazines	957	0.303	0.460
E-books	957	0.064	0.244
Online newspapers	957	0.165	0.371
Audiobooks	957	0.033	0.180
Podcast	957	0.045	0.207

Note: The table reports the share of individuals who reported reading or using each item at least once during the 12 months preceding the survey. "Obs." indicates the number of observations, while the mean represents the proportion of respondents engaging in each activity

Figure 1 shows the distribution of attendance frequencies for selected onsite cultural activities during the 12 months preceding the survey. Percentages represent the share of respondents attending each activity with the reported frequency.

3.2 *Education, Health, Income or Free Time: Which Are the Barriers?*

One possible explanation for the relatively low level of cultural participation concerns the limited interest expressed by a significant share of respondents. Around 25% of individuals declared that they are not interested in cultural activities. According to Stigler and Becker (1977) and Bourdieu (1986), the demand for cultural goods is shaped by past exposure to culture and by the gradual accumulation of "consumption capital". In this perspective, education plays a crucial role in the formation of cultural capital and in the development of preferences for cultural experiences. As reported in Table 1, most people aged over 60 have attained only ISCED level 2, which corresponds to one of the lower levels within the International Standard Classification of Education.

To explore this aspect further, the questionnaire included a short test intended to provide a proxy for respondents' cultural expertise. Participants were asked to identify two well-known artists from a list of five names in three different artistic fields: sculpture, cinema and ballet. The results reported in Table 3 reveal a generally modest level of cultural knowledge. In several cases, respondents were unable to identify even a single correct name. Taken together, the evidence on education and the results of the expertise test suggest that the limited accumulation of cultural capital may represent an important factor behind the relatively low levels of cultural consumption observed among older Italians.

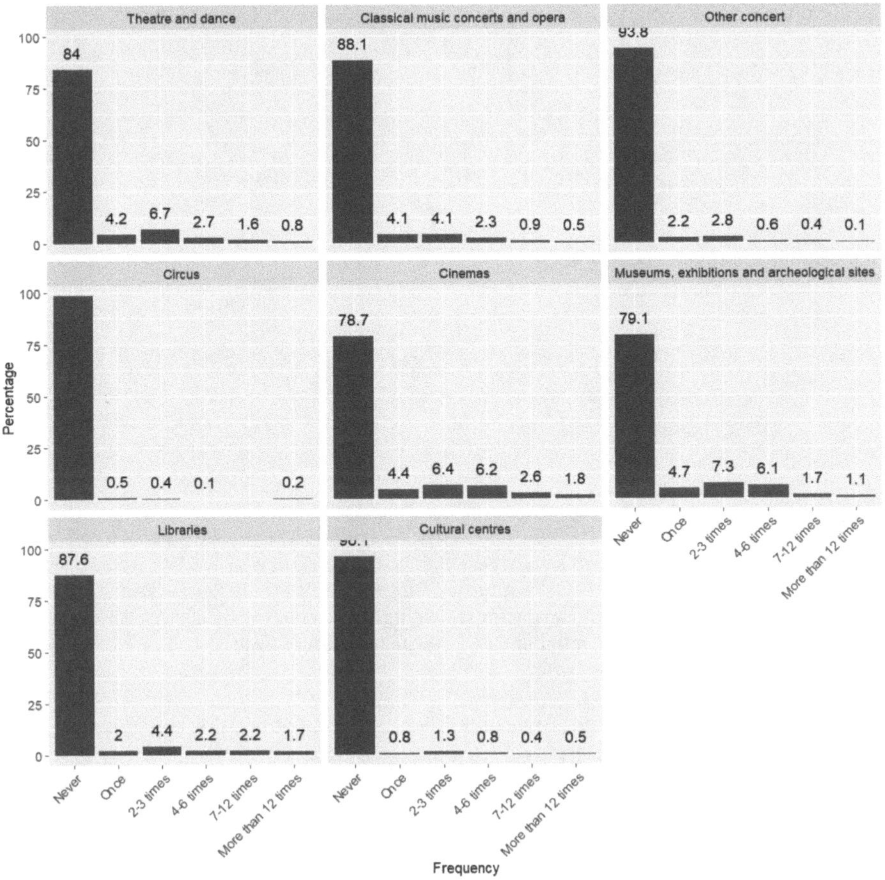

Fig. 1 Frequency of participation in onsite cultural activities during the last 12 months (n = 957)

Table 3 Cultural expertise test results

	Two correct answers		One correct answer		No correct answer	
	Mean	Std. dev.	Mean	Std. dev.	Mean	Std. dev.
Sculpture	0.035	0.184	0.263	0.440	0.702	0.457
Cinema	0.144	0.351	0.542	0.498	0.313	0.464
Ballet	0.057	0.233	0.387	0.487	0.556	0.499

The table reports the distribution of respondents according to the number of correct answers provided in the cultural expertise test (two, one, or none). Means represent the share of respondents in each category. $n = 957$

Health conditions play a pivotal role in determining how individuals engage with culture as they age. While most respondents express general satisfaction with their health, this sentiment follows a downward trajectory as age increases, a trend clearly illustrated in Fig. 2. Since many onsite cultural experiences involve mobility, travel

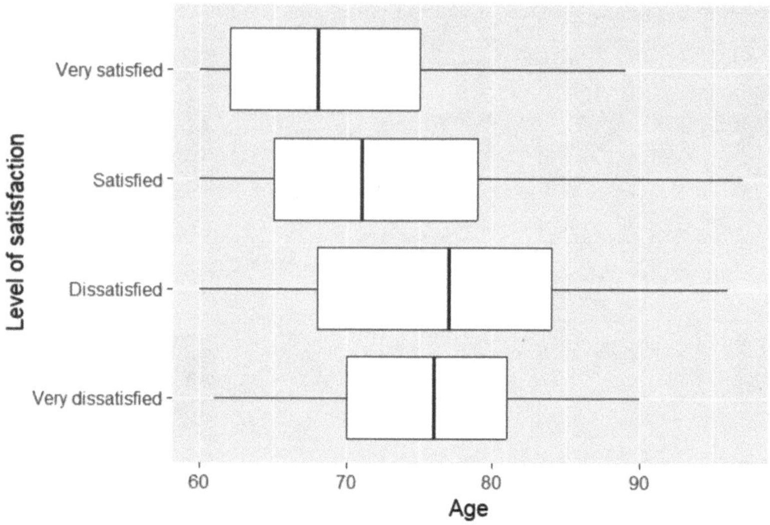

Fig. 2 Age distribution by level of satisfaction with health conditions (n = 957). Note: The figure reports the distribution of respondents' age across different levels of self-reported satisfaction with health conditions. Boxes represent the interquartile range, the central line indicates the median and the horizontal lines extend to the minimum and maximum observed values

or prolonged time outside the home, health-related barriers may significantly limit participation, especially among the oldest age groups.

Admission prices may represent a potential barrier to cultural participation, particularly for individuals with limited financial resources. When respondents were asked about the factors that discourage their attendance at onsite cultural activities, 11.1% indicated that the cost of admission is among the main reasons for not participating.

Although the questionnaire did not collect detailed information on respondents' income, several indicators suggest that a non-negligible share of the sample faces economic constraints, as shown in Table 4. About 21% of individuals reported receiving welfare support, such as the *assegno di inclusione* or a minimum pension. Moreover, less than half of respondents (47%) declared that they would be able to cope with an unexpected expense of €950.

Despite these signals of financial vulnerability, the data do not reveal a statistically significant association between economic hardship and the perception of admission costs as a barrier to cultural participation ($\chi^2 = 0.005$, df = 1, $p = 0.943$). This result can be interpreted in many different ways. One of them is that, within this sample, the price of cultural events does not appear to be the main factor limiting participation in onsite cultural activities.

Table 4 Relative frequencies of opinions on admission costs as a barrier to cultural participation by income level (n = 957)

		Cost as a barrier	
		Yes	No
Income level	Low	.109	.891
	Other	.112	.888

Note: "Income level" is a proxy equal to "low" if the respondent receives a minimum pension, *assegno di inclusione*, or *assegno sociale*, or cannot afford an unexpected expense of €950. Percentages report the share of respondents indicating admission costs as a barrier to onsite cultural participation

Table 5 Frequency of use of the World Wide Web by level of formal education

		Education level		
		ISCED1–2	ISCED 3	ISCED 6–8
Frequency of use of www	Everyday	21.1%	43.0%	74.4%
	Sometimes a week	13.9%	22.9%	10.5%
	Sometimes a month	7.5%	6.1%	3.5%
	Seldom	12.0%	7.0%	4.7%
	Never	45.5%	21.0%	6.9%

Percentages report the distribution of respondents by frequency of Internet use within each education level (ISCED). In addition, 33% of respondents refuse to use the World Wide Web and 23% consider it of limited usefulness

3.3 *Older Adults, Digital and New Technologies*

Older Italians show a limited familiarity with the World Wide Web. About 36.6% of respondents reported that they had not used the Internet at all during the 12 months preceding the survey, while an additional 10.2% declared that they had used it only rarely over the same period. This pattern does not appear to be driven by geographical constraints such as residence in mountain areas, where Internet connections may be slower or less reliable. Rather, the data reveal a clear association between educational attainment and the frequency of Internet use ($\chi^2 = 151.19$, $df = 8$, $p < 0.01$). Individuals with higher levels of education tend to use the web more frequently and appear to be more familiar with digital technologies (Table 5).

The link between educational attainment and familiarity with the World Wide Web raises an important issue. Digital technologies are often presented as a way to broaden access to cultural content and to attract new audiences. However, if the digital divide reflects the same underlying factors that shape traditional patterns of cultural participation, the expansion of online cultural supply may simply reinforce existing inequalities. In such a case, those who are already active cultural consumers are likely to benefit the most from digital opportunities, while individuals who are less engaged in cultural practices may remain excluded from both traditional and online forms of participation.

Table 6 Participation in online cultural activities during the 12 months preceding the interview

	Obs.	Mean	Std. dev.
Online visits to museums or exhibitions	957	0.019	0.136
Theatre or dance performance in streaming	957	0.028	0.166
Classical music concerts or operas in streaming	957	0.036	0.185
Other concert in streaming	957	0.028	0.166
Gaming online	957	0.007	0.085

The table reports the share of respondents who engaged in each online cultural activity at least once during the 12 months preceding the survey. Means indicate the proportion of individuals participating in each activity (n = 957)

Among Italians aged over 60, the Internet is used mainly for activities that replicate traditional media habits. About 26.9% of respondents use the web to read the online versions of newspapers, and 25.1% report being subscribed to at least one audiovisual streaming platform. Interest in other forms of cultural content available online appears much more limited: 69.5% of respondents declared that they are not interested in these types of digital cultural offers. As a consequence, the overall level of online cultural engagement remains rather low, as reported in Table 6.

4 Empirical Investigation

The descriptive evidence presented so far provides a first picture of cultural participation among older Italians and highlights several potential constraints, including limited cultural capital, health conditions and the persistence of a digital divide. Building on this background, the empirical analysis focuses on how different forms of cultural engagement relate to individual outcomes and participation patterns in later life (Coda Moscarola et al., 2025a, 2025b).

Figure 3 summarises these patterns through a bubble plot that compares onsite and online participation across cultural domains. Individuals are first classified according to the cultural activities they attend onsite and then regrouped according to their online engagement, generating 15 possible participation profiles. The categories follow a simple logic: "None" refers to individuals who do not consume culture, while labels such as "Museums only" or "Museums + Theatre" indicate participation in one or more domains. The same classification is applied to online activities to allow comparison between the two modes. The 45-degree identity line represents perfect correspondence between onsite and online behaviour; points on this line indicate identical consumption patterns across both modes.

Participation is concentrated in a limited number of profiles. The largest group is composed of individuals attending museums only, followed by those participating exclusively in theatre activities and by the "Museums + Theatre" combination. More diversified patterns are relatively uncommon, and individuals consuming across all domains ("omnivores") are rare and appear almost exclusively in the onsite mode.

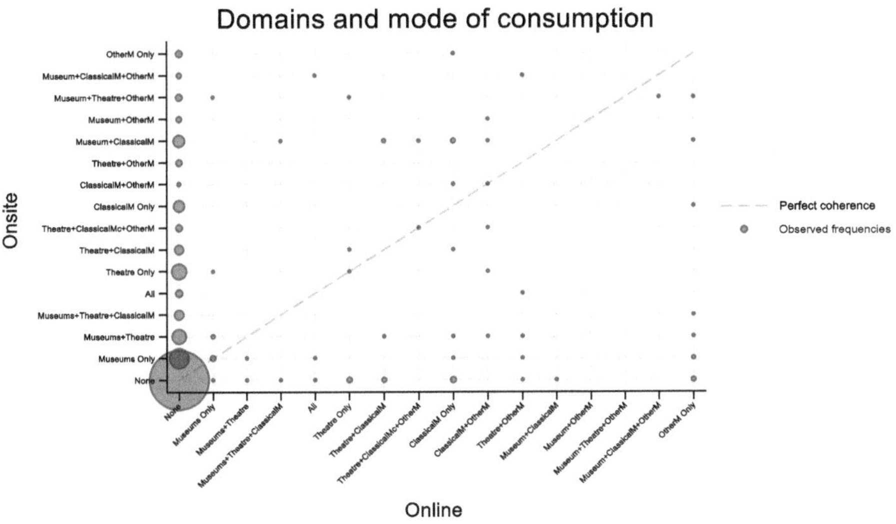

Fig. 3 Cultural consumption domains by mode (onsite vs. online). Bubbles represent combinations of cultural consumption domains. Bubble size reflects the number of individuals in each profile. The 45-degree line indicates perfect correspondence between onsite and online participation

Online engagement involves a smaller share of individuals and is concentrated in fewer domains. While onsite participation displays a broader variety of combinations, online consumption appears more limited. Some regularities nevertheless emerge: museum visitors, both exclusive and combined with theatre, tend to consume museum-related content online, whereas individuals combining museums and classical music onsite, as well as onsite non-consumers, most frequently engage with classical music online.

We then estimate a multinomial logit (mlogit) model. The objective is to identify the individual characteristics associated with participation across different cultural domains. We compare individuals who concentrate their consumption within a single domain (e.g. museums only) with those who extend their participation to additional domains such as theatre, classical music or other concerts. The analysis is carried out separately for each domain and distinguishes between exclusive onsite participation and broader patterns that include both onsite and online engagement. Table 7 summarises the main results.

Before discussing the estimates, it is important to note that the relatively small sample size does not allow strong conclusions for all control variables. For this reason, the discussion focuses only on the most robust and consistent patterns emerging from the estimates.

One of the clearest results concerns individuals who care for children, who are more likely to display broader cultural participation, particularly in the profiles that include all cultural domains. This result is consistent with the idea that cultural activities may also serve educational or recreational purposes when children are

Table 7 Multinomial logit estimates of mono- vs. multi-domain cultural consumption by mode

	Museums				Theatre			
	Onsite		Onsite+online		Onsite		Onsite+online	
	b/se		b/se		b/se		b/se	
2 domains								
Living alone	0.694 (0.406)	*	0.825 (0.428)	*	1.479 (0.707)	**	1.606 (0.669)	**
University	0.368 (0.462)		0.264 (0.474)		0.663 (0.702)		0.727 (0.706)	
Expertise	−0.196 (0.174)		−0.172 (0.173)		−0.194 (0.257)		−0.206 (0.252)	
Zero books at home	−1.038 (1.298)		−0.129 (1.087)		12.899 (1.165)	***	14.146 (0.871)	***
Caregiving children	0.031 (0.018)	*	0.042 (0.023)	*	0.028 (0.022)		0.020 (0.022)	
Often on internet	1.112 (0.499)	**	1.043 (0.492)	**	0.813 (0.503)		0.860 (0.505)	*
3 domains								
Living alone	−0.515 (0.782)		−0.394 (0.709)		1.144 (1.366)		0.980 (1.306)	
University	0.441 (0.783)		0.894 (0.740)		2.787 (0.888)	***	2.538 (0.949)	***
Expertise	0.322 (0.389)		0.498 (0.329)		−1.183 (0.426)	***	−1.090 (0.393)	***
Zero books at home	−13.236 (0.937)	***	−12.935 (0.832)	***	1.017 (1.144)		−0.362 (1.425)	
Caregiving children	0.012 (0.033)		0.030 (0.030)		0.034 (0.028)		0.036 (0.029)	
Often on internet	0.408 (0.747)		0.361 (0.653)		−0.018 (1.148)		0.291 (1.113)	
All domains								
Living alone	0.568 (0.954)		0.869 (0.721)		1.727 (1.149)		1.694 (0.930)	*
University	0.920 (0.883)		0.262 (0.708)		1.863 (1.027)	*	0.895 (0.887)	
Expertise	−0.804 (0.484)	*	−0.153 (0.365)		−0.802 (0.478)	*	−0.132 (0.409)	
Zero books at home	−13.993 (1.257)	***	−13.183 (0.827)	***	−0.024 (1.162)		−0.675 (0.693)	
Caregiving children	0.072 (0.027)	***	0.083 (0.026)	***	0.072 (0.031)	**	0.066 (0.027)	**
Often on internet	0.683 (0.644)		1.113 (0.698)		0.518 (0.676)		1.410 (0.758)	*
Number of observations	183		186		126		139	

Baseline category: Mono-domain consumption (only museums or only theatre). Separate models are estimated for onsite and combined onsite–online participation. In all the specifications, the set of control variables includes: Male, Age, Living alone, University, Credit constrained, Expertise, Zero books at home, Child caregiving, Adult caregiving, Frequent Internet use and the Intercept. Only a selection of estimated coefficients is reported. Robust standard errors in parentheses. *** $p < 0.01$, ** $p < 0.05$, * $p < 0.10$

involved. Living alone is also associated with a higher probability of participating in more than one cultural domain, especially in the museum and theatre specifications. A similar pattern emerges for higher education: holding a university degree tends to be positively related to multi-domain participation, although the statistical significance of this effect appears mainly within the theatre-related models.

By contrast, indicators of limited cultural resources are associated with more restricted participation patterns. In particular, the absence of books at home is strongly correlated with mono-domain consumption in the museum specifications, suggesting that a weaker cultural environment may reduce the likelihood of diversifying cultural activities. Digital familiarity also plays a role. Individuals who frequently use the Internet are more likely to extend their participation beyond a single domain, especially when online cultural consumption is included in the definition of participation.

Finally, neither gender nor cultural expertise shows a consistent association with broader participation across domains. In most specifications, these variables do not reach conventional levels of statistical significance, indicating that the diversification of cultural consumption among older adults is more strongly related to social context and everyday practices than to individual cultural knowledge alone.

5 Conclusion

Population ageing is reshaping the social structure of contemporary societies, and cultural participation among older adults is becoming an increasingly relevant dimension of social inclusion and well-being. The evidence presented in this chapter contributes to this discussion by examining patterns of cultural engagement among Italians aged 60 and over, with particular attention to the interplay between traditional onsite participation and emerging online opportunities.

The analysis highlights a relatively limited and uneven participation in cultural activities among older individuals. While reading and television remain widespread practices, attendance at cultural events requiring physical presence appears much less common and is concentrated within a restricted segment of the population. Several factors contribute to explaining this pattern. Limited cultural capital, health conditions and practical constraints linked to mobility all appear to play a role in shaping the opportunities for participation in later life.

The analysis also shows that the digital transformation of cultural consumption introduces both opportunities and new challenges. In principle, online access to cultural content could reduce some of the traditional barriers to participation, particularly those related to distance, mobility or physical accessibility. However, the empirical evidence suggests that the diffusion of digital cultural consumption among older adults remains limited. A substantial share of respondents report little familiarity with the Internet, and participation in online cultural activities is still confined to a relatively small group of individuals.

This finding raises an important policy issue. If digital access expands primarily among individuals who are already culturally active, the growth of online cultural supply may reinforce existing inequalities rather than reduce them. The results therefore underline the importance of considering older adults as a specific target group in cultural policy. Promoting cultural participation in ageing societies requires addressing both traditional barriers to access and the new forms of exclusion associated with digital technologies. Policies aimed at improving digital literacy, facilitating access to online cultural platforms and designing cultural offers that are accessible to older audiences may play an important role in this context.

At the same time, the evidence suggests that online and onsite cultural participation should not be seen as mutually exclusive alternatives. From a policy perspective, this implies that digital cultural initiatives should be integrated with traditional forms of cultural provision, creating hybrid opportunities that allow older adults to participate according to their preferences, abilities and resources.

More generally, the results presented in this chapter highlight the need to place cultural participation among older adults more firmly within the broader debate on active ageing and social inclusion. As populations continue to age, ensuring that older individuals have meaningful opportunities to engage with cultural life will become an increasingly important component of social policy.

Acknowledgments During the preparation of this work, the authors used ChatGPT 5.2 only as a language editing tool to improve grammar and clarity in English writing. After using this tool/service, the authors reviewed and edited the content as needed and take full responsibility for the content of the published article. We thank an anonymous Referee for helpful comments.

References

Ateca-Amestoy, V., & Castiglione, C. (2023). Live and digital engagement with the visual arts. *Journal of Cultural Economics, 47*, 643–692.

Beaunoyer, E., Dupéré, S., & Guitton, M. J. (2020). COVID-19 and digital inequalities: Reciprocal impacts and mitigation strategies. *Computers in Human Behavior, 111*, 1–9.

Becker, G. S. (1965). A theory of the allocation of time. *The Economic Journal, 75*(299), 493–517.

Bourdieu, P. (1986). The forms of capital. In *Handbook of theory and research for the sociology of education* (pp. 241–258).

Brown, J. L., MacDonald, R., & Mitchell, R. (2015). Are people who participate in cultural activities more satisfied with life? *Social Indicators Research, 122*(1), 135–146.

Coda Moscarola, F., Cuccia, T., De Cristofaro, A., & Zanola, R. (2025a). *Aging with culture: Cultural consumption and well-being in later life*. Mimeo.

Coda Moscarola, F., Seregni, S., & Zanola, R. (2025b). *Cultural participation of older adults in digital era: Expanding access or deepening the divide?* Mimeo.

Creech, A., Hallam, S., McQueen, H., & Varvarigou, M. (2013). The power of music in the lives of older adults. *Research Studies in Music Education, 35*(1), 87–102.

Feder, T. (2023). Access to arts consumption: The stratification of aesthetic life-chances. *Journal of Consumer Culture, 23*(3), 672–691.

Ferraro, A., Cerciello, M., Agovino, M., & Garofalo, A. (2019). The role of cultural consumption in reducing social exclusion: Empirical evidence from Italy in a spatial framework. *Economia Politica, 36*(1), 139–166.

Francourt D., & Finn, S. (2019). *What is the evidence on the role of the arts in improving health and well-being? A scoping review.* Health Evidence Network synthesis report 67. World Wealth Organization Europe.

Goulding, A. (2018). The role of cultural engagement in older people's lives. *Cultural Sociology, 12*(4), 518–539.
Huang, Y., He, Q., & Li, B. (2025). Cultural participation and psychological wellbeing: The mediating role of transcendence. *Humanities & Social Sciences Communications, 12*, 1340.
ISTAT. (2020). *Popolazione per titolo di studio e età (2020).*
ISTAT. (2024a). *Popolazione residente per sesso. età e stato civile al 1 gennaio 2024.*
ISTAT. (2024b). *Classificazioni statistiche e dimensioni dei comuni 30/06/2024.*
ISTAT. (2025). *Censimento e dinamiche della popolazione. Anno 2024.* ISTAT.
Katz-Gerro, T. (1999). Cultural consumption and social stratification: Leisure activities, musical tastes, and social location. *Sociological Perspectives, 42*, 627–646.
Lévy-Garboua, L., & Montmarquette, C. (1996). A microeconometric study of theatre demand. *Journal of Cultural Economics, 20*, 25–50.
Lipp, B., & Peine, A. (2022). Ageing as a driver of progressive politics? What the European silver economy teaches us about the co-constitution of ageing and innovation. *Ageing and Society, 44*(7), 1–13.
Mihelj, S., Leguina, A., & Downey, J. (2019). Culture is digital: Cultural participation, diversity and the digital divide. *New Media & Society, 21*(7), 1465–1485.
Murtin, F., & Zanobetti, L. (2024). The art of living well: Cultural participation and well-being. *Applied Research in Quality of Life, 19*(4), 1763–1790.
Noice, T., Noice, H., & Kramer, A. F. (2013). Participatory arts for older adults: A review of benefits and challenges. *The Gerontologies, 54*(5), 741–753.
Radermecker, A. (2021). Art and culture in the COVID-19 era: For a consumer-oriented approach. *SN Business & Economics, 1*(1), 1–14.
Stigler and Becker. (1977). De Gustibus Non Disputandum. *The American Economic Review, 67*(2), 79–90.
Super, N. (2020). Three trends shaping the politics of aging in America. *Public Policy & Aging Report, 30*(2), 39–45.
Tymoszuk, U., Perkins, R., Spiro, N., Williamon, A., & Fancourt, D. (2020). Longitudinal associations between short-term, repeated, and sustained arts engagement and well-being outcomes in older adults. *Journals of Gerontology: Social Sciences, 75*(7), 1609–1619.
United Nations. (2023). *World social report 2023: Leaving no one behind in an ageing world.*
Vlandas, T., McArthur, D., & Ganslmeier, M. (2021). Ageing and the economy: A literature review of political and policy mechanisms. *Political Research Exchange, 3*(1), 1–23.
Wheatley, D., & Bickerton, C. (2017). Subjective well-being and engagement in arts, culture and sport. *Journal of Cultural Economics, 41*(1), 23–45.

Data Cooperatives and Digital Neomutualism

Giuliana Amore

Abstract Data cooperatives have been introduced in the EU within the Data Governance Act (DGA, EU Regulation n. 868/2022) as providers of data intermediation services "aimed at establishing commercial relationships for the purpose of sharing data between an indeterminate number of data subjects and data controllers, on the one hand, and data users, on the other, through technical, legal, or other means [. . .]." This is both an innovative and incomplete regulation, which therefore requires, from a legal perspective, a systematic framework for the situation in light of the multiple regulatory frameworks involved. This refers in particular to the Third Sector (Third Sector Code), the protection of personal data (General Data Protection Regulation or GDPR), and the new rules for online intermediaries (Digital Services Act [DSA]).

1 Introduction

Data cooperatives have been introduced and regulated within the Data Governance Act (DGA, EU Regulation n. 868/2022) as providers of data intermediation services[1] "aimed at establishing commercial relationships for the purpose of sharing data between an indeterminate number of data subjects and data controllers, on the

[1] This is cooperative data management: a solution for protecting the data of individuals and businesses, and for sharing and equitably distributing the added value generated by the use of data, which is currently in the hands of corporations and multinationals, generating enormous profits. This is referred to as digital neo-mutualism: data cooperatives aggregate data from their members (individuals or businesses) and process it to create value, not just monetary value. They are based on a cooperative, nonpredatory logic. From an economic perspective, see Pentland and Hardjono (2020); about cooperatives, in general, see *ex multis*, F. Casale (2005); L. F. Paolucci (2014); F. Vella et al. (2018).

G. Amore (✉)
Department of Economics and Business, University of Catania, Catania, Italy
e-mail: gamore@unict.it

R. Cellini et al. (eds.), *Cultural, Social, and Political Participation in the Internet Era*, Contributions to Economics, https://doi.org/10.1007/978-3-032-33072-7_7

one hand, and data users, on the other, through technical, legal, or other means [. . .]" (Article 2, n. 11, DGA).

The DGA does not provide a definition of data cooperatives but defines "data cooperative services" as "data intermediation services offered by an organizational structure consisting of data subjects, sole proprietorships or SMEs, who are members of such a structure, whose primary objectives are to assist its members in exercising their rights in relation to certain data, including making informed choices before consenting to data processing, exchanging views on the purposes and conditions of data processing that would best represent the interests of its members in relation to their data, or negotiating the terms and conditions for data processing on behalf of members before granting authorization to the processing of non-personal data or before they give their consent to the processing of personal data."[2]

Therefore, the European legislator identifies the service they provide, in particular focusing on the following elements: data cooperative services are intermediary services; they are offered by an organizational structure composed of data subjects, sole proprietorships, or SMEs, who are members of that structure. The structure's primary objective (which constitutes its defining activity) is to assist its members in exercising their rights in relation to specific data. This assistance may take the form of assistance in making informed choices before consenting to data processing, in exchanging views on the purposes and conditions of data processing that would best represent the members' interests in relation to their data, and in negotiating the terms and conditions for data processing on behalf of members before granting authorization to process nonpersonal data or before they consent to the processing of personal data.

This is both an innovative and incomplete regulation, which therefore requires, from a legal perspective, a systematic framework for the situation in light of the multiple regulatory frameworks involved.[3]

---

[2] Data cooperatives offer a new model for equitable data governance, enabling individuals to collectively control, manage, and benefit from their information, while respecting cooperative principles such as democratic control by members, economic participation, and community interest. Data cooperatives should be distinguished from models such as data trusts. Both "data cooperatives" and "data trusts" aim to give individuals greater control over their data, but they function differently, but data trusts are similar to legal agreements in which trustees manage data on behalf of beneficiaries, focusing on responsible and ethical use. Data cooperatives are member-owned organizations where members collectively decide how their data is used, emphasizing democratic control and benefit-sharing. The key difference lies in governance: trusts rely on trustee decisions, while cooperatives empower members through collective decision-making. As this regard, see in particular, F. Mendonça, *Cooperative di dati: modelli democratici per una gestione etica dei dati*, in arXiv:2504.10058v1 [cs.SI] 14 aprile 2025.

[3] This is particularly evident in recital 31 of EU Regulation 868/2022 (Data Governance Act, DGA), which emphasizes that "data cooperatives aim to achieve a number of objectives, in particular by empowering individuals to make informed choices before consenting to data use, by influencing the terms and conditions set by data user organizations on which data use is subject, so as to offer better choices to individual members of the group, or by finding possible solutions to conflicting views of individual members of a group regarding how data should be used where

This refers in particular to the Third Sector (Third Sector Code), the protection of personal data (General Data Protection Regulation or GDPR), and the new rules for online intermediaries (Digital Services Act [DSA]).

First of all, the DGA specifically emphasizes that "the Commission sees strong potential in using data made available voluntarily by data subjects or other data controllers without seeking (financial) compensation, for purposes of general interest." Recital 15 then defines "data cooperative services [...] as data intermediation services offered by an organizational structure composed of data subjects, sole proprietorships, or SMEs that are members of that structure, whose primary objective is to support its members in exercising their rights in relation to certain data, including making informed choices before consenting to data processing, exchanging views on the purposes and conditions of data processing that would best represent the interests of its members in relation to their data, and negotiating terms and conditions for data processing on behalf of its members before they consent to the processing of non-personal data or before they consent to the processing of personal data."

Now, if it is true that the concept of "data cooperative" is not rigidly defined in the DGA and therefore opens the way to different subjective forms by making generic reference to a structured organization made up of the "members" that compose it, to be identified in the natural persons to whom the data refer (the "data subjects," pursuant to EU Regulation 679/2016), in individual businesses or in small and medium-sized enterprises (SMEs), it is equally true that the "main objectives" of solidarity, variously expressed, of support to its "members" in relation to the use of the data that will be carried out in the provision of the service,[4] make the "cooperative society" appear as the physiologically most suitable entity to fill the role of "data cooperative" in our legal system and in the European one.[5] And, just in light of such solidarity-based objectives, thoughts seem to turn,

---

such data concerns multiple data subjects within that group. In this context, it is important to recognize that the rights under Regulation (EU) 2016/679 are personal rights of the data subject and that the data subject cannot waive them. Data cooperatives could also be a useful tool for sole proprietorships and SMEs, which, in terms of knowledge about data sharing, are often comparable to individuals."

[4] Among these objectives, the definition expressly considers three, mentioning them alternatively and not (necessarily) cumulatively, as is clearly evident from the disjunction "or" between the last and the penultimate one. Specifically, it requires that the aforementioned "organizational structure" act for the primary purpose of: (i) assisting its "members" in exercising the rights recognized by the legal system, facilitating the acquisition of information for the exercise of rights regarding their data, particularly when personal data is involved; (ii) encouraging internal discussion among its "members," based on the "exchange of views on the purposes and conditions of data processing"12, to "best represent the interests of its members in relation to their data"; (iii) "(...) or negotiate the terms and conditions for the processing of data on behalf of the members (...)," that is, agree with third parties, who will use the data, what are the legal and economic conditions aimed at regulating the relationships concerning the use of data, personal and nonpersonal, of its members, natural or legal persons.

[5] F. Bravo (2024).

in our legal system, just as naturally, to L. D. n. 117/2017, containing the so-called Third Sector Code (CTs), which, as is known, has carried out a real work of "institutionalization,"[6] still underway and aimed at reorganizing the nonprofit sector,[7] by promoting its management and improving its transparency. It's a sector defined by legislation through a combination of three criteria: the pursuit of civic, solidarity, and socially beneficial purposes; the performance of activities recognized by the legislator as being of general interest; and, finally, governance capable of preventing the prevalence of purely private interests over broader ones.

According to Article 4 of the Italian Civil Code, "social cooperatives" are also third sector entities, provided they are established to pursue civic and socially beneficial purposes, as well as solidarity-based ones, through the performance—exclusively or primarily—of one or more activities of general interest "in the form of the free provision of [. . .] goods or services, or of mutual assistance." Hence, the potential classification of the data cooperatives mentioned in the DGA as "social cooperatives" under the Third Sector Code. The growing use of new technologies in all areas of life and the massive availability of data held by a small number of market players have led to an exponential growth in the risks highlighted above related to the processing of data of individual data subjects, often unaware of the hidden fate of their information. The development of predictive algorithmic and analytical capabilities has increased the ability of those with such knowledge to anticipate choices and influence citizens' decisions both in information and in debate political and individual behavior. This is why, in the online dimension, it is crucial to ensure that citizens maintain control over aspects such as the content of the information they disseminate and the ways in which it is used and reused by major players in the digital market, as a guarantee of personal freedom in the sense of the right to self-determination. By establishing data cooperatives, the European legislator seems to have recognized the need to support individual data subjects with collective bodies capable not only of assisting them, as a third party could, but also of allowing them to actively participate in the organization and functioning of the entity, contributing to a form of mutual representation and protection of an interest common to other entities to which the intermediated data refers.

As the "data controller" of personal data, the data cooperative will be required to comply with the privacy obligations arising from EU Regulation n. 679/2016 (the so-called GDPR, General Data Protection Regulation)[8] carrying out even just

---

[6] M. Rispoli Farina (2019), 3; G. Ponzanelli (1996), 314, already observes how the growth of the nonprofit sector "confirms the absolutely negligible role of legal rules in the birth and spread of new social phenomena." On the relationship between legal rules and the natural dynamism of third sector entities, see Gori and Zandonai (2018), 11 ss.

[7] F. Bosetti (2021), 361; L. Gori (2022), 1, highlight the difficulty of coining a definition of the "Third Sector." International literature has successfully characterized the Third Sector as "a loose and baggy monster," indicating the extreme complexity of defining the boundaries of a complex of entities, activities, and relationships that lies in an intermediate zone between the State and the market. The expression is of J. Kendall and Knapp (1995), 66 ss. A. Etzioni (1973), 314 ss.

[8] On the protection of personal data, see *ex multis*, D'Orazio et al. (2021).

one of the operations that result in the processing of personal data, deciding the purpose and methods of the processing itself. Indeed, according to Article 4 of the GDPR, such organizations will be "data controllers" whenever they perform any operation applied to personal data, such as the collection, recording, organization, structuring, storage, adaptation or alteration, retrieval, consultation, use, or even simply communication, dissemination, making available, or interconnection of data by any means, including digital means.

Finally, considerations on data cooperatives, as providers of data intermediation services, cannot be concluded without examining the DSA, which, as is well known, imposes prevention and mitigation obligations on the so-called Internet Service Providers (ISPs), i.e., providers of online intermediary services or online platforms, partly regardless of their size and partly exclusively for large digital platforms.

2 Data Cooperatives as ETS (Third Sector Entity)?

According to Article 2, § 1, n. 15, DGA, which defines "data cooperative services," "data intermediation services" may also be performed by a "data cooperative," understood as "[. . .] an organisational structure made up of data subjects, sole proprietorships or SMEs, who are members of such a structure, having as its main objectives those of assisting its members in exercising their rights in relation to certain data, including making informed choices before consenting to data processing, exchanging views on the purposes and conditions of data processing that would best represent the interests of its members in relation to their data, or negotiating the terms and conditions for data processing on behalf of its members before granting authorisation to process non-personal data or before they give their consent to the processing of personal data."

In this regard, it has been correctly observed[9] how the broad legislative provision legitimately suggests that the provision of "data cooperative services" may be carried out, possibly, in forms other than corporate, even though the "cooperative company" is the entity physiologically called upon to fulfill the role of "data cooperative," the "organizational structure" normally aimed at providing data cooperative services: hence, the need to identify—with greater precision—the most appropriate declination among those that the cooperative corporate model offers and can assume.

It seems also appropriate to begin with the recent reform of the Third Sector, which also involved social cooperatives: the most significant change is the expansion of the sectors in which they can operate. With the approval of L. D. n. 112/2017, the traditional provisions of Article 1, letter a) of Law n. 381/1991 were expanded to include social interventions and services pursuant to Article 1, paragraphs 1 and 2, of

[9] See F. Bravo (2024).

Law n. 328/2000[10] and, in particular, "all those activities related to the preparation and provision of free and paid services, or economic benefits intended to eliminate and overcome situations of need and difficulty that human beings encounter in the course of their lives, excluding only those insured by the social security and healthcare systems, as well as those insured through the administration of justice."

This is a provision that, with the exception of the exclusion of specific activities ("insuranced by the social security, healthcare, and justice systems"), could be characterized as "atypical" in that it defines an activity as "social" even in the absence of a specific regulatory mention, provided that it meets the requirements set forth for this purpose—flexibly, openly, and with the characteristics of a "general clause"—by such a provision and identified as the provision of services generally intended to eliminate and/or overcome situations of need and difficulty for the individual. The flexible and open scope of Article 1 of Law n. 328/2000 does not appear to be diminished by the presence of individual cases of "social services," mentioned here and there by the legislator, and seems to maintain a substantial and preeminent atypicality, to the extent that any activity can be considered "social" if it corresponds to the "general clause of social intervention." It is up to the interpreter to assess in concrete terms, on a case-by-case basis, such correspondence based on the specific function performed, in this case, by the (data) cooperative and in light of an evolving interpretation of the very concept of "social activity": this, as is known, in order to adapt the rule and the concept of "social activity and intervention" to the evolving reality through an interpretation-application more in line with social needs.

As highlighted in the DGA itself, in Recital 2, over the past decade, digital technologies have transformed the economy and society, affecting all sectors of activity and daily life. Data is at the heart of this transformation: to make the data-driven economy inclusive for all EU citizens, without digital divides, it should be built in such a way as to enable businesses, particularly micro, small, and medium-sized enterprises (SMEs), and start-ups to thrive, ensuring data access neutrality, data portability, and interoperability, and avoiding lock-in effects. The Commission has therefore proposed establishing common, domain-specific European spaces for data sharing and pooling, where data intermediation services—including those operated by data cooperatives—will play a key role in the data economy, in particular by supporting and promoting voluntary data sharing practices between businesses or facilitating data sharing in the context of obligations established by Union or national law.

Such intermediaries would assist individuals (data subjects) in exercising their rights under Regulation (EU) 2016/679, in particular the right to give and withdraw their consent to data processing, the right to access their data, the right to rectification of inaccurate personal data, the right to erasure or to be forgotten, the right to restriction of processing, and the right to data portability, which allows data subjects to transfer their personal data from one data controller to another. Data cooperatives—according to European legislation—aim to achieve a series of

[10] This provision, in turn, refers to Article 128, par. 2, of L. D. n. 112/1998.

objectives, such as strengthening individuals' position in making informed choices before consenting to the use of their data, influencing the terms and conditions of data user organizations related to data use in order to offer better choices to individual members of the group, or possibly finding solutions to conflicting positions of individual members of a group on how data can be used where such data relates to different data subjects within that group. These objectives are essentially and undeniably "social," pursued through the design and provision of services or economic benefits designed to eliminate and overcome the situations of need and difficulty that human beings (specifically, data subjects) encounter throughout their lives. This is in accordance with the definition of "social activity" contained in Article 1, paragraphs 1 and 2, of Law n. 328/2000.

Once again, from a historical-evolutionary perspective, a type of cooperative appears suited to solving various "collective" problems that have emerged over time and progressively within the social fabric. Consider, in the past, cooperatives established to reduce the marginalization of certain territorial areas, or to address the lack of social services, or the poor quality and diversification of public services, or to overcome the problem of energy supply in neighboring areas at nonmonopolistic prices[11] and now, to implement data sharing between an indeterminate number of data subjects and data owners, on the one hand, and data users, on the other, through technical, legal, or other means: a different and unique collective problem, yet one born from the need to regenerate the new socioeconomic fabric and offer a variety of services to the community. Faced with this natural evolution, the "social" cooperative form—functionally "modernized," so to speak—could take the first steps and come to define and regulate the new formula of "social activity" centered on data sharing (personal and otherwise). Data cooperatives, in fact, aim to improve the well-being, quality of life, and work of those involved in the mutualistic pact, increase forms of participation, and develop the communities in which they operate, with a solidarity-based approach, far removed from traditional capitalist models, capable of producing beneficial effects for the relevant stakeholders.[12]

In other words, the social cooperative appears, on the one hand, to be the most suitable instrument for achieving the objectives of the European legislator and, on the other, appears to offer more thorough protection for data subjects, individual businesses, and SMEs. It is a nonprofit organization that works to meet collective needs and pursue social goals: "removing" and/or "overcoming" difficult situations in which human beings have "evolutionarily" found themselves. In favor of this reconstruction, the entire DGA seems to be systematically militate, undeniably and clearly inspired—between "cooperatives" and "organisations for data altruism" (Article 16 DGA)—by a logic that is not predatory, but rather one of cooperation, solidarity and altruism for the equitable sharing and distribution of the added value produced by the use of data, currently in the hands mostly of corporations and multinationals benefiting from enormous profits: a corporate model, expressly

---

[11] Depedri and Turri (2015), 5, 65 ss.

[12] See F. Bravo (2024).

recognized for the first time as a service and intermediation tool in Regulation (EU) 2022/868, an alternative to the markedly capitalist model currently prevalent, through which to restore centrality to citizens and contribute to making society and the digital economy more supportive and democratic.

In substance, the social cooperative appears to be the best "organizational structure" for carrying out data intermediation services, as it is characterized by the same anthropocentric vision, which leads to ensuring the protection of the individual and social solidarity, toward which the data management model desired by the European legislator is oriented and which distances itself from the business model pursued by the so-called Big Tech, characterized, on the contrary, by the so-called surveillance capitalism.[13]

3 Data Cooperatives and Data Protection Law

Recital 35 specifically states that "this Regulation (DGA) should be without prejudice to the obligation of providers of data intermediation services to comply with Regulation (EU) 2016/679 (GDPR)." Where a data cooperative, by providing intermediation services, processes personal data, the DGA should not undermine the protection of personal data and, where it is a controller or processor as defined in Regulation (EU) 2016/679, it will be bound by the rules of that Regulation. Recitals 4 and 7, then, respectively prescribe that "this Regulation (GDPR) should not be read as creating a new legal basis for the processing of personal data for any of the regulated activities, nor as amending the information obligations provided for by Regulation (EU) 2016/679" (recital 4) and that "as regards personal data, the processing of personal data should be based on one or more of the legal bases for processing provided for in Articles 6 and 9 of Regulation (EU) 2016/679": hence, the necessary compliance of the operations of data cooperatives with the GDPR, with specific reference to the processing of personal data, of course.

In particular, Article 9 GDPR has a "two-phase structure,"[14] by establishing, on one hand, a general prohibition on processing "special categories" and, at the same time, identifying, on the other, a series of exceptions to this prohibition: one of the exceptions to the general prohibition on processing "special categories" data is precisely the case in which the processing is aimed at pursuing specific and legitimate purposes, identified in the articles of association, bylaws, or collective agreement of the foundation, association, or other nonprofit organization, specifically, the data cooperative.

---

[13] Zuboff (2019): the term "surveillance capitalism" refers to the economic order that exploits human experience as raw material for covert commercial practices of extraction, prediction, and sales, in a parasitic economic logic aimed at subverting popular sovereignty. See also L. Petrone (2023), 3, 800 ss.; Resta (2022), 4, 971; Poletti (2022), 1, 45–56; F. Bravo (2020), 83 ss.

[14] R. Tuccillo (2019), 153.

The data cooperative may therefore process the so-called sensitive data, even without the data subject's consent, provided, however, that, from a subjective perspective, the processing concerns only members, former members, or persons with regular contact with the cooperative, and the personal data is not disclosed externally. Essentially, the organization may process "sensitive" data without the data subject's consent when the processing is purely internal. From an objective perspective, for such processing to be lawful, it must pursue specific and legitimate purposes indicated in the bylaws or articles of association: this is in accordance with the so-called principle of purpose, established in Article 5, letter b) of the EU Regulation as one of the foundations of processing, and according to which the collection of data and its subsequent use must have specific and specific purposes, which must be communicated to the data subject and respected. For the data cooperative, as for ETSs in general, the purposes of data processing generally coincide with or are included in the institutional purposes indicated in the bylaws.[15]

Pursuant to the so-called purpose limitation principle, data cooperatives, or more generally, "persons authorized by them to process personal data, under the direct authority of the controller or processor" (according to Article 4, n. 10, GDPR), must collect, process, and use data in a manner compatible and exclusively for specified, explicit, and legitimate purposes: purposes which, as a general rule and as already emphasized, will coincide with those of the entity itself as indicated in its bylaws or articles of association. In this context, the most critical aspect concerns the compatibility or otherwise of the processing carried out (in this case) by a data cooperative with the so-called additional purposes, especially since the Article 12 of the DGA prohibits "data intermediation service providers from using the data for which they provide data intermediation services for purposes other than making them available to data users" and, in Recital 32, emphasizes that "data intermediation service providers only act as intermediaries in transactions and do not use the exchanged data for any other purpose."

In light of the combined provisions of the two Regulations, it appears legitimate to interpret this prohibition restrictively and to consider different purposes, but compatible with that of data sharing, admissible, basing the compatibility assess-

[15] For example, when an organization collects the shared data of its members for inclusion in the membership register, to send correspondence or the club newspaper to their homes, or otherwise to ensure their availability, or collects the data of its beneficiaries to provide services, it may not use such data for purposes other than institutional ones without the authorization and/or specific information provided to the members/beneficiaries. Thus, it may not disclose the name, address, or other information to third parties for marketing, commercial initiatives, or any other purposes not related to the organization.

ment[16] of processing for additional purposes precisely on the instrumentality of any additional purposes with respect to the initial ones. Article 5 (b), GDPR, expressly deems "further processing of personal data for archiving purposes in the public interest, scientific or historical research purposes, or statistical purposes" to be compatible with the initial purposes. Although the data controller is therefore required to specifically and *ex ante* foresee the purposes to be followed in carrying out the processing operations, the carrying out of further processing for different purposes is not excluded: this can occur to the extent that the additional purposes are "compatible" with the purposes for which the data were initially collected. In this regard, the provision of Article 5 (b), GDPR, is "ambiguous," since it is not sufficiently clear which purposes of the processing are "compatible" with the original purpose. The only certainty clearly stated by the European legislator is, in fact, that "further processing of personal data for archiving purposes in the public interest, scientific or historical research purposes, or statistical purposes shall not be considered [. . .] to be incompatible with the initial purposes."

Equally questionable is the merely exemplary or exhaustive nature of the reference to the additional purposes specifically mentioned by the European legislator as "compatible." The solution to this question seems to require a reading of Article 5 (b), GDPR, in conjunction with the subsequent Article 6, paragraph 4, and Recital 50. Therefore, the entity (in this case, the data cooperative) may process personal data for further purposes, not limited to archiving in the public interest, or scientific or historical research or statistical purposes, but generally deemed compatible with the original ones, in light of the context in which the personal data were collected and, in particular, the reasonable expectations of the data subject, the nature of the personal data, the consequences of the envisaged further processing for the data subjects and, finally, the existence of adequate guarantees both in the original processing and in the envisaged further processing.

Thus, with specific reference to a data cooperative, the use of personal data for the interconnection of data subjects and data controllers with data users, data exchange, temporary archiving, curation, conversion, anonymization, and pseudonymization does not appear to be considered "compatible," since Article 12, letter e), DSA specifically provides that "such tools are to be used only upon explicit request or

[16] To determine the compatibility of the new purpose, it is necessary to take into account, among other things, any connection between the purposes for which the personal data were collected and the purposes of the envisaged further processing; the context in which the personal data were collected, in particular with regard to the relationship between the data subject and the data controller; the nature of the personal data, in particular whether special categories of personal data pursuant to Article 9 are being processed, or whether data relating to criminal convictions and offences pursuant to Article 10 are being processed; the possible consequences of the envisaged further processing for the data subjects; the existence of appropriate safeguards, which may include encryption or pseudonymization: in this regard, see Achille (2019). Some important guidelines regarding the purpose compatibility assessment can be found in Opinion 3/2013 of the Article 29 Data Protection Working Party. Although this opinion was written under Directive 95/46/EC, it is nevertheless useful to review the terms of the "compatibility assessment" and combine it with the current provisions of the GDPR.

approval of the controller or data subject." On the contrary, the use of data, for example, for fraud detection or IT security purposes, or the adaptation of exchanged data to improve its usability by users themselves or interoperability, including through data conversion into specific formats, could be considered "compatible."[17]

Furthermore, according to the so-called storage limitation principle, data cooperatives, as data controllers, must retain data for a period of time no longer than necessary to achieve the purposes for which they were collected, unless the retention is for archiving purposes in the public interest, scientific or historical research, or statistical purposes. In this context, it seems appropriate to consider whether a data cooperative can retain, and subsequently process, its members' personal data even after they have left the organization. As already noted, Article 9, paragraph 2, letter d), of the GDPR, permits the use of former members' data (including sensitive data) without specific consent, if such use is carried out within the scope of the organization's activities and with adequate data protection safeguards. However, disclosure to third parties is prohibited (such disclosure requires the former member's specific consent). Therefore, the processing of former members' data, permitted by the Regulation, is purely internal. In particular, the Italian Data Protection Authority has not only specified that, before starting or continuing processing, but the information systems and software used by entities must be configured to minimize the use of identifying personal data and to exclude their processing whenever the purposes pursued in individual cases can be achieved using anonymous data or appropriate methods that allow the data subject to be identified only when necessary. It has also limited the scope of application of the provision from both a subjective and an objective perspective. From the first perspective, the provision clarifies that processing may be carried out by associations, charitable and volunteer organizations, foundations, committees, consortia, and nonprofit organizations: essentially, third sector entities, including data cooperatives in light of the considerations discussed above. From the second perspective, the processing must pursue nonprofit, civic, solidarity, and socially useful purposes as indicated in the Third Sector Code, in Article 5, among which it appears possible to include data sharing for the construction and strengthening of a data-driven digital economy that is inclusive for all citizens of the Union.

But the principle of data retention limitation and the question posed, namely whether or not data cooperatives are permitted to retain, and consequently process, their members' personal data even after they have—for whatever reason or event—left the organization, upon closer inspection, also involves (for such data controllers) the broader and more vexed question of managing digital assets for the period after a person, specifically a member of the organization, has ceased to exist. This is a complex issue, especially given the inadequacy of traditional institutions which, although adapted to the specific characteristics of the digital world, remain

[17] In the event that further processing is incompatible with the original purposes for which the processing was authorized, the entity must act pursuant to an independent legal basis pursuant to Article 6 of the GDPR. On this topic, see F. Resta (2018a), 51 ss. and, in particular, 58.

anchored to a system designed and developed for a profoundly different reality and socioeconomic context. This system therefore needs to be reconsidered in light of the incessant digital evolution that now characterizes and influences every aspect of our era, even beyond the physical death of the individual.

It should be noted that the legal relevance of the issue of posthumous data processing by the data cooperative[18] is mainly attributable to the circumstance that data represents a significant portion of wealth in modern economies. Starting from the consideration that the personal data of an "interested party" (data subject) survive beyond his life, even for an unlimited period of time, thanks to (or because of) current information and communication technologies, the need for recognition of rights and powers of control over such information is undeniable[19] even in the post-mortem phase of the interested party, as a "continuation" of the right to the protection of personal data: the question that arises then concerns not so much the "an," but rather the "who" and on the basis of which rules and principles the protection of data in the so-called post-mortem phase would be due.[20] While it is true that with the principle of storage limitation, established by Article 5, letter e), the GDPR allows both the prolonged retention of data when these, if suitable for identifying the data subject, are processed for archiving purposes in the public interest, statistical purposes, scientific or historical research, and the continuation of the processing of the collected data—where it is achieved and guaranteed that it is impossible for anyone to proceed with the identification of the data subject[21]—it is equally true that this principle undeniably clashes with the right to be forgotten or to have one's data erased, which the interested party can exercise pursuant to Article 17 of the GDPR.[22] In other words, given that the data cooperative can continue to process the data of the deceased former member, it seems necessary to ask whether and who should be granted the right to object to such continued retention by the organization itself or, in general, to take action to protect personal data.

Indeed, Article 2 *terdecies* (entitled "Rights concerning deceased persons") of L. D. n. 101/2018, enacted to adapt national legislation to the provisions of EU Regulation n. 679/2016, generally grants the rights and powers to control the digital content of the deceased data subject to "anyone who has a personal interest, or acts in the data subject's behalf, as his or her agent, or for family reasons worthy of protection," unless otherwise provided by law or by a written, specific, unambiguous, free, and informed prohibition from the data subject, presented or communicated to the data controller. In accordance, therefore, with the position expressed on this matter by the WP29 Working Group in opinion 4/2007 and in

---

[18] See I. Maspes (2020), 5, 583 ss.; G. Resta (2014), 907 ss. e Id. (2019), 86 ss. See also Zeno Zencovich (2018), 99; C. Camardi (2018), 65 ss.; A. Vesto (2020); A. Magnani (2019), 1208 ss.; Tescaro (2014), 10, 316 ss.

[19] G. Resta (2018b), 400 s.

[20] G. Resta, last cited work, 402.

[21] Dell'Utri (2019), 214.

[22] See, *ex multis* M. A. Livi, cit., 292 ss.

substantially similar but more limited terms than Article 13 of the Privacy Code, Article 2 *terdecies* of L. D. n. 101/2018 contains provisions that do not exactly comply with the principles of succession mortis causa and are certainly justified by the objective of protecting those who may suffer harm from the "survival" of such data.[23] The Italian legislator seems to have adopted not so much a "successional" model, but "anomalous,"[24] given the lack of both a real acquisition mortis causa and of merely family "successors" or heirs, but rather an "extension" mechanism[25] to third parties of the protection of the rights of the interested party, justified not only by "family reasons worthy of protection" and therefore by virtue of a family bond or interest, but also from a "personal interest," autonomous and not derived, or from that of the deceased "interested party," based on a fiduciary relationship (mandate). In other words, it does not appear to be a "successional" acquisition, not even an "anomalous" one, but rather an "extraordinary" legitimacy to act and exercise the rights of the deceased interested party, for the post-mortem protection of their personal data: legitimacy independent of the ownership of subjective legal situations[26] and having its source now in a personal or family interest, now in the so-called *post-mortem mandate exequendum.*[27] The broad category of those entitled to exercise the rights of the deceased data subject (in this case, the member of the data cooperative) will therefore include not only the relatives of the data subject, but also the "agent"—as the person charged by the data subject with protecting his or her digital identity after death—and any person who has an interest (financial or merely moral) in the protection (in a broad sense) of the personal data relating to the deceased person[28]: therefore, upon closer inspection, in light of the combined provisions of Articles 5 GDPR and 2 *terdecies*, L. D. n. 101/2018, the data cooperative will not only be able—as data controller—to continue to store and process the personal data of the deceased member (pursuant to Article 5 GDPR), but nothing would seem to exclude the possibility that it could also and possibly exercise the rights of the deceased data subject as a person having, broadly speaking, an interest in the protection of the personal data of one of its deceased members (according to Article 2 *terdecies*, Legislative Decree n. 101/2018).

---

[23] See R. Restuccia (1997), 138.

[24] Zaccaria A., *w. cit.*, 23 ss., 72, 79 s., 94 and 261 ss.; Zoppini (2000), I, 204 and 244; Palazzo and Sassi (2012), 83 ss.

[25] So, Resta G., cit., 411.

[26] See Bargelli (1999), 416.

[27] See Di Staso (2011), 685; Palazzo (2000), 53 s.; Cass., 9.5.1969, n. 1584, in *Foro it.*, vol. 92, n. 12, 3193 ss., which established the admissibility of a *post-mortem exequendum* mandate in our legal system, as it does not conflict with the prohibition on the deceased's wishes from acting posthumously regarding the estate's assets outside of the will. With specific reference to the GDPR, this represents a new application of this mandate, unique to the contemporary era: given the massive amount of data generated by the spread of information technology, destined to outlive the deceased, it is necessary to manage access to blogs, platforms, email accounts, and social networks of users after their death.

[28] Resta G., cit., 415.

4 Data Cooperatives and Digital Services Act

As already noted,[29] the regulation of data cooperatives—as providers of data intermediation services[30]—must also be reconstructed in light of EU Regulation 2022/2065, the DSA, which, as is well known, introduced prevention and mitigation obligations for providers of online intermediary services or online platforms, partly regardless of their size and partly exclusively for large digital platforms. The DSA is intended to apply to all intermediary services that transmit or store information: not only online marketplaces and app stores, but also the so-called collaborative economy platforms, among which—precisely—it seems appropriate to place the services of data cooperatives. The latter, in their role as providers of sharing services, even when operating in the personal data market, connect the "data owner" (the so-called data holder) with the data user (the so-called data user), offering value-added services that undermine the dominant role assumed by overseas multinationals. Through data intermediation cooperatives, "data owners" seize the opportunities of intermediation by granting access and use to other parties, the "data users."[31].

In particular, according to Article 10 of the DGA, data intermediation services include those defined in Article 2, n. 15 of the DGA, as "data intermediation services offered by an organizational structure consisting of data subjects, sole proprietorships, or SMEs that are members of that structure, whose primary objective is to support its members in exercising their rights with respect to certain data, including making informed choices before consenting to data processing, exchanging views on the purposes and conditions of data processing that would best represent the interests of its members in relation to their data, and negotiating terms and conditions for data processing on behalf of its members before they consent to the processing of non-personal data or before they consent to the processing of personal data."

From a subjective perspective, the DSA is therefore not limited to large platforms alone, but extends to all categories of businesses, including micro and small enterprises, which, in light of the DGA, may be members of a data cooperative. From an objective perspective, the DSA will apply to all data intermediary service providers operating broadly within the European Union, regardless of their place of establishment or residence and on the basis of a "substantial connection" with the Union itself. This "substantial connection" exists not only where the cooperatives or

[29] See, *supra*, § 1.

[30] F. Bravo (2021), 1, 199 ss.; Lionello (2021), 3, 675; T. Scholtz (2016).

[31] The "data controller," according to the DGA's terminology, is "the legal person or data subject who, in accordance with applicable Union or national law, has the right to grant access to, or share, certain personal or non-personal data under his or her control." Sharing data allows the data subject, the newly designated "data controller," to grant access or use of the data to the "data user," that is, the "natural or legal person who has legitimate access to certain personal or non-personal data and is authorized to use such data for commercial or non-commercial purposes" (Article 2, DGA). Under the GDPR, the user of personal data is none other than the data controller.

data intermediary service providers are established in the Union, but, in the absence of such an establishment, by virtue of the existence of a significant number of users in one or more Member States or the targeting of their activities toward one or more Member States. The targeting of activities toward one or more Member States may be determined on the basis of all relevant circumstances, such as the use of a language or currency generally used in the Member State in question, the possibility of ordering products or services, or the use of a national top-level domain.[32]

The close connection between the DGA and the DSA is confirmed by the DGA itself, in Article 12, entitled "Conditions for the provision of data intermediation services." This article contains a series of obligations for the provision of data intermediation services, which clearly recall and mirror those set forth in the DSA and the principles contained therein, such as transparency, publicity, and access to data, as well as the prohibition of illegal content.

These obligations, as is known, concern measures to combat illegal content online and the obligation for data intermediation platforms (in this case) to react quickly, in compliance with fundamental rights, such as freedom of expression and data protection; the strengthening of traceability and controls on commercial operators in online markets to ensure the safety of products and services, and a commitment to carry out random checks for the possible reappearance of illegal content; greater transparency and accountability of platforms, for example, by providing clear information on content moderation or on the use of algorithms for recommending content (the so-called recommendation systems)[33]; the ability for users to challenge content moderation decisions; the prohibition of misleading practices and certain types of targeted advertising, such as that directed at minors.

Under the DSA, online platforms and data intermediaries will be subject to fees proportionate to the nature of the services they offer, as well as their size and

[32] The targeting of activities toward a Member State could also be inferred from the availability of an application on the relevant national website, the provision of advertising at the national level or in the language used in the Member State in question, or the management of relationships with members of the organizational structure, for example, the provision of assistance in the language generally spoken in that Member State.

[33] "Recommender systems" are defined as "fully or partially automated systems that an online platform uses to suggest specific information, via its online interface, to recipients of the service or to prioritize such information, including as a result of a search initiated by the recipient of the service, or by otherwise determining the relative order or importance of the information displayed." Pursuant to Articles 27 and 38 of the DSA, all providers of online platforms (including data platforms) must specify in their general terms and conditions the main parameters used in their recommendation systems, as well as the options available to recipients to modify or influence these parameters. Very large ones must also "ensure at least one option for each of their recommendation systems, not based on profiling as defined in Article 4, point 4), of Regulation (EU) 2016/679." Making clear to users the rationale behind this recommendation activity is certainly the first step toward ensuring greater control.

impact. Very large online platforms (and search engines)[34] will have to comply with "additional" and more stringent requirements, from which micro, small, and medium-sized enterprises (SMEs) are exempt. These are defined in Commission Recommendation 2003/361/EC as those with fewer than 250 employees, an annual turnover not exceeding €50 million, or an annual balance sheet total not exceeding €43 million. This is "unless, by virtue of their scope and impact, they meet the criteria to qualify as very large online platforms under the Regulation." In other words, the Digital Services Regulation defines a series of "basic" obligations for all digital service providers (including, specifically, data intermediaries) as well as specific obligations reserved for large ones. In particular, Chapter III defines the due diligence requirements for a transparent and secure online environment in five different sections. First, the provisions establish obligations applicable to all providers of intermediary services, including data, regardless of their size: the obligation to establish a single point of contact to facilitate direct communication with Member State authorities, the Commission, and the Committee; the obligation to designate a legal representative in the European Union for providers who are not established in a Member State but offer their services in the Union; the obligation to indicate in their general terms and conditions any restrictions on the use of their services and to act responsibly in applying and enforcing such restrictions; and transparent reporting obligations regarding the removal of information deemed unlawful or contrary to the providers' general terms and conditions and the disabling of access to such information.

There are obligations applicable to all online platforms, with the exception of those classified as micro or small enterprises pursuant to the Annex to Recommendation 2003/361/EC. These include the obligation for online platforms (including data intermediation platforms) to establish an internal complaints management system regarding decisions taken in relation to allegedly illegal content or information incompatible with their general terms and conditions; to contact certified bodies for the out-of-court resolution of disputes with users of their services; and to take measures in the event of abuse.

Finally, there are additional obligations (in addition to those listed above) for very large online platforms (as defined in Article 33 of the DSA) to manage systemic risks—such as the dissemination of illegal content, adverse impacts on fundamental rights, electoral processes, gender-based violence, or mental health—arising from the operation and use of their services or related to such use and operation, adopting reasonable and effective measures to mitigate such risks. These include preventing systemic risks, subjecting them to independent audits, allowing users to opt out

[34] According to Article 33 of the DSA, very large online platforms and online search engines are those with an average monthly number of active users of the service in the Union of 45 million or more and which are designated as very large online platforms or very large online search engines pursuant to paragraph 4, i.e., on the basis of a decision adopted by the Commission, after consulting the Member State of establishment and in light of the data communicated by the provider of the online platform or online search engine pursuant to Article 24, paragraph 2, or the information requested pursuant to Article 24, paragraph 3, and any other information available to it.

of receiving profiling-based recommendations, and also granting authorities and authorized researchers access to their data and algorithms.

5 Concluding Remarks

Data cooperatives aim to achieve a number of objectives, in particular by empowering individuals to make informed choices before consenting to data use, by influencing the terms and conditions set by data user organizations on which data use is subject, so as to offer better choices to individual members of the group, or by finding possible solutions to conflicting views of individual members of a group regarding how data should be used where such data concerns multiple data subjects within that group. In this context, it is important to recognize that the regulation is innovative and incomplete and, therefore, requires, from a legal perspective, a systematic framework for the situation in light of the multiple regulatory frameworks involved.

This refers in particular to the Third Sector (Third Sector Code), the protection of personal data (General Data Protection Regulation or GDPR), and the new rules for online intermediaries (DSA).

The "main objectives" of solidarity, variously expressed, of support to its "members" in relation to the use of the data that will be carried out in the provision of the service, make the "cooperative society" appear as the physiologically most suitable entity to fill the role of "data cooperative" in our legal system and in the European one. According to Article 4 of the Italian Civil Code, "social cooperatives" are also third sector entities, provided they are established to pursue civic and socially beneficial purposes, as well as solidarity-based ones, through the performance—exclusively or primarily—of one or more activities of general interest "in the form of the free provision of [. . .] goods or services, or of mutual assistance."

As the "data controller" of personal data, the data cooperative will be required to comply with the privacy obligations arising from EU Regulation n. 679/2016 (the so-called GDPR, General Data Protection Regulation), carrying out even just one of the operations that result in the processing of personal data, deciding the purpose and methods of the processing itself. Indeed, according to Article 4 of the GDPR, such organizations will be "data controllers" whenever they perform any operation applied to personal data, such as the collection, recording, organization, structuring, storage, adaptation or alteration, retrieval, consultation, use, or even simply communication, dissemination, making available, or interconnection of data by any means, including digital means.

Finally, the regulation of data cooperatives—as providers of data intermediation services—must also be reconstructed in light of EU Regulation 2022/2065, the DSA, which, as is well known, introduced prevention and mitigation obligations for providers of online intermediary services or online platforms, partly regardless of their size and partly exclusively for large digital platforms.

References

Achille, D. (2019). Art. 5. In A. Barba, & S. Pagliantini (Eds.), *Delle persone*, vol. II, in E. Gabrielli (directed by), *Commentario codice civile.*

Bargelli, E. (1999). Sub art. 13. In C. M. Bianca, & F. Busnelli (Eds.), *Tutela della privacy, (legge 31dicembre 1996, n. 675)*, in *Nuove leggi civ.*, 416.

Bosetti, F. (2021). *Il codice del terzo settore, Comm. al d. lgs. 3 luglio 2017 n. 117.*

Bravo, F. (2020). Il commercio elettronico dei dati personali. In T. Pasquino, A. Rizzo, & M. Tescaro (Eds.), *Questioni attuali in tema di commercio elettronico* (p. 83).

Bravo, F. (2021). Intermediazione di dati personali e servizi di data sharing dal GDPR al data governance act. *Contratto e impresa Europa, 1*, 199.

Bravo, F. (2024). *Le cooperative di dati.* https://site.unibo.it/cooperative-di-dati

Camardi, C. (2018). L'eredità digitale: Tra reale e virtuale. *Dir. inf., 2018*, 65.

Casale, F. (2005). *Scambio e mutualità nella società cooperativa.* Quaderni di Giurisprudenza Commerciale.

D'Orazio, R., Finocchiaro, G., Pollicino, O., & Resta, G. (Eds.). (2021). *Codice della privacy e data protection.*

Dell'Utri, M. (2019). Principi generali e condizioni di liceità del trattamento dei dati personali. In V. Cuffaro, R. D'Orazio, & V. Ricciuto (Eds.), *I dati personali nel diritto europeo* (p. 214).

Depedri, S., & Turri, S. (2015). Dalla funzione sociale alla cooperativa di comunità: un caso studio per discutere sul flebile confine. *Riv. impr. Sociale, 5*, 65.

Di Staso, N. (2011). Il mandato post mortem exequendum. *Fam. pers. succ., 2011*, 685.

Etzioni, A. (1973). The third sector and domestic missions. *Public Administration Review, 33*, 314.

Gori, L. (2022). *Terzo settore e costituzione.*

Gori, L., & Zandonai, F. (2018). I confini del Terzo settore: una mappa costantemente da riscrivere. *Impr. soc., 2018*, 11.

Kendall, J., & Knapp, M. (1995). *A loose and baggy monster. Boundaries, definition and typologies.*

Lionello, L. (2021). La creazione del mercato europeo dei dati: sfide e prospettive. *Diritto del Commercio Internazionale, 3*, 675.

Magnani, A. (2019). Il patrimonio digitale e la sua devoluzione ereditaria. *Vita not., 2019*, 1208.

Maspes, I. (2020). Successione digitale, trasmissione dell'account e condizioni generali di contratto predisposte dagli internet services providers. *I Contratti, 5*, 583.

Palazzo, A. (2000). *Le successioni.*

Palazzo, A. & Sassi, A. (2012). *Trattato della successione e dei negozi successori, 1, Categorie e specie della successione.*

Paolucci, L. F. (2014). *Le società cooperative.*

Pentland, A., & Hardjono, T. (2020). Data cooperatives. In A. Pentland, A. Lipton, & T. Hardjono (Eds.), *Building the new economy.* MIT Press Work in Progress.

Petrone, L. (2023). Il mercato digitale europeo e le cooperative di dati. *Contr. e impr., 3*, 800.

Poletti, D. (2022). Gli intermediari di dati. *European Journal of Privacy Law & Technologies, 1*, 45–56.

Ponzanelli, G. (1996). Quali regole giuridiche per il terzo settore? *Riv. dir. civ., 3*, 313.

Resta, G. (2014). La "morte" digitale. *Dir. inf., 2014*, 907.

Resta, G. (2018a). Art. 5. In Riccio-Scorza-Bellisario (Ed.), *GDPR e normativa privacy.*

Resta, G. (2018b). La successione nei rapporti digitali e la tutela post-mortale dei dati personali. In A. Mantelero & D. Poletti (Eds.), *Regolare la tecnologia: il Reg. UE 2016/679 e la protezione dei dati personali. Un dialogo fra Italia e Spagna* (p. 400).

Resta, G. (2019). La successione nei rapporti digitali e la tutela postmortale dei dati personali. *Contr. e impr., 2019*, 86.

Resta, G. (2022). La regolazione digitale nell'Unione europea—pubblico, privato, collettivo nel sistema europeo di governo dei dati. *Riv. trim. dir. pubbl., 4*, 971.

Restuccia, R. (1997). Sub art. 13. In E. Giannantonio, M. G. Losano, & V. Zeno-Zencovich (Eds.), *La tutela dei dati personali commentario alla L. 675/96.*
Rispoli Farina, M. (2019). Il codice del Terzo settore tra novità e contraddizioni. In D. Di Sabato & O. Nocerino (Eds.), *Il Terzo settore profili critici della riforma.*
Scholtz, T. (2016). *Platform cooperativism: Challenging the corporate sharing economy.*
Tescaro, M. (2014). La tutela postmortale della personalità morale e specialmente dell'identità personale. *Juscivile, 10*, 316.
Tuccillo, R. (2019). Art. 9 GDPR. In A. Barba, and S. Pagliantini (Eds.), *Delle persone*, vol. II, in E. Gabrielli (directed by), *Commentario codice civile.*
Vella, F., Genco, R., & Morara, P. L. (2018). *Diritto delle società cooperative.*
Vesto, A. (2020). *Successione digitale e circolazione dei beni online. Note in tema di eredità digitale.*
Zeno Zencovich, V. (2018). La "datasfera". Regole giuridiche per il mondo digitale parallelo. In Scaffardi (Ed.), *I "profili" del diritto. Regole, rischi e opportunità nell'era digitale* (p. 99).
Zoppini, A. (2000). Le «nuove proprietà» nella trasmissione ereditaria della ricchezza (note a margine della teoria dei beni). *Riv. dir. civ., I*, 204.
Zuboff, S. (2019). *Il capitalismo della sorveglianza, il futuro dell'umanità nell'era dei nuovi poteri.*

Assessing Educational Poverty in Italy over Time: A Multidimensional Approach

Felice Russo, Debora Assisi, and Abbey Walusimbi

Abstract This study examines the degree of educational poverty experencied by pupils in the Italian school system. We analyse educational poverty in Italy using both the multidimensional educational headcount ratio index and the class of additive multidimensional poverty measures proposed by Alkire and Foster (2011), according to the union and intersection methods. These indices allow considering different aspects of educational deprivation, i.e. incidence, breadth, severity, and inequality. We exploit official Italian data collected by INVALSI for various grades of primary and secondary school. INVALSI aims to evaluate all Italian students at different school levels through standardised tests related to achievement in Italian, Mathematics, and English. We first present and discuss our findings on multidimensional educational poverty in the national context over recent years. Furthermore, to highlight heterogeneity across population subgroups, we focus on Italian macro-areas, gender, immigration background (native vs. migrant background), and socio-economic and cultural status. Finally, we briefly discuss the policy implications emerging from our analysis.

1 Introduction

What is the evidence about learning and educational poverty in Italy? This chapter addresses the issue by exploiting data on learning achievements of students participating in several editions of the INVALSI (National Institute for the Evaluation of Education and Training System) survey for various school grades and years. In the context of the Sustainable Development Goals (SDGs) within the "2030 Agenda

---

Supplementary Information The online version contains supplementary material available at https://doi.org/10.1007/978-3-032-33072-7_8.

F. Russo (✉) · D. Assisi · A. Walusimbi
Department of Economic Sciences, University of Salento, Lecce, Italy
e-mail: felice.russo@unisalento.it; debora.assisi@unisalento.it; abbey.walusimbi@unisalento.it

R. Cellini et al. (eds.), *Cultural, Social, and Political Participation in the Internet Era*, Contributions to Economics, https://doi.org/10.1007/978-3-032-33072-7_8

for Sustainable Development", the SDG4 target calls for high-quality education guaranteeing equitable access to all children. Among the indicators proposed to evaluate countries' progress in SDG4, the quality of the education system is expressed in terms of the share of 15-year-old students achieving low performances in the three PISA learning domains, i.e. reading, mathematics, science.[1] Therefore, the alleviation of multidimensional educational poverty (i.e. the acquisition of an insufficient amount of learning) is a crucial issue deserving the attention and intervention of national and international organisations and policymakers.

The existing literature can be broadly classified into two main streams. The first is the measurement of educational poverty, explicitly introduced by Checchi (1998), who addressed the question of how to measure this phenomenon in absolute or relative terms. Since then, other scholars have investigated the extent of educational poverty: (i) by adopting both the absolute and relative approach with different definitions of poverty, expressed as missing certificates, competency levels, years of education (Allmendinger & Leibfried, 2003; Lohmann & Ferger, 2014); (ii) by considering the complexity of the poverty concept, involving incidence, intensity, and inequality among the poor (Denny, 2002; Minzyuk & Russo, 2016; Rios-Neto & Rodrigues, 2013; Sánchez-Garcia et al., 2019; Villar, 2016); and (iii) by considering the multidimensionality of the poverty concept (Minzyuk & Russo, 2016; Agasisti et al., 2021; Sánchez-Antón et al., 2022; Giusti & Schirripa Spagnolo, 2025).

A second stream of literature focuses on the effect on students' learning achievements, derived from various factors that can be influenced by policies and practices, such as: education public expenditure (Agasisti, 2014; Annabi, 2017; Sibiano & Agasisti, 2011); school level variables (Agasisti et al., 2021; Cohen, 2006; Fantuzzo et al., 2005; Ferraro & Põder, 2018; Güzel & Berberoglu, 2005; Henry, 2007; Ma et al., 2013; Ning et al., 2015); teaching practices (Cordero & Gil, 2018; Darling-Hammond, 2000); family background (Lagravinese et al., 2020); and ICT usage (Zhao & Chen, 2023).

Our contribution to the mentioned strands of the literature is limited to the former one and consists in measuring educational poverty in Italy in recent years according to a multidimensional approach. We posit that the students' educational "background" is a multidimensional concept and an exhaustive analysis of the complete learning deprivation status cannot be restricted to a single educational subject (Agasisti et al., 2021). By adopting the definition of underachievers (i.e. students who do not reach a "minimum" proficiency level), we assess the degree of educational poverty in Italy using both the multidimensional educational headcount ratio index and the class of additive multidimensional poverty measures proposed by Alkire and Foster (2011), as we will see below, according to both the union and intersection methods.[2] These indices allow considering different aspects of

[1] PISA is the OECD's Programme for International Student Assessment (www.oecd.org/en/about/programmes/pisa.html)

[2] Starting from school year 2017–18, INVALSI estimates the multidimensional educational headcount ratio index by adopting exclusively the intersection approach for pupils in the last

poverty, i.e. incidence, breadth, severity, and inequality, whose definitions are given in Sect. 2.

The remainder of the chapter is organised as follows: Sect. 2 introduces the methodological approach; Sect. 3 describes the data; Sect. 4 presents the main results; and Sect. 5 concludes.

2 Methodological Aspects

Students' performance on INVALSI standardised tests forms the basis for assessing their cognitive abilities. Drawing from the literature on the economic analysis of poverty, we provide an analytical assessment of pupils' learning through the calculation of composite indices summarising these outcomes, based on the axiomatic approach to the study of poverty.

The issue of poverty measurement involves two challenges: (i) the identification of the poor according to a poverty criterion, often expressed by a poverty line; and (ii) the construction of an indicator aggregating information on the poor into a composite measure summarising the state of learning deprivation. The identification phase consists of several steps requiring the researcher to choose which elementary unit to observe (in our case, the student), the reference variable (standardised test results), and which poverty line to adopt. In this chapter, we adopt both the relative and absolute poverty lines. The set of the educational poor thus consists of students with a result strictly below the predefined threshold for a specific learning subject, and it is assumed that outcomes in various tests are the (indirect) indicators of individual knowledge levels.

2.1 *Unidimensional Approach*

Let $X = (x_1, x_2, x_3, \ldots, x_N)$ be a vector of test results for a specific learning subject, sorted in non-decreasing order, for a set of N students. A synthetic, non-negative poverty indicator P is a real-valued function of the distribution X and a poverty threshold Z, $P = P(X; Z)$. From the contribution of Sen (1976), the axiomatic approach allows for investigating the normative content of poverty indicators: the adopted measure should satisfy properties explicitly deemed desirable by the researcher and/or policymakers.

Here, we recall the most well-known axioms, somewhat minimal, and, where necessary, redefine them for our educational context. The *identification axiom*

year of lower and upper secondary schools (https://serviziostatistico.invalsi.it/en/invalsi_ss_data/eccellenza-accademica-e-dispersione-scolastica-implicita-valori-percentuali/; last accessed 5 July 2026).

requires that the focus of the analysis be the learning levels of the poor population, and a poverty measure should therefore be invariant to what happens above the threshold. The acceptance of *the weak monotonicity axiom* implies that a reduction in the learning levels of a student already identified as poor should, ceteris paribus, lead to an increase in the poverty measure.

There is some complexity in expressing, in terms of learning, a third axiom: the Pigou-Dalton Transfer Principle. Where the analysis focuses on an economic variable such as income, the axiom requires that, ceteris paribus, the transfer of income from a poor unit to any richer one leads to an increase in the poverty measure. However, in an educational context, it is impossible to "transfer units" of learning from one student to another. In line with the unidimensional approach to educational poverty analysis, Denny (2002) provides a rationale for a property that considers the degree of dispersion of learning. With reference to the classic utilitarian framework, the postulate of diminishing marginal utility—together with an additive social welfare function—indicates that the policymaker, faced with assigning a given unit of resource to two individuals, should prefer the poorer of the two. In our study, this is reflected in assuming a policymaker with egalitarian preferences in the distribution of essential learning levels: the main task of educational institutions—and compulsory school in particular—should be ensuring basic and fundamental knowledge, guaranteeing everyone a defined level of learning. Furthermore, Sen (1976) justifies the proposed axiom in terms of relative deprivation: the relative deprivation of knowledge increases with rising inequality of learning among the poor. Analogously, if one has the possibility to improve "the literacy of two individuals by the same amount, then it is better to do so for the less literate of the two" (Denny, 2002, p. 484).

With the *symmetry axiom* (the value of the index depends only on the levels of the observed variable, not on other characteristics such as the student's identity) and the *population independence axiom* (allowing comparison of populations of different sizes by requiring invariance to a replication of the population), we complete the set of minimal axioms considered. Among unidimensional indicators known in the literature, the class of poverty measures proposed by Foster-Greer-Thorbecke (FGT; Foster et al., 1984) is among the most widely used.

2.2 Multidimensional Approach

There has long been unanimous recognition of the multidimensional nature of poverty. In the socio-economic literature, the multidimensional approach extends the number of attributes with which the overall dimension of deprivation must be explained, based on the idea that economic resources alone fail to capture relevant attributes of well-being.

The broader the definition of poverty, the more complex its measurement. A fruitful theoretical framework is that of "capabilities and functionings" (Sen, 1982, 1985). Sen formulates an equity criterion based on the interpretation of needs and interests in the form of basic capabilities. Normative evaluations should consider the capabilities of individuals, not the resources they hold, as resources are simply means to achieve capabilities and obtain functionings. Functionings can be defined as the "states" of doing and being of an individual—the constituent elements of well-being—such as being well-nourished, relating to others, or working in the labour market. Capabilities consist of the ability and possibility of concretely realising basic functionings and lifestyles; they represent what people are able to do and to be. From this perspective, the freedom of a person to choose their own vector of functionings is relevant, and the capabilities measure that degree of freedom.

Looking at the empirical side, the main difficulty lies in measuring individual endowments of capabilities *ex ante*, whereas, with appropriate data, it is possible to determine *ex post* the well-being achieved through the obtained vector of functionings. INVALSI data allow us to determine *ex post* a subset of the vector of functionings expressed in terms of learning achieved for different subjects, and a first approximation of the contribution of cognitive capabilities within the overall set of individual capabilities.

In line with a relative poverty approach, it is possible to characterise poverty in learning as social exclusion—a lack of access to a vector of functionings compared to the rest of the student population.[3] In line with an absolute poverty concept, students are poor in a specific learning dimension if their score is below a minimum competence level identified by INVALSI.

For synthesising deprivation across multiple subjects, the literature offers two main methods differing in their aggregation procedures. The first aggregates deprivation levels on each single dimension and then synthesises through a weighted average over attributes but cannot consider the ways dimensions are distributed among individuals. The second operates the opposite choice—aggregating first over individuals (observing the level of individual multidimensional deprivation) and subsequently determining overall poverty through an aggregation of individual poverty levels.[4] Following Bourguignon and Chakravarty (2003), who define multidimensional poverty as a shortfall from a threshold on each dimension, we adopt the second approach.

This chapter focuses primarily on the class of multidimensional poverty indicators proposed by Alkire and Foster (2011).

In a multidimensional context, data are presented in the form of a matrix of dimension $N \times d$, denoted $\mathbf{X}^{N,d}$. Let x_{ij} indicate the test score of the generic student i in the learning dimension j, with $i = 1, 2, \ldots, N$ and $j = 1, 2, \ldots, d$. A student is poor in the learning dimension j if her score is below a given poverty line Z_j. The vector of poverty thresholds $\mathbf{Z} = (Z_1, \ldots, Z_d)$ collects these cut-offs for all j observed dimensions.

---

3 See Glaesser (2021) on conceptual and empirical issues about the relative poverty approach in education.

4 For a detailed discussion of the implications of this distinction, see Dutta et al. (2003).

Let c_i be the number of learning dimensions in which the generic student is poor, then this student is considered as *globally poor* if her number of learning deprivations (c_i) is equal to or greater than a given cut-off k, with $k \leq d$.

Different levels of this second cut-off, k, may be associated with different approaches towards the multidimensional educational poverty. When $k = 1$ a student is considered globally poor if she is a low performer in *at least* one learning dimension (*union* method). While, when $k = d$, a student is globally poor if she is a low performer in *all* learning domains (*intersection* method). Here, we will adopt both methods. They are specific and extreme cases, depending on the preferred level of k.

As poverty measures, we also adopt the *multidimensional educational headcount ratio* (*MEH*). The *MEH* measures the share of poor students deprived in k learning dimensions, i.e. the incidence of educational poverty, and is defined as:

$$MEH^x = \frac{1}{N}\sum\nolimits_{i=1}^{N}\left[\sum\nolimits_{j=1}^{d} g_{ij}(k)\right]^0, [1]$$

where $g_{ij} = \frac{Z_j - x_{ij}}{Z_j}$ for student i is the poverty gap in the specific learning dimension j; $g_{ij} > 0$ if $x_{ij} < Z_j$ and $c_i \geq k$, otherwise $g_{ij} = 0$.

Thanks to the dual cut-off described above, AF propose a class of poverty indicators of the FGT type, appropriately modified to account for dimensions in multidimensional settings, a family M_a such that:

$$M_\alpha^x = \frac{1}{Nd}\sum\nolimits_{i=1}^{N}\sum\nolimits_{j=1}^{d} w_j\left(g_{ij}(k)\right)^\alpha, [2]$$

where w_j is the weight assigned to dimension j, with $\sum_{j=1}^{d} w_j = d$, and α is a non-negative parameter measuring the sensitivity to changes in the intensity and the inequality aversion within the group of poor students in the learning dimension j.[5]

Different values of α yield different measures emphasising distinct aspects of poverty. When $\alpha = 0$, we obtain the *adjusted educational headcount ratio (M0)*, measuring both incidence and breadth of poverty, with the latter expressed as the

[5] The weighting system determines the relative importance of each learning domain in calculating the aggregate poverty index and, additionally, influences the range of possible poverty identification criteria. When equal weights are used ($w_j = 1, \forall j$), the identification cut-off k ranges from 1 to d, and according to $k = 1$ a student is identified as poor if deprived in at least one dimension (union approach), whereas, when $k = d$ a student is identified as poor only if deprived in all dimensions (intersection approach). In this case, a student i is considered as globally poor if $c_i \geq k$. However, when some dimensions receive higher weights than others, the deprivation count c_i becomes the *weighted* sum of deprivations. Consequently, the minimum possible value for the cut-off k, equivalent to a union approach, is the smallest weight among all dimensions: $k = \min(w_j)$, while the maximum possible value for k remains d.

number of learning deprivations experienced by poor students. The *M0* satisfies the dimensional monotonicity axiom: if an already-poor individual becomes deprived in another dimension, the indicator increases. From a purely methodological perspective, therefore, the *M0* provides a more comprehensive description of the educational poverty phenomenon than the *MEH*, as the former explicitly considers its multidimensional nature. When $\alpha = 1$, we obtain the *adjusted educational poverty gap index* (*M1*), capturing incidence, breadth, and—measured by the magnitude of the poverty gaps—the depth of poverty. When $\alpha = 2$, Eq. 2 reduces to the *adjusted educational poverty severity index* (*M2*), which also accounts for inequality within the poor by attaching higher weights to students experiencing larger poverty gaps. Notably, when $\alpha > 1$, we are assuming a policymaker with egalitarian preferences in the distribution of essential learning levels.

Learning dimensions are considered independent attributes, and all indicators within the AF class can be decomposed by groups (e.g. socio-economic background, gender), a property particularly relevant for policymakers assessing heterogeneity. Once the educationally globally poor have been identified, all indicators within the AF class are also decomposable by learning dimension.

3 Data

Our purpose is to analyse the Italian educational system with a specific focus on the measurement of educational poverty. Among available data on learning outcomes, the OECD's PISA survey provides highly standardised data comparing competencies of representative samples of 15-year-old students across countries in reading, mathematics, and science. However, we focus on official Italian data collected by INVALSI because its census-based coverage of the entire student population enables fine-grained analysis at the provincial level, a level for which the PISA sample is not representative.[6] Moreover, INVALSI tracks five specific grade levels throughout the educational cycle, unlike PISA, which only assesses 15-year-olds.

Starting in school year 2004–05, INVALSI administers yearly standardised tests to all Italian students at different school levels (primary and secondary education). Notably, test scores have statistical properties similar to income data, as they are individual and continuous observations.

The INVALSI assessment is a low-stakes test, results do not affect students' academic progression or grades, but schools receive feedback for improvement, and the results help the central government assess school system performance and allow comparisons within and between schools across space and over time. The main INVALSI survey is census-based, involving administration by teachers in each school and class. Additionally, a probabilistic sample of schools is tested under

[6] On the relationship between PISA and INVALSI results, see Giangiacomo et al. (2024).

Table 1 INVALSI data coverage across grades and school years (2020–21/2024–25)

School year	Second grade-Primary School	Fifth grade-Primary School	Third year-Middle School	Second year-High School	Fifth year-High School
2020–21	X	X	X		X
2021–22	X	X	X	X	X
2022–23	X	X	X	X	X
2023–24	X	X	X	X	X
2024–25			X		X

Note: Table created by authors

external observers' control, providing higher data quality by minimising teachers' cheating (Longobardi et al., 2018). The sample is representative only at the regional level.

Currently, the INVALSI assessment framework entails yearly standardised tests in Italian language, Mathematics, and English (reading and listening) administered to student cohorts in the 2nd and 5th grades of primary school; the 3rd year of lower secondary school; and the 2nd and 5th years of upper secondary school. Five original databases are thus usually available, each containing scores for approximately half a million pupils per grade and subject.[7] Participation in the census-based survey is mandatory for all public and private schools across the national territory and ensures the anonymity of the tests.[8] Our study is thus based on INVALSI national census data from the last five available school years (2020–21 to 2024–25; no 2019–20 due to Covid-19). The data coverage is not uniform across all grade levels, as detailed in Table 1.

In addition to raw test scores normalised between 0 and 100, INVALSI provides a score transformation based on the Rasch model, named *WLE* scores. This methodology is based on a probabilistic model estimating latent parameters from observed data, explaining how the probability of observing a certain response pattern varies as a function of only two parameters: individual ability (unique to each person) and item difficulty (unique to each question). If the one-dimensionality and local independence assumptions underlying Item Response Theory (the framework within which the Rasch model is situated) are satisfied, the estimated ability is independent of the type or difficulty of the set of items. Every year, the WLE-Rasch score scale has a national mean set at 200 points with a standard deviation of 40, and thus scores are expressed on a relative, not absolute, scale.

[7] Participation rates for the census-based survey are documented in annual INVALSI Reports (see https://www.invalsiopen.it/risultati/; last accessed 6 July 2026).

[8] Since 2018, the tests have been carried out in two different ways: in primary schools, they were administered to pupils in paper format, whereas in lower and upper secondary schools, the tests were administered to students online via computer (*Computer-Based Test*—CBT).

Since 2017, INVALSI has adopted an advanced psychometric methodology, still based on Item Response Theory, to make test results directly comparable across years through a process known as "linking". Before this procedure, scores were year-specific: a score of 200 in 2015 did not mean the same as 200 in 2016 because the tests were different. Thanks to linking, a WLE-score of 210 in Mathematics in 2023 represents the same ability level as 210 in 2021 or 2024, allowing both tracking of results over time and analysis of convergence or divergence between geographical areas or social groups. This methodological innovation enabled the computation and comparison of the multidimensional educational poverty indices presented and discussed in Sect. 4, ensuring that competency thresholds and measures are, respectively, stable and comparable across school years from 2017 onwards.[9]

Regarding the poverty line, i.e. the level of learning below which the student is considered educationally poor, we employ either absolute or relative poverty thresholds, contingent upon the data available for each grade level.

For secondary education (3rd year of lower secondary school, 2nd and 5th years of upper secondary school), we refer to an *absolute* educational poverty line.[10] For Italian language and Mathematics, INVALSI identifies five increasing competence levels ranging from 1 (low-skilled) to 5 (high-skilled), with level 3 considered the minimum required competence level in terms of the goals prescribed by the National Guidelines. For English (listening and reading), results are expressed on the CEFR (Common European Framework of Reference for Languages) scale, and the National Guidelines indicate that students should attain the A2 level at the end of lower secondary school, whilst for the last year of upper secondary the adequacy threshold is the B2 level (see INVALSI, 2021, p. 75). Students below the minimum proficiency level in a specific learning subject are considered "educationally poor" in that domain.

For primary education (2nd and 5th grades), no analogous absolute thresholds are available, so we employ a *relative* poverty line defined as 85% of the national median of the WLE-Rasch scores.[11]

An overview of test subjects and grades is presented in Table 2.

[9] A limited number of observations with missing data were excluded from the sample; these cases arose when students were present for one standardised test but absent for another.

[10] The threshold limits for learning subjects in secondary education were sourced from the INVALSI Statistical Department. See "Descrizione analitica e sintetica dei Livelli di competenza con cut-off livelli INVALSI" at https://serviziostatistico.invalsi.it/invalsi_ss_data/dati-regionali-di-area-geografica-e-nazionali-campionari/. See also https://www.invalsiopen.it/wp-content/uploads/2019/10/Editoriale1_ladispersionescolasticaimplicita.pdf (last accessed 6 July 2026).

[11] Legislative Decree No. 62/2017 introduced an English language assessment (reading and listening) in the fifth grade of primary school, with pupils expected to achieve CEFR level A1.

Table 2 Summary of INVALSI tests: grades involved and subjects

		Italian language	Mathematics	English reading	English listening
Primary school	Second grade	X	X		
	Fifth grade	X	X	X	X
Middle school	Third year	X	X	X	X
High school	Second year	X	X		
	Fifth year	X	X	X	X

Note: Table created by authors

4 Main Results

This section describes the main findings of the multidimensional analysis, where all available learning domains are jointly considered.[12]

The weights determine the relative importance of each learning domain: for grades with two subjects (Primary 2nd grade and High School 2nd year), equal weights of 1 are used with $k = 1$ (union) and $k = 2$ (intersection). For grades with four subjects, the weights are 1.3 for Italian, 1.3 for Mathematics, and 0.7 each for English reading and listening, with cut-offs $k = 1.3$ (union) and $k = 4$ (intersection). Under these weights, when $k = 1.3$, a pupil is identified as globally deprived if poor in at least one of Italian, Mathematics, or English (where English learning poverty requires being poor in both reading and listening). When $k = 4$, a student is globally poor only if low performing in all subjects.[13]

The estimates are structured to highlight heterogeneity across population subgroups: macro-areas (North-West, North-East, Centre, South, South and Islands), gender (male vs. female), immigration background (native vs. migrant background), and socio-economic and cultural status (ESCS).[14]

[12] All tables detailing the *MEH, M0, M1,* and *M2* indices are provided in the online Appendix, available at https://doi.org/10.1007/978-3-032-33072-7_8. Results were computed by the authors using the Distributive Analysis Stata Package (DASP) software (Abdelkrim & Duclos, 2007).

[13] Our choice aligns with INVALSI indications. For instance, when a student fails to reach level A2 (end of first cycle) in *both* reading and listening, the pupil is considered "fragile in English learning" (see INVALSI, 2024, p. 132, https://www.invalsiopen.it/risultati/; last accessed 6 July 2026). We assign a slightly higher weight to overall English learning compared to Mathematics and Italian, as English functions as a "gateway skill" whose absence has a multiplier effect on future poverty risk by limiting access to global knowledge, high-value employment, and international networks.

[14] The ESCS index is a composite indicator measuring a student's family background and socio-economic advantages, constructed by INVALSI by combining: (i) the highest level of education of the parents; (ii) the highest occupational status of the parents; (iii) the availability of educational resources at home, typically measured by the number of books in the household.

4.1 Italy

The national picture reveals differentiated trends according to the union method (Table A1-Panel A, online Appendix). In Primary School 2nd grade, a clear deterioration is recorded: the *MEH* increased from 0.343 (2020–21) to 0.398 (2023–24), a 16% rise. The *M1* and *M2* indices show even sharper increases (+45.5% and + 66.7%, respectively), indicating that not only has the number of students in educational poverty grown, but their competence deficit and inequality have also deepened. In the 5th grade, the situation appears more stable, with a slight decline in most indicators. In Lower Secondary School, index values remain high (*MEH* around 0.53–0.54) but show a slight tendency towards improvement in *M1* and *M2* (−7.3% and − 15.4%, respectively). In Upper Secondary School, the phenomenon is most acute: *MEH* in the 5th year remains at very high levels (0.667 in 2020–21, 0.669 in 2024–25), though an improvement for all indicators is observed in 2023–24 (*MEH* drops to 0.625).

The more stringent intersection method (Table A1-Panel B, online Appendix) confirms the critical issues, although absolute values are lower.[15]

4.2 Italian Macro-Areas

The analysis across five macro-areas—North-West (Aosta Valley, Piedmont, Lombardy, and Liguria), North-East (Bolzano, Trento, Veneto, Friuli-Venezia Giulia, and Emilia-Romagna), Centre (Tuscany, Umbria, Marche, and Lazio), South (Abruzzo, Molise, Campania, and Puglia), and South and Islands (Basilicata, Calabria, Sicily, and Sardinia)—reveals significant territorial inequalities (see online Appendix, Tables A3−A12).

From this section onwards, Panel A of each table reports the educational poverty indices and their percentage changes over time, while Panel B provides the relative contribution of each macro-area to the corresponding national total.

4.2.1 Primary School—Second Grade (Tables A3 and A4)

In Primary 2nd grade (Panel A), a worrying and widespread deterioration is recorded between 2020–21 and 2023–24, applying both the union and intersection methods.

With the union method ($k = 1$), all indicators (*MEH, M0, M1, M2*) show high percentage increases across all macro-areas, especially in the North-West and North-East, where the *M2* index (which attaches higher weights to students experiencing

[15] Table A2 (online Appendix) reports a decomposition of the multidimensional educational poverty indices at the national level, showing which learning domains contribute the most to educational poverty.

larger poverty gaps and thus accounts for inequality within the poor) doubles or more. The Centre, traditionally more high performing, also sees significant increases. The South and Islands start from higher absolute values, but percentage growth over the 4-year period for *M1* and *M2* is significantly lower than in the North. This suggests a generalised deterioration of basic skills (Italian and Mathematics) across the country, with acceleration precisely in historically stronger areas.

With the intersection method ($k = 2$), a clear worsening is observed between 2020–21 and 2023–24 for the *M2* index, in particular for northern and central regions. While the Centre remains the highest-performing area over the entire period, the North-East has emerged as the lowest-performing macro-area in 2023–24 according to *M2*.

The relative weight (Panel B) of northern regions on national educational poverty increased during the period for those indices accounting for the magnitude of poverty gaps and inequality (*M1, M2*) in 2023–24, indicating the problem is no longer just a Southern issue but is becoming a national phenomenon.

4.2.2 Primary School—Fifth Grade (Tables A5 and A6)

In Primary 5th grade, the picture is mixed and more complex. With the union method ($k = 1.3$), even though the southern regions start from higher absolute values, a clear improvement is observed between 2020–21 and 2023–24, particularly in the South, where the *M2* index decreased by 29.4%. In contrast, northern regions show substantial stability or slight deterioration. This trend might reflect a partial recovery of the southern regions after initial negative pandemic peaks, while the North may be experiencing longer-term effects.

With the intersection method ($k = 4$), the improvement in the South and the South and Islands is even more pronounced (up to, respectively, −60% and − 33.3% for *M2*), while the North-West remains stable. This indicates that recovery efforts in the southern regions are having an effect, particularly on the most vulnerable students.

The relative contribution (Panel B) of the southern regions to national indices of extreme educational poverty (intersection method) decreased between 2020–21 and 2023–24, consistent with the improvement observed in Panel A. The North-West, however, saw its relative weight increase, confirming a growing educational emergency in the northern regions.

4.2.3 Middle School—Third Year (Tables A7 and A8)

Using the absolute proficiency threshold (Panel A), data show a clear and positive improving trend from 2020–21 to 2024–25, especially with the intersection method ($k = 4$). The North and Centre show steady progress. Percentage decreases are very significant in magnitude, particularly in the South (up to −46.7% for *M2*), signalling a generalised reduction in absolute multidimensional educational poverty in middle schools, perhaps due to targeted interventions on achieving minimum competencies.

The relative contribution (Panel B) of the South to national educational poverty for *M1* and *M2* decreased over the 5-year period, although it remains amongst the areas with the greatest weight, while the northern regions saw their relative contribution increase.

4.2.4 High School—Second Year (Tables A9 and A10)

In High School 2nd year (Panel A), the situation appears stable or slightly worsening between 2021–22 and 2023–24. With the union method ($k = 1$), the North-West records small increases in all indices, while the South and Islands show slight decreases.

With the intersection method ($k = 2$), the increase in the North-West is more marked (+14.3% for *M2*), highlighting growing difficulties in Northern high schools for students who do not achieve the adequacy thresholds in either discipline.

The relative contribution (Panel B) of the North-West to national educational poverty increased steadily over all 3 years, while that of the southern regions slightly decreased. The Centre maintains a stable contribution.

4.2.5 High School—Fifth Year (Tables A11 and A12)

In High School 5th year (Panel A), the picture is contrasting. With the union method ($k = 1.3$), a clear improvement is observed in 2023–24, followed by a rebound in 2024–25, bringing values almost back to 2020–21 levels, particularly in northern and central regions. The South and Islands show the most consistent improvements over the 5-year period. With the intersection method ($k = 4$), the improvement between 2020–21 and 2024–25 is more evident, especially in the South and Islands (up to −20% for *M2*). However, the 2024–25 results interrupt the positive trend, suggesting a fragile and not yet stabilised situation.

The relative contribution (Panel B) to extreme educational poverty shifted significantly between 2020–21 and 2024–25: while the weight of the South increased, that of the South and Islands decreased, pointing to diverging trajectories within the Mezzogiorno.

Notably, Panel B reveals a clear and significant pattern regarding the geographic distribution of educational poverty in Italy. Overall, we observe that: (i) for North-West, North-East, and Centre, their relative contribution to national educational poverty tends to decrease when moving from the *MEH* index to the *M2* index; (ii) for South and South and Islands, their relative contribution, conversely, tends to increase when moving from *MEH* to *M2*. Notably, in the 2nd grade of Primary School, this pattern weakens or even reverses in the most recent school year (2023–24), suggesting that “intense” educational poverty might also be increasing in the North, making the geography of the educational issue more homogeneous. However, for most of the period analysed, the identified trend remains significant and politically

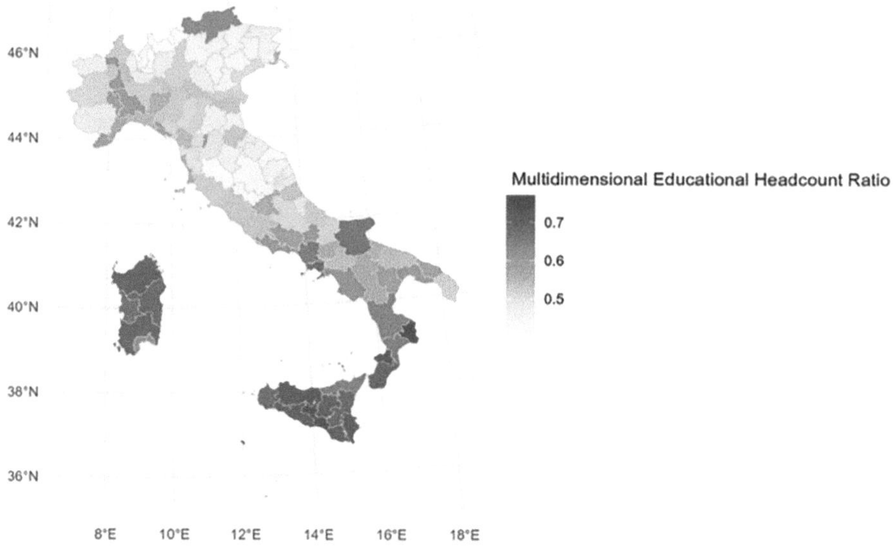

Fig. 1 Provincial *MEH*: 3rd year Middle School cohort (2024–25)—Union. Source: Authors' calculations on INVALSI data

relevant. As a result, in the North and Centre students in educational poverty tend to experience more limited and homogeneous difficulties—in fewer subjects or with less profound deficiencies—while in the southern regions the educational poverty presents different *qualitative* characteristics. In the latter regions, students are more likely to experience poverty that is more intense and unequal (i.e. the values of poverty measures increase in $\boldsymbol{\alpha}$).

The following maps (see Figs. 1, 2, 3 and 4) illustrate the *MEH* at the provincial level based on the most recent INVALSI survey (2024–25) for the last year of Middle School and High School. According to the union method, index values are considerably high (ranging around 0.50–0.70 for Middle School; around 0.60–0.70 for High School). The stark contrast between the two methods is revealing: while many students face some learning challenges (union), the intersection method—with much lower values (0.10–0.25 and 0.20–0.40, respectively)—identifies a smaller, critically vulnerable group facing profound, cross-disciplinary failure.

All maps reveal a strong North-South divide. The final year of upper secondary school shows the highest levels of educational poverty, suggesting that the phenomenon intensifies significantly between lower and upper secondary school. The union map (Fig. 3) shows almost the entire southern part of the country in the highest value bracket (>0.7) for this student cohort, signalling the need to act promptly to prevent the accumulation of learning gaps.

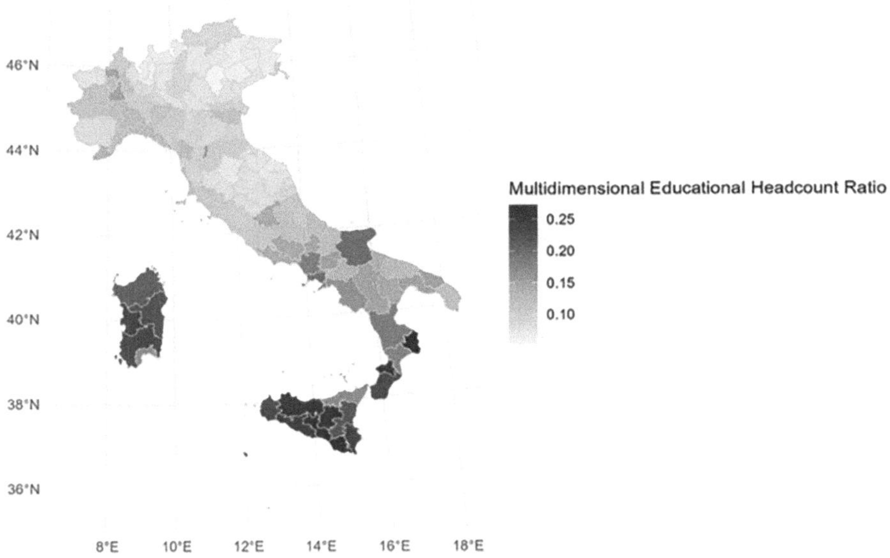

Fig. 2 Provincial *MEH*: 3rd year Middle School cohort (2024–25)—Intersection. Source: Authors' calculations on INVALSI data

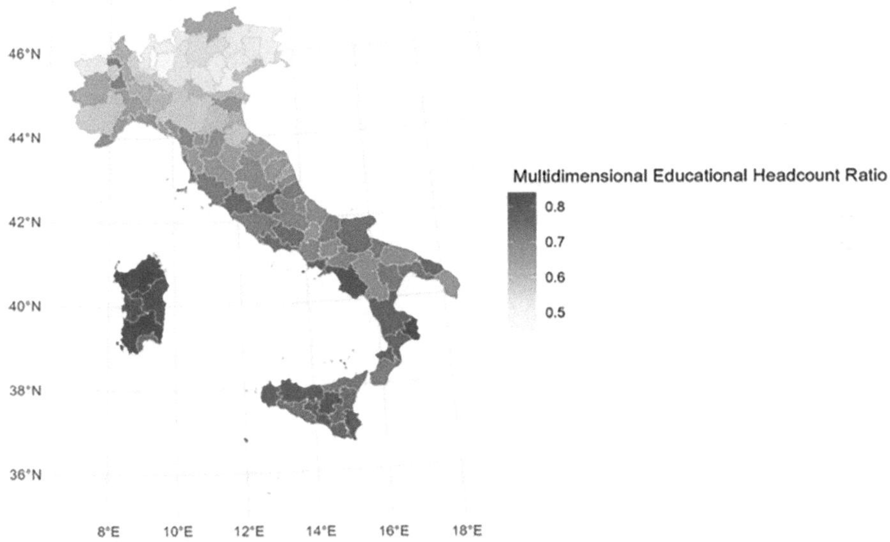

Fig. 3 Provincial *MEH*: 5th year High School cohort (2024–25)—Union. Source: Authors' calculations on INVALSI data

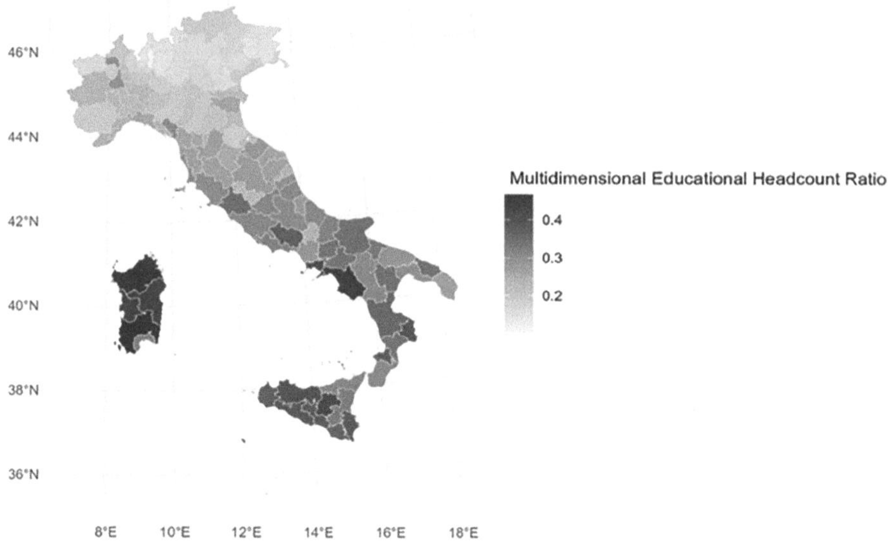

Fig. 4 Provincial *MEH*: 5th year High School cohort (2024–25)—Intersection. Source: Authors' calculations on INVALSI data

4.3 Disaggregation by Gender

Gender analysis reveals a consistent and systematic gap to the disadvantage of male pupils. Across all school cycles and for almost all years, the educational poverty indices for males are higher than those for females and the national average (see online Appendix, Tables A13 and A14, Panel A). The phenomenon is pronounced in secondary school (e.g. in the 5th year of upper secondary school in 2020–21, the *MEH* for males was 0.672 compared to 0.661 for females). The *M1* and *M2* indices are also consistently higher, indicating that males are not only more frequently in educational poverty but also that their learning deficit is, on average, wider and more unequally distributed. Female students show systematically lower index values, suggesting greater resilience to educational poverty (see online Appendix, A15 and A16, Panel A). However, an increase in indices is also observed for females in the 2nd grade of primary school, a sign that the deterioration in that cycle affects both genders, albeit from different starting levels.

Panel B confirms this imbalance: the relative contribution of males to the total indices is almost always above 50% and tends to increase moving from *MEH* to *M2,* confirming their overrepresentation in the most severe situations of educational poverty.

4.4 Disaggregation by Migrant/Native Status

The most profound and alarming gap is the one between students with a migrant background (i.e. pupils born abroad) and native students.

The index values are markedly higher at every school cycle for migrant students (see online Appendix, Tables A17 and A18, Panel A). In upper secondary school, according to the union method, the *MEH* for migrant students consistently exceeds 0.80, a value indicating an almost universal condition of educational poverty in this group. The *M1* and *M2* indices are also far higher, signifying a very deep competence gap. Although some trends show slight improvements in certain years, the 2024–25 data confirm the gravity of the situation. When we turn to the results of the intersection method, it emerges that improvements over the period are more apparent at the end of primary and middle school.

In contrast, the values for natives are significantly lower and align with, or are slightly below, the national average (see online Appendix, A19 and A20, Panel A). This confirms that the relevant national average is influenced by the high incidence of the phenomenon among students born abroad. The trend for natives mirrors the national one, with a weakening in the 2nd grade of primary school and relative stability or slight improvement in the other cycles.

Panel B for migration status confirms that, despite representing a fraction of the student population, migrant students contribute disproportionately to the educational poverty indices, especially in those measuring also depth and severity (*M1*, *M2*, respectively) of educational deprivation. This relative contribution is particularly high in lower secondary school and the 2nd year of upper secondary school, key transition phases.

4.5 Disaggregation by Socio-Economic Status (ESCS)

Findings point to significant and enduring disparities stratified by socio-economic status (Tables A21–A26, online Appendix).[16] Students in the first (lowest) ESCS tertile consistently experience the highest levels of deprivation. For instance, under the union method, the *M0* for the first tertile (0.440) is more than double that of the third tertile (0.203) in the 2022–23 middle school year. Under the intersection method, the *M0* for the first tertile (0.186) is over three times that of the third tertile (0.056).

The evolution over time reveals a striking divergent path. In middle school (3rd year), there is a remarkable improvement for the most disadvantaged: the

[16] The socio-economic status (ESCS) is not available for the 2nd grade in primary school in INVALSI data over the period analysed. In Tables A21–A26, the sum of the results on the relative contribution of ESCS tertiles to the specific overall multidimensional educational poverty index is not equal to one due to missing data on ESCS values.

M0 for the first tertile fell from 0.541 (2020–21) to 0.421 (2024–25), a reduction of 22.18%. Declines in *M1* (−30.77%) and *M2* (−34.78%) indicate decreasing depth and severity. Under the intersection method, *M1* and *M2* fell by 48.33% and 52.94%, respectively, suggesting that targeted interventions have been effective. However, in primary school, poverty indices for the first tertile remain high with no clear improving trend. The final year of high school shows stagnation: the *M0* remained persistently high (0.582 in 2020–21 vs. 0.583 in 2024–25), highlighting that challenges accumulate and are not resolved by the end of secondary education for the most disadvantaged students.

5 Conclusive Comments

In this chapter, we applied the multidimensional approach to analysing educational poverty in Italy. Using INVALSI test results for Italian, Mathematics, and English for the school years 2020–21 to 2024–25, we assessed the degree of educational deprivation across five grade levels. Students were chosen as the elementary unit of analysis and, according to data availability, both absolute and relative poverty approaches were adopted. In line with the axiomatic approach, we focused on indicators from the Alkire and Foster (2011) class, allowing for characterising different aspects of educational poverty.

The analysis paints an evolving picture. Primary 2nd grade shows a worrying generalised deterioration, especially in the North. Primary 5th grade presents a mixed picture, with signs of recovery in the southern regions. Middle School shows a positive trend in reducing absolute educational poverty. High School exhibits stability with slight deterioration in the North, while the southern regions show improvements. A common thread is the increase in the relative contribution of northern regions, signalling that critical issues are no longer confined to the Mezzogiorno but are becoming a national issue requiring differentiated interventions. Notably, in the southern regions, the relative contribution tends to increase when moving from *MEH* to *M2*, where the latter gives greater weight to students with larger poverty gaps. With the intersection method, indicator values always decrease—sometimes considerably—and findings from the union method are substantially confirmed.

Moreover, (i) there exists an educational gender gap unfavourable to males, manifesting as higher probability, intensity, and severity of the phenomenon; (ii) a great structural challenge is the gap between native and migrant students: even with some progress under the intersection method, the incidence, breadth, depth, and severity of educational poverty among migrants remain of a different order of magnitude, indicating that Italy has not yet effectively integrated this component into its educational system; and (iii) socio-economic background remains a powerful determinant: while there is compelling evidence of targeted efforts reducing multidimensional poverty in Middle School, persistent challenges in Primary School and stagnation in High School call for continuous, coordinated policy from early years through to the end of secondary education.

Overall, these results constitute a significant step in strengthening an informational base that allows policymakers to gain a deeper awareness of the degree of learning poverty in Italy. The decomposability characteristics of the indicators for population subgroups allow for identifying the areas where results appear most concerning. If educational poverty is seen not only as indicating a low level of learning but above all as "a normative concept rooted in an understanding of poverty as an unacceptable state in a particular society" (Lohmann & Ferger, 2014, p. 1), the effort to identify whether different subsets of the population are differently poor could foster poverty reduction policies directing educational resources effectively where appropriate. The public policy perspective influences the choice among various measures: for example, policymakers attentive to learning inequality among the poor should be particularly sensitive to measures assigning higher weights to students in the bottom part of the distribution. Furthermore, if we believe that school failure weakens commitment and motivation to learn, Primary school results should be evaluated with the utmost attention.

From a local perspective, the southern regions remain candidates for investments in educational policies aimed at reducing educational deficiencies. Findings reveal that the North-South divide is not only quantitative (more pupils in difficulty) but above all qualitative, as educational poverty is more heterogeneous and polarized in the southern regions: alongside students with mild difficulties, there seems to exist a segment of educational "ultra-poor" with extreme deprivations.

Future research should investigate the determinants of educational poverty through multilevel regression models, allowing for considering the hierarchical structure of educational processes and identifying which factors—at the individual, family, and school level—explain the variance in individual risks of educational poverty.[17] If there were a significant role for school-level factors, the policy implications would be more substantial.

References

Abdelkrim, A., & Duclos, J. Y. (2007). *DASP: Distributive analysis stata package*. PEP, World Bank, UNDP and Université Laval.

Agasisti, T. (2014). The efficiency of public spending on education: An empirical comparison of EU countries. *European Journal of Education, 49*, 543–557.

[17] It is worth recalling that we released several databases displaying the estimated values of both the multidimensional educational headcount ratio and Alkire-Foster multidimensional poverty indices for each Italian province. These datasets are first provided looking at the national context and are further broken down by gender, migrant status and socio-economic background (ESCS), according to both union and intersection methods. Practitioners wishing to utilize estimates of the *M0* or *M1* indices—whether as dependent or explanatory variables in an econometric model—can access the relevant databases via the following web page: https://ameliadp.grins.it/. On econometric modelling for AF Measures, see Alkire et al. (2015).

Agasisti, T., Longobardi, S., Prete, V., & Russo, F. (2021). The relevance of educational poverty in Europe: Determinants and remedies. *Journal of Policy Modeling, 43*, 692–709.

Alkire, S., & Foster, J. (2011). Counting and multidimensional poverty measurement. *Journal of Public Economics, 95*, 476–487.

Alkire, S., Foster, J. E., Seth, S., Santos, M. E., Roche, J. M., & Ballo, P. (2015). Multidimensional poverty measurement and analysis: Chapter 10—Some regression models for AF measures. *OPHI Working Paper* No. 91. Retrieved July 6, 2026, from https://ophi.org.uk/sites/default/files/OPHIWP091_Ch10.pdf (also in Alkire, S., Foster, J. E., Seth, S., Santos, M. E., Roche, J. M., & Ballo, P. (2015). *Multidimensional poverty measurement and analysis*. Oxford: Oxford University Press).

Allmendinger, J., & Leibfried, S. (2003). Education and the welfare state: The four worlds of competence production. *Journal of European Social Policy, 13*, 63–81.

Annabi, N. (2017). Investments in education: What are the productivity gains? *Journal of Policy Modeling, 39*, 499–518.

Bourguignon, F., & Chakravarty, S. (2003). The measurement of multidimensional poverty. *Journal of Economic Inequality, 1*, 25–49.

Checchi, D. (1998). Povertà ed istruzione: Alcune riflessioni e una proposta di indicatori. *Politica Economica, 14*, 245–282.

Cohen, J. (2006). Social, emotional, ethical, and academic education: Creating a climate for learning, participation in democracy, and well-being. *Harvard Educational Review, 76*, 201–237.

Cordero, J. M., & Gil, M. (2018). The effect of teaching strategies on student achievements: An analysis using TALIS-PISA-link. *Journal of Policy Modeling, 40*, 1313–1331.

Darling-Hammond, L. (2000). Teacher quality and student achievement. *Education Policy Analysis Archives, 8*, 1.

Denny, K. (2002). New methods for comparing literacy across populations: Insights from the measurement of poverty. *Journal of the Royal Statistical Society Series A, Royal Statistical Society, 165*, 481–493.

Dutta, I., Pattanaik, P. K., & Xu, Y. (2003). On measuring deprivation and the standard of living in a multidimensional framework on the basis of aggregate data. *Economica, 70*, 197–221.

Fantuzzo, J., Grim, S., & Hazan, H. (2005). Project start: An evaluation of a community-wide school-based intervention to reduce truancy. *Psychology in the Schools, 42*, 657–667.

Ferraro, S., & Põder, K. (2018). School-level policies and the efficiency and equity trade-off in education. *Journal of Policy Modeling, 40*, 1022–1037.

Foster, J. E., Greer, J., & Thorbecke, E. (1984). A class of decomposable poverty measures. *Econometrica, 52*, 761–766.

Giangiacomo, P., Falzetti, P., & Bagnarol, C. (2024). Do national and international surveys speak the same language? In P. Falzetti (Ed.), *Surveys on students: INVALSI national and international tests. VI seminar "INVALSI data: A tool for teaching and scientific research"* (pp. 130–146). FrancoAngeli.

Giusti, C., & Schirripa Spagnolo, F. (2025). A quantile approach for measuring multidimensional educational poverty in Italy. *Social Indicators Research, 179*, 29–45.

Glaesser, J. (2021). Relative educational poverty: Conceptual and empirical issues. *Quality and Quantity, 56*, 2803–2820.

Güzel, C. I., & Berberoglu, G. (2005). An analysis of the programme for international student assessment 2000 (PISA2000) mathematical literacy data for Brazilian, Japanese and Norwegian students. *Studies in Educational Evaluation, 31*, 283–314.

Henry, K. L. (2007). Who's skipping school: Characteristics of truants in 8th and 10th grade. *The Journal of School Health, 77*, 29–35.

INVALSI (2021). Rapporto Prove INVALSI 2021. INVALSI. Retrieved July 6, 2026, from https://www.invalsiopen.it/risultati/risultati-prove-invalsi-2021/

INVALSI (2024). Rapporto Prove INVALSI 2024. INVALSI. Retrieved July 6, 2026, from https://www.invalsiopen.it/risultati/risultati-prove-invalsi-2024/

Lagravinese, R., Liberati, P., & Resce, G. (2020). The impact of economic, social and cultural conditions on educational attainments. *Journal of Policy Modeling, 42*, 112–132.

Lohmann, H., & Ferger, F. (2014). Educational poverty in a comparative perspective: Theoretical and empirical implications. *SFB 882 Working Paper Series* No. 26, DFG Research Center, Bielefeld University.

Longobardi, S., Falzetti, P., & Pagliuca, M. M. (2018). Quis custiodet ipsos custodes? How to detect and correct teacher cheating in Italian student data. *Statistical Methods & Applications, 27*, 515–543.

Ma, X., Jong, C., & Yuan, J. (2013). Exploring reasons for the East Asian success in PISA. In H.-D. Meyer & A. Benavot (Eds.), *PISA, power, and policy: The emergence of global educational governance* (pp. 225–246). Symposium Books.

Minzyuk, L., & Russo, F. (2016). La misurazione multidimensionale della povertà in istruzione in Italia. *Politica Economica/Journal of Economic Policy, 32*, 65–122.

Ning, B., Van Damme, J., Van Den Noortgate, W., Yang, X., & Gielen, S. (2015). The influence of classroom disciplinary climate of schools on reading achievement: A cross-country comparative study. *School Effectiveness and School Improvement, 26*, 586–611.

Rios-Neto, E. L. G., & Rodrigues, C. G. (2013). Educational quality and deprivation: Elasticity comparisons based on reading test scores from PISA 2000 and 2009. *Mimeo*. Retrieved July 6, 2026, from https://iussp.org/sites/default/files/event_call_for_papers/IUSSP_2012_ExtendedAbstract_RiosNeto.pdf

Sánchez-Antón, M.-D.-C., Badillo-Amador, R., Marco-Gil, M.-D.-C., LLinares-Ciscar, J. V., Álvarez-Díez, S., & Sánchez-Garcia, J. F. (2022). Analysis of the educational poverty in Spain by subjects, regions and gender. *Social Indicators Research, 162*, 829–861.

Sánchez-Garcia, J. F., Sánchez-Antón, M.-D.-C., Badillo-Amador, R., Marco-Gil, M.-D.-C., & LLinares-Ciscar, J. V., and Álvarez-Díez, S. (2019). A new extension of Bourguignon and Chakravarty index to measure educational poverty and its application to the OECD countries. *Social Indicators Research, 145*, 479–501.

Sen, A. K. (1976). Poverty: An ordinal approach to measurement. *Econometrica, 44*, 219–231.

Sen, A. K. (1982). *Choice, welfare and measurement*. Basil Blackwell.

Sen, A. K. (1985). *Commodities and capabilities*. North-Holland.

Sibiano, P., & Agasisti, T. (2011). Efficiency of public spending in education: A challenge among Italian regions. *Investigaciones de Economia de la Education, 6*, 503–516.

Villar, A. (2016). Educational poverty as a welfare loss: Low performance in the OECD according to PISA 2012. *Modern Economy, 7*, 441–449.

Zhao, C., & Chen, B. (2023). ICT in education can improve students' achievements in rural China: The role of parents, educators and authorities. *Journal of Policy Modeling, 45*, 320–344.

Part II
Lawfulness, Firms' Performance and Social Cohesion

Does Fraud Risk Affect Legality Ratings? Evidence from Italian Listed Firms

Angela Maria Greco, Mariastella Messina, and Davide Rizzotti

Abstract Within the framework of the United Nations *2030 Agenda for Sustainable Development*, Goal 16 (*Peace, Justice and Strong Institutions*) aims to combat all forms of organized crime and significantly reduce corruption and illegality. In this context, Law No. 190 of November 6, 2012, introduced the Legality rating, which serves as an institutional mechanism designed to promote ethical behavior and integrity among Italian firms. This study examines whether the elements considered in the attribution of the legality rating can indirectly capture factors associated with financial statement manipulation. Results reveal no significant relationship between the legality rating and the likelihood of fraudulent reporting, suggesting that the rating captures formal compliance rather than substantive financial integrity. The findings highlight the need to enrich the legality rating framework with quantitative indicators of financial misconduct to enhance its role as a comprehensive integrity metric.

1 Introduction

Ensuring corporate behavior integrity has become a cornerstone of sustainable governance. While numerous initiatives aim to foster transparency and compliance, few have attempted to link legality certification with financial reporting integrity. In Italy, the *Legality Rating* (LR) was conceived as a tool to reward ethical conduct; however, its effectiveness in signaling deeper forms of misconduct, such as financial statement fraud, remains unexplored. The LR, issued by the Italian Competition Authority (Autorità Garante della Concorrenza e del Mercato, ICA), certifies a

A. M. Greco · M. Messina (✉) · D. Rizzotti
Department of Economics and Business, University of Catania, Catania, Italy
e-mail: angelamaria.greco@unict.it; mariastella.messina@unict.it; rizzotti@unict.it

R. Cellini et al. (eds.), *Cultural, Social, and Political Participation in the Internet Era*, Contributions to Economics, https://doi.org/10.1007/978-3-032-33072-7_9

firm's adherence to legality, ethical behavior, and good governance standards. The LR score is determined by compliance with the requirements outlined in Article 2 of the Implementing Regulation (Resolution No. 28361, July 28, 2020). From a governance perspective, the LR demonstrates that a firm which adopts it have integrity-based governance practices and that its top management has not been convicted of crimes such as corruption, environmental violations, or workplace safety regulations.

The LR ensures the formal absence of criminal infiltration within a company. However, corporate illegality may also manifest through more subtle behaviors, particularly financial statement manipulation. Prior research indicates that more than half of individuals involved in corporate fraud engage in financial reporting misconduct, which represents a central issue in the agency theory framework (Meckling & Jensen, 1976).

In order to evaluate the effectiveness of the LR assignment procedure, this study investigates whether the attributes considered in awarding the LR are also capable of indirectly identifying firms prone to financial statement manipulation. Specifically, the study tests the existence of a statistical association between the possession of LR and the probability of fraudulent financial reporting.

The empirical analysis focuses on firms listed on the Italian Stock Exchange during 2024. Data on the LR were obtained from the official ICA website, while financial statement data used to assess manipulation risk were extracted from AIDA database. This study applies statistical techniques to test whether the LR is associated with earnings manipulation or accounting fraud risk indicators.

The findings reveal no statistically significant relationship between possession of an LR and a low probability of financial statement manipulation. Among firms holding an LR, 18% exhibit a high risk of fraudulent financial reporting. Although the LR effectively certifies formal compliance with legal and ethical requirements, it does not fully capture the complex and multifaceted nature of fraud.

The absence of a significant association implies that the LR, as currently structured, may overlook certain dimensions of unethical financial behavior. Consequently, enhancing the requirements by incorporating financial ratios and indicators capable of identifying less visible yet economically relevant forms of illegality would be appropriate. Integrating these measures could strengthen the role of LR as a comprehensive tool of both formal compliance and substantive corporate integrity.

The remainder of this chapter is structured as follows. Section 1 introduces the research context and outlines the main objectives of the study. Section 2 provides an overview of the Italian legislative framework governing the LR, presents a review of the existing literature on financial statement fraud, and develops the research hypotheses. The sample selection process, research design, and methodological approach employed in the empirical analysis are described in Sect. 3. Section 4 reports the descriptive statistics, empirical results, and findings' discussion. Finally, Sect. 5 concludes the chapter by summarizing the main results, discussing their implications, and outlining directions for future research.

2 Background

Legality refers to conformity with the law and adherence to legal norms. Conversely, *illegality* encompasses a range of punishable behaviors that may be perpetrated either by individuals, acting in pursuit of personal interests to the detriment of others, or by organized entities such as criminal organizations (e.g., Mafia, Camorra). These behaviors manifest through various forms, including fraud, corruption, tax evasion, financial statement manipulation, money laundering, organized crime, and criminal infiltration of legitimate economic and political structures.

Legality assumes a pivotal role within the framework of the United Nations 2030 Agenda for Sustainable Development, specifically through Goal 16, which promotes peaceful and inclusive societies, universal access to justice, and the establishment of accountable and effective institutions at all levels.

Among the multiple objectives encompassed by Goal 16 are: the reduction of all forms of violence; the promotion of the rule of law at both national and international levels; the guarantee of equal access to justice; the reduction of illicit financial; the mitigation of corruption and abuse of power in all their manifestations; the establishment of accountable, inclusive, participatory, and representative decision-making processes; and the protection of fundamental freedoms in accordance with national legislation and international agreements.

Within this framework, this study focuses on the specific objective of "*developing effective, accountable, and transparent institutions at all levels.*" In this context, the LR represents a strategic instrument for Italian enterprises. It is designed to promote and institutionalize ethical conduct, transparency, and corporate responsibility principles, thereby fostering a business environment that aligns with the broader aims of sustainable development and good governance.

2.1 Legality Rating

LR is a voluntary certification issued by the ICA. It serves as an instrument for assessing and promoting ethical and lawful corporate conduct. The rating is expressed through a score ranging from a minimum of one star to a maximum of three stars, depending on the degree of compliance with the requirements established under Article 2 of the Implementing Regulation (Resolution No. 28361 of July 28, 2020).

To qualify for the LR, firms must meet the following four minimum prerequisites:

- Headquarters is located in Italy.
- Sales of at least two million euros in the year before the request.
- Company registration at least 2 years before the request year.
- Compliance with the ICA's substantive requirements.

The substantive requirements of the ICA are as follows: the directors and shareholders of the applicant companies must not have been recipients of preventive or cautionary measures, nor have they been issued a sentence of conviction under criminal law; and the use of traceable payment systems for transactions exceeding the legal limit set for cash exchanges (Bertacchini et al., 2024).

Starting from the first star, which is earned by meeting the four prerequisites, an additional star is earned for each additional requirement completed from the list below.

The list of additional requirements is as follows:

- Commitment to protocols that aim to prevent and fight organized crime.
- The tracing of payments for amounts lower than the limit set by law as the maximum cash exchange amount.
- Implementing corporate compliance systems or organizational frameworks to ensure conformity control.
- Implementation of organizational processes to ensure CSR compliance.
- Registration on a "white list" of entities not associated with organized crime.
- Adopting ethical codes endorsed by trade associations.
- Adopting organizational models that aim to prevent and combat corruption.

The certification remains valid for 2 years from the date of issuance and may be renewed upon request. At the governance level, the attainment of the LR demonstrates that the company operates within an integrated and ethically oriented governance framework, where senior management has no criminal convictions for offenses such as those related to workplace safety, environmental violations, or corruption.

Despite its strengths as a reputational and compliance tool, the LR framework largely emphasizes the formal and procedural aspects of legality. Thus, it may fail to identify subtler manifestations of illegality, such as fraudulent financial reporting, which undermines both the transparency and effectiveness of Goal 16 objectives.

2.2 *Fraudulent Financial Reporting*

Fraudulent financial reporting (FFR) refers to the intentional misstatement or omission of amounts or disclosures in financial statements to deceive stakeholders regarding a firm's actual economic condition. FFR entails a deliberate violation of accounting principles with the explicit objective of distorting perceptions of performance, solvency, and stability (Nicolò et al., 2023), unlike unintentional errors or aggressive yet legally permissible earnings management practices.

Elliott and Willingham (1980) conceptualize FFR as a deliberate act of deception by management that misleads investors and creditors through falsified financial statements. Similarly, Wallace (1995) described FFR as a deceptive scheme supported by fabricated documentation and misrepresentations, while Spathis (2002) characterized it as the intentional falsification of figures that fail to reflect the firm's true financial situation. Synthesizing these perspectives, Dalnial et al. (2014) concluded that FFR represents the preparation of financial statements with the explicit intention to deceive users of financial information.

Given its implications, FFR has attracted substantial attention from the public, regulatory authorities, and academic community. It poses significant risks not only to individual organizations and their stakeholders but also to public confidence in the integrity of capital markets (Beasley et al., 2010a, 2010b).

In the literature, FFR is frequently analyzed within the theoretical framework of the fraud triangle, which posits that pressure, opportunity, and rationalization are the primary antecedents of fraudulent behavior. Among these, financial pressure is often identified as the most critical determinant: firms experiencing financial distress or approaching bankruptcy are more likely to manipulate financial statements to conceal deteriorating performance (Dutzi & Rausch, 2016). Under distress, managers may be incentivized to overstate revenues, defer loss recognition, or adjust accruals to maintain access to external financing, comply with debt covenants, or safeguard their reputational capital (Barniv et al., 2002; Xu, 2021).

Empirical evidence corroborates these theoretical expectations. Xu (2021) documented that U.S. firms approaching bankruptcy systematically intensify real earnings management (such as overproduction or R&D expenditure cuts) during the 5 years preceding failure, often in conjunction with accrual-based earnings manipulation. Similarly, Dutzi and Rausch (2016) synthesized findings indicating that distressed firms may pursue upward earnings management to project stability or downward manipulation to obtain more favorable bankruptcy outcomes, illustrating the context-dependent nature of reporting strategies in periods of distress. Franceschetti et al. (2013) analyze European SMEs and reveal that firms nearing insolvency frequently adopt income-decreasing accounting choices in anticipation of bankruptcy negotiations.

Additionally, the literature identifies accounting anomalies (such as abnormal depreciation, inflated receivables, and aggressive capitalization of expenditures) as early warning indicators of both corporate failure and potential manipulation. Serrano-Cinca et al. (2019) demonstrate that these anomalies, rooted in earnings management practices, constitute powerful predictors of bankruptcy, underscoring the overlap between financial distress and fraud risk. Expanding on this perspective, Shahana et al. (2023) provided a systematic review of fraud detection research, highlighting that recent advances in data mining and machine learning have significantly enhanced the ability to identify red flags in distressed firms. Nonetheless, persistent challenges, such as class imbalance, data noise, and asymmetric misclassification costs, continue to limit the practical implementation of such models.

2.3 Hypotheses Development

FFR clearly falls within the previously delineated theoretical boundaries of illegality. It represents a deliberate and concealed activity undertaken to unlawfully pursue the private interests of a limited group of individuals (internal or external to the organization) at the expense of corporate transparency, stakeholder trust, and market efficiency.

A preliminary critical analysis of the LR framework reveals a noteworthy limitation. The current assessment model primarily emphasizes compliance-oriented and organizational dimensions, reflecting a predominantly procedural conception of corporate legality. In contrast, financial indicators receive limited attention within the evaluation process. This imbalance raises questions regarding the LR's comprehensiveness as a preventive tool against complex forms of financial misconduct.

Such observations lead to a broader theoretical reflection: *do the elements considered in determining the LR and its associated score merely ensure the formal absence of criminal infiltration, or can they also guarantee the substantive integrity of financial reporting practices?* In other words, *does the LR function as an effective proxy for corporate ethical behavior and financial transparency, or does it primarily capture the compliance-oriented dimension of legality without encompassing the risk of deceptive financial disclosure?*

Despite the growing relevance of the LR as an instrument of reputational capital and institutional trust, the extant literature lacks empirical evidence linking these aspects and FFR (Hernandez Aros et al., 2026). This research gap precludes an informed understanding of whether the LR may serve as a reliable signal of financial reporting quality and integrity. Accordingly, to address this gap and in line with our research question, we formulate the following null hypothesis:

H_0: There is no relation between the presence of LR and presence of FRR

3 Sample Selection and Design of the Research

3.1 Methodology and Data Collection

The research design is based on regression analysis between the LR and FRR. The hypothesis was tested on firms listed on the Italian stock exchange in 2024. The data related to the RL were obtained from the ICA website. The financial reporting data used for M-score and corporate governance data are extracted from the AIDA database.

3.2 Dependent Variable

The LR is a voluntary request and was measured as a dummy variable. If the firm has obtained the LR for the 2-year period, the variable assumes a value of 1; if the firm has not obtained or has not requested the LR, the variable assumes a value of 0.

3.3 Explanatory Variable

The Beneish M-Score (Beneish, 1999), a statistically derived composite index extensively employed in the accounting and auditing literature to infer the probability of earnings manipulation, is used to proxy the explanatory variable FFR. By integrating a set of diagnostic financial ratios, the model serves as an empirical instrument to differentiate between firms exhibiting normal accounting behavior and those potentially engaging in deceptive financial reporting practices.

The Beneish M-Score functional form is defined as follows:

$$\text{M-score} = -4.84 + 0.92 * \text{DSRI} + 0.528 * \text{GMI} + 0.404 * \text{AQI} + 0.892 * \text{SGI} \\ +0.115 * \text{DEPI} - 0.172 * \text{SGAI} + 4.679 * \text{TATA} - 0.327 * \text{LVGI}$$

where:

DSRI = (Net Receivable$_t$/Sales$_t$)/(Net Receivable$_{t-1}$/Sales$_{t-1}$)

GMI = [(Sales$_{t-1}$ − COGS$_{t-1}$)/Sales$_{t-1}$]/[(Sales$_t$ − COGS$_t$)/Sales$_t$]

AQI = [1 − (Current Asset$_t$ + PPE$_t$/Total Asset$_t$)]/[1 − (Current Asset$_{t-1}$ + PPE$_{t-1}$/Total Asset$_{t-1}$)]

SGI = Sales$_t$/Sales$_{t-1}$

DEPI = [Depreciation$_{t-1}$/(Depreciation$_{t-1}$ + PPE$_{t-1}$)]/[(Depreciation$_t$/(Depreciation$_t$ + PPE$_t$)]

SGAI = [SGA Expenses$_t$/Sales$_t$]/[SGA Expenses$_{t-1}$/Sales$_{t-1}$]

TATA = Total Accruals$_t$/Total Assets$_t$

VGI = [(Total Long Term Debt$_t$ + Current Liabilities$_t$)/Total Asset$_t$]/[(Total Long Term Debt$_{t-1}$ + Current Liabilities$_{t-1}$)/Total Asset$_{t-1}$]

If the M-score is greater than −1.78, it gives way to a red flag, indicating that the possibility of manipulation occurring in the organization, or it could also indicate a strong likelihood of the firm being a manipulator.

Given the above, FRR is a dummy variable. Specifically, it assumes a value of 1 if the firm's M-score is greater than −1.78; in this case, there is a risk of fraudulent reporting activities. The variable assumed a value of 0 if the firm's M-score is less than −1.78; in this case, there is no\ a risk of fraudulent reporting activities.

3.4 Control Variables

Previous studies (Devarajar et al., 2022; Girau et al., 2019; Mousavi et al., 2022; Razali & Arshad, 2014) have shown that the characteristics of corporate governance have a significant impact on fraudulent financial reporting. Poor corporate governance increases the occurrence of fraud in an organization (Beasley, 1996; Farber, 2005a, 2005b).

Based on these studies, we verify the effects of some corporate governance characteristics to obtain the LR. Specifically, we considered the following as control variables: board independence (hereafter BOARDIND); board size (hereafter BOARDSIZ); CEO duality (hereafter CEODUAL).

Existing corporate governance theories state that BOARDIND as an essential ingredient for achieving statutory board responsibilities and plays a critical role in the supervision and enhancement of corporate reputation while ensuring a strong governance framework (Hoitash, 2011; Hundal, 2017; Jensen, 1993; Yeoh, 2019). Previous studies have shown that a higher percentage of independent directors reduces the likelihood of financial statement fraud (Beasley, 1996; Razali & Arshad, 2014). However, some studies (Devarajar et al., 2022; Shan, 2013) have found no significant association between BOARDIND and corporate fraud.

The literature provided mixed results about the effect of BOARDSIZ on monitoring activities. Some authors (Abbott et al., 2004; Alzoubi & Selamat, 2012; De Andres et al., 2005; Lipton & Lorsch, 1992) have indicated that smaller boards are more effective in monitoring functions. Karamanou and Vafeas (2005) argued that BOARDSIZ that is too small or too large is expected to be ineffective. Other studies (Abbott et al., 2000) have found no effects of BOARDSIZ on the quality of financial reporting. Razali and Arshad (2014) found no association between BOARDSIZ and fraudulent financial reporting.

The CEO's duality role suggests the possibility of a conflict of interest in the decision-making process (Fama & Jensen, 1983). However, some studies (Girau et al., 2019; Shan, 2013) have found no significant association between CEODUAL and corporate fraud.

Given the heterogeneity of the empirical evidence described above, the null hypothesis for these control variables is also formulated.

According to previous studies (Anderson et al., 2004; Carcello & Neal, 2000), BOARDIND was measured as the number of independent directors to the board size.

BOARDSIZ was measured as the number of directors on board according to previous studies (Allegrini & Greco, 2013; Anderson et al., 2004; DeFond & Francis, 2005; Raghunandan & Rama, 2007).

According to previous studies (Abbott et al., 2003; Michelon & Parbonetti, 2012; Tsui et al., 2001), CEODUAL was considered a dummy variable that assumes a value of 1 if CEO is also the chairman of the board, and 0 otherwise.

Finally, we include as a control variable firms' localization (hereafter referred to as NORTH, CENTER, SOUTH), and industry (hereafter IND).

3.5 Model

We examine the hypothesized relations using the following regression model:

$$\text{LR} = \alpha_0 + \alpha_1 * \text{FFR} + \alpha_2 * \text{BOARDIND} + \alpha_3 * \text{BOARDSIZ} + \alpha_4 * \text{CEODUAL}$$
$$+\alpha_5 * \text{NORTH} + \alpha_6 * \text{CENTER} + \alpha_7 * \text{SOUTH} + \alpha_8 * \text{IND} + \text{Error}$$

where LR dummy variable with a value of 1 if the firm has obtained the LR, and 0 otherwise.

FRR dummy value with a value of 1 if the firm is in the grey zones or distress zones and/or if its M-score is greater than −2.22, and 0 otherwise.

BOARDIND the number of independent directors to the board size.

BOARDSIZ the number of directors on the board.

CEODUAL dummy variable that assumes a value of 1 if CEO is also the chairman of the board, and 0 otherwise.

NORTH dummy variable with a value of 1 if the firm has headquarters in the north area, and 0 otherwise.

CENTER dummy variable with a value of 1 if the firm has headquarters in the center area, and 0 otherwise.

SOUTH dummy variable with a value of 1 if the firm has headquarters in the south area, and 0 otherwise.

IND dummy variable for each industry with a value of 1 if the firm belongs to the specific industry, and 0 otherwise.

4 Statistics, Results, and Discussion

4.1 Descriptive Statistics

The initial sample includes firms listed on the Italian Stock Exchange with 2024 financial statements in the AIDA database. The preliminary sample comprised 285 firms. Companies operating in the banking and insurance sectors, as well as holding companies, were excluded because of their specific accounting and regulatory characteristics. Furthermore, additional firms were removed from the dataset due to missing information related to the explanatory or control variables. The final sample consisted of 218 firms.

In 2024, 16% of the sample (34 firms) obtained an LR. Similarly, 16% of the firms (34 firms) reported an M-score greater than −1.78, suggesting the potential presence of earnings manipulation or, at least, a high likelihood of classification as potential manipulators according to Beneish's model.

Regarding geographical distribution, 72% of the firms (158 firms) are located in Northern Italy, 22% in the Central regions, and 6% in the South.

Information on industry classification is reported in Table 1.

Table 1 shows that 34.86% of the sample operates in the "Manufacturing" industry, followed by the "Information and communication services" with 9.27% of the sample, "Professional, scientific, and technical activities" with 16.51% of the sample, and "Wholesale and retail trade" with 10.09% of the sample.

Table 1 Firm industry

Industry	Firms	%
Manufacturing	76	34.86%
Electricity and gas supply	6	2.75%
Water supply, sewerage, and waste management	2	0.92%
Building	11	5.05%
Wholesale and retail trade	22	10.09%
Transportation and warehousing	4	1.83%
Accommodation and food services	1	0.46%
Information and communication services (ICT)	42	19.27%
Real estate activities	6	2.75%
Professional, scientific, and technical activities	36	16.51%
Rentals, travel agencies, and business support services	9	4.13%
Education	1	0.46%
Artistic, sports, and entertainment activities	2	0.92%
	218	**100%**

Table 2 Board size and board independence

	Board size	Board independence (%)
Average	8	32.75%
Median	7	30.00%
Minimum	2	0.00%
Maximum	18	91.67%

Table 3 LR and M-score

	Firms	%
Firms with a legality rating and a high probability of accounting manipulation	6	18%
Firms with legality ratings and a low probability of accounting manipulation	28	82%
Total	**34**	**100%**

Table 2 reports data about the board of directors' size and board independence.

The CEO duality analysis shows that in 42% of the sample (91 firms), the CEO is also the chairman of the board.

By comparing firms with LR and those with an M-score greater than −1.78 (Table 3), 18% of the sample (6 firms on 34) despite having the LR presents a high risk of FFR activities.

4.2 *Regression Analysis and Results*

The analysis employs a logistic regression model (Table 4), which is an appropriate choice given that the dependent variable, LR, is dichotomous. The model exhibits a pseudo-R-squared value of 0.14, which falls within the range defined by the

Table 4 Results of the regression analysis

	B	S.E.	Wald	gl	Sign.
M-score is greater than −1.78	0.120	0.555	0.047	1	0.829
Board size	−0.021	0.083	0.064	1	0.800
Board independence (%)	−0.003	0.012	0.061	1	0.805
CEO duality	−0.315	0.444	0.504	1	0.478
Center	−1244	0.832	2233	1	0.135
North	−1113	0.725	2360	1	0.124
Manufacturing sector	19.584	28420.394	0.000	1	0.999
Supply of electricity, gas, steam, and air conditioning	0.224	32806.971	0.000	1	1000
Water supply, sewerage networks, and waste management services	−0.579	39556.820	0.000	1	1000
Constructions	20.663	28420.394	0.000	1	0.999
Wholesale and retail trade	19.840	28420.394	0.000	1	0.999
Transportation and storage	0.083	34788.630	0.000	1	1000
Accommodation and food service activities	42.445	49225.944	0.000	1	0.999
Information and communication services (ICT)	19.959	28420.394	0.000	1	0.999
Real estate activities	−0.053	32799.729	0.000	1	1000
Professional, scientific, and technical activities	17.594	28420.394	0.000	1	1000
Administrative and support service activities	20.043	28420.394	0.000	1	0.999
Education	0.199	49225.945	0.000	1	1000
Constant	−19.807	28420.394	0.000	1	0.999

Cox and Snell R-squared (0.111) and the Nagelkerke *R*-squared (0.191), indicating a satisfactory level of explanatory power. Furthermore, the Hosmer–Lemeshow goodness-of-fit test was not statistically significant ($p = 0.139$), suggesting that the model provided an adequate fit to the observed data.

The absence of a statistically significant relationship between the dependent variable LR and the explanatory variable FRR leads to the nonrejection of the null hypothesis. This evidence suggests that the parameters currently adopted for LR attribution may not fully encompass the complex and multidimensional nature of illicit or irregular practices within firms. In this sense, the criteria used to define LR appear to be only partially effective in capturing the underlying dynamics of corporate misconduct. Furthermore, the data reveal that the LR attribution process remains largely unrelated to the governance variables that significantly affect FRR, highlighting a possible misalignment between the mechanisms driving risk attribution and those influencing the quality and reliability of financial reporting. This finding raises important questions regarding the adequacy of existing models in reflecting the interplay between governance structures, ethical conduct, and risk assessment within organizations.

5 Conclusions

This study builds on the distinction between formal legality and substantive corporate integrity. While the LR captures compliance with legal and organizational requirements, the literature on corporate governance (Beasley, 1996; Farber, 2005a, 2005b; Saona et al., 2020) shows that effective internal monitoring mechanisms are key in reducing fraudulent financial reporting. At the same time, fraud detection research (Beneish, 1999; Serrano-Cinca et al., 2019; Shahana et al., 2023) emphasizes the role of quantitative financial indicators in identifying manipulation. By linking these streams, this study tests whether a formal, compliance-based certification, such as the LR, can act as a proxy for financial reporting integrity.

Using a sample of 218 nonfinancial firms listed on the Italian Stock Exchange in 2024 and applying the Beneish M-Score model as an established indicator of potential earnings manipulation, this study explored whether the possession of the LR is statistically associated with a lower probability of financial statement fraud. The empirical evidence does not support this hypothesis. Approximately 18% of firms awarded an LR show a high risk of manipulation. The lack of association between LR and FFR highlights a structural gap between legality-based certification systems and data-driven fraud detection mechanisms, reinforcing the central role of internal governance quality and financial indicators in explaining earnings manipulation.

These findings offer several important insights. First, they suggest that the LR, as currently designed, captures formal compliance with legal and ethical standards but not substantive financial integrity. The rating's criteria emphasize the absence of criminal convictions and the adoption of compliance-oriented governance practices. However, they do not incorporate metrics capable of detecting aggressive accounting or earnings manipulation behaviors. Consequently, the LR appears to function more as a symbolic assurance mechanism, demonstrating conformity with procedural requirements, rather than as a diagnostic tool for identifying deeper governance or ethical vulnerabilities.

Second, the absence of significant effects from traditional corporate governance variables reinforces the notion that the LR operates largely outside the domain of internal monitoring effectiveness. This is particularly noteworthy given that prior research consistently identified governance quality as a moderating factor in reducing fraud and earnings manipulation (Beasley, 1996; Farber, 2005a, 2005b; Saona et al., 2020). The lack of alignment between LR and governance-related mechanisms raises questions about whether LR sufficiently reflects the internal structures that safeguard transparency and accountability.

From a theoretical standpoint, this research contributes to the emerging literature at the intersection of legality assessment, corporate governance, and financial reporting quality (Bokhari et al., 2023; Velte, 2023). It extends the debate on how institutional certification systems can effectively signal firms' actual behavioral integrity. The findings suggest that the legality/integrity gap remains a significant challenge: firms may appear compliant with external legality frameworks while engaging in internal opportunistic financial reporting practices. This dynamic underscores the complexity of corporate integrity measurement and the limitations of static compliance-based indicators.

From a policy and regulatory perspective, the results highlight the need for reform and enrichment of the LR framework. The LR could incorporate quantitative financial and governance metrics alongside current qualitative requirements to enhance its capacity as a genuine integrity indicator. Integrating early-warning indicators would allow regulators to detect more nuanced forms of illegality that remain invisible under purely compliance-oriented assessments. Moreover, coordination between the ICA and financial supervisory bodies could foster a multidimensional model of legality evaluation, blending legal compliance, ethical governance, and financial transparency into a unified framework.

This study suggests that stakeholders should not rely solely on legality ratings as proxies for corporate ethical behavior or financial soundness. Instead, the LR should be interpreted as a component of a broader due diligence process, complemented by financial analysis and continuous monitoring mechanisms.

Nevertheless, this study has certain limitations that should be acknowledged. The analysis is limited to one country, 1 year, and listed companies, which may restrict the generalizability of the results. Moreover, the Beneish M-Score is a probabilistic model and cannot definitively identify fraudulent reporting, although it is widely used. Future studies could extend the temporal coverage, employ panel data to analyze trends over time, or adopt machine learning-based fraud detection models to test the robustness of these findings. Comparative cross-country research could also investigate whether analogous legality certification systems in other jurisdictions exhibit similar limitations. The extended analysis of non-listed companies could provide useful information to identify other relevant characteristics.

In conclusion, while the LR represents a commendable institutional innovation for promoting ethical business conduct and reinforcing the rule of law, its current configuration does not adequately capture the multifaceted and covert nature of financial fraud. Strengthening the LR through the integration of financial, behavioral, and governance-based indicators could transform it from a mere formal compliance instrument into a comprehensive and dynamic tool of corporate integrity assessment. Such a reform would not only align the LR more closely with the principles of Goal 16 of the UN 2030 Agenda but would also contribute to the creation of a more transparent, responsible, and sustainable economic ecosystem in Italy and beyond.

References

Abbott, L. J., Park, J., & Parker, S. (2000). The effects of audit committee activity and independence on corporate fraud. *Managerial Finance, 26*(11), 55–67.

Abbott, L. J., Parker, S., Peters, G. F., & Raghunandan, K. (2003). The association between audit committee characteristics and audit fees. *Auditing: A Journal of Practice and Theory, 22*(2), 17–32.

Abbott, L. J., Parker, S., & Peters, G. F. (2004). Audit committee characteristics and restatements. *Auditing: A Journal of Practice and Theory, 23*(1), 69–87.

Allegrini, M., & Greco, G. (2013). Corporate boards, audit committees and voluntary disclosure: Evidence from Italian listed companies. *Journal of Management and Governance, 17*(1), 187–216. https://doi.org/10.1007/s10997-011-9168-3

Alzoubi, E. S. S., & Selamat, M. H. (2012). Proposing conceptual framework for reducing earning management using ownership structure mechanism: Jordanian companies perspective. *Journal of Finance, Accounting and Management, 3*(2), 58.

Anderson, R. C., Mansi, S. A., & Reeb, D. M. (2004). Board characteristics, accounting report integrity, and the cost of debt. *Journal of Accounting and Economics, 37*, 315–342.

Barniv, R., Agarwal, A., & Leach, R. (2002). Predicting bankruptcy resolution. *Journal of Business Finance and Accounting, 29*(3–4), 497–520. https://doi.org/10.1111/1468-5957.00440

Beasley, M. S. (1996). An empirical analysis of the relation between the board of director composition and financial statement fraud. *The Accounting Review, 71*(4), 443–465.

Beasley, M. S., Hermanson, D. R., Carcello, J. V., & Neal, T. L. (2010a). *Fraudulent financial reporting: 1998–2007: An analysis of US public companies*.

Beasley, M. S., Hermanson, D. R., Carcello, J. V., & Neal, T. L. (2010b). *Fraudulent financial reporting: 1998–2007: an analysis of U.S. public companies* (p. 453). Association Sections, Divisions, Boards, Teams.

Beneish, M. D. (1999). The detection of earnings manipulation. *Financial Analysts Journal, 55*(5), 24–36. https://doi.org/10.2469/faj.v55.n5.2296

Bertacchini, F., Magri, C., & Gabrielli, G. (2024). What is in a rating? Exploring the link between the Italian legality rating and earnings management. *Business Strategy and the Environment*, 1494–1509. https://doi.org/10.1002/bse.4059

Bokhari, S. A. A., Ali, M., Albort-Morant, G., Latan, H., de Sousa Jabbour, A. B. L., Ullah, S., et al. (2023). Bridging the gap: The moderating roles of institutional quality and compliance on the link between CSR and financial performance. *Journal of Cleaner Production, 404*, 136897.

Carcello, J. V., & Neal, T. L. (2000). Audit committee composition and auditor reporting. *The Accounting Review, 75*(4), 453–467.

Dalnial, H., Kamaluddin, A., Sanusi, Z. M., & Khairuddin, K. S. (2014). Accountability in financial reporting: Detecting fraudulent firms. *Procedia - Social and Behavioral Sciences, 145*, 61–69. https://doi.org/10.1016/j.sbspro.2014.06.011

De Andres, P., Azofra, V., & Lopez, F. (2005). Corporate boards in OECD countries: Size, composition, functioning and effectiveness. *Corporate Governance: An International Review, 13*(2), 197–210. https://doi.org/10.1111/j.1467-8683.2005.00418.x

DeFond, M. L., & Francis, J. R. (2005). Audit research after Sarbanes–Oxley. *Auditing: A Journal of Practice and Theory, 24*, 5–30.

Devarajar, M., Shaharudin, M. S., Pitchay, A. A., Haron, H., & Ganesan, Y. (2022). Corporate governance and fraudulent financial reporting among Malaysian public listed companies. *International Journal of Law, Government and Communication, 7*(29), 81–95. https://doi.org/10.35631/ijlgc.729007

Dutzi, A. a., & Rausch, B. (2016). Earnings management before Bankruptcy: A review of the literature. *Journal of Accounting and Auditing: Research and Practice, 2016*, 1–21. https://doi.org/10.5171/2016.245891

Elliott, R. K., & Willingham, J. J. (1980). *Management fraud: Detection and deterrence*. Petrocelli Books.

Fama, E., & Jensen, M. (1983). Agency problems and residual claims. *Journal of Law and Economics, 26*(2), 327–349.

Farber, D. B. (2005a). Restoring trust after fraud: Does corporate governance matter? *The Accounting Review, 80*(2), 539–561. https://doi.org/10.2308/accr.2005.80.2.539

Farber, D. B. (2005b). Restoring trust after fraud: Does corporate governance matter? *The Accounting Review, 80*(2), 539–561.

Franceschetti, B. M., Koschtial, C., & Felden, C. (2013). Break-up analysis: A method to regain trust in business transactions. In D. Mancini, E. Vaassen, & R. Dameri (Eds.), *Accounting information systems for decision making. Lecture notes in information systems and organisation* (Vol. 3). Springer. https://doi.org/10.1007/978-3-642-35761-9_12

Girau, E. A., Ag Kee, D. K. H., Bujang, I., & Jidwin, A. P. (2019). The empirical analysis of corporate fraud and corporate governance in Malaysia. *The Business and Management Review, 10*(3), 1–7.

Hernandez Aros, L., Sarmiento Morales, J. J., & Moreno Hernández, J. J. (2026). Structured framework for dealing with types of financial statement fraud, integrating common modalities, variables, strategies, and patterns. *Journal of Risk and Financial Management, 19*(2), 157.

Hoitash, U. (2011). Should independent board members with social ties to management disqualify themselves from serving on the board? *Journal of Business Ethics, 99*(3), 399–423. https://doi.org/10.1007/s10551-010-0660-5

Hundal, S. (2017). Multiple directorships of corporate boards and firm performance in India. *Corporate Ownership and Control, 14*(4), 150–164. https://doi.org/10.22495/cocv14i4art13

Jensen, M. C. (1993). The modern industrial revolution, exit, and the failure of internal control system. *Journal of Finance, XLVIII*(July), 831–880.

Karamanou, I., & Vafeas, N. (2005). The association between corporate boards, audit committees, and management earnings forecasts: An empirical analysis. *Journal of Accounting Research, 43*(3), 453–486. https://doi.org/10.1111/j.1475-679X.2005.00177.x

Lipton, M., & Lorsch, J. W. (1992). A modest proposal for improved corporate governance. *The Business Lawyer*, 59–77.

Meckling, W. H., & Jensen, M. C. (1976). Theory of firm. Managerial behavior, agency costs and ownership structure. *Journal of Financial Economics, 3*(4), 305–360.

Michelon, G., & Parbonetti, A. (2012). The effect of corporate governance on sustainability disclosure. *Journal of Management and Governance, 16*(3), 477–509. https://doi.org/10.1007/s10997-010-9160-3

Mousavi, M., Zimon, G., Salehi, M. a., & Stępnicka, N. (2022). The effect of corporate governance structure on fraud and money laundering. *Risks, 10*(9), 1–25. https://doi.org/10.3390/risks10090176

Nicolò, D., Shahana, T., Lavanya, V., Rashid, A., Bernate-valbuena, M., Saona, P., Altman, E. I., et al. (2023). Labor tax avoidance and its determinants: The case of mafia firms in Italy. *European Management Review, 190*(2), 184–192. https://doi.org/10.1016/j.sbspro.2014.06.032

Raghunandan, K., & Rama, D. V. (2007). Determinants of audit committee diligence. *Accounting Horizons., 21*(3), 265–279.

Razali, W. A. A. W. M., & Arshad, R. (2014). Disclosure of corporate governance structure and the likelihood of fraudulent financial reporting. *Procedia - Social and Behavioral Sciences, 145*, 243–253. https://doi.org/10.1016/j.sbspro.2014.06.032

Saona, P., Muro, L., & Alvarado, M. (2020). How do the ownership structure and board of directors' features impact earnings management? The Spanish case. *Journal of International Financial Management and Accounting, 31*(1), 98–133.

Serrano-Cinca, C., Gutiérrez-Nieto, B., & Bernate-Valbuena, M. (2019). The use of accounting anomalies indicators to predict business failure. *European Management Journal, 37*(3), 353–375.

Shahana, T., Lavanya, V., & Rashid, A. (2023). State of the art in financial statement fraud detection: A systematic review. *Technological Forecasting and Social Change, 192*(May 2022).

Shan, Y. G. (2013). Can internal governance mechanisms prevent asset appropriation? Examination of type I tunneling in China. *Corporate Governance: An International Review, 21*(3), 225–241. https://doi.org/10.1111/corg.12022

Spathis, C. T. (2002). Detecting false financial statements using published data: Some evidence from Greece. *Managerial Auditing Journal, 17*(4), 179–191. https://doi.org/10.1108/02686900210424321

Tsui, J., Jaggi, B., & Gul, F. (2001). CEO domination, discretionary accruals and audit fees. *Journal of Accounting, Auditing, and Finance, Summer*, 189–203.

Velte, P. (2023). The link between corporate governance and corporate financial misconduct. A review of archival studies and implications for future research. *Management Review Quarterly, 73*(1), 353–411.

Wallace, W. A. (1995). *Auditing*. South-Western College Publishing.

Xu, C. (2021), *Real earnings management in bankrupt firms* (pp. 22–38). December 2020. https://doi.org/10.1002/jcaf.22483.

Yeoh, P. (2019). Corporate governance codes in the UK: The risk of over-reliance. *Business Law Review, 40*, 19.

The Effects of Financial and Nonfinancial Indicators on Mafia-Related Dissolution: An Analysis of Italian Municipalities

Eleonora Cardillo, Angela Maria Greco, and Mariastella Messina

Abstract The dissolution of Italian municipalities due to mafia infiltration represents an extraordinary measure to protect administrative legality and preserve the democratic principles of public action. In line with Goal 16 of the United Nations 2030 Agenda, this study analyzes the association between dissolutions due to mafia-related crimes and a series of financial, nonfinancial, and contextual indicators. The analysis, conducted on a sample of 745 Italian municipalities with over 15,000 inhabitants in the 3-year period 2019–2021, uses a linear regression model to identify the determinants of the phenomenon. The results highlight a significant link between dissolution and the institution's structural deficits, as well as the influence of factors related to staff composition and socioeconomic conditions.

1 Introduction

Goal 16 of the United Nations 2030 Agenda calls for building fair, accountable, and transparent institutions at all levels of government. Institutional sustainability cannot be reduced solely to administrative efficiency or financial soundness; it must also include the public entity's ability to operate within an ethical and legal framework. The importance of Goal 16 is also evident in Italian legislation, which provides for the dissolution of municipalities in the event of serious cases of infiltration. However, dissolution, while representing an emergency response to a pathological situation, raises questions regarding the financial and nonfinancial factors, as well as the contextual factors, that can identify or predict infiltration itself. In public administration, anti-corruption policies and control processes represent a relevant area of investigation for addressing institutional and sociopolitical aspects, as well as accounting practices. Studies of corruption at the local level have highlighted that the presence of weak and inefficient institutions contributes to increasing the

E. Cardillo · A. M. Greco · M. Messina (✉)
Department of Economics and Business, University of Catania, Catania, Italy
e-mail: eleonora.cardillo@unict.it; angelamaria.greco@unict.it; mariastella.messina@unict.it

R. Cellini et al. (eds.), *Cultural, Social, and Political Participation in the Internet Era*, Contributions to Economics, https://doi.org/10.1007/978-3-032-33072-7_10

negative effects of corruption (Dimant & Tosato, 2018; Mohamadi et al., 2017). Since public resources can be misused, promoting good local governance becomes a strategic lever for reducing the degree of corruption in the behavior of public officials (Arifin et al., 2015; Graycar & Villa, 2011).

The study aims to explore the effects of financial, nonfinancial, and contextual indicators on the dissolution of mafia-related entities. Specifically, financial indicators are primarily represented by structural deficit parameters. Nonfinancial indicators refer to the internal size of the municipality and consider data relating to staff turnover, gender, and education of employees and managers, length of service, age, and political mandate. Contextual data refers to the resident population and its per capita taxable income.

The statistical analysis was conducted on a sample of 745 Italian municipalities with more than 15,000 inhabitants in the period 2019–2021.

The results show that the intertwining of financial fragility, sociocultural factors of public employees/managers, and the socioeconomic context impacts the actions of criminal organizations within local authorities.

The added value of this study lies in its adoption of an integrated and multidimensional approach to the phenomenon of mafia infiltration in Italian municipalities (Daniele & Geys, 2015; Mastrorocco & Di Cataldo, 2021). In particular, the contribution is twofold: on the one hand, it provides empirical evidence confirming the role of structural deficits and socioeconomic conditions as signals of vulnerability (Padovani et al., 2024); on the other hand, it introduces innovative findings on nonfinancial factors, showing that even qualified and highly experienced personnel may facilitate illicit dynamics, highlighting the role of so-called "invisible facilitators." This leads to a predictive and preventive perspective that enriches the academic debate and provides practical tools for monitoring and governing local administrations.

The chapter is structured as follows: Sect. 2 introduces the topic of fair, accountable, and transparent institutions; Sect. 3 examines the regulatory aspects and literature on municipal dissolutions due to mafia infiltration; Sect. 4 presents the hypotheses; Sect. 5 describes the methodology and model used; Sect. 6 analyzes the data and results obtained; and, finally, Sect. 7 highlights the chapter's conclusions.

2 Fair, Accountable, and Transparent Institutions

Several studies (Veltri et al., 2023) identify corruption as a key challenge within Sustainable Development Goal 16, emphasizing its multidimensional and interdisciplinary nature. Goal 16, "*Peace, justice and strong institutions*," promotes the rule of law at both national and international levels, ensuring access to justice while fostering accountable, inclusive, and transparent institutions (Goetz & Jenkins, 2016; Vimercati, 2022). Achieving this goal requires combating crime and mafia-type organizations, which significantly hinder economic growth and sustainable development. In contexts where corruption and organized crime generate severe institutional dysfunction, profound social and economic instability emerges.

The academic literature has devoted considerable attention to Goal 16. For instance, Hope (2020) analyzes the target of substantially reducing corruption and bribery in all their forms, proposing indicators and policy strategies to improve performance. Central to these efforts is the promotion of transparency, which helps curb antisocial behavior and supports impartial administrative action (Singh, 2021). However, mafia-related activities and corruption are complex, pervasive phenomena that are difficult to regulate due to their deeply embedded territorial dimensions (Ahen, 2022).

Consequently, effective responses require coordinated institutional action and governance mechanisms capable of detecting and addressing corruption and organized crime (Di Gennaro & Aurilia, 2022). In this vein, Mathew et al. (2025) examine the relationship between white-collar crime and SDG 16, highlighting its societal impacts and proposing measures such as strengthening regulatory frameworks and enhancing transparency and accountability. Ultimately, addressing corruption demands a comprehensive understanding of its roots and systemic effects, enabling stakeholders to adopt proactive, preventive, and transformative interventions rather than merely reactive approaches (Ahen, 2022; Cincimino et al., 2024).

3 The Dissolution of Municipalities Due to Mafia

Goal 16 aligns with existing Italian legislation, particularly Article 143 of the Consolidated Law on Local Authorities (TUEL—Legislative Decree 267/2000), which provides for the dissolution of municipal or provincial governments in cases of serious organized crime infiltration. This measure functions as an extraordinary preventive tool to safeguard legality, administrative transparency, and constitutional principles. Dissolution may be enacted by the Council of Ministers, upon proposal of the Minister of the Interior, when concrete, consistent, and significant evidence demonstrates direct or indirect links between local officials and mafia-type organizations, or forms of influence that compromise institutional integrity. The procedure requires a thorough investigation and well-substantiated reasoning based on objective evidence. Following dissolution, an extraordinary commission assumes administrative control for 18 months, extendable by 6 months, with the aim of restoring legality and transparency.

The literature on dissolution due to mafia infiltration has progressively expanded, adopting multidisciplinary perspectives ranging from accounting and financial analysis to organizational analysis, tracing the economic, political, and local governance effects. Existing studies can be traced back to three main lines of investigation: (1) the identification of anomalous accounting and financial patterns in dissolved municipalities, often with predictive or diagnostic purposes; (2) the analysis of the impact of mafia infiltration and dissolution on public spending processes, procurement and the composition of the political class; (3) the in-depth analysis of the organizational aspects and internal control mechanisms of local authorities exposed to the phenomenon.

Within the first strand, several studies have documented recurring accounting patterns in municipalities dissolved for mafia reasons. Eboli et al. (2021) find a systematic accumulation of payment and collection arrears, a contraction in capital expenditure, and low levels of debt, thus outlining an anomalous financial profile. Iezzi and Pauselli (2025) built predictive models to prevent the risk of infiltration. The results highlighted that municipalities in the periods preceding dissolution tend to experience higher operating costs, lower spending on education and social services, budgetary rigidity, and an inappropriate allocation of public funds, with a concentration in sensitive sectors such as construction and waste management.

The second strand includes studies that analyze the influence of mafia infiltration on public spending and procurement. Barone and Narciso (2015) and Ravenda et al. (2020) highlight how the presence of mafia alters resource allocation mechanisms, increasing corruption and inefficiencies. Daniele and Geys (2015) highlight that dissolution also produces significant effects on the selection of the political class and on the composition of spending, which is more oriented toward construction and waste, rather than education, transport, and security. Similar results are reported by Mastrorocco and Di Cataldo (2021), who confirm the impact of infiltrations on the allocation of resources in the budget and on financial planning capacity.

The third strand analyzes organizational aspects and internal control systems. Guarini et al. (2022), given the fragmentation of internal control activities in Italian municipalities, propose a framework for redesigning the internal control system, with a view to fully integrating administrative processes, information, and risk management. Monteduro et al. (2024) found that municipalities surrounded by a higher percentage of corrupt municipalities tended to be more exposed to corruption. Furthermore, the probability of engaging in corruption was significantly higher in municipalities with a weak organizational capacity to resist the spread of corruption. Daniele and Galletta (2015) show how the effects of dissolution can extend to neighboring municipalities, where there is a contraction in public investment due to fears of increased controls, suggesting an indirect but significant effect on the local administrative context.

In summary, the literature highlights how dissolution for mafia-related reasons produces profound effects not only on the political-administrative level but also on the accounting, organizational, and financial systems of local authorities. An analysis of the effects of special administration cannot ignore the investigation of accounting and governance aspects, which, when properly interpreted, can serve as tools for safeguarding administrative integrity and rebuilding institutional trust in areas affected by mafia infiltration.

To this end, the study aims to statistically investigate the association between the dissolution of Italian municipalities for mafia-related reasons and the presence of structural deficits, nonfinancial factors, and contextual factors, with the aim of identifying useful indicators that can provide further interpretations of the dissolution process and which can be leveraged to prevent or manage corrupt practices.

4 Hypothesis Development

4.1 *Dissolution for Mafia and Financial Indicators*

The impact of a financial deficit on the risk of corruption, and consequently on the potential for criminal infiltration in local government, has received considerable attention in the literature. Studies predominantly highlight the detrimental effects of mafia infiltration and corruption phenomena on the financial structure of local authorities. Dalla Chiesa (2014) provides a detailed account of how mafia infiltration undermines governance and accounting procedures, often resulting in structural deficits due to excessive debt levels, unregulated expenditure, and instances of misappropriation. Ravenda et al. (2020) reveal that mafia infiltration is associated with greater cost overruns in public procurement contracts, signaling inefficiencies and financial imbalances linked to corrupt mechanisms. Occhiuzzi (2020) underscores that mafia infiltration leads to administrative dysfunctions, including irregularities in financial transactions and inefficiencies in public service delivery. Eboli et al. (2021) emphasize that criminal networks not only engender inefficient management but also disrupt standard financial planning and control processes. Research consistently shows that mafia infiltration impairs governance quality, generating structural deficits, particularly through reduced revenue collection, elevated costs, and diminished accountability. Dagnes et al. (2020), focusing on three northwestern Italian regions, demonstrate that "mafiosi" are primarily business-oriented and occupy varied positions within networks facilitating illegal exchanges. The distortions induced by mafia processes impose substantial aggregate and collective costs, manifesting as inefficient resource allocation, curtailed economic innovation, and restricted market access. Daniele and Giommoni (2021) find that budget constraints may prompt local authorities to curtail spending, thereby reducing their exposure to corruption. Padovani et al. (2024) suggest that municipalities at higher risk of mafia contamination exhibit more severe structural deficits. Few contributions have examined the role of accounting values in predicting or detecting corruption-related phenomena (Arifin et al., 2015; Paterson et al., 2019). Some studies (Funk & Owen, 2020) propose that future research should analyze irregularities stemming from mismanagement in municipalities, developing vulnerability frameworks through verification systems to uncover corrupt practices.

In line with the foregoing, the first hypothesis is formulated as follows:

H1: There is a positive association between the dissolution for mafia of Italian municipalities and their structural financial deficit situation.

4.2 *Dissolution for Mafia and Nonfinancial Indicators*

Beyond traditional financial indicators, the literature on local authorities and organized crime has emphasized the importance of socioinstitutional nonfinancial variables in explaining the vulnerability of local governments to mafia infiltration (Marasabessy et al., 2022; Onyango, 2024; Schepisi et al., 2023; Travaglino & Abrams, 2019; Yeboah-Assiamah et al., 2016). These include variables related to employee/manager characteristics (training, gender, age, turnover) and political factors (political turnover). Regarding training, Akbar and Vujić (2014) highlight the importance for multinational corporations of investing in manager training to counter corrupt behaviors through cultural responses, and for governments to identify public policies that focus not on hierarchies but on empowerment and transparency. The research further underscores the need to develop anti-corruption education and training programs for both public and private sector managers. For Hauser (2019), regular employee training is considered one of the most effective methods for preventing corruption; the results of the empirical analysis conducted on business professionals demonstrate that higher training levels are positively correlated with the probability of rejecting corruption. Pliscoff Varas and Lagos Machuca (2021) present the results of questionnaires administered to participants in ethical training workshops for central and local government employees in Chile. The findings indicate that, following the workshops, improvements in ethical frameworks were observed among participants, with particularly significant positive effects on managerial aspects for women and newly hired public sector employees.

Several contributions highlight the ability of mafia-type organizations to exert control by appropriating the cultural values of territories and persuading citizens to represent them (Schepisi et al., 2023; Travaglino & Abrams, 2019). Thus, attitudes and normative knowledge of the phenomenon carry weight in relation to such processes, and counteraction measures should aim at targeted and effective legal training interventions. For Debski et al. (2018), culture is an important dimension to consider when analyzing the relationship between female participation in society and corruption, as omitting cultural characteristics may produce a spurious correlation between increased female participation rates alone and reduced corruption levels. Alatas et al. (2009) analyze data collected in Australia, India, Indonesia, and Singapore to highlight gender differences in behavior toward a common corruption problem. The authors show that, while women in Australia are less tolerant of corruption than men, no significant gender differences are observed in India, Indonesia, and Singapore. Consequently, the results suggest that gender differences highlighted in prior studies may not be universal but rather strongly influenced by the reference cultural context.

Regarding gender, Frank et al. (2011) argue that the nexus between gender and corruption can be analyzed from three perspectives. First, gender may play a role in understanding corrupt behavior; differences between men and women could be observed in their propensity to give and receive bribes and to engage in corrupt reciprocity networks. For instance, based on interviews with taxi drivers in Colombia, Lambsdorff and Fink (2006) find that female public transport police officers appear more difficult to corrupt. Second, the effects of corruption on the policy objective of improving gender equality could be examined. As with other goals and reforms, gender policies can evidently be undermined by certain types of corruption; thus, identifying and addressing these aspects can enhance the effectiveness of gender policies. Third, some facets of corruption may affect victims differently by gender. Men may experience corruption differently from women; identifying who is more vulnerable to specific aspects of corruption can be useful for designing countermeasures (Nyamu-Musembi, 2007). Dollar et al. (2001) and Swamy et al. (2001) demonstrate that women are less involved in corruption cases and less tolerant of corruption. Cross-national data show that corruption is less severe where women hold a greater share of parliamentary seats and top government bureaucracy positions and represent a larger portion of the workforce. Women, along with older and less affluent individuals, exhibit greater aversion to corrupt behaviors (Gatti et al., 2003). The study by Decarolis et al. (2023) examines the correlation between gender and bureaucratic corruption in Italian and Chinese public contexts, reporting that women are less likely to be investigated for corruption than men. Pessa et al. (2025) conduct a study on selected political scandals in Brazil and Spain that addresses gender differences in corruption networks. The research finds that men are more likely to be involved in multiple scandals than women, and moreover, scandals predominantly involving women are quite rare.

Concerning age, Zhang et al. (2019), using data from a survey of Chinese government employees, found that corruptibility decreases significantly with increasing age. Zhang et al. (2025) conducted a survey of Taiwanese public employees, with results revealing that corruptibility decreases significantly with age. Abbink (2004), assuming that for the German federal government regular staff turnover represents a preventive measure against corruption in public administration, analyzes the effects of such a policy and concludes that it contributes significantly to reducing corruption levels and the frequency of inefficient decisions attributable to corrupt practices.

Finally, regarding political turnover, that is, the continuity or discontinuity of local governments' political orientation over time, it has received attention in relation to infiltration risk. The literature (Golden & Picci, 2005; Rose-Ackerman, 1999; Treisman, 2000) has emphasized how prolonged control by the same party or political alignment can reduce the effectiveness of accountability mechanisms, fostering opaque practices, low transparency, and reduced political alternation. In municipalities subject to dissolution for mafia, such political continuity is often accompanied by the entrenchment of informal networks and the weakening of institutional controls. Conversely, political discontinuity, especially if accompanied by turnover in top figures (e.g., the mayor), can constitute a breaking point with prior collusive practices and an opportunity for administrative renewal.

In line with the foregoing, the second hypothesis is formulated as follows:

H2: There is a negative association between the dissolution for mafia of Italian municipalities and nonfinancial indicators.

4.3 Dissolution for Mafia and Contextual Indicators

In the Italian context, the relationship between mafia, per-capita income, and population is crucial for understanding managerial shortcomings or anomalous mechanisms in public action.

Regarding resident population, larger size and organizational complexity of municipalities typically hinder oversight of public resource use and facilitate opaque behaviors. Population growth, particularly in urban or high-density areas, generates increasing demand for essential public services, such as infrastructure, healthcare, education, and transportation, that often exceeds the administrative and fiscal capacity of local authorities. In such settings, inefficiencies in public spending management can create spaces of opacity that favor mafia infiltration, especially where control mechanisms are weak. Thus, more articulated and complex administrative management, arising from higher population incidence in a given territory, may be associated with elevated corruption risk (Goel & Nelson, 1998). Recent studies highlight how demographic and territorial fragmentation in Italy heightens corruption risk and inefficiencies in public tenders, elements frequently exploited by criminal organizations for economic gain (Gara et al., 2024).

With reference to a community's socioeconomic welfare level, unethical and nontransparent behaviors diminish in the presence of higher per-capita taxable income. Low per-capita fiscal income often signals a narrow tax base, weak collection capacity, and fragile institutions, all conditions that foster the underground economy and clientelist practices tied to organized crime. In territories marked by low institutional quality and strong mafia presence, difficulties in mobilizing stable fiscal revenues exacerbate structural imbalances and constrain public entities' financial autonomy, intensifying the vicious cycle of administrative inefficiency, corruption, and fiscal pressure. Corruption risk thus decreases in contexts of higher institutional quality and greater community welfare (Dimant & Tosato, 2018; Jetter & Parmeter, 2018).

In line with the foregoing, the third hypothesis is formulated as follows:

H3: There is an association between the dissolution for mafia of Italian municipalities and context variables.

Articulated as:

H3a: There is a positive association between the dissolution for mafia of Italian municipalities and the increase in resident population.

H3b: There is a negative association between the dissolution for mafia of Italian municipalities and the increase in per-capita taxable income.

5 Research Design

5.1 Methodology

To test the hypotheses, a linear regression analysis was conducted. The sample consisted of 745 Italian municipalities with a population greater than 15,000, analyzed over the 3-year period 2019–2021. The choice of sample was justified by the possibility of obtaining more precise data on both cases of mafia-related dissolutions and indicators. The total number of observations was 2235.

5.2 Dependent Variable and Explanatory Variables

The dependent variable, dissolution due to mafia-related events (SPM), is a binary variable that takes the value 1 if the entity under analysis was disbanded due to mafia-related events in the year under analysis and 0 otherwise.

Regarding the financial variable, the entity's structural deficit situation (DEF-STRUCTURAL) was considered. In this regard, in compliance with the provisions of Article 242, paragraphs 1 and 2 of the TUEL, local entities that exhibit serious and incontrovertible financial imbalance, detectable by analyzing eight indicators and exceeding the limits of more than three of the indicators, are in structural deficit. This variable is a binary variable that takes value 1 if the entity exceeded more than three of the established limits in the year under analysis and 0 otherwise.

The nonfinancial variables concern the characteristics of the local entity's employees and managers and data relating to the political component. In particular, the variables analyzed are:

- *Human resource turnover rate* (TURNOVER) is given by the ratio of permanent employees and managerial staff who left work during the year to the total permanent and managerial staff as of December 31 of the year under consideration.
- *Staff feminization rate* (FEMP) is given by the ratio of permanent female employees and managerial staff to the total permanent and managerial staff as of December 31 of the year under consideration.
- *Management feminization rate* (FEMD) is given by the ratio of female managerial staff to the total managerial staff as of December 31 of the year under consideration.
- *Staff with a high school diploma* (FORMP) is given by the ratio of permanent female employees and managerial staff with a high school diploma to the total permanent and managerial staff as of December 31 of the year under consideration.
- *Management personnel with a degree or higher qualification* (FORMD) is calculated as the ratio of management personnel with a degree or higher qualification to the total management personnel as of December 31 of the year in question.
- *Personnel with no more than 20 years of service* (ANZSERV) is calculated as the ratio of permanent employees to management personnel with 20 years or less of service, and permanent employees to management personnel as of December 31 of the year in question.
- *Personnel under 35 years of age* (UNDER35) is calculated as the ratio of permanent employees to management personnel under 35 years of age, and permanent employees to management personnel as of December 31 of the year in question.

- *Political mandate* (POLM): This indicator indicates whether there has been a change in political mandate and therefore in party in the years analyzed. This parameter is a binary variable that takes the value 1 if there was a change in mandate in the year analyzed compared to the previous year and 0 otherwise.
- *Change of mayor* (SINDCAM): This indicator indicates whether there was a change in mayor in the year analyzed compared to the previous year, regardless of political party; this indicator is a binary variable that takes the value 1 if there was a change in mayor in the year analyzed compared to the previous year and 0 otherwise.

Finally, the context variables analyzed are:

- *Population* (POP): Indicates the population resident in the municipality as of January 1 of the year analyzed.
- *Taxable income* per capita (REDP): Given by the ratio between taxable income at the municipal level and the number of inhabitants resident in the municipality in the year analyzed.
- *Geographic location of the institution* (NORTH–CENTER–SOUTH) and the year of observation (2019–2020–2021) were considered as control variables.

5.3 Data Collection

Data for the dependent variable SPM and the explanatory variables POP and REDP were obtained from the ANAC website; data for structural deficit parameters were obtained by accessing the institutional area of the municipal websites and consulting the appendices to the financial statements; data on local authority employees and managers were obtained from the ISTAT website—section "Budget indicators and data on institutional unit personnel"; finally, data on political mandates and mayors were obtained from the OPENDATA website.

5.4 Model

To test the hypotheses, the following model is used:

$$
\begin{aligned}
\mathrm{SMP} = {} & \alpha_0 + \alpha_1 * \mathrm{DEFSTRUCTURAL} + \alpha_2 * \mathrm{TURNOVER} + \alpha_3 * \mathrm{FEMD} \\
& + \alpha_5 * \mathrm{FORMD} + \alpha_7 * \mathrm{ANZSERV} + \alpha_8 * \mathrm{UNDER35} \\
& + \alpha_9 * \mathrm{POLM} + \alpha_{10} * \mathrm{SINDCAM} + \alpha_{11} * \mathrm{POP} + \alpha_{12} * \mathrm{REDP} \\
& + \alpha_{13} * \mathrm{NORTH} + \alpha_{14} * \mathrm{CENTER} + \alpha_{15} * \mathrm{SOUTH} + \alpha_{16} * 2019 \\
& + \alpha_{17} * 2020 + \alpha_{18} * 2021 + \mathrm{Error}.
\end{aligned}
$$

The variables are specified as follows:

- DEFSTRUCTURAL. Dichotomous variable with a value of 1 if the thresholds for more than three of the eight deficit parameters are exceeded, and a value of 0 otherwise.
- TURNOVER. Percentage of employees and managers who left work during the year.
- FEMP. Percentage of female employees and managers.
- FEMD. Percentage of female managers.
- FORMP. Percentage of employees and managers with a high school diploma or higher.
- FORMD. Percentage of managers with a high school diploma or higher.
- ANZSERV. Percentage of employees and managers with less than 20 years of service.
- UNDER35. Percentage of employees and managers under 35 years of age.
- POLM. Dichotomous variable that takes on the value of 1 if there was a change in mandate in the year being analyzed compared to the previous year and the value of 0 otherwise.
- SINDCAM. Dichotomous variable that takes on the value of 1 if in the year analyzed there was a change of mayor compared to the previous year and the value of 0 otherwise.
- POP. Population residents in the municipality as of January 1 of the year under review.
- REDP. Ratio of taxable income at the municipal level to the number of inhabitants resident in the municipality in the year under review.
- NORTH. Dichotomous variable that takes the value 1 if the local authority is in Northern Italy and 0 otherwise.
- CENTER. Dichotomous variable that takes the value 1 if the local authority is in Central Italy and 0 otherwise.
- SOUTH. Dichotomous variable that takes the value 1 if the local authority is in Southern Italy and 0 otherwise.
- 2019. Dichotomous variable that takes the value 1 if the observation year is 2019 and 0 otherwise.
- 2020. Dichotomous variable that takes the value 1 if the observation year is 2020 and 0 otherwise.
- 2021. Dichotomous variable that takes the value 1 if the observation year is 2021 and value 0 otherwise.

6 Data Analysis and Results

6.1 Descriptive Statistics

The sample analyzed is distributed across the country as shown in Fig. 1; the regions that host more than 45% of the analyzed municipalities are Sicily, Puglia, Campania,

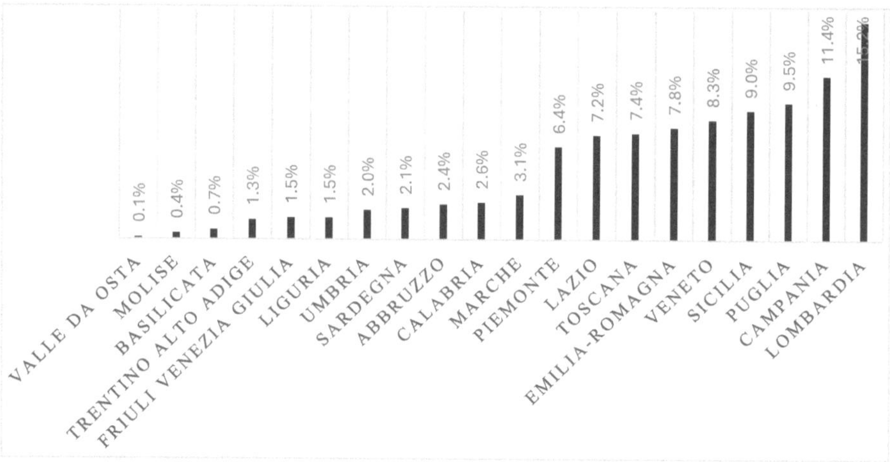

Fig. 1 Sample distribution by region

and Lombardy. The sample is 42% in Northern Italy, 20% in Central Italy, and 38% in the South.

In the 3-year period analyzed (2019–2021), 31 municipalities were affected by the dissolution order for mafia-related reasons; in particular, in 2019, the municipalities involved amounted to 2% of the sample (16 municipalities), in 2020, 0.70% of the sample (5 municipalities), and in 2021, 1% (10 municipalities). The 31 municipalities are all located in Southern Italy. Regarding the DEFSTRUCTURAL financial variable, the data show that 7% of the sample (52 municipalities) were in a structural deficit situation. Analyzing each year, in 2019, 1.9% of the sample (14 municipalities) was in a deficit situation, in 2020, 2.15% of the sample (16 municipalities), and in 2021, 2.95% (22 municipalities).

As shown in Table 1, the average turnover rate for employees and managers was 19% in 2019, 20% in 2020, and 22% in 2021. While not showing significant fluctuations over time, an increasing trend is observed. The average feminization rate for employees and managers was 53% in 2019 and 2020 and 54% in 2021, demonstrating a consistent trend over time. The feminization rate for managers also exhibited a similarly consistent trend, although it remained lower, at 31% in 2019 and 2021 and 30% in 2020. Almost all managers (99% in 2019 and 2020, and 100% in 2021) have a bachelor's degree or higher, and a very high percentage of employees and managers (81% in 2019, 82% in 2020, and 83% in 2021) have a high school diploma or higher. Regarding the average rate of staff with less than 20 years of service, the data show that for 2019, the value was 50%, with an increasing trend in 2020, reaching a rate of 54%, and in 2021, 57%. The percentage of employees and managers under 35 years of age was very low in the 3-year period considered, averaging 3% in 2019, 4% in 2020, and 6% in 2021. The sample analyzed covers municipalities with more than 15,000 inhabitants; the average population over the

Table 1 Average value of nonfinancial and contextual variables

Variable	Average value 2019	2020	2021
TURNOVER	19%	20%	22%
FEMP	53%	53%	54%
FEMD	31%	30%	31%
FORMD	99%	99%	100%
FORMP	81%	82%	83%
ANZSERV	50%	54%	57%
UNDER35	3%	4%	6%
POP	48.150	48.060	47.786
REDP	13.421 €	13.161 €	13.952 €

Table 2 Data relating to the change of mandate and the change of mayor

	2019		2020		2021	
SINDCAM	154	21%	78	10%	75	10%
POLM	123	17%	56	8%	56	8%

3-year period considered was 48,000. The average per capita taxable income also remained constant at €13,500.

Table 2 shows that in 2019, regardless of political party, a change in mayor occurred in 21% of the sample (154 municipalities); this figure decreased to 10% of the sample in the following 2 years. Regarding changes in political mandate, in 2019, this occurred in 17% of the sample (123 municipalities), while it affected 8% in 2020 and 2021.

The Pearson correlation analysis (Table 3) shows that the dependent variable SPM is negatively associated with FEMP ($p < 0.01$), FORMP ($p < 0.05$), UNDER35 ($p < 0.01$), REDP ($p < 0.01$), NORTH ($p < 0.01$), CENTER ($p < 0.01$), and SOUTH ($p < 0.01$). However, there is a positive association between the dependent variable SPM and the financial explanatory variable DEFSTRUCTURAL ($p < 0.01$).

6.2 *Results of the Regression Analysis*

To test the hypotheses, we performed a linear regression analysis. Table 4 shows the results of the analysis.

The data reveals a positive and statistically significant association between SPM and the financial variable DEFSTRUCTURAL ($p < 0.01$). This means that in the event of a mafia-related dissolution, the municipality is found to be in a position of structural deficit. Regarding the association between SPM and nonfinancial variables, there is a positive and statistically significant association with the FORMP variable ($p < 0.01$) and a negative and statistically significant association with the ANZSERV variable ($p < 0.05$). The analysis therefore shows that local authorities dissolved due to mafia-related reasons have a high percentage of permanent employees and managers with a high school diploma or higher. Furthermore, it

Table 3 Pearson correlations

	SPM	DEFSTRUCTURAL	TURNOVER	FEMD	FEMP	FORMD	FORMP	ANZSERV	UNDER35	SINDCAM	POLM	POP	REDP	NORTH	CENTER	SOUTH	2019	2020	2021
DEFSTRUCTURAL	0.087b	–																	
TURNOVER	0.039	0.044[a]	–																
FEMD	−0.005	−0.028	-0.057[a]	–															
FEMP	−0.115[b]	−0.148[b]	−0.146[b]	0.213[b]	–														
FORMD	0.010	0.017	0.014	0.007	0.018	–													
FORMP	−0.053[a]	−0.112[b]	−0.059[b]	0.027	0.365[b]	−0.011	–												
ANZSERV	−0.032	0.020	0.133[b]	−0.044	0.097[b]	−0.039	0.134[b]	–											
UNDER35	−0.077[b]	−0.094[b]	0.242[b]	0.009	0.188[b]	−0.019	0.177[b]	0.171[b]	–										
SINDCAM	0.030	−0.008	0.003	0.033	−0.011	0.030	−0.030	−0.052[a]	−0.049[a]	–									
POLM	0.034	−0.003	0.000	0.032	0.020	0.029	0.000	−0.052[a]	−0.073[b]	0.808[b]	–								
POP	−0.009	−0.007	−0.087[b]	0.061[a]	0.029	0.014	0.016	0.014	−0.028	−0.002	0.014	–							
REDP	−0.177[b]	−0.193[b]	−0.124[b]	0.177[b]	0.697[b]	0.016	0.316[b]	−0.028	0.297[b]	−0.039	−0.004	0.108[b]	–						
NORTH	−0.101[b]	−0.135[b]	−0.078[b]	0.114[b]	0.606[b]	−0.009	0.195[b]	−0.152[b]	0.270[b]	−0.025	−0.003	−0.011	0.741[b]	–					
CENTER	−0.059[b]	−0.064[b]	−0.041	0.031	0.082[b]	−0.019	0.112[b]	0.181[b]	−0.003	0.001	−0.005	0.041	0.048[a]	−0.423[b]	–				
SOUTH	0.151[b]	0.191[b]	0.112[b]	−0.152[b]	−0.684[b]	0.027	−0.290[b]	0.006	−0.272[b]	0.024	0.007	−0.022	−0.793[b]	−0.670[b]	−0.389[b]	–			
2019	0.046[a]	−0.020	−0.097[b]	0.001	−0.029	−0.036	−0.076[b]	−0.174[b]	−0.196[b]	0.142[b]	0.138[b]	0.001	−0.017	0.000	0.000	0.000	–		
2020	−0.043[a]	−0.009	−0.037	−0.012	0.002	−0.031	0.005	0.004	−0.055[b]	−0.067[b]	−0.069[b]	0.000	−0.067[b]	0.000	0.000	0.000	−0.500[b]	–	
2021	−0.003	0.029	0.134[b]	0.011	0.027	0.068[a]	0.072[b]	0.170[b]	0.250[b]	−0.075[b]	−0.069[b]	−0.001	0.085[b]	0.000	0.000	0.000	−0.500[b]	−0.500[b]	–

[a] The correlation is significant at the 0.05 level (two-tailed)
[b] The correlation is significant at the 0.01 level (two-tailed)

Table 4 Regression model—determinants of dissolution due to mafia

Dependent variables: SPM				
Explanatory variables[a]	Expected sign	Coefficient	*t*	Value
(Constant)		0.029	0.602	0.548
DEFSTRUCTURAL	+	0.061	3.355	0.001
TURNOVER	−	−0.005	−0.168	0.867
FEMP	−	−0.020	−0.615	0.539
FEMD	−	0.008	0.799	0.424
FORMD	−	0.010	0.268	0.789
FORMP	−	0.076	2.817	0.005
ANZSERV	−	−0.054	−2.510	0.012
UNDER35	−	−0.067	−0.749	0.454
SINDCAM	−	−0.008	−0.531	0.596
POLM	−	0.010	0.657	0.511
POP	+	5990	0.409	0.682
REDP	−	−4156	−3.102	0.002
CENTER		−0.009	−1.244	0.214
SOUTH		−0.001	−0.087	0.931
2019		0.012	1.961	0.050
2021		0.010	1.647	0.100
R-squared 0.049				
F 4070				
P < 0.01				

[a]The explanatory variable NORTH and the year 2020 variable were automatically excluded

appears that in the event of a dissolution, the percentage of seniority of less than 20 years is lower. Finally, the association between SPM and context variables is negative and statistically significant with the REDP variable ($p < 0.01$). The results therefore show that in municipalities dissolved due to mafia-related crimes, per capita taxable income is lower.

7 Conclusions

The analysis reveals significant results, highlighting critical accounting issues and contextual factors associated with mafia infiltration in the municipalities examined. A first noteworthy finding is the positive association between the dissolution of municipalities due to mafia-related activities and the presence of structural deficits. This confirms our hypothesis linking mafia-related activities to financial imbalances. Therefore, entities experiencing structural deficits may constitute contexts where illicit procedures and activities can flourish (Di Cataldo & Mastrorocco, 2018; Ravenda et al., 2020; Eboli et al., 2021). Consolidated debt situations, a decline in investment spending, and the presence of difficult-to-repay deficits may be indicators not only of poor planning and management but also of the risk of mafia infiltration or corruption (Arifin et al., 2015; Funk & Owen, 2020; Paterson et al., 2019). Regarding nonfinancial variables, the results in some cases show data that are discordant with the hypotheses formulated. Statistical analysis revealed a positive and statistically significant association between the dissolution of municipalities due to mafia involvement and the presence of personnel with a high school diploma or higher qualification. This highlights that regular employee training is not always an effective method to combat the phenomenon (Hauser, 2019).

The results of the analysis therefore do not confirm our hypothesis and lead us to believe that illicit dynamics may also be linked to the participation of structured personnel with adequate training. This reflection reinforces the presence of so-called invisible "*facilitators*" who represent key players in the mafia phenomenon (Allum et al., 2019). Indeed, it is often these qualified individuals who, by combining illegal and legal activities, create illicit profit activities that accompany criminal acts (Mete & Sciarrone, 2017). This area of activity is often developed by public and private sector professionals and by people in positions of responsibility such as managers who, despite operating invisibly, make mafia organizations viable and possible (Allum et al., 2019). The analysis also highlights that municipalities dissolved due to mafia-related issues have a high percentage of personnel with more than 20 years of seniority. This confirms our hypothesis that shorter-serving personnel, likely younger ones, are less likely to suffer or tolerate mafia or illicit activities (Zhang et al., 2025). With respect to context variables, the results reveal a negative and statistically significant association with the variable per capita taxable income. This leads us to affirm that in poorer contexts, and in any case with lower income levels, the mafia infiltrates with the aim of providing easier economic means and creating opportunities for illicit enrichment. The growth in the well-being of a territory and a community therefore constitutes a deterrent to the emergence of mafia activities (Dimant & Tosato, 2018; Jetter & Parmeter, 2018). The results therefore suggest that ineffective or inadequate administrative action can lead to cases of social degradation and a decline in the population's well-being, which becomes fertile ground for criminal organizations. When local institutions act virtuously and responsibly, for example, by creating economic opportunities and offering adequate services, they not only improve their administrative management but also foster a more livable and ethical environment.

This study contributes to defining the context of the mafia phenomenon by identifying factors that, when associated with it, represent warning signs to monitor. Institutions and governments are responsible for promoting actions that can curb the mafia and monitoring management and accounting frameworks, as well as associated human and social factors. Therefore, the study has implications for both the administrative and management context of municipalities and the organization of the human capital that drives administrative action. Specifically, on the one hand, the study expands the analytical framework offered by previous literature, which has primarily focused on the repressive and normative aspects of dissolution (Daniele & Geys, 2015; Mastrorocco & Di Cataldo, 2021), introducing an approach that integrates financial and nonfinancial indicators with social variables. On the other hand, it offers an operational interpretation of the phenomenon, suggesting the systematic use of these indicators as useful predictive tools for preventing and monitoring the risk of mafia infiltration. In this sense, the research follows recent studies aiming to develop predictive models for identifying vulnerable contexts (Iezzi & Pauselli, 2025; Ferraresi & Gucciardi, 2022).

From a practical perspective, the findings underscore the importance of strengthening internal control systems in municipalities, especially in contexts with structural deficits and socioeconomic weakness. Targeted interventions to train and develop human capital within the institution, as well as promoting a culture of public ethics, can reduce the critical areas where corrupt behaviors thrive (Hauser, 2019; Lagos & Pliscoff, 2020). These considerations are perfectly aligned with Goal 16 of the 2030 Agenda, which promotes accountable, transparent, and effective institutions.

However, the study has some limitations. The sample focuses only on municipalities with more than 15,000 inhabitants, excluding smaller municipalities that could be equally, if not more, exposed to mafia-related risks. Furthermore, it would be useful to analyze additional elements, such as individual deficit indicators, and to assess the association of mafia-related dissolutions with each of them, to obtain a more detailed picture of the most critical accounting areas.

References

Abbink, K. (2004). Staff rotation as an anti-corruption policy: An experimental study. *European Journal of Political Economy, 20*(4), 887–906.

Ahen, F. (2022). International mega-corruption Inc.: The structural violence against sustainable development. *Critical Perspectives on International Business, 18*(2), 178–200.

Akbar, Y., & Vujić, V. (2014). Explaining corruption: The role of national culture and its implications for international management. *Cross Cultural Management, 21*(2), 191–218.

Alatas, V., Cameron, L., Chaudhuri, A., Erkal, N., & Gangadharan, L. (2009). Gender, culture, and corruption: Insights from an experimental analysis. *Southern Economic Journal, 75*(3), 663–680.

Allum, F., Marinaro, I. C., & Sciarrone, R. (Eds). (2019). *Italian mafias today: Territory, business and politics*. Edward Elgar Publishing.

Arifin, T., Trinugroho, I., Prabowo, M. A., Sutaryo, S., & Muhtar, M. (2015). Local governance and corruption: Evidence from Indonesia. *Corporate Ownership and Control, 12*(4CONT1), 194–199.

Barone, G., & Narciso, G. (2015). Organized crime and business subsidies: Where does the money go? *Journal of Urban Economics, 86*, 98–110.

Cincimino, S., Gnoffo, S., La Rosa, F., & Paternostro, S. (2024). Entrepreneurship and organised crime: A systematic review and research agenda based on three decades of scholarship. *Journal of Small Business and Enterprise Development.*

Dagnes, J., Donatiello, D., Moiso, V., Pellegrino, D., Sciarrone, R., & Storti, L. (2020). Mafia infiltration, public administration and local institutions: A comparative study in Northern Italy. *European Journal of Criminology, 17*(5), 540–562.

Dalla Chiesa, F. (2014). *Manifesto dell'antimafia* (Vol. 92). Einaudi.

Daniele, G., & Galletta, S. (2015). *Come cambiano i comuni sciolti per mafia*. La Voce.

Daniele, G., & Geys, B. (2015). Organised crime, institutions and political quality: Empirical evidence from Italian municipalities. *Economic Journal, 125*(586), F233–F255.
Daniele, G., & Giommoni, T. (2021). Corruption under austerity. *SSRN Electronic Journal, 2020*.
Debski, J., Jetter, M., Mösle, S., & Stadelmann, D. (2018). Gender and corruption: The neglected role of culture. *European Journal of Political Economy, 55*(September 2016), 526–537.
Decarolis, F., Fisman, R., Pinotti, P., Vannutelli, S., & Wang, Y. (2023). Gender and bureaucratic corruption: Evidence from two countries. *Journal of Law, Economics, and Organization, 39*(2), 557–585.
Di Cataldo, M., & Mastrorocco, N. (2018). *Organised crime, captured politicians and the allocation of public resources*. Trinity Economics Papers.
Di Gennaro, G., & Aurilia, R. (2022). Corruption and policy-making: How corruption models favor mafias—The case study of Italy. In *Corruption-new insights*. IntechOpen.
Dimant, E., & Tosato, G. (2018). Causes and effects of corruption: What has past decade's empirical research taught us? A survey. *Journal of Economic Surveys, 32*(2), 335–356.
Dollar, D., Fisman, R., & Gatti, R. (2001). Are women really the 'fairer' sex? Corruption and women in government. *Journal of Economic Behavior and Organization*.
Eboli, M., Toto, A., & Ziruolo, A. (2021). Mafia infiltrations in Italian municipalities: Two statistical indicators. *Applied Economics, 53*(24), 2693–2712.
Ferraresi, M., & Gucciardi, G. (2022). Political alignment, centralisation, and the sense of government unpreparedness during the COVID-19 pandemic. *European Journal of Political Economy, 73*, 102144.
Frank, B., Lambsdorff, J. G., & Boehm, F. (2011). Gender and corruption: Lessons from laboratory corruption experiments. *European Journal of Development Research, 23*(1), 59–71.
Funk, K. D., & Owen, E. (2020). Consequences of an anti-corruption experiment for local government performance in Brazil. *Journal of Policy Analysis and Management, 39*(2), 444–468.
Gara, M., Iezzi, S., & Siino, M. (2024). *Corruption risk indicators in public procurement: A proposal using Italian open data*. No. September.
Gatti, R., Paternostro, S., & Rigolini, J. (2003) *Individual attitudes toward corruption: Do social effects matter?* World Bank Policy Research Working Paper N. 3122. https://doi.org/10.1596/1813-9450-3122
Goel, R. K., & Nelson, M. A. (1998). Corruption and government size: A disaggregated analysis. *Public Choice, 97*(1–2), 107–120.
Goetz, A. M., & Jenkins, R. (2016). Gender, security, and governance: The case of sustainable development goal 16. *Gender and Development, 24*(1), 127–137. https://doi.org/10.1080/13552074.2016.1144412
Golden, M. A., & Picci, L. (2005). Proposal for a new measure of corruption, illustrated with Italian data. *Economics and Politics, 17*(1), 37–75.
Graycar, A., & Villa, D. (2011). The loss of governance capacity through corruption. *Governance, 24*(3), 419–438.
Guarini, E., Magli, F., & Martinelli, M. (2022). La prospettiva del "Sistema di Controllo Interno Integrato" nella Pubblica Amministrazione: Riflessioni a partire dal caso Regione Lombardia. *Management Control, 2*, 63–89.
Hauser, C. (2019). Fighting against corruption: Does anti-corruption training make any difference? *Journal of Business Ethics*, Springer Netherlands, *159*(1), 281–299.
Hope, K. R. (2020). Corruption reduction as a target of the sustainable development goals: Applying indicators and policy frameworks. In *The emerald handbook of crime, justice and sustainable development* (pp. 105–130). Emerald Publishing Limited.
Iezzi, S., & Pauselli, C. (2025). *Quaderni dell'antiriciclaggio*.
Jetter, M., & Parmeter, C. F. (2018). Sorting through global corruption determinants: Institutions and education matter—Not culture. *World Development, 109*, 279–294.
Lagos, N., & Pliscoff, C. (2020). Implementando los sistemas de integridad en el sector público chileno: Reflexiones a partir del manual de la Organización para la Coope ración y el Desarrollo

Económico sobre integridad pública. *Revista Chilena de la Administración del Estado, 3*, 35–48.
Lambsdorff, J., & Fink, H. (2006). Combating corruption in Colombia: Perceptions and achievements. *Passauer Diskussionspapiere: Volkswirtschaftliche Reihe, V-44-06*, 1–75.
Marasabessy, A. C., Suanto, Hayati, E., & Utaminingsih, S. (2022). Internalization values of character education as a solution for degradation of civility of the nation. *Cetta: Jurnal Ilmu Pendidikan, 5*(2), 150–159.
Mastrorocco, N., & Di Cataldo, M. (2021). *Organised crime, captured politicians and the allocation of public resources (No. tep0420)*. Department of Economics.
Mathew, S. N., Soundar, K. G., Martin, N. R., & Dwivedi, R. (2025). Legally aided leeches—Combating the menace of white-collar crimes with respect to sustainable development goals-16. In *Rule of law in context: Globalisation and Indian resonances to sustainable development* (pp. 25–40). Routledge.
Mete, V., & Sciarrone, R. (2017). The boundaries of mafias: Relationships and business in the 'grey area'. In *Redefining organized crime: A challenge for the European Union?* (pp. 293–315). Hart.
Mohamadi, A., Peltonen, J., & Wincent, J. (2017). Government efficiency and corruption: A country-level study with implications for entrepreneurship. *Journal of Business Venturing Insights, 8*(June), 50–55.
Monteduro, F., D'Onza, G., & Mussari, R. (2024). Corruption spreads: Understanding interorganizational corruption contagion in municipal governments. *International Journal of Public Sector Management, 37*(1), 108–123.
Nyamu-Musembi, C. (2007). *Gender and corruption in the administration of justice* (pp. 121–128). Global Corruption Report.
Occhiuzzi, F. (2020). The dissolution of municipal councils due to organized crime infiltration. *European Journal of Interdisciplinary Studies, 6*(2), 16–29.
Onyango, G. (2024). How mafia-like bureaucratic cartels or thieves in suits run corruption inside the bureaucracy, or how Government Officials Swindle citizens in Kenya! *Deviant Behavior, 45*(5), 689–707.
Padovani, E., Porcelli, F., & Zanardi, A. (2024). The determinants of the financial distress of Italian municipalities: How much is it due to inadequate resources? *International Tax and Public Finance*, 1494–1533.
Paterson, A. S., Changwony, F., & Miller, P. B. (2019). Accounting control, governance and anti-corruption initiatives in public sector organisations. *The British Accounting Review, 51*(5).
Pessa, A. A. B., Martins, A. F., Prates, M. V., Gonçalves, S., Masoller, C., Perc, M., & Ribeiro, H. V. (2025). Structural roles and gender disparities in corruption networks. *Scientific Reports, 15*(1), 1–12.
Pliscoff Varas, C., & Lagos Machuca, N. (2021). Implementación de sistemas de integridad como estrategia de control de la corrupción en el Gobierno Central de Chile. *Gestión y Política Pública, 30*(3), 81–114.
Ravenda, D., Giuranno, M. G., Valencia-Silva, M. M., Argiles-Bosch, J. M., & García-Blandón, J. (2020). The effects of mafia infiltration on public procurement performance. *European Journal of Political Economy, 64*(July).
Rose-Ackerman, S. (1999). Political corruption and democracy. *Connecticut Journal of International Law, 14*, 363.
Schepisi, M., Liuzza, M. T., Frisanco, A., Giannini, A. M., & Aglioti, S. M. (2023). Attitudes towards Italian Mafias Scale (AIMS): Development and validation. *PeerJ, 11*, 1–25.
Singh, N. R. (2021). Transparency in institutions: Critical factor for achievement of sustainable development goals. In *Peace, justice and strong institutions* (pp. 960–974). Springer International Publishing.
Swamy, A., et al. (2001). Gender and corruption. *Journal of Development Economics 64*(1), 25–55.
Travaglino, G. A., & Abrams, D. (2019). How criminal organisations exert secret power over communities: An intracultural appropriation theory of cultural values and norms. *European Review of Social Psychology, 30*(1), 74–122.

Treisman, D. (2000). The causes of corruption: A cross-national study. *Journal of Public Economics, 76*(3), 399–457.
Veltri, S., Bruni, M. E., Iazzolino, G., Morea, D., & Baldissarro, G. (2023). Do ESG factors improve utilities corporate efficiency and reduce the risk perceived by credit lending institutions? An empirical analysis. *Utilities Policy, 81*, 101520.
Vimercati, B. (2022). Regions and Goal 16: The institutional dimension of sustainable development. Participatory, open and inclusive decision-making. *Regioni, 50*(1–2), 187–235.
Yeboah-Assiamah, E., Asamoah, K., Bawole, J. N., & Musah-Surugu, I. J. (2016). A socio-cultural approach to public sector corruption in Africa: Key pointers for reflection. *Journal of Public Affairs, 16*(3), 279–293.
Zhang, Y., Jancsics, D., & Graycar, A. (2019). Introduction to PAR symposium of understanding and reducing public corruption. *Public Administration Review, 79*, 519.
Zhang, Y., Hung, W. J., Dong, H. K., & Chen, D. Y. (2025). Public Employees' whistleblowing intention: Explanation by an adapted theory of planned behavior. *Public Administration, 103*(1), 115–135.

Exploring the Impact of Soft Preventive Judicial Measures on Business Resilience and Performance Under Organised Crime Infiltration: Evidence from a Multi-Case Analysis

Giovanni Scirè and Enzo Bivona

Abstract Organised crime infiltration in legitimate businesses threatens market functioning, firm governance and local economic development. In Italy, alongside seizure and confiscation, the Anti-Mafia Code introduced continuity-preserving "soft" preventive measures—judicial administration (Art. 34) and judicial control (Art. 34-bis)—aimed at interrupting criminal influence while keeping firms operating. Yet, firm-level evidence on their economic and organisational consequences remains limited. This study adopts an organisational resilience perspective and investigates how firms' operating and financial conditions evolve around these interventions. We conduct a comparative multi-case analysis of 11 firms subjected to Arts. 34/34-bis, identified through judicial records and matched with peer groups by sector, size and geography using AIDA data. We reconstruct trajectories across pre-intervention, intervention, and post-intervention phases using four indicators: value of production, current ratio, net income and debt-to-equity. Findings suggest that soft preventive measures mainly operate as contingent stabilisers: they support operational continuity, but liquidity, profitability and capital structure remain fragile, especially after the judicial phase. The study contributes by opening the firm-level process between preventive judicial intervention and economic outcomes, offering mechanism-oriented evidence that complements existing research on anti-mafia policies.

1 Introduction

Organised crime (OC) infiltration into legitimate businesses poses a persistent threat to economic development, institutional trust, and the stability of local productive

G. Scirè (✉) · E. Bivona
Department of Political Sciences and International Relations (DEMS), University of Palermo, Palermo, Italy
e-mail: giovanni.scire01@unipa.it; enzo.bivona@unipa.it

R. Cellini et al. (eds.), *Cultural, Social, and Political Participation in the Internet Era*, Contributions to Economics, https://doi.org/10.1007/978-3-032-33072-7_11

systems (Pinotti, 2015; Savona & Berlusconi, 2015). Infiltration can take multiple forms, ranging from coercion and collusion to laundering and the capture of procurement opportunities, thereby blurring the boundary between legal and illegal activity (Bafundi et al. 2026; Scirè & Bivona 2026; Von Lampe, 2016; Zabyelina et al., 2022). At the firm level, these dynamics may reshape governance and strategic choices and distort market behaviour through protected positions, opportunistic access to liquidity, and the displacement of competitors (Calamunci & Drago, 2020; Riccardi, 2014; Von Lampe, 2016). Empirical evidence links OC presence to distortions in productivity and performance, particularly among SMEs in local clusters, and clarifies behavioural mechanisms through which criminal groups penetrate lawful organisations (Fourie et al., 2023; Ganau & Rodríguez-Pose, 2018).

Evidence from the National Agency for the Administration and Destination of Assets Seized and Confiscated from Organised Crime (ANBSC) indicates that, when traditional ablative measures are applied, around 68% of infiltrated firms enter liquidation or bankruptcy after criminal influence is removed (ANBSC, 2023; Nicolò, 2025, p. 130). The Italian Anti-Mafia framework has therefore complemented seizure and confiscation with continuity-preserving preventive measures, notably judicial administration (Art. 34) and judicial control (Art. 34-bis), designed to interrupt infiltration while preserving going-concern status without transferring ownership (Visconti, 2019). These measures seek to restore corporate legality while safeguarding production and employment continuity (Bivona, 2012, 2019; Calamunci, 2022b). Judicial administration temporarily replaces management under court supervision, whereas judicial control introduces oversight while management remains in place. Although both instruments pursue continuity-oriented objectives, they may also introduce governance discontinuities that disrupt routines and resource flows on which firms relied (Bivona, 2019; Calamunci et al., 2021; Visconti, 2019).

Despite their growing policy relevance, rigorous firm-level evidence on the economic and organisational consequences of "soft" preventive measures remains limited. Prior research has focused on macro-level patterns or accounts, leaving less explored the micro-dynamics through which operating and financial conditions evolve around intervention (Calamunci & Drago, 2020; Chircop et al., 2023; Pinotti, 2015). Moreover, the removal of criminal influence is frequently treated as a sufficient condition for recovery, whereas the organisational processes that enable (or prevent) a return to stable, lawful value creation receive less attention (Nicolò, 2025).

To address this gap, we adopt a resilience perspective, treating soft preventive measures as an institutional shock and a trigger for organisational reconfiguration. We define resilience as the capability to restore and sustain value creation after the judicial removal of OC influence, without relying on, or remaining exposed to, criminal ties. This framing is consistent with resilience research emphasising absorption, adaptation, and recovery, grounded in sensemaking and learning (Duchek, 2020; Hillmann & Guenther, 2021; Weick et al., 2005; Williams et al., 2017).

Empirically, we apply a comparative multi-case design to firms subjected to Art. 34 or Art. 34-bis. Cases are identified through direct analysis of judicial records, improving selection accuracy relative to exclusive reliance on commercial databases such as AIDA, which may include firms involved in non-criminal proceedings and provide limited information on infiltration timing and intensity (Calamunci & Drago, 2020; Costanzo & Mazzuca, 2025; Greco & Messina, 2024). Financial and operating data are collected from AIDA, and trajectories are reconstructed across pre-intervention, intervention, and post-intervention phases using indicators of value of production, liquidity, profitability and capital structure. Each case is benchmarked against a tailored peer group matched by sector, size and geography to contextualise performance and interpret post-intervention patterns as recovery, stabilisation or persistent fragility.

2 Organised Crime Infiltration and Preventive Governance: Economic, Legal and Managerial Perspectives

OC infiltration into lawful firms is a multidimensional phenomenon that reshapes managerial behaviour, market structures and governance mechanisms. OC penetrates the legal economy to launder capital, exercise territorial control and consolidate influence over relevant economic nodes (Sciarrone, 2011; Sciarrone & Storti, 2016). Infiltration strategies typically combine money laundering, tax fraud, monopolistic practices and coercive rent extraction, blurring the boundary between licit and illicit activity and generating hybrid governance arrangements that are often difficult to detect through accounting evidence alone (Chircop et al., 2023; Von Lampe, 2016). Recent scholarship notes that digital transformation can expand concealment opportunities and facilitate novel criminal business models, including through crypto-related channels, further complicating detection and governance (Arnone et al., 2025; Nazzari & Riccardi, 2024).

A growing empirical literature examines the economic consequences of OC infiltration using firm-level financial statements. Evidence suggests heterogeneous financial profiles: OC-linked firms may display short-run turnover advantages or expanded credit access, alongside weaker fundamentals such as lower profitability, reduced cash buffers and higher default risk (Bianchi et al., 2022). Accounting-based analyses of firms under judicial administration similarly highlight indebtedness and liquidity constraints; in some cases, liquidity improves after intervention while profitability and operating efficiency deteriorate, indicating difficulties in restoring a sustainable economic equilibrium once illicit advantages and informal channels are removed (Greco & Messina, 2024). More broadly, prior research emphasises substantial heterogeneity among infiltrated firms, reflecting different economic roles and modes of interaction with criminal organisations, ranging from operational support and capital laundering to direct competition in lawful markets (Fabrizi et al., 2017; Parbonetti, 2021). Beyond firm-level outcomes, OC presence can distort local competitive dynamics by acting as a barrier to entry and reducing productivity growth, particularly in territorially embedded SMEs, thereby eroding agglomeration benefits and influencing firms' strategic positioning (Ganau & Rodríguez-Pose, 2018; Slutzky & Zeume, 2024). Overall, while infiltrated firms may sometimes benefit from informal protection in the short run, longer-run trajectories often reflect structural inefficiencies and rising legal exposure, undermining sustainability and reputational capital (Arellano-Bover et al., 2024; Pinotti, 2015; Scirè & Bivona, 2026).

From a compliance and policy perspective, Italy has historically relied on ablative tools (seizure and confiscation) to disrupt criminal assets; however, these instruments can generate substantial collateral damage through liquidation, organisational disruption and the reallocation of productive resources (Bivona, 2012; Esposito & Ricci, 2014, 2015). To mitigate such externalities, the Anti-Mafia Code introduced continuity-preserving "soft" preventive measures, judicial administration (Art. 34) and judicial control (Art. 34-bis), designed to sever criminal ties while maintaining business continuity. Judicial administration involves the temporary replacement of governance bodies under court supervision, whereas judicial control imposes monitoring while management remains in place (Calamunci, 2022b;Colacurci, 2023 ; Visconti, 2019). The aim is to safeguard productive capacity and employment and to attenuate criminally induced market distortions. Consistent with this logic, prior work suggests that judicial administration may generate positive spillovers for lawful peers by reducing illicit competitive advantages (Calamunci & Drago, 2020; Chircop et al., 2023), although legal scholarship cautions that interpretative divergence and normative fragmentation may limit operational effectiveness when implementation is uneven (Colacurci, 2023; Visconti, 2019).

A recurrent limitation in this research area concerns case identification and the timing of infiltration and intervention. Many studies identify target firms through administrative or commercial datasets such as AIDA (Calamunci & Drago, 2020; Greco & Messina, 2024). However, such sources may include firms affected by non-criminal proceedings (e.g. bankruptcy or distress) and typically provide limited information on the onset, intensity and organisational penetration of infiltration (Costanzo & Mazzuca, 2025). Moreover, financial statements may offer delayed or ambiguous signals given the lag between de facto criminal control and judicial recognition, meaning that designs relying solely on accounting indicators risk capturing only residual traces or misclassifying distressed but non-infiltrated firms (Calamunci, 2022a). For these reasons, several authors advocate integrating commercial data with judicial documentation, case studies and seizure-related evidence to improve validity and interpretability and to better capture the organisational mechanisms through which infiltration operates (Fourie et al., 2023; Riccardi & Berlusconi, 2016).

These methodological and institutional issues point to the importance of a managerial and organisational perspective. At the firm level, a central question is how organisations navigate the institutional discontinuity induced by judicial intervention and which capabilities enable a return to viable, lawful conditions. Obstacles may include weakened managerial competences, dependence on informal networks and inadequate internal control systems, which hinder reintegration into legitimate markets even after criminal influence is removed (Calamunci, 2022b).

From a managerial standpoint, recovery is more likely when intervention goes beyond formal compliance and supports planning and control, performance management and learning routines oriented to the medium–long term (Bivona, 2019). Organisational resilience provides a useful lens, as it can be understood as a dynamic capability encompassing anticipation, coping and adaptation, supported by sensemaking and organisational learning (Duchek, 2020; Weick et al., 2005; Williams et al., 2017). Importantly, in infiltration contexts, enforcement may also trigger cycles of adaptation and counter-adaptation, reflecting the counter-resilience of criminal actors and increasing competitive and institutional pressure on firms in transition (Ayling, 2009).

Drawing on the above contributions, resilience in firms emerging from OC influence can be interpreted as a multidimensional challenge involving (i) operational continuity and the restoration of productive capacity, (ii) financial adjustment and (iii) the rebuilding of legitimacy and trust with key stakeholders. In this perspective, soft preventive measures may facilitate short-run coping through monitoring and compliance; however, prior work suggests that durable adaptation requires organisational mechanisms such as robust planning and control, codified learning routines, and stakeholder engagement aimed at repairing reputation and trust. Absent these levers, firms risk forms of "compliance without viability", whereby formal obligations are met, but the lawful economic model is not rebuilt on sustainable bases (Bivona, 2012, 2019; Calamunci, 2022b).

3 Methodology

3.1 Research Design and Case Selection

This study adopts a comparative multi-case design (Eisenhardt, 1989; Eisenhardt & Graebner, 2007; Yin, 2018) to trace operating and financial trajectories of firms subjected to "soft" preventive measures under the Italian Anti-Mafia Code, namely judicial administration (Art. 34) and judicial control (Art. 34-bis), following OC infiltration. The analysis covers three phases (pre-intervention, intervention, post-intervention) through a replicable protocol for comparative interpretation. This approach is a distinctive methodological feature of the study and is suited to complex, relatively rare preventive policies whose implications unfold through context-dependent legal, organisational, financial and territorial mechanisms. Accordingly, the design does not aim to estimate average causal effects or provide statistical generalisation; rather, it reconstructs trajectories and mechanisms linking preventive judicial intervention to organisational resilience, financial viability and lawful market repositioning. The study thus complements large-sample empirical approaches by opening the firm-level "black box" between legal intervention and economic outcome.

Consistent with recent methodological approaches (Calamunci, 2022a; Costanzo & Mazzuca, 2025), cases were identified through direct access to judicial archives. We included only firms for which judicial decisions explicitly recognised either ascertained infiltration or a high risk of infiltration in the reasoning of the decision and excluded inactive or liquidating firms and cases with insufficient information. For each proceeding, duration and phase boundaries were reconstructed from case files, improving case timing and selection accuracy relative to approaches relying exclusively on commercial datasets.

Financial data for case and peer firms were collected from AIDA (Bureau van Dijk/Moody's). The quantitative analysis focuses on 2015 onwards, reflecting financial-statement availability and staggered intervention timing, while documentary evidence covers an approximately 10-year horizon. We computed four indicators aligned with business resilience and financial viability: (i) value of production (€), (ii) current ratio, (iii) net income (€) and (iv) debt-to-equity ratio (D/E). Operationally, the value of production captures continuity and short-term coping; current ratio and debt-to-equity ratio capture financial resilience; and net income indicates whether stabilisation is accompanied by a viable post-judicial economic model. This indicator set is consistent with peer benchmarking approaches and prior empirical work on firm performance and OC-related interventions (Albuquerque et al., 2013; Bakke et al., 2020; Calamunci & Drago, 2020; Greco & Messina, 2024). To limit outlier influence in small samples, peer-group annual values were aggregated using the median; phase-level values were computed as medians of annual observations within each phase for both the case firm and its peer group.

3.2 Peer-Group Construction, Sample Overview and Comparative Strategy

For each case firm, we built a matched peer group by sector (NACE), size (assets band), and geography, prioritising NUTS-3 where feasible; when local comparables were unavailable, we broadened the scope up to the national level. Whenever possible, we also checked that peer firms were not subject to preventive measures within the observation window. Table 1 reports cases, peer-group parameters, and the geographic scope adopted.

The empirical strategy combines two complementary comparison levels: (i) intra-firm analysis, comparing each case firm across phases (pre-intervention vs intervention vs post-intervention), and (ii) inter-firm analysis, benchmarking each case firm against its peer-group phase values within each phase. Accordingly, the objective is not to estimate average causal effects of judicial administration or judicial control on firm performance. Rather, peer groups are used as contextual benchmarks to assess whether case-firm trajectories are broadly aligned with, or diverge from, comparable firms operating in similar sectoral, dimensional and territorial conditions. In this sense, the comparative strategy supports a mechanism-

Table 1 Case firms and peer groups (overview)

ID	NACE	Region	Measure	Dur. (years)	Peer (n)	Assets band	Geo. scope
1	4120	Calabria	Art. 34-bis	2	8	80%–120%	NUTS-3
2	4931	Calabria	Art. 34-bis	2	20	80%–120%	NUTS-0
3	7739	Calabria	Art. 34-bis	1	18	80%–120%	NUTS-1
4	5229	Lombardy	Art. 34	1	7	50%–150%	NUTS-3
5	3811	Campania	Art. 34-bis	2	9	50%–150%	NUTS-2
6	8129	Lazio	Art. 34	2	4	20%–500%	NUTS-0
7	5010	Sicily	Art. 34	1	10	20%–500%	NUTS-0
8	4690	Sicily	Art. 34	3	9	80%–120%	NUTS-2
9	4120	Piedmont	Art. 34	1	8	50%–150%	NUTS-2
10	3249	Emilia-Romagna	Art. 34-bis	1	11	50%–150%	NUTS-0
11	4120	Sicily	Art. 34	2	13	80%–120%	NUTS-3

Source: Authors' own elaboration based on AIDA database and judicial records

oriented interpretation of firm-level trajectories, while avoiding claims of strict causal identification or statistical generalisation.

4 Results from Selected Case Firms and Peer Groups

This section reports the results of the comparative analysis of firms subject to preventive judicial measures following OC infiltration. We examine trajectories across three phases, pre-intervention, intervention and post-intervention, using both intra-firm and inter-firm comparisons. While the documentary analysis draws on judicial records spanning approximately a decade, the quantitative assessment focuses on 2015–2023 due to financial-statement availability and the staggered timing of interventions. The focus is on operational capacity, liquidity, profitability and capital structure.

4.1 Intra-Firm Performance Dynamics Across Phases

To assess how firms evolve across phases, we computed percentage changes for each indicator as follows:

$$\Delta\% = \frac{(Firm\ Value_{t+1} - Firm\ Value_t)}{Firm\ Value_t} \times 100 \tag{1}$$

Table 2 Medians of intra-firm dynamics (% change between phases)

Indicator	Δ% Intervention-pre	Δ% Post-intervention	Δ% Post-pre
Value of production (€)	12.88	13.61	26.73
Current ratio	7.55	8.60	−7.75
Net income (€)	−2.10	−100.31	24.20
Debt-to-equity ratio	−21.21	22.66	34.71

Source: Authors' own elaboration based on AIDA database and judicial records

where t denotes the initial phase (pre-intervention or intervention) and $t + 1$ the subsequent phase (intervention or post-intervention). This standardisation improves comparability across heterogeneous cases.

Overall, patterns are heterogeneous across firms and indicators. Value of production often increases during intervention and remains stable or grows post-intervention, suggesting that the measures do not generally obstruct operations. By contrast, net income and liquidity show mixed trajectories, and improvements under supervision frequently do not consolidate after exit. Leverage often declines during intervention but increases in the post-intervention phase for several firms.

To summarise firm-level percentage changes across the sample, Table 2 reports medians to limit the influence of outliers and extreme observations.

At the median level, operational capacity improves overall (Post-Pre +26.73), whereas liquidity contracts (Post-Pre −7.75). Net income shows instability, with no median improvement during intervention (Intervention-Pre −2.10) and a sharp post-intervention deterioration (Post-Intervention −100.31) followed by partial recovery over the full horizon (Post-Pre +24.20). Leverage declines during intervention (D/E – 21.21) but increases thereafter (Post-Intervention +22.66; Post-Pre +34.71). Taken together, these results suggest operational stabilisation combined with persistent fragility in profitability, liquidity, and capital structure. They should be interpreted cautiously, given the relatively short post-intervention window.

4.2 Inter-Firm Benchmarking: Comparison with Peer Groups

We benchmarked each case firm against a matched peer group (sector, size, geography). Percentage differentials were computed as:

$$\Delta_t\,(\%) = \frac{(Firm\ Value_t - Peer\ Value_t)}{Peer\ Value_t} \times 100 \qquad (2)$$

where t denotes the phase (pre-intervention, intervention, post-intervention). This enables standardised relative comparisons across heterogeneous firms.

To summarise these patterns, Table 3 reports the mean percentage differentials between case firms and peer groups across phases. On average, case firms outperform peers in value of production across phases, whereas the current ratio remains below peer levels and deteriorates over time. Net income differentials

Table 3 Mean percentage differentials between case firms and peer groups (Δ%)

Indicator	Mean Δ% pre	Mean Δ% intervention	Mean Δ% post
Value of production (€)	65.22	40.09	61.22
Current ratio	−2.11	−10.91	−17.66
Net income (€)	−62.34	−77.11	−57.06
Debt-to-equity ratio (D/E)	5.35	−11.47	141.05

Source: Authors' own elaboration based on AIDA database and judicial records

are negative in all phases, with substantial dispersion across cases. D/E improves relative to peers during intervention but increases sharply post-intervention, signalling a relative deterioration in capital structure after exit. Overall, the evidence points to composite effects: operational continuity appears comparatively resilient, while liquidity, profitability and post-intervention leverage remain fragile. The next section discusses these findings, considering the literature and implications for organisational resilience and policy design.

5 Discussion

This study explored firm-level implications of "soft" preventive judicial measures under Arts. 34 and 34-bis for businesses affected by OC infiltration. By triangulating judicial records with financial statement data and benchmarking each case against matched peers, we traced pre-intervention, intervention and post-intervention trajectories in operational capacity, liquidity, profitability and capital structure. These dimensions operationalise resilience: value of production captures continuity and operational coping; liquidity and capital structure reflect financial resilience; and profitability and post-intervention trends indicate whether short-term stabilisation evolves into adaptive viability. Heterogeneity across indicators and cases suggests that judicial supervision operates mainly as a contingent stabiliser rather than a uniform recovery lever.

These findings also clarify the empirical positioning of the chapter. Prior quantitative and accounting-based studies have examined the territorial, market and firm-performance consequences of OC and anti-mafia enforcement, including productivity effects, peer-firm spillovers, financial-statement profiles and outcomes under judicial administration (Bianchi et al., 2022; F. Calamunci & Drago, 2020; Chircop et al., 2023; Ganau & Rodríguez-Pose, 2018; Pinotti, 2015; Slutzky & Zeume, 2024). Legal and managerial scholarship, in turn, has clarified the institutional rationale, procedural features and governance challenges of continuity-preserving preventive measures (Bivona, 2019; Calamunci, 2022b; Colacurci, 2023; Visconti, 2019). This chapter complements these strands by focusing on the within-firm process that links judicial intervention to observed economic outcomes. The comparative multi-case design is therefore not used to claim strict causal identification, but to examine how similar preventive measures generate heterogeneous trajectories depending on organisational, financial, sectoral and territorial conditions.

A first insight concerns operational continuity. Intra-firm medians and peer benchmarks indicate that the value of production generally improves across phases and outperforms peers. This is consistent with the rationale of Arts. 34/34-bis to preserve production and employment, often by stabilising firms' dealings with the public administration while severing criminal influence (Bivona, 2019; Calamunci et al., 2021), and with evidence that reducing criminal distortions can improve local market functioning (Calamunci & Drago, 2020; Chircop et al., 2023). However, operational continuity does not automatically translate into economic resilience: it captures short-term coping capacity, whereas resilience requires lawful routines and a financially sustainable business model after the judicial phase.

Liquidity and profitability display fragile and uneven trajectories. Intra-firm dynamics show that improvements achieved during supervision often do not consolidate post-intervention, while peer comparisons reveal persistent gaps in liquidity and net income. These findings qualify the assumption, often implicit in evaluations of traditional preventive measures, that removing criminal influence is sufficient for "recovery" (Nicolò, 2025). They are also consistent with evidence that infiltrated or supervised firms may retain indebtedness and liquidity constraints, and that restoring sustainable economic equilibrium becomes difficult once illicit advantages and informal channels are removed (Bianchi et al., 2022; Greco & Messina, 2024). From an organisational perspective, this pattern supports a resilience interpretation in which short-run coping may occur under external oversight, but durable adaptation depends on sensemaking, learning, and rebuilding lawful routines and stakeholder relations (Duchek, 2020; Weick et al., 2005; Weick & Sutcliffe, 2001; Williams et al., 2017).

Capital structure dynamics further underline post-intervention fragility. While leverage tends to stabilise during intervention, it worsens sharply in the post-intervention phase when benchmarked against peers. In the absence of a systematic improvement in profitability relative to peers, this pattern suggests that post-intervention borrowing may be associated more with working-capital pressures and transition costs than with value-creating investment. This is consistent with the view that infiltrated firms operate in hybrid environments where governance discontinuities, damaged stakeholder trust and constrained access to legitimate finance can persist after formal exit (Von Lampe, 2016; Zabyelina et al., 2022). From this perspective, worsening debt-to-equity ratios are not merely accounting symptoms, but signals of an incomplete recovery process when legal exit is not accompanied by financial restructuring and renewed access to legitimate credit.

Overall, our findings reinforce a dynamic and multidimensional view of exit from OC influence. Preventive judicial measures can help stabilise operations and restore legality, but outcomes remain heterogeneous and path-dependent, shaped by firm-specific capabilities and by sectoral and territorial conditions (Ganau & Rodríguez-Pose, 2018; Pinotti, 2015; Slutzky & Zeume, 2024). In this sense, "soft" measures appear necessary to interrupt infiltration while preserving continuity, yet not sufficient to ensure durable, lawful viability without complementary managerial and institutional conditions that support post-intervention reconfiguration.

6 Conclusions

This study analysed, through a comparative multi-case design, the economic–financial and organisational trajectories of 11 firms affected by OC infiltration and subject to "soft" preventive measures under the Italian Anti-Mafia Code, judicial administration (Art. 34) and judicial control (Art. 34-bis). By identifying cases directly from judicial documentation rather than relying exclusively on commercial databases, the study reduced the risk of false positives and improved the accuracy of timing and contextual relevance (Calamunci & Drago, 2020; Riccardi & Berlusconi, 2016). We excluded inactive or liquidating firms and retained only cases in which the anti-mafia rationale was explicitly stated in judicial decisions. Combining judicial records with AIDA data, we traced three phases, pre-intervention, intervention and post-intervention, across four indicators (value of production, current ratio, net income and debt-to-equity ratio), benchmarked against peer groups matched by NACE sector, firm size and NUTS geographic area. Given this design, the study should be read as a mechanism-oriented comparative analysis, not as an attempt to estimate average causal effects of such measures. Peer groups contextualise observed trajectories, while judicial records support reconstruction of intervention timing, rationale and content. The study complements existing research by opening the firm-level process linking preventive judicial intervention to organisational adjustment, financial rebalancing, stakeholder trust and lawful market repositioning.

Theoretically, the study interprets infiltrated firms as organisations in vulnerable transition, where resilience is a dynamic capability articulated through coping and adaptation (Duchek, 2020). The framework links empirical evidence to stages of organisational response: short-term coping during judicial intervention, post-intervention reconfiguration and reconstruction of economic, financial and relational viability. Stabilisation induced by preventive measures appears necessary but not sufficient for durable viability, which depends on organisational learning and renewed legitimacy in stakeholder relations (Weick & Sutcliffe, 2001; Williams et al., 2017). In hybrid competitive and institutional environments (Von Lampe, 2016; Zabyelina et al., 2022), marked by criminal counter-resilience (Ayling, 2009) and market distortions affecting SMEs (Ganau & Rodríguez-Pose, 2018; Slutzky & Zeume, 2024), "soft" measures can be viewed as corrective devices enabling post-intervention reconfiguration under managerial and institutional conditions. Anti-mafia interventions may also attenuate local market distortions and benefit lawful peers (Chircop et al., 2023).

Policy implications point to the need to embed Arts. 34 and 34-bis in a post-intervention accompaniment ecosystem combining managerial mentoring and strengthened management control (budgeting, infra-annual reporting, treasury and cash-flow monitoring), working-capital support, compliance arrangements, and territorial partnerships with business associations, chambers of commerce and banks (Bivona, 2019; Calamunci, 2022b; Visconti, 2019). Where these levers are activated, short-term stabilisation is more likely to translate into economic and legal resilience; where they are absent, firms risk moving from illegality to competitive marginalisation, especially in institutionally fragile contexts (Pinotti, 2015).

Future research should expand the sample and compare outcomes under Art. 34 and Art. 34-bis more systematically. Although these cases remain rare, complex and context-dependent, broader samples and consistent comparative protocols could support cautious analytical generalisation and strengthen inference, while preserving attention to firm-level mechanisms (Costanzo & Mazzuca, 2025). Judicial administration and judicial control are necessary responses to OC infiltration, yet sustainable recovery remains contingent on managerial and institutional factors. The observed gap between short-term stabilisation and medium-term viability, especially in liquidity and capital structure, highlights the need for systemic strategies that complement formal legality with organisational, financial, and relational capital, thereby strengthening economic legality within affected territories.

Acknowledgements We thank an anonymous referee and the editors for their valuable comments. The views and opinions expressed are solely those of the authors. Detailed case-level tables are available from the authors upon reasonable request in pseudonymised form.

References

Albuquerque, A. M., De Franco, G., & Verdi, R. S. (2013). Peer choice in CEO compensation. *Journal of Financial Economics, 108*(1), 160–181. https://doi.org/10.1016/j.jfineco.2012.10.002

ANBSC. (2023). *Relazione sull'attività svolta* (Vol. 2023). Anno.

Arellano-Bover, J., De Simoni, M., Guiso, L., Macchiavello, R., Marchetti, D. J., & Prem, M. (2024). Mafias and firms. *Quaderni Dell'antiriciclaggio, 24*. https://uif.bancaditalia.it/pubblicazioni/quaderni/2024/quaderno-24-2024/quaderno-24-2024.pdf

Arnone, G., Scirè, G., & Bivona, E. (2025). The (mis)use of cryptocurrencies by criminal organizations: A systematic literature review. *Digital Finance*. https://doi.org/10.1007/s42521-025-00148-1

Ayling, J. (2009). Criminal organizations and resilience. *International Journal of Law, Crime and Justice, 37*(4). https://doi.org/10.1016/j.ijlcj.2009.10.003

Bafundi, A., Ciappei, C., Fabrizi, M. et al. (2026). The mafia influence in the business context: Infiltration of criminal firms in the public procurement market. *Journal of Management and Governance*. https://doi.org/10.1007/s10997-026-09789-9

Bakke, T., Mahmudi, H., & Newton, A. (2020). Performance peer groups in CEO compensation contracts. *Financial Management, 49*(4), 997–1027. https://doi.org/10.1111/fima.12296

Bianchi, P. A., Marra, A., Masciandaro, D., & Pecchiari, N. (2022). Organized crime and firms' financial statements: Evidence from criminal investigations in Italy. *The Accounting Review, 97*(3), 77–106. https://doi.org/10.2308/TAR-2019-0079

Bivona, E. (2012). Aspetti critici nei processi di risanamento e sviluppo duraturo delle aziende confiscate alla criminalita' organizzata. In *Il bene dell'azienda Scritti in onore di Vittorio Coda* (pp. 321–355). Giuffrè Editore.

Bivona, E. (2019). Sistema di Controllo Interno e prevenzione delle infiltrazioni della criminalità organizzata. *Management Control, 1*, 51–68. https://doi.org/10.3280/MACO2019-SU1004

Calamunci, F. M. (2022a). A review of methods in research on organized crime infiltration of legitimate businesses. In *The private sector and organized crime* (pp. 26–38). Routledge. https://doi.org/10.4324/9781003198635-3

Calamunci, F. M. (2022b). What happens in criminal firms after godfather management removal? Judicial administration and firms' performance. *Small Business Economics, 58*(1). https://doi.org/10.1007/s11187-020-00439-4

Calamunci, F., & Drago, F. (2020). The economic impact of organized crime infiltration in the legal economy: Evidence from the judicial Administration of Organized Crime Firms. *Italian Economic Journal, 6*(2), 275–297. https://doi.org/10.1007/s40797-020-00128-x

Calamunci, F. M., De Benedetto, M. A., & Silipo, D. B. (2021). Anti-mafia law enforcement and lending in mafia lands. Evidence from judicial Administration in Italy. *The B.E. Journal of Economic Analysis & Policy, 21*(3), 1067–1106. https://doi.org/10.1515/bejeap-2020-0353

Chircop, J., Fabrizi, M., Malaspina, P., & Parbonetti, A. (2023). Anti-mafia police actions, criminal firms, and peer firm tax avoidance. *Journal of Accounting Research, 61*(1), 243–277. https://doi.org/10.1111/1475-679X.12455

Colacurci, M. (2023). La giurisprudenza del Tribunale di S.M. Capua Vetere sul d.lgs. n. 231/2001 e le misure di prevenzione patrimoniali antimafia: il controllo giudiziario volontario nella prassi. In *Verso una riforma della responsabilità da reato degli enti. Dato empirico e dimensione applicativa* (pp. 331–362). Società editrice il Mulino.

Costanzo, G. D., & Mazzuca, M. (2025). Interdisciplinary approach and quantitative methodologies for the analysis of mafia phenomena: A contribution from economic and statistical sciences. *Il Nuovo Diritto Delle Società, 6*.

Duchek, S. (2020). Organizational resilience: A capability-based conceptualization. *Business Research, 13*(1). https://doi.org/10.1007/s40685-019-0085-7

Eisenhardt, K. M. (1989). Building theories from case study research. *Academy of Management Review, 14*(4), 532–550. https://doi.org/10.5465/amr.1989.4308385

Eisenhardt, K. M., & Graebner, M. E. (2007). Theory building from cases: Opportunities and challenges. *Academy of Management Journal, 50*(1), 25–32. https://doi.org/10.5465/amj.2007.24160888

Esposito, P., & Ricci, P. (2014). Public (dis)value: A case study. In *Studies in public and non-profit governance* (Vol. 3, pp. 291–300). https://doi.org/10.1108/S2051-663020140000003012

Esposito, P., & Ricci, P. (2015). How to turn public (dis)value into new public value? Evidence from Italy. *Public Money and Management, 35*(3). https://doi.org/10.1080/09540962.2015.1027499

Fabrizi, M., Malaspina, P., & Parbonetti, A. (2017). Caratteristiche e modalità di gestione delle aziende criminali. *Rivista di Studi e Ricerche sulla criminalità organizzata, 3*(1).

Fourie, M., Steenkamp, P., McIntyre-Louw, J.-L., & Oellermann, C. (2023). Exploring infiltration behaviour by organised crime groups. *Journal of Money Laundering Control, 26*(1), 159–171. https://doi.org/10.1108/JMLC-10-2021-0117

Ganau, R., & Rodríguez-Pose, A. (2018). Industrial clusters, organized crime, and productivity growth in Italian SMEs. *Journal of Regional Science, 58*(2), 363–385. https://doi.org/10.1111/jors.12354

Greco, A. M., & Messina, M. (2024). Characteristics of Italian firms in the judicial administration: Can financial ratios be red flags of criminal infiltrations? *Corporate Ownership and Control, 21*(3, special issue), 116–132. https://doi.org/10.22495/cocv21i3siart10

Hillmann, J., & Guenther, E. (2021). Organizational resilience: A valuable construct for management research? *International Journal of Management Reviews, 23*(1). https://doi.org/10.1111/ijmr.12239

Nazzari, M., & Riccardi, M. (2024). Cleaning mafia cash: An empirical analysis of the money laundering behaviour of 2800 Italian criminals. *European Journal of Criminology, 21*(4), 583–608. https://doi.org/10.1177/14773708231224981

Nicolò, D. (2025). *Mafia and firm performance. The effect of organized crime and its judicial removal*. Franco Angeli. https://series.francoangeli.it/index.php/oa/catalog/book/1465

Parbonetti, A. (2021). *La presenza delle mafie nell'economia: profili e modelli operativi (first)*. Padova University Press. http://hdl.handle.net/11159/7262

Pinotti, P. (2015). The economic costs of organised crime: Evidence from southern Italy. *The Economic Journal, 125*(586), F203–F232. https://doi.org/10.1111/ecoj.12235

Riccardi, M. (2014). When criminals invest in businesses: Are we looking in the right direction? An exploratory analysis of companies controlled by mafias. In *Organized crime, corruption and crime prevention* (Vol. 9783319018393, pp. 197–206). Springer International Publishing. https://doi.org/10.1007/978-3-319-01839-3_23

Riccardi, M., & Berlusconi, G. (2016). Measuring organised crime infiltration in legal businesses. In *Organised crime in European businesses*. doi:https://doi.org/10.4324/9781315640617.

Savona, E. U., & Berlusconi, G. (2015). Organized crime infiltration of legitimate businesses in Europe: A pilot project in five European countries. Final report of project ARIEL—Assessing the Risk of the Infiltration of Organized Crime in EU MSs Legitimate Economies: A pilot project in 5 EU countries (www.arielproject.eu).

Sciarrone, R. (2011). *Alleanze nell'ombra. Mafie ed economie locali in Sicilia e nel Mezzogiorno*. Fondazione Res.

Sciarrone, R., & Storti, L. (2016). *Complicità trasversali fra mafia ed economia. Servizi, garanzie, regolazione. Stato e Mercato* (p. 108). doi:https://doi.org/10.1425/85087

Scirè, G., & Bivona, E. (2026). Mapping organized crime as a stakeholder: A risk-based and responsive governance perspective. *Regulation & Governance*, 1–16. https://doi.org/10.1111/rego.70194

Slutzky, P., & Zeume, S. (2024). Organized crime and firms: Evidence from Antimafia enforcement actions. *Management Science, 70*(10), 6569–6596. https://doi.org/10.1287/mnsc.2021.00859

Visconti, C. (2019). Il controllo giudiziario 'volontario': una moderna 'messa alla prova' aziendale per una tutela recuperatoria contro le infiltrazioni mafiose. In G. Amarelli & S. Sticchi (Eds.), *Le interdittive antimafia e le altre misure di contrasto all'infiltrazione mafiosa negli appalti pubblici* (pp. 237–253). Giappichelli.

Von Lampe, K. (2016). *Organized crime: Analyzing illegal activities, criminal structures, and extra-legal governance*. SAGE Publications Ltd.

Weick, K. E., & Sutcliffe, K. (2001). *Managing the unexpected: Assuring high performance in an age of uncertainty*. Jossey-Bass.

Weick, K. E., Sutcliffe, K. M., & Obstfeld, D. (2005). Organizing and the process of sensemaking. *Organization Science, 16*(4). https://doi.org/10.1287/orsc.1050.0133

Williams, T. A., Gruber, D. A., Sutcliffe, K. M., Shepherd, D. A., & Zhao, E. Y. (2017). Organizational response to adversity: Fusing crisis management and resilience research streams. *Academy of Management Annals, 11*(2). https://doi.org/10.5465/annals.2015.0134

Yin, R. K. (2018). *Case study research and applications. Design and methods*. SAGE Publications.

Zabyelina, Y., Thachuk, K. L., & Savona, E. U. (2022). *The private sector and organized crime*. Routledge. https://doi.org/10.4324/9781003198635

From Seizure to Social Value: Descriptive Evidence on the Management and Reuse of Confiscated Assets

Pierpaolo Parrotta, Marco Stimolo, Alessandro Stringhi, Marianna Marino, and Giovanni Immordino

Abstract The social reuse of assets confiscated from organized crime has become an increasingly important instrument for promoting social justice, inclusion, and territorial regeneration. While this model has attracted growing policy attention in Italy and, more recently, at the European level, limited evidence is available on how organizations actually manage confiscated assets and address the challenges associated with their reuse. This chapter provides descriptive evidence based on an original nationwide survey of social cooperatives managing confiscated assets. We examine the characteristics of the assets, the main managerial and institutional challenges faced by organizations, the strategies adopted to overcome them, and the policy recommendations emerging from practitioners' experience. The findings highlight the importance of community engagement, inter-organizational networks, managerial capabilities, and supportive institutions in ensuring the long-term sustainability and social impact of confiscated asset reuse initiatives.

P. Parrotta (✉) · M. Stimolo
Department of Economics and Statistics, University of Siena, Siena, Italy
e-mail: pierpaolo.parrotta@unisi.it; marco.stimolo@unisi.it

A. Stringhi
Department of Business Administration, Prague University of Economics and Business, Prague, Czech Republic
e-mail: alessandro.stringhi@vse.cz

M. Marino
Laboratory for the Analysis of compleX Economic Systems, IMT Lucca Institute for Advanced Studies, Lucca, Italy
e-mail: marianna.marino@imtlucca.it

G. Immordino
Department of Economics and Statistics, University of Naples Federico II, Naples, Italy
e-mail: giovanni.immordino@unina.it

R. Cellini et al. (eds.), *Cultural, Social, and Political Participation in the Internet Era*, Contributions to Economics, https://doi.org/10.1007/978-3-032-33072-7_12

1 Introduction

The reuse of confiscated assets for social purposes has emerged as a powerful tool for promoting social justice, inclusion, and territorial regeneration. In Italy, the legal framework governing the reuse of assets seized from organized crime has enabled a broad spectrum of non-profit organizations and public institutions to transform these once symbols of illegality into community goods. This model is increasingly gaining relevance at the European level. Directive (EU) 2024/1260 (2024) aims to harmonize Member States' approaches to the social reuse of confiscated assets, including the adoption of national strategies for asset recovery and the development of training programmes for asset managers. Despite its potential, however, the process of assigning, managing, and enhancing confiscated assets entails a range of operational, financial, legal, and social challenges.

This chapter examines how social cooperatives engaged in the reuse of confiscated assets operate, focusing on the challenges they face, the strategies they adopt, and the policy implications that emerge. Our analysis draws on original data from a nationwide survey conducted between September 2024 and February 2025, covering 106 social cooperatives managing one or more assets confiscated from criminal organizations in Italy. The survey combines structured questions with open-ended responses, allowing us to capture both qualitative patterns and insights.

We focus on social cooperatives as they represent a particularly suitable organizational setting for analysing the management of confiscated assets. Compared with other organizational forms, they are structurally closer to traditional firms, being subject to stricter reporting and governance requirements (D.Lgs. 112/2017, 2017), while at the same time pursuing explicit social objectives. Moreover, social cooperatives exhibit a greater degree of internal homogeneity, whereas associations encompass a wide variety of missions and organizational models, making them less amenable to systematic analysis. Focusing on social cooperatives therefore allows us to identify more consistent managerial practices and to derive insights that are potentially scalable across different European contexts.

Existing studies have examined the economic and social consequences of asset confiscation. Calamunci et al. (2023) show that anti-mafia reassignment policies affect housing prices differently depending on the destination of confiscated properties, with heterogeneous effects across territories and forms of reuse. Boeri et al. (2024) show that while the confiscation of mafia assets initially exerts a negative, localized effect on nearby property values, their subsequent re-allocation generates positive—though temporary—spillovers. Fiorillo et al. (2026) find that the confiscation of real estate assets from mafia organizations increases trust in government institutions and the legal system in Southern regions, whereas in Central and Northern regions this effect is weaker and mainly confined to local levels of government.

While this literature provides important insights into the consequences of confiscation policies, contributions from management scholars have largely focused on case-based evidence (e.g., Bisogno, 2023; Cavotta & Dalpiaz, 2022). As a result, the organizational mechanisms through which confiscated assets are effectively managed and reused remain underexplored, and a systematic understanding of best practices and managerial capabilities is still lacking.

We contribute to filling this gap by shifting the focus from the effects of confiscation policies to the governance and management of confiscated assets. Leveraging original survey data, we provide an empirically grounded analysis of both the characteristics of confiscated assets and the strategies adopted by managing organizations to address key challenges, including financial sustainability, workforce integration, institutional coordination, and community engagement. Our findings highlight the coexistence of strong civic motivation and organizational heterogeneity, alongside persistent constraints related to financial viability, legal complexity, and human resource management. By identifying patterns in practices and strategies, we contribute to the development of more effective support mechanisms for organizations involved in the social reuse of confiscated assets.

2 Asset Characteristics

Consistent with the geographical distribution of confiscated assets,[1] our sample shows that most confiscated assets assigned to entities are in areas with historical criminal activity. However, the presence in Northern Italy highlights the trans-regional expansion of organized crime over time. The widespread participation of non-profit organizations across regions supports the broader applicability and replicability of the social reuse model (see Fig. 1). This suggests that, beyond countering local criminal legacies, the model has evolved into a nationwide tool for social innovation, inclusion, and local development.

As shown in Fig. 2, most assets consist of properties with agricultural, building, or mixed-use potential (37.6%), underscoring the centrality of land-based and multi-functional assets in the social reuse model. These often include farmland, abandoned structures, or partially developed sites.

Residential properties such as apartments and detached houses make up a substantial portion of the assets (31.2%). These are frequently repurposed for housing initiatives, community living, or support services, including shelters for vulnerable populations (e.g., women, minors, or migrants). Commercial or industrial premises (8.8%)—including warehouses and office spaces—are less common but particularly valuable for economic integration strategies, such as vocational training, social enterprises, or logistics-based activities. Finally, villas, multi-level buildings, and small accommodation facilities (22.4%) represent a significant share. These often lend themselves to tourism, hospitality, and cultural initiatives, enabling organizations to combine economic sustainability with public engagement and

[1] See Let's tell the good: The Practices of Social Reuse of Confiscated Assets from Mafias (Libera, 2024). www.libera.it/documenti/schede/raccontiamo_il_bene_pubb_en.pdf.

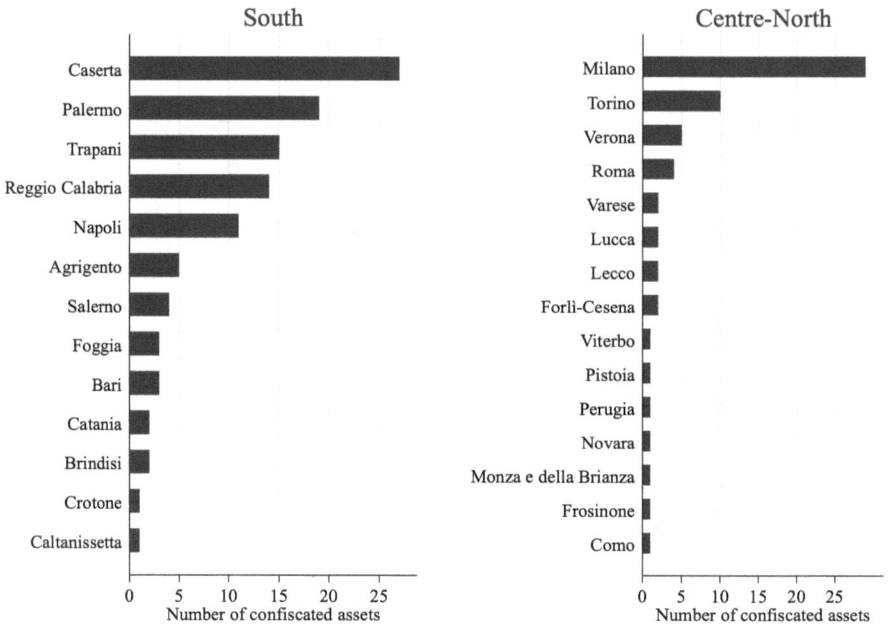

Fig. 1 Confiscated assets by province

awareness-raising. The distribution reflects the wide spectrum of properties seized from organized crime, and the multiple functional opportunities these assets offer for social purposes, whether through residential, agricultural, commercial, or multi-functional reuse schemes.

The data retrieved from the interviews inform us on the physical condition of confiscated assets at the time of assignment, which is often problematic, posing a major operational and financial challenge for the organizations involved. Nearly half of all assets (45.9%) were reported to be in poor or very poor condition, requiring substantial investment for renovation, adaptation, or basic usability. About a third of properties are in good or very good condition (28.9% combined), while just one case (0.6%) reported an excellent state. A further 21.8% fall into the "fair" category, likely requiring moderate repair or upgrades. This distribution underscores the burden placed on social cooperatives and other entities managing the reuse process, who often must secure external funding, navigate bureaucratic hurdles, and manage delays before the assets can be put to effective social use. Against this backdrop, the next section examines in greater detail the main challenges faced by organizations managing confiscated assets.

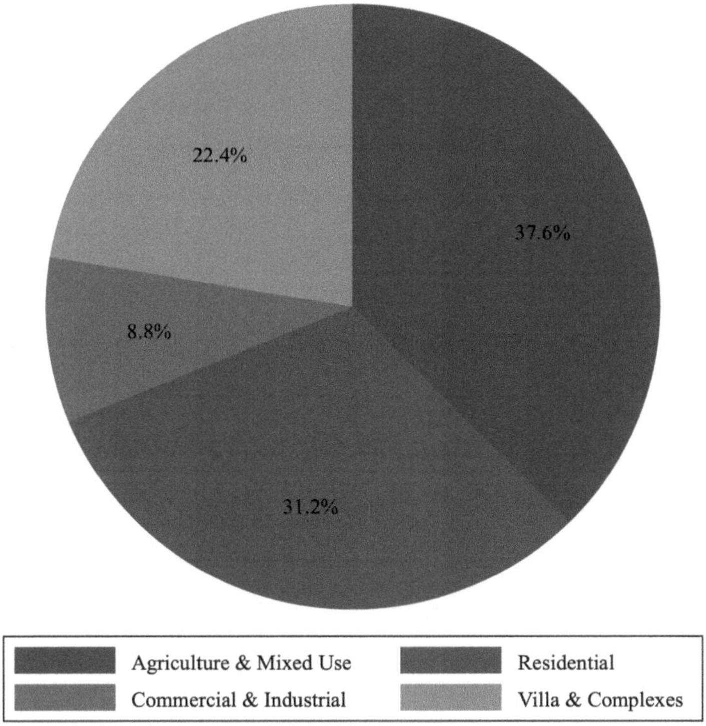

Fig. 2 Confiscated assets by type

3 Main Challenges

The interview data indicate a complex set of challenges (see Fig. 3) encountered by organizations involved in the reuse of confiscated assets, reflecting the broader social, economic, and institutional contexts in which these initiatives operate. The reported categories are not mutually exclusive, i.e., respondents could indicate more than one challenge.

Community relations and the promotion of a culture of legality emerge as the most frequently cited challenge, standing clearly above all others. This underscores the centrality of building trust, legitimacy, and social acceptance in local contexts often marked by the persistent legacy of organized crime. In many cases, managing organizations operate in environments where mistrust towards institutions is widespread and where criminal networks may still exert social or economic influence. As a result, fostering community engagement requires continuous effort, including outreach activities, transparency, and the active involvement of local stakeholders.

Economic sustainability and access to funding represent the second most frequently reported concern, highlighting the difficulty of securing stable financial

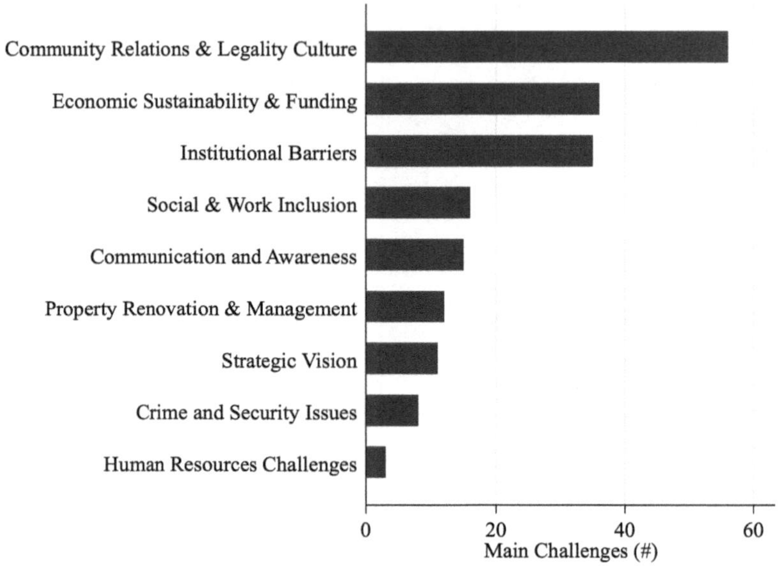

Fig. 3 Main challenges

resources and ensuring long-term viability. Many interviewees point to persistent constraints, including delays in public payments, limited access to credit, and the inherent tension between achieving economic sustainability and pursuing strong social objectives.

Next, *institutional barriers* also emerge as a major challenge, reflecting the weight of administrative complexity, regulatory constraints, and delays in public procedures. Respondents frequently report difficulties related to fragmented regulations, lengthy authorization processes, and cumbersome bureaucratic requirements. In addition, limited coordination between public authorities and managing entities further complicates institutional dialogue and slows decision-making.

Communication and public awareness emerge as another relevant challenge. Several organizations report persistent difficulties in making their activities visible and socially valued. Effectively communicating the mission, impact, and symbolic significance of confiscated assets requires not only resources, but also specific skills and strategic capabilities that are not always available within these organizations. Moreover, limited visibility may reduce community support, hinder participation, and constrain opportunities for partnerships and fundraising.

In the middle-lower part of the distribution, we find *social and work inclusion* and *property renovation and management*. These dimensions point to the dual nature of asset reuse initiatives, which combine economic activity with strong social objectives. Organizations face the challenge of integrating disadvantaged individuals—often with fragile or irregular work trajectories—into stable and productive roles, requiring tailored training, supervision, and continuous support.

However, they must cope with the technical and financial burden of restoring and maintaining assets that are frequently in poor condition, entailing significant upfront investments and ongoing maintenance costs.

Strategic vision follows closely, highlighting the difficulty of long-term planning and organizational development in a context characterized by uncertainty, resource constraints, and institutional complexity. Limited managerial capacity, short funding cycles, and the need to respond to urgent operational issues may hinder the ability of organizations to adopt forward-looking strategies and scale their activities over time.

Crime and security issues and *human resource challenges* are the least frequently mentioned categories. Although they appear at the bottom of the ranking, they remain non-negligible and may be particularly salient in specific territorial contexts. Security concerns can still arise in areas with a strong criminal presence, potentially affecting both staff and beneficiaries, while human resource constraints—such as difficulties in attracting and retaining qualified personnel—can further limit organizational effectiveness. Together, these factors suggest that even less frequently reported challenges may have significant implications for the sustainability and resilience of asset reuse initiatives. Moreover, the influence of criminal clans may persist in local community relations beyond direct security issues, as reflected in the prominence of community engagement among the most frequently reported challenges.

While the evidence discussed above highlights the multiple and interrelated challenges faced by organizations managing confiscated assets, it also points to the emergence of a set of adaptive strategies aimed at overcoming these issues. In response to operational, financial, and institutional barriers, organizations adopt a variety of practices to enhance their effectiveness and ensure the sustainability of their activities. The next section examines these strategies, shedding light on the mechanisms through which asset reuse initiatives can be strengthened.

4 Adopted Strategies

The strategies adopted by organizations to address the challenges outlined above reveal a diverse yet interconnected set of practices aimed at enhancing both operational effectiveness and social impact (see Fig. 4).

Partnerships and networking (31.1%) emerge as the most frequently adopted strategy, underscoring the central role of collaboration in this context. Organizations actively build alliances with other third-sector entities, public institutions, and, in some cases, private-sector partners to access complementary resources, share knowledge, and coordinate service provision. These networks not only facilitate resource pooling and economies of scale but also enhance visibility and legitimacy, particularly in environments where individual organizations may face capacity constraints.

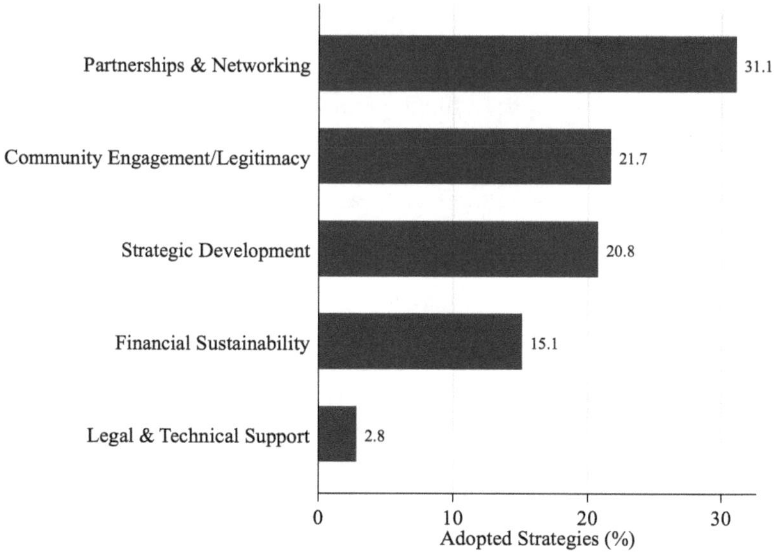

Fig. 4 Adopted strategies

Community engagement and legitimacy (21.7%) represent another key strategic dimension, closely aligned with the challenges related to trust and local embeddedness. Organizations invest in communication campaigns, educational initiatives, and participatory practices aimed at fostering community involvement and reshaping local perceptions of confiscated assets. These efforts are crucial to transforming such assets from symbols of illegality into shared community resources, thereby strengthening social acceptance and long-term sustainability.

Strategic development (20.8%) reflects a growing emphasis on planning, professionalization, and organizational learning. Many respondents highlight the importance of defining clear objectives, adopting medium- to long-term planning horizons, and developing managerial capabilities. In a context characterized by uncertainty and resource constraints, flexibility and an entrepreneurial mindset emerge as key factors enabling organizations to adapt to changing conditions while remaining aligned with their social mission.

Financial sustainability (15.1%) is addressed through a range of strategies aimed at diversifying revenue streams and reducing dependence on unstable funding sources. These include the development of income-generating activities, participation in public calls and grants, and the exploration of private funding opportunities. Such approaches reflect the need to balance economic viability with social objectives, often requiring innovative business models that integrate market-oriented activities with social value creation.

Legal and technical support (2.8%), although less frequently mentioned, highlights the importance of access to specialized expertise in navigating regulatory frameworks, administrative procedures, and technical requirements. This dimension is particularly relevant given the complexity and fragmentation of the legal environment surrounding confiscated assets.

Taken together, these strategies point to a set of practices that goes beyond mere asset management, aiming instead at the regeneration of social and economic value. While each organization may emphasize a primary strategic axis, our qualitative evidence suggests that these approaches are often combined, with strong complementarities emerging between networking, community engagement, and financial planning. This integrated approach appears crucial for addressing the multi-dimensional challenges associated with the reuse of confiscated assets.

5 Recommendations for Startups

The reflections shared by managers of confiscated assets provide a nuanced picture of the challenges and requirements involved in launching and sustaining initiatives based on such properties. Their insights combine practical guidance with broader strategic considerations, highlighting not only operational needs but also the values and institutional conditions underpinning successful asset reuse. These responses, shown in Fig. 5, offer valuable inputs for policy design, particularly in supporting new entrants and strengthening the broader ecosystem of asset reuse.

A central theme emerging from the advice highlights the importance of a clear and feasible project idea. Respondents consistently emphasize the need for

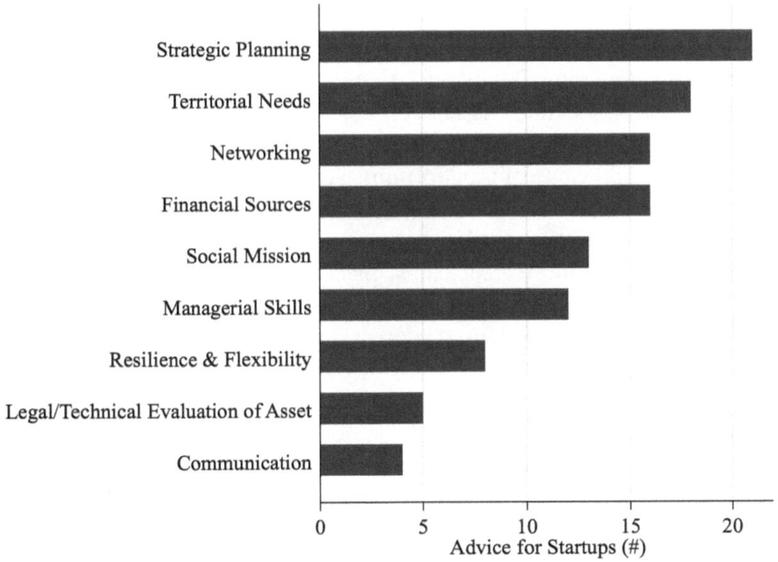

Fig. 5 Recommendations for startups

a realistic business plan, grounded in economic sustainability and aligned with the specific characteristics of the assigned asset. This entails conducting a thorough assessment of local needs, defining clear objectives, and structuring implementation in manageable phases. A well-developed strategy is seen not only as a managerial tool, but as a key condition for credibility and long-term impact.

Another recurring recommendation relates to territorial embeddedness. Successful initiatives tend to be those deeply rooted in their local context, capable of engaging with communities and responding to their needs. Managers stress the importance of early and continuous interaction with local stakeholders, as well as the ability to build trust and foster a sense of shared ownership around the project. Thus, community engagement emerges as both a strategic and a normative dimension of asset reuse.

Closely connected to this is the emphasis on partnerships and networking. Given the complexity of managing confiscated assets, operating in isolation is rarely viable. Building alliances with public institutions, third-sector organizations, and experienced actors is considered essential for accessing resources, sharing knowledge, and enhancing legitimacy. In several cases, respondents explicitly recommend that startups join consortia or umbrella organizations to benefit from guidance, advocacy, and operational support.

Financial readiness also represents a critical factor. Many respondents highlight the importance of securing initial resources—through public funding, foundations, or private sources—to sustain activities during the early stages. Access to credit, guarantee mechanisms, and diversified revenue streams are all seen as key to ensuring economic viability. In the absence of adequate financial support, organizations may struggle to carry out necessary renovations or maintain operations in the startup phase.

Beyond these operational aspects, several managers stress the importance of a strong ethical orientation. Managing a confiscated asset is not merely an economic activity, but a socially embedded mission. This requires an organizational culture grounded in transparency, accountability, and commitment to social impact, reflecting the symbolic value of transforming assets linked to criminal activities into collective goods.

Human capital is another crucial dimension. Respondents emphasize the need to build competent and motivated teams, invest in training, and develop complementary skills within the organization. The quality of human resources is widely perceived as a decisive determinant of success, particularly in contexts characterized by complexity and uncertainty.

In this regard, organizational resilience and flexibility are equally important. Navigating administrative procedures, legal constraints, and evolving local conditions requires the ability to adapt, respond creatively to emerging challenges, and maintain a long-term perspective despite initial difficulties.

Effective communication also plays a central role. Transparent and consistent communication strategies are essential to build legitimacy, engage stakeholders, and foster community support. This includes not only promoting the project's activities but also conveying its broader social and symbolic significance.

Finally, respondents stress the importance of thorough due diligence on the assigned assets. This involves assessing their legal status, physical condition, and regulatory constraints, including permits, renovation needs, and functional suitability. Such a preliminary evaluation is essential to avoid unforeseen costs and ensure the feasibility of the project. In parallel, legal and administrative preparedness is crucial, as organizations must navigate complex regulatory frameworks. Access to legal and technical expertise, particularly in the early stages, is therefore strongly recommended.

Overall, the testimonies suggest that successful entry into the field of confiscated asset reuse requires a combination of strategic clarity, territorial sensitivity, and collaborative capacity. From a policy perspective, these findings point to the importance of providing pre-assignment technical support, facilitating access to funding and credit guarantees, offering legal assistance, and promoting networks of exchange and mentorship. More broadly, they highlight the need to frame confiscated assets not simply as properties to be allocated, but as instruments of civic regeneration. Supporting new initiatives in this domain thus means investing not only in organizational capacity but also in the broader goal of fostering sustainable, legitimate, and inclusive local development.

6 Suggested Policy Changes

The responses from confiscated asset managers highlight a set of concrete, actionable priorities for policy reform aimed at improving the effectiveness and sustainability of asset reuse initiatives (see Fig. 6).

The most recurrent request concerns the acceleration and simplification of bureaucratic processes related to confiscation, assignment, and authorization. Lengthy delays, unclear procedures, and regulatory ambiguities are seen as major obstacles that hinder timely and effective reuse. Respondents call for faster assignment processes, standardized procedures, and clearer evaluation criteria.

Access to funding emerges as another critical issue. Many responses emphasize the need for stronger and more stable financial support to cover renovation costs, sustain startup phases, and ensure long-term viability. Suggested measures include facilitating access to credit through guarantees or revolving funds, re-allocating resources from confiscations, and designing financial instruments tailored to non-profit organizations managing complex social projects.

A recurring concern relates to the mismatch between required investments and the duration of asset concessions. Respondents stress the importance of extending or ensuring the renewal of concessions, particularly when significant investments are needed, to reduce uncertainty and enable long-term planning.

Several responses also highlight the poor physical and legal conditions of assets at the time of assignment. There is a clear need to ensure that properties are transferred in usable and compliant conditions, or that adequate funding and information

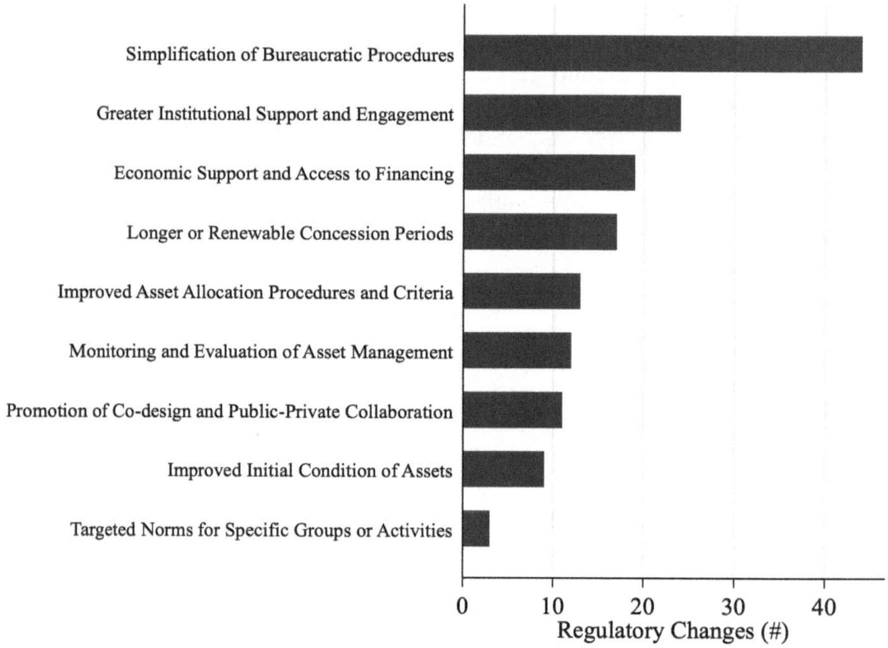

Fig. 6 Suggested policy changes

are provided to support their recovery. Greater transparency in documentation and access to asset records are also considered essential.

Strengthening institutional support is another key priority. Respondents call for more active involvement of public authorities at local, regional, and national levels, including structured support throughout the assignment process and participatory planning mechanisms. Institutional proximity is seen as crucial for building trust and enhancing the legitimacy of reuse initiatives.

Finally, respondents point to the need for improved monitoring systems that account not only for economic performance but also for social and territorial impact, as well as for targeted regulatory measures to promote inclusive employment and address the specific constraints of smaller or marginal areas.

7 Conclusions

This chapter provides an empirically grounded analysis of the characteristics, challenges, and strategies associated with the social reuse of confiscated assets in Italy, drawing on original survey data from social cooperatives directly involved in their management.

The evidence highlights the multi-faceted nature of asset reuse initiatives. On the one hand, confiscated assets offer significant opportunities for local development and inclusion, as reflected in their diverse functional uses across residential, agricultural, and commercial domains. On the other hand, their often poor physical condition and complex institutional environment generate substantial operational and financial constraints.

Our findings show that organizations operate within a highly demanding context, characterized by interrelated challenges. Specifically, issues related to community legitimacy, financial sustainability, and institutional barriers emerge as the most pressing, underscoring that the success of asset reuse depends not only on managerial capacity but also on broader social and governance conditions.

At the same time, quite a few organizations show a strong capacity for adaptation. The strategies they adopt—ranging from partnerships and community engagement to strategic planning and revenue diversification—highlight the importance of collaboration, local embeddedness, and organizational learning. These practices suggest that effective asset reuse is not the result of isolated interventions, but rather of coordinated and multi-dimensional efforts.

The recommendations provided by experienced managers further reinforce this perspective, pointing to the need for strategic clarity, financial preparedness, and strong territorial integration, as well as for ethical commitment and organizational resilience. Taken together, these insights contribute to identifying a set of enabling conditions for successful asset reuse initiatives.

From a policy perspective, the findings suggest several priorities. These include strengthening pre-assignment support mechanisms, facilitating access to funding and credit, simplifying administrative procedures, and promoting training and capacity-building programmes for asset managers. In this regard, the recent European Directive (EU) 2024/1260—which calls for national strategies and training initiatives—offers a timely framework for scaling and institutionalizing these practices at the European level.

In conclusion, the sustainable reuse of confiscated assets requires a combined effort: while non-profit organizations need resilience and creativity, institutional backing and policy innovation are essential to unlock the full potential of these experiences as drivers of social inclusion, local development, and anti-mafia culture.

Acknowledgements We are especially grateful to Libera, Associazioni, nomi e numeri CONTRO LE MAFIE for generously providing access to its unique dataset on entities managing confiscated assets, without which this research would not have been possible. We thank Federica Muzzicato and Andrea Sereni for their valuable research assistance. The views and opinions expressed in this chapter are solely those of the authors.

References

Bisogno, M. (2023). Transition management strategies of confiscated mafia-type firms: The role of public administrations and nonprofit organizations. *Journal of Public Budgeting, Accounting and Financial Management, 35*(6), 121–139.

Boeri, F., Di Cataldo, M., & Pietrostefani, E. (2024). Localized effects of confiscated and re-allocated real estate mafia assets. *Journal of Economic Geography, 24*(2), 219–240.

Calamunci, F. M., Ferrante, L., Scebba, R., & Torrisi, G. (2023). Mafia doesn't live here anymore: Antimafia policies and housing prices. *Journal of Regional Science, 63*(4), 1001–1025.

Cavotta, V., & Dalpiaz, E. (2022). Good apples in spoiled barrels: A temporal model of firm formalization in a field characterized by widespread informality. *Journal of Business Venturing, 37*(2), 106188.

Decreto Legislativo 112 3/7/2017. (2017). *Revisione della disciplina in materia di impresa sociale*. Gazzetta Ufficiale della Repubblica Italiana.

Directive 2024/1260/EU. (2024). *European Parliament and of the Council of 24 April 2024*.

Fiorillo, D., Mosca, M., & Pennacchio, L. (2026). Institutional trust and the confiscation of real estate assets from organised crime. *Journal of Institutional Economics, 22*.

Part III
Entrepreneurship and Social Inclusion

Entrepreneurial Education and Non-WEIRD Countries: Might AI Make a Difference?

Veronica Scuotto, Theofilos Tzanidis, and Enrico di Taranto

Abstract This chapter examines the transformative potential of Artificial Intelligence (AI) in reshaping Entrepreneurial Education (EE) for non-WEIRD—-Western, Educated, Industrialised, Rich, and Democratic—countries. Beginning with the foundational critique of WEIRD samples in social and behavioural science, and extending the recent roadmap for non-WEIRD entrepreneurship research, this chapter argues that the most urgent and under-theorised challenge in the global EE literature is not the integration of AI per se, but the contextual adaptation of AI-enabled pedagogies to the specific socio-economic, linguistic, infrastructural, and institutional realities of non-WEIRD national settings. To address this challenge, the chapter proposes the AI-EENI framework—AI-Enabled Entrepreneurial Education for Non-WEIRD Inclusion. The framework is a six-layer predictive-prescriptive model that leverages internationally validated secondary datasets and AI forecasting methodologies to generate actionable EE interventions without the requirement for primary data collection in fragile or resource-constrained contexts. The AI-EENI framework integrates DARQ+ technologies—Distributed ledger, AI, Reality technologies, and Quantum computing—into a coherent, contextually sensitive architecture for non-WEIRD EE delivery. This framework is applied to Ghana as practical evidence. The chapter contributes to the growing literature on AI in education, non-WEIRD entrepreneurship, and responsible technology deployment, whilst offering practical prescriptions for educators, policymakers, and international development agencies working towards SDG 4.

V. Scuotto (✉) · E. di Taranto
Department of Economics Management and Institutions, University of Naples Federico II, Naples, Italy
e-mail: veronica.scuotto@unina.it; enrico.ditaranto@unina.it

T. Tzanidis
Business School, University of West of Scotland, Paisley, Scotland
e-mail: theo.tzanidis@uws.ac.uk

R. Cellini et al. (eds.), *Cultural, Social, and Political Participation in the Internet Era*, Contributions to Economics, https://doi.org/10.1007/978-3-032-33072-7_13

1 Introduction

Academics working at the intersections of management, education, and development have been interested in education, entrepreneurship, and technology for many years. However, despite decades of work, there remains one curious inconsistency in this research: most theories, empirical evidence, and instructional recommendations that form the worldwide body of knowledge on entrepreneurial education (EE) have been built from and tested on samples that are anything but 'normal'. Non-WEIRD populations—those who are not Western, Educated, Industrialised, Rich, and Democratic—are a population type defined in Henrich et al.'s (2010) critique of behavioural science. Their analysis demonstrated that WEIRD subjects are 'frequent outliers' across a wide range of psychological, behavioural, and economic measures, yet have been systematically treated as representative of universal human behaviour. With approximately six billion people living outside WEIRD contexts, this epistemological distortion is not merely an academic inconvenience; it has material consequences for the design and delivery of educational and entrepreneurial programmes that are ostensibly intended to serve these majority-world populations.

Shepherd et al. (2025) have recently crystallised this critique into a formal roadmap for the entrepreneurship research field, arguing that the discipline's theoretical foundations built on American and Northern European datasets, validated in WEIRD institutional environments, and published in WEIRD-dominated journal ecosystems may be systematically unfit for the contexts in which the majority of entrepreneurial activity actually takes place. The implication for EE is profound: if the theoretical models that inform EE programmes are themselves products of WEIRD epistemology, then those programmes risk reproducing inequality rather than alleviating it.

AI is both a manifestation of the problem and, if leveraged correctly, part of the solution. Artificial intelligence is the defining technology of our time, rapidly widening the gap between what's possible in education and who has access to these opportunities. By 2030, generative AI could automate 70% of work activities in nearly every job, according to the McKinsey Global Institute (2023). This automation has the potential to create trillions of dollars of value. For non-WEIRD economies—many of which have large, young, entrepreneurially active populations but limited access to quality EE infrastructure—this trajectory represents an existential inflection point: an opportunity to leapfrog legacy educational systems, or a risk of accelerating the already substantial gap between WEIRD and non-WEIRD entrepreneurial ecosystems.

This chapter synthesises the current state of the literature on AI and EE in non-WEIRD contexts and identifies the conditions under which AI can genuinely transform entrepreneurial education for the populations it most needs to serve.

The original contribution of this chapter is the AI-EENI framework—AI-Enabled Entrepreneurial Education for Non-WEIRD Inclusion—a six-layer predictive-prescriptive model. The framework will be able to design evidence-based, contextually appropriate EE interventions for non-WEIRD settings without the logistical, ethical, and financial burdens of primary data collection in fragile or resource-constrained environments. The answer lies in a secondary data approach that combines AI-driven analysis of internationally validated aggregate datasets with predictive modelling, adaptive content generation, and DARQ-enabled delivery architecture.

2 The WEIRD Paradigm and Its Discontents: Entrepreneurship in Non-Western Contexts

The intellectual provocation embedded in Henrich et al.'s (2010) analysis of the WEIRD problem—published in one of the most-cited papers in the history of behavioural and brain sciences—extends far beyond its original psychological domain. When these authors demonstrated that participants from WEIRD societies exhibit distinctive patterns of visual perception, fairness norms, cooperation, moral reasoning, and self-conception that place them at the statistical periphery of the global human distribution, the implications reverberated across every social science that had similarly built its empirical foundations on WEIRD convenience samples. Entrepreneurship research was no exception.

The entrepreneurship field's theoretical canon is deeply embedded in WEIRD intellectual traditions. The foundational individual-opportunity nexus of Shane and Venkataraman (2000)—perhaps the most cited framework in entrepreneurship scholarship—was developed from and validated against samples drawn almost exclusively from WEIRD economies. Alvarez and Barney's (2007) distinction between discovery and creation theories of entrepreneurial action, whilst theoretically powerful, assumes institutional contexts—functioning legal systems, enforceable contracts, intellectual property protections, reliable financial infrastructure—that characterise WEIRD economies but are absent or unreliable in many non-WEIRD settings. Sarasvathy's (2001) effectuation theory, which proposes that expert entrepreneurs begin with available means rather than predetermined goals, offers more contextual flexibility, but was itself developed from think-aloud protocols with 27 expert entrepreneurs, all from North American technology ventures.

Welter (2011) is one of the earliest scholars to formally call for contextualised entrepreneurship theory. She calls upon researchers to consider the historical, temporal, institutional, spatial, and social contexts in which entrepreneurs behave. This contextualisation agenda has gained significant traction in the subsequent decade, as evidenced by the proliferation of studies examining entrepreneurship in emerging economies (Bruton et al., 2008) and in contexts of poverty (Bruton et al., 2013; Sutter et al., 2019). However, Shepherd et al. (2025) argue persuasively that despite this growth, the field remains structurally biased: studies on non-WEIRD contexts constitute a small minority of published output in the field's leading journals, and the theoretical frameworks employed in these studies are still predominantly imported from WEIRD scholarship rather than developed indigenously.

This structural bias has specific consequences for entrepreneurial education. EE programmes designed on the basis of WEIRD theoretical frameworks and pedagogical models carry embedded assumptions about individual agency, market orientation, risk tolerance, and institutional support that may be systematically misaligned with the realities of non-WEIRD entrepreneurs. Shantz et al. (2018), in their qualitative study of rural entrepreneurs in Ghana, found that informal institutions of collectivism and fatalism shaped entrepreneurs' occupational identities in ways that directly constrained the uptake of innovative practices that EE programmes sought to promote. Chatterjee et al. (2022), studying women entrepreneurs in rural India who had completed a solar energy entrepreneurship training programme, found that outcome divergence was not a function of programme quality but of the alignment—or misalignment—between programme assumptions and participants' socio-economic realities, family support structures, and prior work experience.

The market imperfection logic that underlies entrepreneurial opportunity theory (Alvarez & Barney, 2007; Shane & Venkataraman, 2000) takes on a distinctive character in non-WEIRD economies. Drawing on Chrisman et al. (2026), entrepreneurial opportunities in non-WEIRD settings are frequently constituted by imperfections in product or factor markets that generate transactional gains through goods and services for future use. However, the uncertainty associated with these opportunities—what Knight (1921) characterised as unmeasurable, as distinct from the probabilistically assessable risk that can be hedged through mathematical tools—is substantially higher in non-WEIRD contexts, where institutional voids, regulatory fragility, and social capital constraints compound the fundamental unknowability of entrepreneurial futures (Ramoglou, 2021; Ramoglou & McMullen, 2024). McMullen and Shepherd (2006) argued that entrepreneurial action requires the actor to bear uncertainty until a unique opportunity can be identified; in non-WEIRD contexts, this threshold is considerably higher and the resources available to bear it considerably fewer.

It is within this structural context that the question of AI's role in non-WEIRD EE acquires its full significance. Learning poverty—defined by the World Bank as the share of ten-year-olds who cannot read and understand a simple text—affects approximately 70% of children in low- and middle-income countries (World Bank et al., 2022), with rates reaching 89% in sub-Saharan Africa and 78% in South Asia. These figures represent not merely an educational deficit but an entrepreneurial one: the cognitive foundations upon which entrepreneurial competences—analytical reasoning, strategic planning, risk assessment, and financial literacy—are built remain underdeveloped across the majority of the non-WEIRD world's student population. Any EE intervention, whether AI-enabled or otherwise, must reckon with this foundational reality.

3 Artificial Intelligence in Education: From Promise to Pedagogical Practice

AI has been introduced into educational settings at a growing pace over the last decade. A large amount of scholarship has developed across engineering, cognitive science, educational technology, and educational management. Zhai et al. (2021), in their comprehensive review of AI in education from 2010 to 2020, documented exponential growth in both the volume and diversity of AI Educational (AIEd) research, with applications ranging from intelligent tutoring systems and automated assessment to learning analytics, natural language processing for feedback, and predictive modelling of student outcomes. Zawacki-Richter et al. (2019), whose systematic review examined research on AI applications in higher education, identified a troubling pattern in this growth: the field was dominated by computer scientists and technologists, with educators and pedagogical scholars substantially underrepresented—a disciplinary imbalance with direct implications for the relevance and usability of AI tools in real educational settings.

The arrival of large language models—exemplified by the GPT series (OpenAI), Claude (Anthropic), and Gemini (Google DeepMind)—and the rapid diffusion of generative AI tools from 2022 onwards has introduced a qualitative shift in the AIEd landscape. Where earlier AI applications in education were primarily assistive—supporting teachers' administrative tasks, providing automated feedback, or identifying at-risk students through learning analytics—generative AI opens the possibility of AI as a co-constructor of educational content, a personalised tutor, and a creative partner in entrepreneurial scenario development. Kasneci et al. (2023), in an influential multi-author analysis, identified a dual character to this shift: generative AI offers genuine opportunities for personalised learning at scale, real-time adaptive feedback, and support for complex cognitive tasks; but it simultaneously introduces risks of over-reliance, erosion of critical thinking, academic integrity violations, and the propagation of AI-generated misinformation.

For EE specifically, Bell and Bell (2023) provide the most direct engagement with the implications of the generative AI era. Their analysis, structured around the 'about', 'for', and 'through' entrepreneurship taxonomy first articulated by Pittaway and Cope (2007) and codified by the Quality Assurance Agency (QAA, 2018), argues that whilst all three dimensions of EE are affected by generative AI, the teaching 'about' entrepreneurship—factual knowledge about entrepreneurial processes, markets, and financing—is most immediately and comprehensively disrupted. AI tools can now generate high-quality case studies, market analyses, business plan templates, and competitive intelligence reports on demand, rendering many of the traditional content delivery functions of EE programmes potentially redundant. The implication, which Bell and Bell (2023) make explicit, is that the distinctive and irreplaceable value of human EE lies in facilitating learning 'through' entrepreneurship—the experiential, reflective, and identity-forming dimensions of entrepreneurial practice that cannot be simulated by even the most sophisticated generative AI.

Winkler et al. (2023) extend this analysis through a framework of inquiry questions across four domains: General AI in EE; Drivers and Policies; Accountability and Ethics; and Learning Innovation. Their contribution is notable for its explicit recognition that the adoption of AI in EE is not a purely pedagogical or technological question but a deeply political one, shaped by institutional incentives, accreditation pressures, funding architectures, and regulatory environments. This political dimension is particularly consequential in non-WEIRD contexts, where the absence of robust national regulatory frameworks for AI in education creates both opportunities for rapid innovation and risks of unmitigated harm.

The potential of AI to address educational disadvantage is documented by Katona and Katonane Gyonyoru (2025) in a controlled experimental study involving 122 participants over 13 weeks. They found that students from socially disadvantaged backgrounds achieved higher learning outcomes and engagement when taught with AI-based adaptive programming compared to students who received standard instruction. The mechanism was personalisation: AI-driven adaptive systems were able to identify and respond to individual learning gaps in real time, providing targeted support that a single teacher managing a large class could not replicate. This finding is directly relevant to non-WEIRD EE contexts, where class sizes are frequently large, teacher training is variable, and the heterogeneity of student preparedness is extreme.

The broader UNESCO policy architecture provides the normative context for AI in education globally. The UNESCO Beijing Consensus (2019)—the first international document on AI for SDG 4, adopted at a conference attended by more than 50 government ministers from over 100 Member States—established the principle that AI in education must be equitable, inclusive, and pedagogically grounded rather than merely technologically impressive. The subsequent UNESCO Recommendation on the Ethics of AI (2021b)—the first global standard on AI ethics, applicable to all 194 Member States—extended these principles to a broader ethical framework encompassing human rights and dignity, justice and fairness, transparency, accountability, and environmental sustainability. The Global Education Monitoring Report (UNESCO, 2023) reinforced this normative architecture with its central finding that educational technology, including AI, serves its highest purpose when it complements rather than displaces human teaching, and when its deployment is governed by educational goals rather than commercial interests.

4 AI and Entrepreneurial Education: A Contested but Necessary Convergence

The convergence of AI and entrepreneurial education represents one of the most dynamic and contested intersections in the contemporary management and education literature. Chen et al. (2024), in their scoping review of AI in entrepreneurship education, document a rapid proliferation of research interest since 2018, whilst simultaneously identifying a conspicuous gap: most existing AI applications in EE focus on narrow technical interventions—automated assessment, data analytics for student monitoring, basic chatbot tutoring—rather than on the sophisticated pedagogical designs that the field requires for diagnosis, prediction, intervention, and recommendation. They call explicitly for future research to examine how AI can support the full developmental curve of entrepreneurial learning, from initial diagnosis of students' entrepreneurial mindset and competency baseline through to the co-creation of entrepreneurial ventures within AI-augmented incubation environments.

Thottoli et al. (2025), in their systematic review of 167 articles spanning three decades of university incubation research, document the slow but gathering transformation of incubation centres by AI. Their analysis identifies AI-enabled services, including intelligent business plan evaluation, automated market intelligence, investor matching algorithms, and predictive modelling of venture survival prospects. However, they note a persistent concentration of these innovations in WEIRD institutional settings—American research universities, European innovation hubs, East Asian technology parks—with minimal documented application in sub-Saharan African, South Asian, or other non-WEIRD incubation contexts. This geographic concentration mirrors the broader pattern identified by Shepherd et al. (2025) and represents a structural gap that the AI-EENI framework is designed to address.

The economic stakes are considerable. The McKinsey Global Institute's modelling on generative AI's economic impact (McKinsey Global Institute, 2023) suggests that automation of up to 70% of business activities by 2030 will fundamentally restructure the skills premium in labour markets globally. If we think about countries whose comparative advantage lies today in labour-intensive sectors—agriculture, manufacturing, extractive industries, informal services—then this trend points to a pressing need for skills transformations in these non-WEIRD economies. EE that equips non-WEIRD populations with the entrepreneurial competences to create and manage AI-enabled ventures, rather than merely to participate in AI-automated labour markets as low-wage operatives, is not a luxury but a developmental imperative.

Kooli (2023) offers a critical perspective that is essential to the balance of this analysis. His examination of AI chatbots in education and research identifies ethical risks—bias, privacy violations, academic integrity erosion, and the reinforcement of existing inequalities through algorithmic design—that are disproportionately acute in contexts where regulatory oversight is weak, data protection frameworks are nascent, and users' ability to critically evaluate AI outputs is constrained by limited prior exposure to advanced technologies. The implication is not that AI should be withheld from non-WEIRD educational contexts but that its deployment in these contexts requires more rigorous ethical governance than has been applied in WEIRD settings where regulatory infrastructure is more robust.

5 The AI-EENI Framework: A Predictive-Prescriptive Model for Non-WEIRD Entrepreneurial Education

To address this concern on how AI can be adapted in EE in non-WEIRD countries, we offer a new framework named AI-EENI -AI-Enabled Entrepreneurial Education for Non-WEIRD Inclusion (see Fig. 1). The framework relies on a sequential six-layer predictive-prescriptive architecture designed to address the specific methodological and pedagogical challenges of deploying AI-enabled entrepreneurial edu-

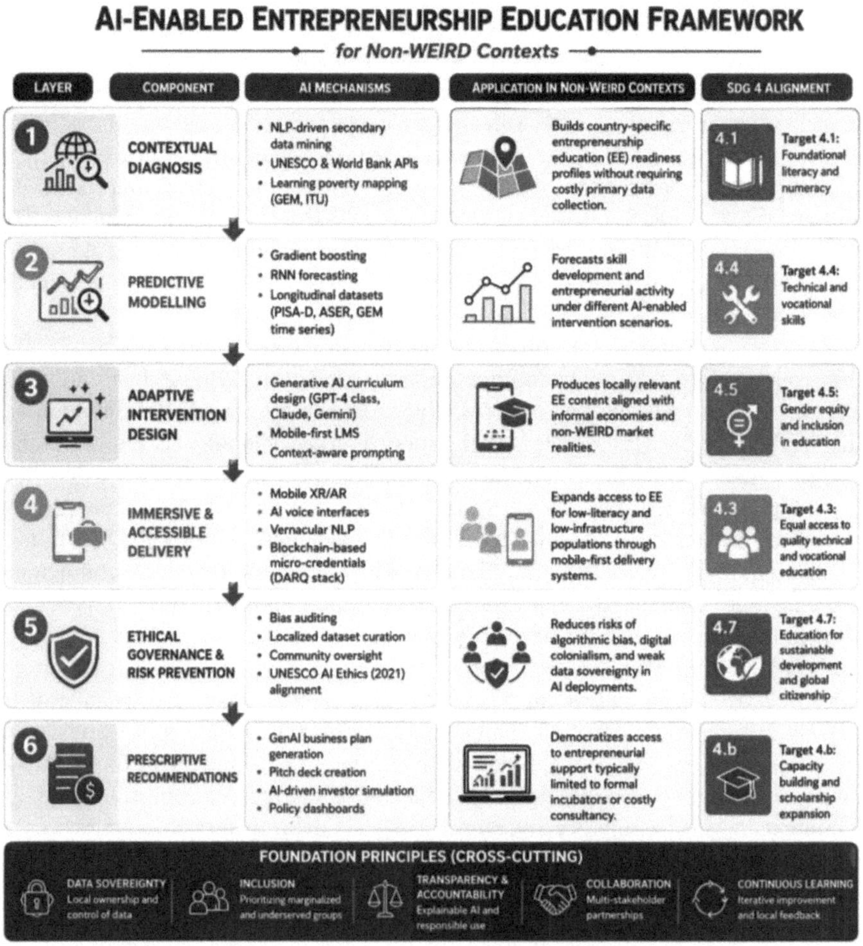

Fig. 1 The AI-EENI framework: six layers, mechanisms, and non-WEIRD applications. *Source*: Adapted from Chen et al. (2024) and Accenture (2019). Framework applied with reference to UNESCO (2021a) SDG 4 target structure. AI-generated figures created by Swedish software architect Knut Sveidqvist, https://mermaid.ai/web/, 2026

cation in non-WEIRD national contexts. The framework has three defining characteristics that distinguish it from prior approaches in the literature.

First, it is secondary data-dependent by design. Recognising the documented ethical, logistical, and financial constraints on primary data collection in fragile and resource-constrained settings—constraints emphasised by Shepherd et al. (2025) and by the broader literature on research ethics in development contexts—the AI-EENI framework generates its diagnostic, predictive, and prescriptive outputs exclusively from internationally validated aggregate datasets. These include the World Bank Learning Poverty Index, the GEM Annual Reports GEM (2025), the UNESCO Institute for Statistics global education database, the GSMA Mobile Economy reports, the ITU ICT Development Index, the UN Human Development Index, and where available, national-level educational assessment data such as Uwezo (East Africa). This design choice allows the framework to generate contextually specific, evidence-based EE prescriptions for any non-WEIRD national context for which these secondary data sources provide coverage, without the requirement for field research.

Second, the framework integrates DARQ+ technologies into a coherent pedagogical delivery architecture. Rather than treating AI in isolation, the AI-EENI framework situates AI within the broader DARQ technology cluster (Accenture, 2019), recognising that the transformative potential of AI in non-WEIRD EE is maximised when combined with distributed ledger technologies for portable credentialing, reality technologies for immersive experiential learning, and quantum-computing-enabled data processing for predictive modelling at scale. This integration reflects the Accelerated and Immersive Education model developed by Tzanidis (2023) who demonstrates that immersive technologies can dramatically compress learning timelines whilst simultaneously deepening learner engagement and knowledge retention.

Third, the framework is explicitly ethical-by-design. Layer five—Prevention and Ethical Governance—is not an addendum to the framework but an architecturally constitutive element that shapes the design and deployment parameters of all other layers. This reflects the recognition, grounded in the critical AI ethics literature of Buolamwini and Gebru (2018), Mohamed et al. (2020), and Floridi et al. (2018), that algorithmic systems deployed in non-WEIRD contexts carry specific risks of bias, digital colonialism, and data sovereignty violation that cannot be adequately addressed through post-hoc auditing but must be embedded in the architecture of the system from the outset.

The framework builds upon and extends the six-step diagnostic-predictive model proposed by Chen et al. (2024) —diagnosis, prediction, intervention, delivery, prevention, and recommendation (see Fig. 1)—by integrating DARQ+ technology deployment, specifying secondary data sources for each diagnostic layer, and providing explicit ethical governance mechanisms. Figure 1 presents the complete AI-EENI framework.

6 Applying the AI-EENI Framework: Sub-Saharan Africa

Sub-Saharan Africa is an interesting and very challenging case for studying the AI-EENI framework because whilst it has some of the highest levels of necessity entrepreneurship, it also faces some of the greatest challenges with regards to education. It is unique because it has high levels of entrepreneurial desire but low levels of entrepreneurial capacity (GEM, 2024). Ghana exhibits one of the most dynamic entrepreneurial ecosystems in West Africa, with a TEA rate of approximately 25% (GEM, 2024), driven by a combination of demographic youth dividend, a relatively stable institutional environment, and persistent market imperfections in key sectors, including agribusiness, health services, and financial inclusion. Opportunity creation in Ghana is, as Alvarez and Barney (2007) would characterise it, responsive to localised informational asymmetries—precisely the conditions under which AI-enabled diagnostic tools could generate the greatest marginal informational value for aspiring entrepreneurs. The informal sector accounts for an estimated 80% of Ghana's total employment, reflecting the scale of necessity-driven entrepreneurship and the limited absorptive capacity of formal labour markets.

A major structural barrier is learning poverty: 'According to World Bank (2022), sixty per cent of Ghanaian children aged 10 cannot read and comprehend a simple text'. Learning basic literacy skills alone limits the development of higher-level entrepreneurial skills. In contrast, competencies such as analytical thinking, strategic planning, and the effective application of technology are considered crucial for entrepreneurial success.

6.1 Layer 1: Contextual Diagnosis

Applying the diagnostic layer of the AI-EENI framework to Ghana reveals a profile characterised by high entrepreneurial intent but comparatively low entrepreneurial preparedness; persistent gender disparities in STEM education that limit female participation in technology-driven entrepreneurship; and a nascent but rapidly expanding EdTech sector—exemplified by platforms such as Eneza Education and Farmerline—that demonstrates local institutional appetite for digital learning solutions. NLP-driven analysis of Ghana's National Entrepreneurship and Innovation Plan (Government of Ghana, 2017) and the National Education Sector Plan identifies a policy commitment to entrepreneurship as a development lever, but surfaces a critical implementation gap at the level of secondary and tertiary EE pedagogy. The diagnostic also reveals significant geographic heterogeneity: urban centres, particularly Accra and Kumasi, exhibit substantially higher entrepreneurial ecosystem density than rural and peri-urban areas, reflecting the spatial concentration of EE infrastructure that mirrors patterns identified by Newman and Alvarez (2022) in their study of women entrepreneurs in Kumasi.

6.2 Layers 2 and 3: Predictive Modelling and Adaptive Intervention

Predictive modelling drawing on World Bank longitudinal educational attainment data and GEM time-series for Ghana suggests that targeted AI integration in secondary and tertiary EE—delivered primarily through mobile platforms—could improve composite entrepreneurial skill development indicators meaningfully within a decade, contingent upon sustained mobile infrastructure investment and teacher capacity development. The adaptive intervention design for Ghana prioritises GenAI-generated EE case studies reflecting the informal sector and agribusiness context; WhatsApp-based AI tutoring, given the platform's estimated penetration of over 80% among urban and peri-urban youth (Yeboah & Nyagorme, 2022); and vernacular NLP tools supporting instruction in Twi and Ga for learners whose primary language is not English. The effectuation logic of Sarasvathy (2001) is particularly well-suited to the Ghanaian entrepreneurial context: AI-EE tools that train learners to start with available means—personal networks, locally available resources, platform technology—rather than optimal conditions will generate more robust entrepreneurial behaviour than tools that presuppose WEIRD institutional environments.

6.3 Layers 4, 5, and 6: Delivery, Governance, and Prescriptions

Smartphone-based AR applications represent the most immediately realisable immersive delivery mechanism. Blockchain micro-credentialing presents a particularly high-impact opportunity: in a context where formal educational certification frequently fails to reach rural and peri-urban learners, distributed ledger-based skills recognition—as proposed by Sharples and Domingue (2016)—offers a portable, verifiable, and institutionally recognised alternative. The primary ethical risk in Ghana is gender bias: most commercially available AI EE tools are trained on WEIRD entrepreneurship datasets that systematically underrepresent female-led, informal, and African business models. Mitigation requires the curation of Ghanaian-specific entrepreneurial success case studies for AI training data augmentation and regulatory alignment with the Ghana Data Protection Act (Act 843, 2012). At the prescriptive level, the framework recommends a public–private partnership between the Ghana NEIP, mobile network operators (MTN Ghana, Vodafone Ghana), and EdTech developers to zero-rate AI-EE content; integration of AI-generated business planning modules into the National Board for Professional and Technician Examinations (NABPTEX) curriculum; and the establishment of AI-enabled virtual incubation hubs accessible via USSD for feature-phone users in rural areas. A summary of the six layers is presented in Table 1.

Table 1 Application of the AI-EENI framework in a non-WEIRD national context

Indicator	Sub-Saharan Africa-Ghana
TEA rate (GEM, 2024)	~25%
Learning poverty (World Bank et al., 2022)	~60%
Mobile penetration (GSMA, 2024)	~79%
AI-EE priority mechanism (Layers 3–4)	WhatsApp AI tutors; mobile GenAI for agribusiness; AR business simulations
Primary ethical risk (Layer 5)	Gender bias in AI training data; informal sector underrepresentation
Policy entry point (Layer 6)	NEIP + MTN/Vodafone zero-rating; NABPTEX curriculum integration

Table 1 presents a comparative summary of key diagnostic indicators, priority AI-EE interventions, principal ethical risks, and policy entry points related to the single case study.
Sources: GEM (2024), World Bank et al. (2022), GSMA (2024, 2025), UNESCO (2023), ASER Centre (2023)

7 Cross-Cutting Themes and Framework Validation

The application of the AI-EENI framework across non-WEIRD national contexts reveals both the structural universality of the model's analytical logic and the imperative of contextual adaptation at each operational layer.

Three cross-cutting themes emerge from the comparative analysis with particular salience for the theoretical development of the AI-EENI framework and its broader applicability to the non-WEIRD EE challenge.

Mobility Comes First: First, mobile infrastructure remains the bottom line across countries. The deployment of AI-EE hinges on indispensable mobile connectivity infrastructure in the country. Mobile Internet users across Africa will total 615 million by 2030, up from 416 million this year, per the GSMA (2025). This growth will outstrip any other digital infrastructure investments across the continent. UNESCO's (2013) policy guidelines for mobile learning identified 13 unique benefits of mobile-first educational delivery, including expanded reach, immediate feedback, personalised learning pathways, and anytime-anywhere accessibility—all of which are directly applicable to the AI-EE challenge. Hence, no AI-EE intervention for non-WEIRD contexts that is not mobile-first, low-bandwidth-optimised, and offline-functional can claim serious intent to reach the populations it is ostensibly designed to serve.

The second cross-cutting issue is gender-transformative design as a moral and economic imperative. Women represent an unequal amount of entrepreneurs driven by necessity and lacking EE or incubation programs in Ghana. Rietveld and Patel (2022), analysing GEM data from 97 countries, confirm that gender inequality directly moderates the gender entrepreneurship competency gap—a finding with direct implications for the design of AI training datasets, the selection of EE case study exemplars, and the governance mechanisms embedded in Layer 5 of the AI-EENI framework. AI-EE tools that fail to actively embed gender-transformative design across all six layers will not merely fail to close existing gender entrepreneurship gaps but risk algorithmically amplifying them.

The third cross-cutting theme concerns the irony of deploying AI-EE when learning poverty prevails. Settings in which non-WEIRD EE is most urgently needed are settings where learners are least likely to have the prerequisite reading and math skills needed to use even the best-designed AI-EE applications. This creates a sequencing challenge: AI-EE tools deployed without foundational literacy support will generate the algorithmic exclusion that Layer 5 of the framework is designed to prevent. The resolution proposed by the AI-EENI framework is architectural rather than sequential: Layer 4 mandates voice-based, visually rich, vernacular-language AI interfaces that can function below text-literacy thresholds, allowing EE content to be delivered and received by learners who would be excluded by text-dominant AI tools. Katona and Katonane Gyonyoru's (2025) experimental evidence—demonstrating that AI-adaptive education significantly improves outcomes for socially disadvantaged learners.

8 Ethical Governance: Prevention as a Design Imperative

The ethical dimensions of AI deployment in non-WEIRD contexts cannot be adequately addressed through the retrospective auditing and regulatory mechanisms that characterise AI governance in WEIRD settings. This is not because WEIRD governance mechanisms are adequate—they are not, as the continuing revelations of algorithmic bias, surveillance capitalism, and data sovereignty violations in WEIRD contexts attest—but because non-WEIRD contexts lack the institutional, legal, and civil society infrastructure that makes even imperfect retrospective governance possible. The argument for prevention-by-design is therefore both principled and pragmatic.

Buolamwini and Gebru's (2018) gender shades study remains the most cited empirical demonstration of algorithmic bias in commercial AI systems, and its findings bear direct repetition in the context of non-WEIRD AI-EE deployment. Error rates for darker-skinned women in commercial facial recognition systems were up to 34.7 percentage points higher than for lighter-skinned men—a disparity that was directly attributable to the racial and gender composition of the training datasets, rather than to any inherent technical limitation of the underlying algorithms. The lesson is broad: AI learns to replicate what's in the data it is trained on, including the patterns of exclusion, misrepresentation, and bias. If our training data is mostly sourced from WEIRD entrepreneurship settings, then our AI-EE tools will internalise WEIRD assumptions about entrepreneurship into their generative text, evaluation metrics, and personalisation frameworks. Mohamed et al. (2020) situate this technical problem within a broader political economy. Their decolonial AI analysis identifies three patterns through which AI development recapitulates historical colonial relationships: the extraction of data from non-WEIRD communities without meaningful consent or benefit-sharing; the imposition of WEIRD-trained AI systems as universal solutions to problems defined by WEIRD institutions; and the epistemic subordination of non-WEIRD knowledge systems, cultural contexts, and value frameworks to WEIRD AI architectures. The UNESCO Recommendation on the Ethics of AI (2021b)—with its emphasis on human rights, dignity, cultural diversity, and environmental sustainability—provides the normative framework for resisting these patterns, but the recommendation's implementation in non-WEIRD contexts requires more than policy commitment: it requires the active co-design of AI-EE systems with the communities they are intended to serve.

Floridi et al.'s (2018) ethical framework for AI, which identifies five core principles (beneficence, non-maleficence, autonomy, justice, and explicability) and provides 20 concrete recommendations for a 'good AI society', provides a further normative reference point for the prevention layer of the AI-EENI framework. The explainability principle is particularly relevant to non-WEIRD EE contexts: AI systems that cannot explain their recommendations in culturally accessible terms will not be trusted by the learners and educators they are designed to serve, regardless of their technical performance. Community ownership of AI-EE infrastructure—through locally governed data cooperatives, community AI literacy programmes, and participatory system design processes—is the structural mechanism through which the prevention layer's commitments can be operationalised. In this frame emerges a critical debate on data sovereignty, which is the principle that communities and nations have the right to govern the collection, storage, and use of data about their members. Data sovereignty is a foundational dimension of ethical AI-EE governance in non-WEIRD contexts that has received insufficient attention in the existing literature. The AU Data Policy Framework (2022) and the AU Convention on Cyber Security and Personal Data Protection (2023) represent significant African continental governance innovations, but their implementation at the national and institutional level remains uneven. For the AI-EENI framework, data sovereignty has practical implications for the design of Layer 1 (Contextual Diagnosis): the secondary datasets that power the diagnostic layer must be deployed in ways that respect national data sovereignty, avoid creating dependencies on foreign data infrastructure, and build local analytical capacity rather than extracting data for analysis in WEIRD institutional settings.

9 Conclusions, Limitations, and Future Research Directions

This chapter contributes to the broader agenda articulated by Shepherd et al. (2025) for non-WEIRD entrepreneurship research by demonstrating that AI can be deployed as a methodological tool to generate non-WEIRD-relevant EE knowledge without the constraints that have historically limited primary research in these contexts. The secondary data approach embedded in the AI-EENI framework is not a second-best substitute for primary research but a strategically appropriate methodology for the conceptual and prescriptive work that the field currently needs:

mapping the landscape of non-WEIRD EE readiness, identifying the highest-impact intervention points, and generating testable predictions about AI-EE programme outcomes that can guide the primary empirical research agenda.

There are a number of caveats that should be mentioned. The scenario modelling predictions presented in this AI-EENI framework are only as good as the quality, timeliness, and cross-national comparability of the secondary data used to build it. Learning poverty rates, TEA indices, and mobile penetration statistics are subject to methodological heterogeneity across national statistical agencies, temporal lags that may reduce forecasting accuracy in rapidly changing contexts, and the counterfactual assumptions embedded in scenario modelling that are necessarily speculative. The framework is grounded in the theoretical synthesis and secondary data analysis presented in this chapter, rather than in direct engagement with the educators, students, and institutional stakeholders whose agency is ultimately determinative of programme success or failure.

Future research should pursue three complementary agendas. First, primary empirical validation studies should employ the community co-design principles advocated by the prevention layer of the AI-EENI framework, which are essential to test the framework's prescriptions against lived entrepreneurial and educational experience. The roadmap provided by Shepherd et al. (2025) for non-WEIRD entrepreneurship research offers specific guidance on methodological approaches for this validation agenda, including narrative and life history approaches that can capture the contextual richness that quantitative secondary data analysis necessarily flattens. Second, longitudinal impact studies—measuring entrepreneurial and economic outcomes of AI-EENI-aligned programmes in other non-WEIRD contexts over periods sufficient to capture the skill development and venture creation effects projected by the predictive modelling layer—would provide the evidence base necessary to move from conceptual model to policy-grade intervention framework aligned with the SDG 4 agenda.

The broader significance of this research extends beyond the single case analysis. The approximately six billion people who live outside WEIRD countries represent not merely the majority of the world's current and future entrepreneurial activity, but the majority of the entrepreneurial capacity that will be required to address the development, climate, and inclusion challenges codified in the Sustainable Development Goals. Artificial intelligence, deployed thoughtfully, contextually, and ethically through frameworks such as AI-EENI, represents a genuine structural opportunity to close the entrepreneurial education access gap that has historically privileged WEIRD populations.

References

Accenture. (2019). *Technology Vision 2019: The post-digital era is upon us—are you ready for what's next?* Accenture. Retrieved from https://newsroom.accenture.com/news/2019/emerging-post-digital-world-provides-new-opportunities-for-businesses-to-deliver-personalized-realities-and-experiences-according-to-accenture-technology-vision-2019

Alvarez, S. A., & Barney, J. B. (2007). Discovery and creation: Alternative theories of entrepreneurial action. *Strategic Entrepreneurship Journal, 1*(1–2), 11–26.
ASER Centre. (2023). *Annual status of education report (ASER) 2023*. ASER Centre.
AU. (2022). *AU data policy framework*. African Union Commission.
Bell, R., & Bell, H. R. (2023). Entrepreneurship education in the era of generative artificial intelligence. *Entrepreneurship Education, 6*(3), 229–244.
Bruton, G. D., Ahlstrom, D., & Obloj, K. (2008). Entrepreneurship in emerging economies: Where are we today and where should the research go in the future? *Entrepreneurship Theory and Practice, 32*(1), 1–14.
Bruton, G. D., Ketchen, D. J., & Ireland, R. D. (2013). Entrepreneurship as a solution to poverty. *Journal of Business Venturing, 28*(6), 683–689.
Buolamwini, J., & Gebru, T. (2018). Gender shades: Intersectional accuracy disparities in commercial gender classification. *Proceedings of Machine Learning Research, 81*, 77–91.
Chatterjee, I., Shepherd, D. A., & Wincent, J. (2022). Women's entrepreneurship and well-being at the base of the pyramid. *Journal of Business Venturing, 37*(4), 106222.
Chen, L., Ifenthaler, D., Yau, J. Y.-K., & Sun, W. (2024). Artificial intelligence in entrepreneurship education: A scoping review. *Education + Training, 66*(6), 589–608.
Chrisman, J. J., Jack, S., Kellermanns, F. W., Rosenbusch, N., & Wennberg, K. (2026). Knowledge accumulation: Entrepreneurial opportunity and uncertainty. *Entrepreneurship Theory and Practice, 50*(1), 3–20.
Floridi, L., Cowls, J., Beltrametti, M., Chatila, R., Chazerand, P., Dignum, V., Luetge, C., Madelin, R., Pagallo, U., Rossi, F., Schafer, B., Valcke, P., & Vayena, E. (2018). AI4People—An ethical framework for a good AI society: Opportunities, risks, principles, and recommendations. *Minds and Machines, 28*(4), 689–707.
GEM. (2024). *GEM 2023/2024 Global Report: 25 years and growing*. Global Entrepreneurship Research Association. Retrieved from https://www.gemconsortium.org/report/global-entrepreneurship-monitor-gem-20232024-global-report-25-years-and-growing
GEM. (2025). *GEM 2024/2025 Global Report: Entrepreneurship reality check*. Global Entrepreneurship Research Association. Retrieved from https://www.gemconsortium.org/report/gem-20242025-global-report-entrepreneurship-reality-check-4
Government of Ghana. (2017). *National Entrepreneurship and Innovation Programme (NEIP)*. Government of Ghana.
GSMA. (2024). *The mobile economy Sub-Saharan Africa 2024*. GSMA Intelligence.
GSMA. (2025). *The mobile economy Africa 2025*. GSMA Intelligence.
Henrich, J., Heine, S. J., & Norenzayan, A. (2010). The weirdest people in the world? *Behavioral and Brain Sciences, 33*(2–3), 61–83.
Kasneci, E., Sessel, K., Kuechemann, S., Bannert, M., Dementieva, D., Fischer, F., Gasser, U., Groh, G., Guennemann, S., Huellermeier, E., Krusche, S., Kutyniok, G., Michaeli, T., Nerdel, C., Pfeffer, J., Poquet, O., Sailer, M., Schmidt, A., Seidel, T., Stadler, M., Weller, J., Kuhn, J., & Kasneci, G. (2023). ChatGPT for good? On opportunities and challenges of large language models for education. *Learning and Individual Differences, 103*, 102274.
Katona, J., & Katonane Gyonyoru, K. I. (2025). AI-based adaptive programming education for socially disadvantaged students: Bridging the digital divide. *TechTrends, 69*, 925–942.
Knight, F. H. (1921). *Risk, uncertainty, and profit*. Houghton Mifflin.
Kooli, C. (2023). Chatbots in education and research: A critical examination of ethical implications and solutions. *Sustainability, 15*(7), 5614.
McKinsey Global Institute. (2023). *The organization of the future: Enabled by gen AI, driven by people*. McKinsey & Company. Retrieved from https://www.mckinsey.com/capabilities/people-and-organizational-performance/our-insights/the-organization-of-the-future-enabled-by-gen-ai-driven-by-people
McMullen, J. S., & Shepherd, D. A. (2006). Entrepreneurial action and the role of uncertainty in the theory of the entrepreneur. *Academy of Management Review, 31*(1), 132–152.
Mohamed, S., Png, M.-T., & Isaac, W. (2020). Decolonial AI: Decolonial theory as sociotechnical foresight in artificial intelligence. *Philosophy and Technology, 33*, 659–684.

Newman, A. B., & Alvarez, S. A. (2022). Questioning boundedly rational frameworks in practice: The case of women entrepreneurs in Kumasi, Ghana. *Journal of Business Venturing, 37*(4), 106205.

Pittaway, L., & Cope, J. (2007). Entrepreneurship education: A systematic review of the evidence. *International Small Business Journal, 25*(5), 479–510.

QAA. (2018). *Enterprise and entrepreneurship education: Guidance for UK higher education providers*. Quality Assurance Agency for Higher Education.

Ramoglou, S. (2021). Knowable opportunities in an unknowable future? On the epistemological paradoxes of entrepreneurship theory. *Journal of Business Venturing, 36*(2), 106090.

Ramoglou, S., & McMullen, J. S. (2024). "What is an opportunity?": From theoretical mystification to everyday understanding. *Academy of Management Review, 49*(2), 273–298.

Rietveld, C. A., & Patel, P. C. (2022). Gender inequality and the entrepreneurial gender gap: Evidence from 97 countries (2006–2017). *Journal of Evolutionary Economics, 33*, 595–620.

Sarasvathy, S. D. (2001). Causation and effectuation: Toward a theoretical shift from economic inevitability to entrepreneurial contingency. *Academy of Management Review, 26*(2), 243–263.

Shane, S., & Venkataraman, S. (2000). The promise of entrepreneurship as a field of research. *Academy of Management Review, 25*(1), 217–226.

Shantz, A. S., Kistruck, G., & Zietsma, C. (2018). The opportunity not taken: The occupational identity of entrepreneurs in contexts of poverty. *Journal of Business Venturing, 33*(4), 416–437.

Sharples, M., & Domingue, J. (2016). The blockchain and kudos: A distributed system for educational record, reputation and reward. In K. Verbert, M. Sharples, & T. Klobučar (Eds.), *Adaptive and adaptable learning. EC-TEL 2016. Lecture notes in computer science* (Vol. 9891, pp. 490–496). Springer.

Shepherd, D. A., Wincent, J., & Chase, S. R. (2025). What if we are the WEIRD ones? A call (and roadmap) for more non-WEIRD entrepreneurship research. *Entrepreneurship Theory and Practice, 49*(5), 1223–1260.

Sutter, C., Bruton, G. D., & Chen, J. (2019). Entrepreneurship as a solution to extreme poverty: A review and future research directions. *Journal of Business Venturing, 34*(1), 197–214.

Thottoli, M. M., Cruz, M. E., & Al Abri, S. S. S. (2025). The incubation revolution: Transforming entrepreneurial education with artificial intelligence. *Asia Pacific Journal of Innovation and Entrepreneurship, 19*(1), 2–23.

Tzanidis, T. (2023). *Accelerated and immersive education: Integrating DARQ+ technologies in higher education pedagogy*. University of the West of Scotland [Internal Research Report].

UNESCO. (2013). *UNESCO policy guidelines for mobile learning*. UNESCO. Retrieved from https://unesdoc.unesco.org/ark:/48223/pf0000219641

UNESCO. (2019). *Beijing consensus on artificial intelligence and education*. UNESCO. Retrieved from https://unesdoc.unesco.org/ark:/48223/pf0000368303

UNESCO. (2021a). *AI and education: Guidance for policy-makers*. Retrieved from https://www.unesco.org/en/articles/ai-and-education-guidance-policy-makers

UNESCO. (2021b). *Recommendation on the ethics of artificial intelligence*. UNESCO. Retrieved from https://www.unesco.org/en/articles/recommendation-ethics-artificial-intelligence

UNESCO. (2023). *Global education monitoring report 2023: Technology in education—a tool on whose terms?* UNESCO. Retrieved from https://unesdoc.unesco.org/ark:/48223/pf0000385723

Welter, F. (2011). Contextualizing entrepreneurship—Conceptual challenges and ways forward. *Entrepreneurship Theory and Practice, 35*(1), 165–184.

Winkler, C., Hammoda, B., Noyes, E., & Van Gelderen, M. (2023). Entrepreneurship education at the dawn of generative artificial intelligence. *Entrepreneurship Education and Pedagogy, 6*(4), 579–589.

World Bank, UNESCO, UNICEF, FCDO, USAID, & Bill & Melinda Gates Foundation. (2022). *The state of global learning poverty: 2022 update*. World Bank Group.

Yeboah, S. T., & Nyagorme, P. (2022). Students' acceptance of WhatsApp as teaching and learning tool in distance higher education in sub-Saharan Africa. *Cogent Education, 9*(1), 2077045.

Zawacki-Richter, O., Marín, V. I., Bond, M., & Gouverneur, F. (2019). Systematic review of research on artificial intelligence applications in higher education—Where are the educators? *International Journal of Educational Technology in Higher Education, 16*(1), 1–27.

Zhai, X., Chu, X., Chai, C. S., Jong, M. S. Y., Istenic, A., Spector, M., Liu, J.-B., Yuan, J., & Li, Y. (2021). A review of artificial intelligence (AI) in education from 2010 to 2020. *Complexity, 1*, 8812542.

Gender Equality in Governance and Social Topics of Italian Sustainability Reports. First Evidence Under the CSRD

Simona Catuogno and Roberto Tizzano

Abstract Gender equality is a key driver in addressing inequalities in business and society while creating value for the broader ecosystem. In governance and management literature, gender diversity is widely recognized as a mechanism that positively affects economic performance, earnings quality and disclosure transparency. However, research on gender equality disclosure within ESG reporting remains limited, despite its growing relevance for competitiveness and sustainability performance. Drawing on legitimacy theory, this study explores how gender equality is disclosed within governance and social topics of sustainability reports and examines whether increased disclosure reflects a genuine commitment to gender-related policies. The analysis is based on content analysis of hand-collected data from 420 nonfinancial reports issued by 105 Italian firms during the transition to the European Sustainability Reporting Standards (ESRSs). The findings reveal an overall improvement in gender equality disclosure related to both sustainable governance and social inclusion. Moreover, recent legislation appears to have enhanced the standardization and comparability of reporting and to have supported women's participation in governance and social areas. Nonetheless, evidence of the effective implementation of gender equality programs remains limited. The study provides theoretical and practical insights into corporate approaches to gender equality and its integration into sustainability reporting, contributing to the debate on the role of gender equality in strengthening ESG performance in the post-ESRS context.

1 Introduction

The transition to a sustainable economy needs a gender perspective, which is crucial for addressing inequalities in business and society while creating value for

S. Catuogno (✉) · R. Tizzano
Department of Economics and Statistics, University of Naples Federico II, Naples, Italy
e-mail: simona.catuogno@unina.it; roberto.tizzano@unina.it

R. Cellini et al. (eds.), *Cultural, Social, and Political Participation in the Internet Era*, Contributions to Economics, https://doi.org/10.1007/978-3-032-33072-7_14

the entire ecosystem. The adoption of the 2030 Sustainable Development Goals (SDGs), particularly Goal 5 (Gender equality) and Goal 10 (Reduced inequalities), emphasizes the critical role of women's participation in achieving ESG performance objectives. The introduction of the EFRAG European Sustainability Reporting Standards (ESRSs) in 2024 represented a significant change in corporate sustainability disclosure since they moved the reporting from voluntary to mandatory. Under the Corporate Sustainability Reporting Directive (CSRD), large companies and SMEs involved in their value chain are now required to report on material impacts, risks, and opportunities connected to ESG issues, including gender-related policies, actions and targets. This requirement reflects a heightened focus on transparency and accountability of gender issues among the strategies of good governance and social inclusion as they contribute to the sustainable growth and competitiveness of organizations.

Women's human and relational sensitivity to social inclusion closely aligns with ESG goals, offering a pathway to integrate the gender dimension into corporate practices and reporting effectively. Despite their superior ability to establish and maintain interpersonal ties, women are still underrepresented at institutional, political, and economic levels, and there is a huge gender gap in employment and leadership. Yet the Italian story about principles versus regulation acknowledges that the effective participation of women on boards and in supervisory bodies is highly connected to compulsory quotas (Mazza et al., 2024).

The topic of gender diversity is well developed in governance and management literature, where it emerges as a pivotal mechanism that positively impacts economic performance (Arena et al., 2023; Baima et al., 2021; Reguera-Alvarado et al., 2017), earnings quality (El-Dyasty & Elamer, 2023), and transparency of disclosures (Mnif & Cherif, 2021). Some studies have investigated how female relational skills enhance value creation for the whole environment (Arena, Catuogno, Kunz, & Pastore, 2024; Arena, Catuogno, Paoloni, & Pastore, 2024). At the same time, others have documented a beneficial effect on ESG performance (García-Meca & Martinez-Ferrero, 2025; Paolone et al., 2024; Sánchez-Hernández et al., 2025; Yahya, 2025). However, a comprehensive investigation on the disclosure of gender equality among the ESG reporting topic is still lacking in the academic debate, even if the issue is extremely relevant to achieving strategic competitiveness and improving ESG performance.

Taking together the results of the preceding research, we explore the disclosure of gender equality among governance and social topics of nonfinancial reports of Italian firms and investigate whether the increasing focus on gender equality disclosure genuinely reflects a commitment to adopt policies that foster the benefits of women's participation in the workplace and improve strategic and ESG performance. For the investigation of gender equality, we resort to the perspective of the legitimacy theory (Dowling & Pfeffer, 1975), which states that companies are encouraged to disclose information to increase transparency and accountability, legitimize their status, and enhance reputation in society. Using the content analysis on hand-collected data for a sample of 420 nonfinancial reports released by 105 Italian firms during the period 2021–2024, we observe an improvement in the disclosure of gender equality related to both sustainable governance and social inclusion. Moreover, we find that the new legislation has undoubtedly fostered standardization and comparability of sustainability reports, as well as women's participation in both governance and social areas. However, we still notice a gap in the actual implementation of gender equality policies during the period.

The study offers theoretical and practical insights into the level of corporate sensitivity to gender equality and its integration into sustainability reporting, both as mandatory requirement and voluntary but market-expected choice. We also contribute to the broader understanding of the role gender equality plays in improving ESG performance, setting a baseline for further exploration of the topic in the post-ESRS era.

2 Legitimacy Theory and Gender Equality in Sustainability Reports

Legitimacy theory posits that companies must align with societal and contractual expectations to maintain their social approval to operate (Shocker & Sethi, 1973). Legitimacy is a fundamental requirement for company survival (Dowling & Pfeffer, 1975) and survival is in jeopardy whenever society believes that the entity has violated the contract (Deegan et al., 2002). As the contractual and societal expectations change over time, managers will have different perceptions of whether operations are within the boundaries and norms of what society identifies as acceptable behaviors (O'Donovan, 2002). Thus, if managers believe that firm operations are in accordance with social expectations, they will voluntarily disclose them in their reports to remain legitimate and improve reputation (Cormier & Gordon, 2001).

Among voluntary information, legitimacy theory encourages companies to disclose on equitable opportunities for all genders for societal benefit (Mehnaz & Yang, 2025). Disclosing female representation in governance, management, and employment improves the firm's legitimacy by indicating that they promote gender equality strategies and policies to facilitate social inclusion and pursue sustainable development objectives (Isidro & Sobral, 2015). Hence, the presence of women on the board or in other senior positions has the potential to positively impact various stakeholder groups, including investors, customers, and the community, thus contributing to the development of the firm's image. As gender equality gains prominence in global sustainability agendas, the disclosure of gender-related aspects is critical to corporate legitimacy. Companies that fail to address gender equality risk reputational damage, financial penalties, and weakened stakeholder trust (Deegan et al., 2002; O'Donovan, 2002).

Previous studies have specifically investigated the human dimension of gender equality in management and governance, which chiefly refers to the knowledge, skills, and proficiency that female directors hold and employ to magnify economic performance. In the context of corporate governance, gender diversity emerges as a pivotal mechanism. Research indicates that gender-diverse boards act as enhanced control mechanisms, given the broader range of perspectives and viewpoints they bring to the meetings and their potential to improve board independence (Reguera-Alvarado et al., 2017). As the board of directors performs the functions of defining the company's strategy, appointing, monitoring and rewarding managers, and linking the company with the external context (Abdullah, 2014), it is of fundamental importance to guarantee appropriate gender diversity among directors that is strongly associated with firm performance in the interests of its shareholders (Baima et al., 2021; Kılıç & Kuzey, 2016). Additionally, independent women on the board mitigate the riskiness related to technology innovation, ameliorating the conflicting interests among shareholders, debtholders, and societal governance (Arena et al., 2023). Female executive directors and females in audit committees positively impact financial reporting quality, exercise effective monitoring, and attenuate agency conflict (El-Dyasty & Elamer, 2023). Female participation on the board also has the power to reduce the level of earnings management (Mnif & Cherif, 2021).

Besides the human dimension of gender equality, other studies have investigated the relational skills of women, showing that female relational capital based on networking and other knowledge-sharing practices enhances strategic competitiveness in terms of value creation for the entire ecosystem (Arena et al., 2024a). Furthermore, the relational capital of women in the decision-making process contributes to the co-creation of economic, public, and social value (Arena et al., 2024).

Another strand of research has explored the involvement of female capital in connection with ESG performance. Sánchez-Hernández et al. (2025) investigated how female representation on boards and sustainability committees influences the readability of sustainability reports, reducing lexical complexity. The findings also reveal that female industry expert directors enhance report readability. Furthermore, female education and international business experience positively impact readability by lowering linguistic complexity. García-Meca and Martinez-Ferrero (2025) found that gender-diverse boards and female executive directors effectively prevent ESG misconduct, especially in countries with strong national policies that support gender equality, demonstrating the complementary role of gender diversity and national equality policies. In addition, female CEOs are more likely to restrain irresponsible ESG practices, especially when they are supported by a critical mass of women directors or executives. Paolone et al. (2024) investigated the effects of board gender diversity on ESG performance, finding a positive linkage with the ESG scores. Yahya (2025) focused on the relationship between women as CEOs or board chairpersons and ESG performance, showing that women have leadership characteristics that increase the weighted average of environmental and social performance.

In the realm of sustainability reporting, previous international sustainability standards such as SDGs and GRI promoted gender-sensitive metrics among the ESG reporting topics however, with the transition to ESRSs, the disclosure of material issues related to gender equality is no longer optional. It becomes a strategic requirement essential for aligning ESG performance metrics with stakeholder expectations.

Overall, by embedding gender equality initiatives into corporate policies and strategies, firms can improve economic competitiveness, earnings quality, transparency of sustainability reporting, and ESG performance, promoting sustainable governance and a more inclusive and equitable business culture. Therefore, based on the previous literature, we will analyze the sustainability reports of the sample companies to investigate how the disclosure of gender equality related to both sustainable governance and social inclusion has evolved over time. Moreover, we will distinguish between formal compliance with the ESRS disclosure requirements and substantial disclosure with reference to the effective implementation of plans, actions, targets, and KPIs, investigating whether the increasing focus on gender equality disclosure has reflected a real commitment to enlarge women's participation in the workplace with the aim of improving ESG performance.

Therefore, our analysis focuses on the following research questions:

RQ1: Do firms pursue sustainable governance by improving the disclosure of gender equality among governance topics?

RQ2: Do firms pursue social inclusion by improving the disclosure of gender equality among social topics?

RQ3: Has the new legislation under the CSRD generated an overall improvement in the gender equality performance?

3 Methodology

This section provides the description of the empirical strategy employed to examine the nonfinancial reports released by Italian nonfinancial firms with the final objective of identifying and evaluating the characteristics of sustainability disclosure, the disclosure of governance and social material topics related to gender equality, and the actual implementation of policies aimed at improving gender equality performance in terms of increased female participation in governance and social perspectives.

3.1 Empirical Strategy and Sample Selection

The empirical setting consists of a panel of Italian companies observed over the period 2021–2024, to enable the analysis of both cross-sectional and longitudinal variations during the critical transition period to the new European regulation under the CSRD. The analysis involved three steps.

First, we identified the sample from the population of Italian companies publishing sustainability, nonfinancial, or integrated reports, referring to the CONSOB

Table 1 Sample distribution by sector

Sectors	Percentages
Manufacturing	43.8%
Services	26.7%
Trade and construction	10.5%
Energy and utilities	11.4%
Finance, telecommunication, and others	7.6%
Total	100%

Source: Authors' elaboration

Table 2 Sample distribution by geographical location

Geographical location	Percentages
North	75.20%
Centre	21.90%
South	2.90%
Total	100%

Source: Authors' elaboration

database on listed companies' nonfinancial disclosure and to the *Osservatorio Bilanci Sostenibilità*, a digital archive that collects and makes accessible sustainability reports produced by Italian companies. The initial lists from these sources were composed of 214 companies.

The second step involved systematically consulting the websites of the selected companies to verify the availability of sustainability reports for multiple years. Firms represent different sectors, as shown in Table 1, and different geographical locations, as reported in Table 2, with the exclusion of 44 companies operating in the financial sector due to their distinct regulatory framework and reporting practices.

All available reports were downloaded for each company, and a manual screening was conducted to ensure the completeness and comparability of the reporting documents, given variations in language, report titles, formats, and publication platforms across firms and over time. Among the 170 nonfinancial firms, only 105 published eligible sustainability reports, bringing the final sample of 420 firm-year observations. The final sample included companies subject to mandatory requirements, as well as those that voluntarily publish sustainability reports. These reports constitute the primary source of nonfinancial disclosure data analyzed in the study.

We also classified the sample companies by size (small, medium, and large) on the basis of the number of employees, turnover, and total assets and observed that 99 companies fell into the category of large companies while only six were classified as SMEs.

The third step encompassed a manual content analysis (Corvino et al., 2019; Guthrie et al., 2004) aimed at detecting the disclosure of policies, actions, and targets specifically employed to promote sustainable governance and social inclusion by increasing female participation in work life and by implementing measures aimed at reducing inequalities. To ensure consistency and accuracy in the manual textual analysis, only reports published in the Italian language were included

Table 3 Characteristics of sustainability reports

Characteristics	Description
Mandatory or voluntary base	In scope of NFRD or CSRD
Adopted reporting standards	GRI or ESRSs
Approach to materiality	Reference to impact or double materiality
Integration with financial reporting	Included in management report or separate

Source: Authors' elaboration

in the sample. This selection criterion was adopted to allow the extraction of disclosure information using a text mining dictionary approach (Harymawan et al., 2020) specifically developed to process Italian language corporate disclosures. The dictionary was constructed based on terms and expressions identified in prior gender studies and operationalized through a structured keyword list stored in an external database. This methodological framework provided a comprehensive basis for evaluating the interplay between corporate sustainability reporting and material gender related issues in the Italian context.

3.2 Characteristics of Sustainability Reports and Gender Equality

Our manual content analysis on the sample of 420 sustainability reports was aimed at detecting the key drivers of corporate reporting and practices to assess whether firms pursue sustainable governance (RQ1) and social inclusion (RQ2) by improving the disclosure of gender equality among governance and social topics. We also investigated whether the new legislation under the CSRD produced an overall improvement in the implementation of gender equality policies (RQ3).

To these aims, as illustrated in Table 3, sustainability reports were analyzed to evaluate whether ESG information is presented as mandatory and voluntary disclosures, depending on whether companies were or were not in scope of NFRD 2014/95/EU or CSRD 2022/2464/EU. Then we identified the reporting standards adopted by companies in the years 2021–2024, distinguishing between reports prepared according to the Global Reporting Initiative (GRI) or the European Sustainability Reporting Standards (ESRSs). We subsequently investigated whether and how firms assessed the materiality of gender related topics, focusing on the impact of materiality or the double materiality concept. We finally examined the positioning of information, identifying whether ESG disclosure is included in the management reports or presented separately in order to understand the degree of integration with financial reporting.

Our content analysis was then aimed at providing an answer to our RQ1 and RQ2, as presented in Table 4, by detecting the disclosure of the material topics specifically implemented to increase female participation in corporate governance and working

Table 4 Governance and social topics related to gender equality

Topic related to gender equality	ESG dimension
% women on boards	Governance (RQ1)
% women in supervisory bodies	Governance (RQ1)
% women in management	Social (RQ2)
% employed women	Social (RQ2)
Gender pay gap	Social (RQ2)
Female parental leave	Social (RQ2)
Training hours for women	Social (RQ2)

Source: Authors' elaboration

Table 5 Mandatory or voluntary base of sustainability report

Base of sustainability report	2021	2022	2023	2024
Voluntary	33.3%	33.3%	39%	39%
Mandatory	66.7%	66.7%	61%	61%

Source: Authors' elaboration

life and overcome inequalities among their own workforces. Using a text mining dictionary approach, we searched for seven disclosure information related to gender equality in the governance and/or the social section of the sustainability reporting in which the subject was disclosed as a material topic.

We also explored the reporting of the material topics of gender equality by sectors to make some comparisons.

Ultimately, in order to respond to RQ3, we observed whether gender equality performance has increased under the legal constraint of CSRD and ESRSs. We specifically explored whether firms have heightened the percentage of female participation on boards, supervisory bodies, management and employment and whether there has been an implementation of additional actions to reduce the pay gap, improve work-life balance, or enhance training programs for female talents.

4 Discussion of the Findings

With reference to the main characteristics of corporate reporting, starting from 2024, the CSRD replaced the previous NFRD, introducing more stringent requirements on information to be provided within the sustainability reporting. Companies under the CSRD obligation are required to release mandatory and audited sustainability reports, while all the other firms outside the scope are expected to publish voluntary sustainability reports to disclose comparable information to stakeholders. Table 5 shows the distribution of the sample firms considering the mandatory or the voluntary nature of their published sustainability reports.

The reduction in mandatory reporting in 2023 and 2024 was due to the exit of some companies from the scope of application for changes in size or legal status. For instance, the NFRD mandated reporting for public interest entities and large listed companies. In 2023, however, some companies delisted from

Table 6 Adopted reporting standards

Reporting standards	2021	2022	2023	2024
GRI	100%	100%	100%	34.3%
ESRSs	0%	0%	0%	65.7%

Source: Authors' elaboration

Table 7 Approach to materiality

Approach to materiality	2021	2022	2023	2024
Impact materiality	96.2%	82%	76.2%	16.2%
Double materiality	3.8%	18%	23.8%	83.8%

Source: Authors' elaboration

Table 8 Integration with financial reporting

Positioning of ESG disclosures	2021	2022	2023	2024
Management reports	13.3%	15.23%	17.14%	59.04%
Separate	86.6%	84.76%	82.85%	40.95%

Source: Authors' elaboration

regulated markets, while others changed their status to benefit corporations. These companies, however, continued to prepare sustainability reports on a voluntary basis to ensure transparency in ESG information and accountability to stakeholders for their actions.

CSRD has also required companies in scope to adopt the ESRSs. Due to the regulatory change, Table 6 highlights the reporting framework adopted by companies over time.

Data in Table 6 reveal that, as expected, a large number of firms in 2024 started to adopt the ESRSs. However, comparing the percentage of firms obliged to release sustainability reporting under CSRD (61%) with the percentage of firms adopting the ESRSs (65.7%), we understand that also voluntary sustainability reports have been redacted using the ESRS.

From 2024 onwards, companies under the scope of CSRD must conduct a double materiality analysis to disclose information on their risks and opportunities arising from ESG issues, and on the impact of their activities on people and the environment. Table 7 shows firms' approach to materiality with the aim of capturing whether, under the GRI framework before 2024, firms have anticipated the assessment of the double materiality of the ESG reporting topics.

Despite the adoption of the GRI, which only prescribes the impact materiality analysis, many companies have also conducted a financial materiality assessment to gradually prepare for the implementation of the new CSRD regulation but also to capture the financial aspects of sustainability reports and protect their business from potential risks.

Table 8 provides evidence of the positioning of sustainability reports as part of the financial statement and specifically in the management report or as a separate document. Companies' choice reflects the degree of integration of sustainability with financial issues.

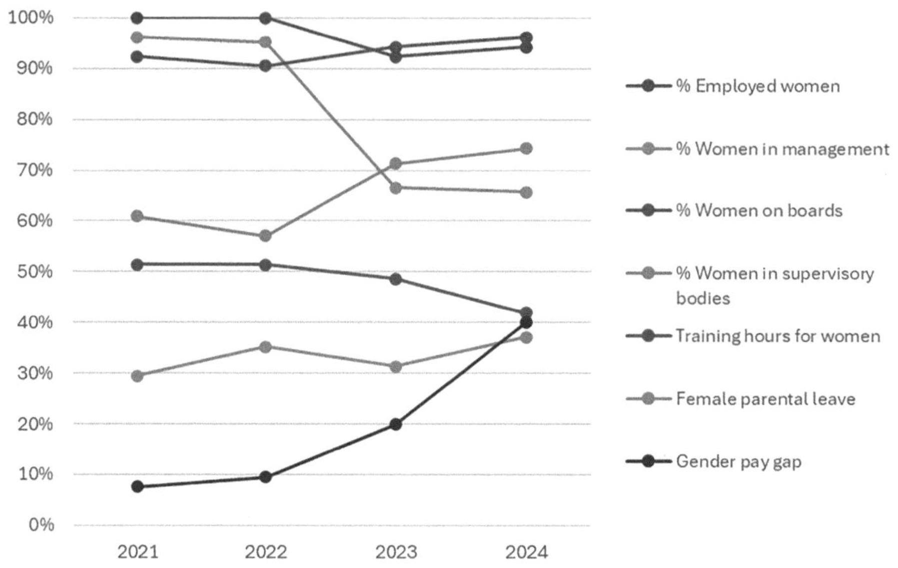

Fig. 1 Disclosure of gender equality by year. Source: Authors' elaboration

There has been a steady increase in companies that have included sustainability reporting within their annual report since 2021, as required by the CSRD. This may be due to companies' awareness of the interconnection between sustainability and financial issues. It is no coincidence that sustainability issues, in addition to being influenced by corporate decisions, can in turn significantly impact corporate performance and the overall performance of the business.

With reference to the formal compliance with the ESRSs disclosure requirements related to gender equality, our content analysis was aimed at providing an answer to our RQ1 and RQ2 by investigating among the sampled firms those that disclosed gender related issues as material topics in their sustainability reports to increase female participation in corporate governance and work life and overcome inequalities among their own workforces. Therefore, we focused on the extent of the reporting coverage in terms of the number of disclosed topics related to gender equality, as identified in our empirical design. This helped identify how much each specific gender topic was reported during the 4 years of analysis (Fig. 1). Then the level of reporting has been divided into the three ranges of low (companies disclosing from 0 to 33%), medium (companies disclosing between 33% and 66%), and high (companies disclosing above 66%) disclosure, according to the respective percentages (Table 9).

Data relating to female employees (S) and to women on boards of directors (G) are those with the highest level of disclosure throughout the entire time frame, while the gender pay gap (S) shows the most significant growth, especially in 2024. Disclosure of women in managerial positions (S) shows the greatest decline, while disclosure of women in supervisory bodies (G) considerably improves.

Table 9 Level of disclosure of gender equality by year

Disclosure of gender equality	ESG	2021	2022	2023	2024
% employed women	S	High	High	High	High
% women in management	S	High	High	Medium	Medium
% women on boards	G	High	High	High	High
% women in supervisory bodies	G	Medium	Medium	High	High
Training hours for women	S	Medium	Medium	Medium	Medium
Female parental leave	S	Low	Medium	Low	Medium
Gender pay gap	S	Low	Low	Low	Medium

Source: Authors' elaboration

Differences in disclosure levels may depend on the importance companies place on the single topics or on the limited quantity or quality of available information. In some cases, the lack of information may reflect a decision to protect reputation when performance in that area is weak. In any case, 2024 was the first year of application of the ESRSs, and therefore, there may have been an incomplete adaptation to the new requirements.

Figure 2 shows the distribution of firms disclosing each topic of gender equality by sector. The objective is to verify the evolution of gender equality disclosure over the years within each sector and the differences which may occur among them.

The disclosure of the gender pay gap (S) is always increasing over the years and among sectors. Disclosure of female participation on boards (G), management (S), and among employees (S) is always high, with peaks of 100% over time and in each sector, followed by women's participation in supervisory bodies (G). Differently, disclosures of female parental leave (S), training hours for women (S), and gender pay gap (S) exhibit lower level of disclosure during the 4 years of observation and among sectors.

The distribution by sectors shows evidence of varying levels of disclosure, with some topics reported more than others. Generally, the "Finance, Telecommunications, and Other" sector reached peaks of 100% between 2021 and 2022 for the disclosure of three topics, namely, women's participation on board (G), management (S) and among employee (S), while for four topics, namely women's participation on board (G), management (S), supervisory bodies (G) and gender pay gap (S), it showed a higher percentage of disclosure between 2023 and 2024. The "Manufacturing" sector, on the other hand, is the least communicative.

Finally, in order to respond to RQ3 related to the investigation, the substantial disclosure related to the effective implementation of plans, actions, targets, and KPIs, we examined the evolution of each gender issue to understand whether the more stringent disclosure requirements have also led to an improvement in gender equality performance in terms of increased female participation in governance and social perspectives. Figure 3 highlights the tendency of each gender issue before the transition to the new legislation under the CSRD and in the first year of application of the Directive.

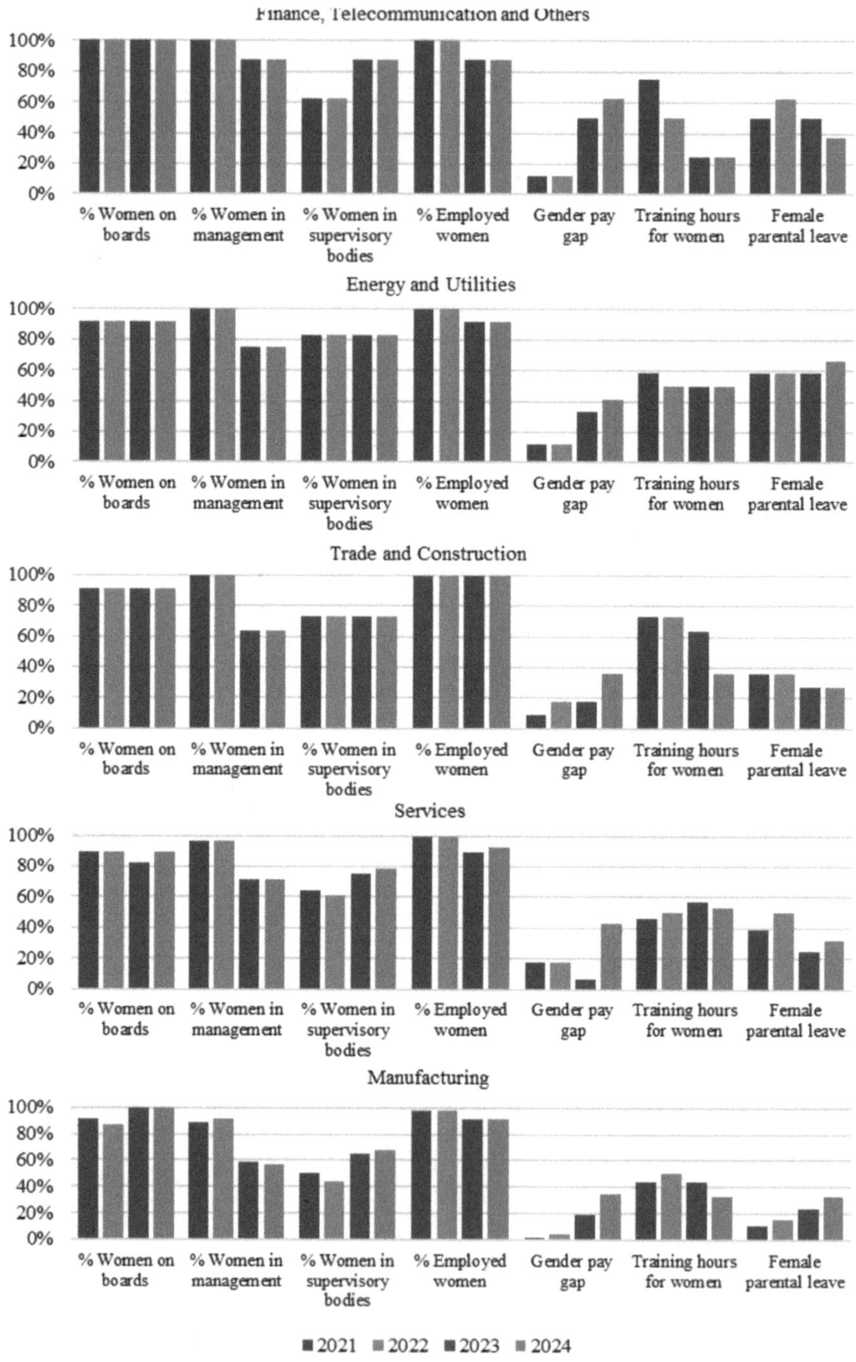

Fig. 2 Disclosure of gender equality by sector. Source: Authors' elaboration

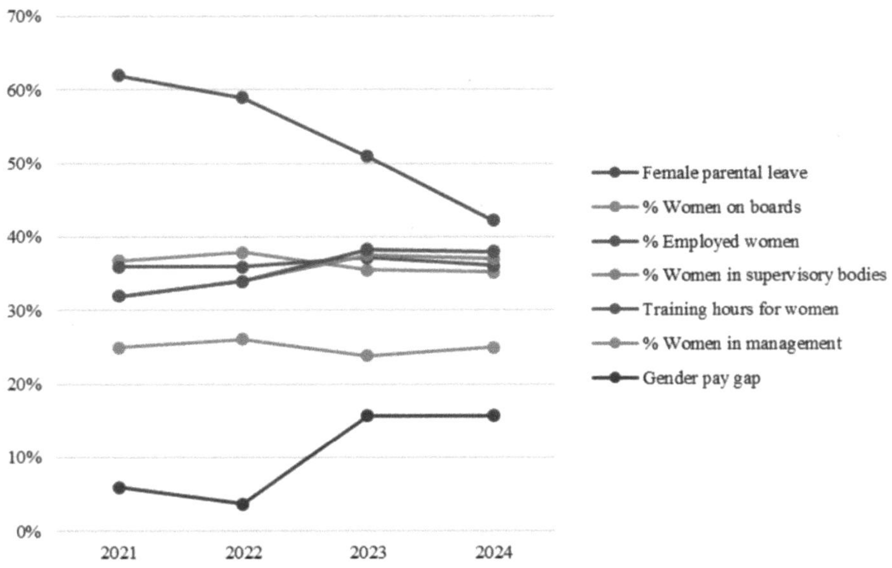

Fig. 3 Gender equality performance over time. Source: Authors' elaboration

Figure 3 should be interpreted in conjunction with Fig. 1 to understand the relevance of variations in gender equality in relation to the number of disclosing companies.

Participation of women on the board (G), women in management (S), and women among employees (S) is almost stable, with a quite steady number of firms disclosing the topics. Involvement of women in supervisory bodies (G) and training hours for women (S) increased with slight differences in the number of disclosed topics. Female parental leave (S) decreased with a small increase in firms disclosing the topic, however it can also be interpreted as a positive indicator of the implementation of more gender equality programs of work-life balance for both women and men. Finally, the gender pay gap (S) dramatically increased, even though the trend is not completely reliable since the number of firms disclosing the topic significantly increased during the period.

Overall, with reference to RQ1 and RQ2, we find an increasing and high level of disclosure in the governance-related material matters and find an increasing and medium-high level of disclosure in the social-related material matters of gender equality. In line with the expectation of legitimacy theory, firms have strengthened the disclosure of gender equality related to both sustainable governance and social inclusion to increase transparency and accountability of their sustainability reporting, enhance reputation, and gain trust from stakeholders.

Moreover, with reference to RQ3 related to gender equality performance, we find that the transition to the ESRSs has fostered standardization and comparability of data. The new legislation has also led to an improvement of some items related to gender equality in both governance and social perspectives. Women's involvement on the board and in supervisory boards, which is essential for promoting fairness in all the other areas of organization, could enhance financial performance and lead to more responsible and sustainable practices (Paolone et al., 2024), however it is still below the minimum quota of 40% required by Law No. 120 of 12 July 2011, the so-called Golfo-Mosca. Similarly, gender equality is traditionally connected with social development as women bring different ways of thinking, are more attuned to social responsibility and create superior value not only for shareholders but also for the broader society (Moulton, 2009; Steccolini, 2019). However, we still observe a gap in the actual implementation of equitable policies and initiatives related to female employment, training hours, and pay as acknowledged by previous studies (Adapa et al., 2016; Flynn et al., 2015).

5 Comments and Conclusions

By using the standpoint of the legitimacy theory as theoretical motivation according to which corporate bodies are pushed to disclose gender equality related to sustainable governance and social inclusion in their sustainability reports to reach social consensus and strategic objectives of value creation for the entire ecosystem, we conduct a content analysis on hand-collected data on a sample of nonfinancial reports of 105 Italian firms during the period 2021–2024 to explore the disclosure of gender equality among governance and social topics and investigate whether the increasing focus on gender equality genuinely reflects a commitment to adopt policies that improve ESG performance during the transition period to the ESRSs. We observe an improvement in the disclosure of gender equality related to both sustainable governance and social inclusion. Moreover, we find that the new legislation has undoubtedly fostered standardization and comparability of data together with an improvement of some items related to women's participation in governance and social perspectives. However, we still observe a gap between the improved formal compliance with the ESRSs disclosure requirements of gender equal and the substantial implementation of gender equality initiatives during the period of observation.

To conclude, beyond disclosure, sustainable governance and social inclusion from the perspective of gender equality performance is yet to come.

Our study contributes to the ongoing research on gender studies and sustainable development, offering some evidence on the role gender equality plays in improving ESG performance, setting a reference point for further exploration of the topic in the post-ESRS era.

Moreover, we intend to raise awareness among standard setters and regulators and contribute to the cultural development of corporate practices through several recommendations aimed at creating a more gender equal and sustainable economy. First, female representation in the prominent ESG roles is now an essential requirement rather than an optional consideration to meet the needs of all stakeholders. Second, failing to address gender inequities across the sustainability domains undermines the overall effectiveness of ESG strategies. Third, quotas are not enough and much more can be done to understand how work-life balance programs for women and men can support gender equality. Finally, female leaders in ESG roles should become positive role models for other women, emphasizing the need to create gender equal and inclusive corporate environments, contrasting barriers that prevent firms from fully realizing the improvement of economic and ESG performance.

Future research could corroborate our results by employing statistical methodology to evaluate the effect of firm size, sector, and profitability on the material assessment of gender equality. The relationship with corporate governance models, employee engagement, rewards for sustainability initiatives, stakeholder engagement, and work-life balance measures could also be scrutinized to provide a nuanced understanding of corporate sustainability reporting practices and their intersections with gender equality initiatives.

References

Abdullah, S. N. (2014). The causes of gender diversity in Malaysian large firms. *Journal of Management and Governance, 18*(4), 1137–1159.

Adapa, S., Rindfleish, J., & Sheridan, A. (2016). 'Doing gender' in a regional context: Explaining women's absence from senior roles in regional accounting firms in Australia. *Critical Perspectives on Accounting, 35*, 100–110.

Arena, C., Catuogno, S., & Naciti, V. (2023). Governing FinTech for performance: The monitoring role of female independent directors. *European Journal of Innovation Management, 26*(7), 591–610.

Arena, C., Catuogno, S., Paoloni, P., & Pastore, P. (2024a). Shared value in female entrepreneurship. A publicness frame in the field of knowledge sharing. *Journal of Knowledge Management, 28*(9), 2485–2518.

Arena, C., Catuogno, S., Kunz, A., & Pastore, P. (2024b). Relational dimension of women in small businesses for the value co-creation. *Small Business, 3*.

Baima, G., Forliano, C., Santoro, G., & Vrontis, D. (2021). Intellectual capital and business model: A systematic literature review to explore their linkages. *Journal of Intellectual Capital, 22*(3), 653–679.

Cormier, D., & Gordon, I. M. (2001). An examination of social and environmental reporting strategies. *Accounting, Auditing and Accountability Journal, 14*(5), 587–617.

Corvino, A., Caputo, F., Pironti, M., Doni, F., & Bianchi Martini, S. (2019). The moderating effect of firm size on relational capital and firm performance: Evidence from Europe. *Journal of Intellectual Capital, 20*(4), 510–532.

Deegan, C., Rankin, M., & Voght, P. (2002). Firms' disclosure reactions to major social incidents: Australian evidence. *Accounting Forum, 24*(1), 101–130.

Dowling, J., & Pfeffer, J. (1975). Organizational legitimacy: Social values and organizational behavior. *Pacific Sociological Review, 18*(1), 122–136.

El-Dyasty, M. M., & Elamer, A. A. (2023). Female leadership and financial reporting quality in Egypt. *Journal of Applied Accounting Research, 24*(3), 583–605.

Flynn, A., Earlie, E. K., & Cross, C. (2015). Gender equality in the accounting profession: One size fits all. *Gender in Management: An International Journal, 30*(6), 479–499.

García-Meca, E., & Martinez-Ferrero, J. (2025). Understanding the role of gender diversity in ESG misconduct. The moderating effect of gender equality policies. *Sustainability Accounting, Management and Policy Journal, 16*(3), 816–844.

Guthrie, J., Petty, R., Yongvanich, K., & Ricceri, F. (2004). Using content analysis as a research method to inquire into intellectual capital reporting. *Journal of Intellectual Capital, 5*(2), 282–293.

Harymawan, I., Soeprajitno, N., Widya, R. R., Ratri, M. C., & Paramitasari, Y. I. (2020). Text mining on sustainability reporting: A case study. *Journal of Security and Sustainability Issues, 9*(1), 1–15.

Isidro, H., & Sobral, M. (2015). The effects of women on corporate boards on firm value, financial performance, and ethical and social compliance. *Journal of Business Ethics, 132*, 1–19.

Kılıç, M., & Kuzey, C. (2016). The effect of board gender diversity on firm performance: Evidence from Turkey. *Gender in Management: An International Journal, 31*(7), 434–455.

Mazza, T., Furlotti, K., Medioli, A., & Tibiletti, V. (2024). Mandatory gender quotas: The impact on board and committee meetings. *Management Research Review, 47*(1), 45–63.

Mehnaz, L., & Yang, C. (2025). Women in accounting research: A review of gender diversity, equity and inclusion. *Meditari Accountancy Research, 33*(7), 30–59.

Mnif, Y., & Cherif, I. (2021). Female board directorship and earnings management. *Pacific Accounting Review, 33*(1), 114–141.

Moulton, S. M. (2009). Putting together the publicness puzzle: A framework for realized publicness. *Public Administration Review, 69*(5), 899–900.

O'Donovan, G. (2002). Environmental disclosures in the annual report: Extending the applicability and predictive power of legitimacy theory. *Accounting, Auditing and Accountability Journal, 15*(3), 344–371.

Paolone, F., Pozzoli, M., Chhabra, M., & Di Vaio, A. (2024). Cultural and gender diversity for ESG performance towards knowledge sharing: Empirical evidence from European banks. *Journal of Knowledge Management, 28*(11), 106–131.

Reguera-Alvarado, N., De Fuentes, P., & Laffarga, J. (2017). Does board gender diversity influence financial performance? Evidence from Spain. *Journal of Business Ethics, 141*, 337–350.

Sánchez-Hernández, M. D. M., Martínez-Ferrero, J., & García-Meca, E. (2025). Board gender diversity, female expertise, and female internationalization: Exploring influences on the readability of sustainability reporting. *Corporate Social Responsibility and Environmental Management, 32*(4), 4343–4357.

Shocker, A. D., & Sethi, S. P. (1973). An approach to incorporating social preferences in developing action strategies. *California Management Review, 15*(4), 97–115.

Steccolini, I. (2019). New development: Gender (responsive) budgeting. A reflection on critical issues and future challenges. *Public Money and Management, 39*(5), 379–383.

Yahya, H. (2025). Female leadership and ESG performance of firms: Nordic evidence. *Corporate Governance: The International Journal of Business in Society, 25*(1), 109–127.

Good Practices in Socialisation to Sustainable Entrepreneurship Among Young Women: Evidence from the INTERGEN Project

Emilio Chiodo, Carola Continenza, Maria Laura Fornaci, Rita Salvatore, and Maria Saide Liperi

Abstract This chapter presents the theoretical and methodological framework used by the INTERGEN project to identify "good practices" for socialising young women into sustainable entrepreneurship. By referring to relational sociology and adopting the capability approach, the study defines good practices as situated learning opportunities able to activate transformative processes rather than rigid, replicable models. Through a qualitative and participatory methodology, 31 practices were mapped and classified into four different areas related to immaterial support (education and mentoring), entrepreneurship services, networking, and integrated actions. Particular attention is given to rural contexts, where women emerge as key actors of socio-ecological innovation. Methodologically, the selection involved qualitative criteria (i.e. effectiveness and innovativeness) and stakeholder consultation to ensure social validity. The chapter concludes by proposing evidence-informed policy design principles, advocating for integrated, intersectional, and context-sensitive frameworks. It emphasises that fostering sustainable female entrepreneurship requires moving beyond fragmented measures towards creating relational ecosystems, enhancing women's agency.

E. Chiodo (✉)
Department of Bioscience and Technology for Food, Agriculture and Environment, University of Teramo, Teramo, Italy
e-mail: echiodo@unite.it

C. Continenza
Department of Education Sciences, Roma Tre University, Rome, Italy
e-mail: carola.continenza@uniroma3.it

M. L. Fornaci · M. S. Liperi
Fondazione Giacomo Brodolini, Rome, Italy
e-mail: fornaci@fondazionebrodolini.eu; liperi@fondazionebrodolini.eu

R. Salvatore
Department of Political Science, University of Teramo, Teramo, Italy
e-mail: rsalvatore@unite.it

R. Cellini et al. (eds.), *Cultural, Social, and Political Participation in the Internet Era*, Contributions to Economics, https://doi.org/10.1007/978-3-032-33072-7_15

1 Introduction: Theoretical Foundations and Methodological Criteria for the Selection of Good Practices

This chapter examines the theoretical, methodological, and empirical framework developed within the project INTERGEN—*The Socialisation of Young Unemployed Women into Sustainable Entrepreneurship* for the identification and evaluation of practices aimed at fostering the socialisation of young women into sustainable entrepreneurship. Drawing on the capability approach and a relational understanding of social action, the contribution reflects on the criteria adopted for selecting and assessing practices, while also discussing the epistemological and methodological implications involved in using the notion of "good practice" within complex and context-sensitive policy fields. Against this background, the chapter combines theoretical reflection with empirical analysis in order to explore how practices may contribute to fostering women's agency, empowerment, and socio-economic inclusion.

Section 1 outlines the conceptual and methodological assumptions underpinning the study and discusses the main theoretical limits related to the use of good practices as analytical and policy tools. Section 2 presents the empirical framework and reconstructs the different phases of the research process developed for the identification, selection, and analysis of the mapped experiences. Section 3 discusses the main results emerging from the mapping activity, with particular attention to the different areas of intervention and to the specific role of rural contexts. Finally, Sect. 4 develops a set of evidence-informed principles for policy design grounded in the findings and interpretive insights generated within the project.

Building on the theoretical and methodological assumptions outlined previously, the INTERGEN project focused on identifying and analysing practices aimed at supporting young women facing gender and generation-based disadvantages in their pathways towards sustainable entrepreneurship.

The primary objective was not merely to identify virtuous experiences already implemented, but to highlight practices capable of activating transformative pathways that are sustainable over time and aligned with an inclusive vision of development (cf. Carrà, 2008). Within this framework, good practices were not conceived as pre-defined models to be mechanically replicated, but rather as situated configurations of relations, strategies, actors, and resources embedded in relational dynamics that shape social action (Donati, 2013), and capable of fostering the emergence of a new generation of female entrepreneurs oriented towards sustainability in all its dimensions: environmental, social, economic and, consistent with the specific focus of the project, also generational and gender-related.

Accordingly, the concept of good practice has been interpreted through a processual and contextual lens, attentive to the transformative potential of practices in their capacity to respond adaptively and innovatively to the needs of individuals and territories. In this regard, the concept of good practice was also interpreted through the lens of the capability approach (Sen, 1999), understood as the effective capacity to choose and realise one's life project. The practices mapped within the project were therefore assessed in terms of their ability to expand the real opportunities available to young women, strengthening their autonomy, agency, and capacity to actively participate in the construction of a more equitable and sustainable economy. As Sen (1999) argues, development cannot be reduced to economic growth or to the implementation of well-designed programmes; rather, it must be conceived as a process aimed at expanding the substantive freedoms that individuals are able to enjoy.

From this perspective, capabilities are not solely dependent on individual endowments but are deeply embedded in economic, social, and institutional contexts, and are shaped by interconnected instrumental freedoms such as access to education, information, democratic participation, and social protection. Strengthening young women's capacity for self-determination, therefore, requires multi-level interventions involving a plurality of actors, public institutions, private organisations, and third-sector actors, capable of generating enabling environments that support endogenous and sustainable processes of empowerment. The good practices identified within INTERGEN can be situated within this horizon, insofar as they operate as concrete levers to sustain women's freedom of choice and action, and facilitate their active involvement in shaping their life trajectories. Therefore, sustainable female entrepreneurship can be understood as emerging within a relational ecosystem, namely a dynamic and context-dependent network of social, institutional, territorial, and environmental relations through which resources, trust, knowledge, and opportunities are collectively produced and negotiated. Entrepreneurial agency is not conceived as an individual attribute alone, but as the outcome of interconnected processes involving communities, institutions, support networks, and local development dynamics.

Building on this perspective, the analysis was grounded in the assumption that, to be effective, practices should not be limited to the transmission of technical skills or the promotion of self-employment. Rather, they should be understood as devices of social transformation, capable of strengthening project-oriented capacities, activating relational resources, and generating enabling conditions that support young women's engagement with sustainable entrepreneurship. Therefore, good practices have been interpreted as generative contexts, within which learning emerges through the interaction between actors, experiences, and environments, and through the continuous integration of cognitive, operational, and relational dimensions (Misino, 2003). In this framework, and in line with the indications provided by the RUS Coordination Committee (RUS, 2024), the INTERGEN project adopted a set of reference dimensions that made it possible to structure the identification and analysis of practices on a more solid methodological basis. This also reflects a broader concern in the literature with the risks associated with decontextualised approaches to best practice selection, emphasising that practices cannot be assessed independently of the objectives they pursue and the conditions that sustain their effectiveness (cf. Davies & Kochhar, 2000).

Within the INTERGEN project, a good practice was understood as an already implemented and documented experience, specifically aimed at promoting sustainable entrepreneurship among young women facing gender and generation-based disadvantages. Such practices were selected for their demonstrated capacity to strengthen project-related competences, foster autonomy, and support processes of socio-economic inclusion.

The selection process was structured around a set of criteria with the aim of identifying practices capable of generating positive impacts in line with the principles of sustainability and social equity. From a reflexive perspective, however, the value attributed to these practices did not rest solely on the results achieved, but also on their ability to activate processes of learning and contextual adaptation, offering useful insights for the design of future interventions that are sensitive to the specificities of local contexts and target groups. In the course of the mapping and analysis of promising practices, attention was therefore not limited to exemplary or widely recognised cases. Instead, the focus also included experiences that, within specific contexts, proved capable of producing relevant and assessable outcomes, even if not universally codified as "best" cases. In this regard, particular importance was attributed to the social validity of practices, understood as their capacity to be recognised, appropriated, and shared by the actors involved, and to generate meanings and opportunities for further development.

On the basis of these assumptions, a set of methodological criteria was defined to guide, in a systematic way, the selection and analysis of the practices identified. These criteria, shared among project partners and external experts, made it possible to assess the mapped experiences in relation to their coherence with the INTERGEN project's objectives of sustainability and inclusion. The criteria adopted were the following: effectiveness; efficiency; sustainability; innovativeness; reproducibility and transferability; relevance to the theoretical framework. A further key element in the evaluation of good practices, as highlighted in the specialised literature, concerns the development of a robust monitoring and evaluation system to complement these analytical criteria (Aggett et al., 2012; Peters & Heron, 1993). Identifying evaluation dimensions alone is not sufficient; it is equally necessary to rely on operational tools capable of continuously tracking the evolution of practices, enabling timely adjustments where needed, and ensuring transparent sharing of data among the actors involved (RUS, 2024, pp. 40–41). Only through a structured and continuous attention to medium and long-term outcomes is it possible to fully grasp the transformative potential of the practices analysed. At the same time, as will be discussed in the following section, it is important to avoid reducing evaluation to measurement alone. An excessive reliance on quantifiable indicators risks obscuring the complexity of contexts and overlooking the lessons that emerge from unforeseen developments, particularly when an overemphasis on replicability leads to simplifying processes that should instead be understood in their situated and irreducible specificity.

1.1 Theoretical and Epistemological Limits in the Use of Good Practices

The use of the concept of good practice entails certain theoretical and epistemological risks, particularly when it is interpreted in a reductive and mechanistic manner. The idea of isolating a set of "winning" variables to replicate them in different contexts may generate an imitative or even misleading effect, which overlooks the complexity and uniqueness of local situations. A practice that was successful in a given context may be ineffective, if not counterproductive, if transposed elsewhere without considering the environmental, institutional, and social conditions that enabled its effectiveness (cf. Stame, 2015). On the contrary, approaches that embrace complexity and are equipped with adequate tools to interpret it are becoming increasingly prominent. Rather than simplifying, this perspective seeks to grasp the plurality of effects, economic, social, and political, and recognise that each intervention represents a unique configuration of elements and mechanisms. A good practice, rather than being a model to be rigidly applied, is a learning opportunity that can foster critical reflection and creative adaptation.

In this context, the approach that focuses on the analysis of the mechanisms activated in specific contexts is useful: it is not so much a question of verifying whether a project has achieved its predetermined objectives, but of understanding what happens when certain actors located in a certain social and cultural environment react to the stimuli and dynamics introduced by the intervention. The focus then shifts to what works, for whom, under what circumstances, overcoming the idea of linear causality in favour of a more situated and generative understanding of change (cf. Stame, 2015). Unexpected effects, whether positive or negative, are an integral part of the project experience and deserve to be understood and evaluated. Not only is it possible to succeed in unforeseen ways, but it is also possible to fail despite having achieved the expected results if these turn out to be counterproductive. What is needed, therefore, is an evaluative approach that does not merely measure deviations from the initial objectives but is able to observe processes at their turning points, grasping the decisions that generate learning, redefinition of purposes, and openness to new possibilities. The selection of good practices is not limited to certifying already successful experiences but becomes a strategic tool to orient public action towards forms of sustainable innovation, collaboration, and participatory construction of change.

This critical approach is linked to a more mature view of the concept of "lessons learned", which breaks away from any claim to mechanical generalisability. Rather than identifying replicable formulas, it is a matter of grasping the situated and often unpredictable nature of the solutions that emerge. The so-called good practices should not be read as exportable models, but as context-dense narratives offering broad guidelines useful to decision-makers in other contexts. It is therefore crucial to be able to recognise obstacles and to value those alternative trajectories that emerge in moments of uncertainty, often thanks to the ability of the actors involved to critically reinterpret reality and open up new spaces for action.

In this light, good practices do not represent mere evidence to be transferred, but generative events marked by an unrepeatable interweaving of local factors, intuitions, contingencies, and learnings. For this reason, any attempt to crystallise in prescribed norms what has worked risks emptying practices of their transformative significance. Their strength lies in their testimony that change is possible, even if not reproducible in the same form. The resulting learning is more like an informed trust that encourages recognising weak signals, experimenting with unconventional solutions, and adapting tools and objectives to changing contexts. This also calls for a critical review of the idea of the usefulness of evaluation: instrumental use, which aims to provide ready-made recommendations, gives way to reflexive use capable of nurturing the strategic thinking of actors and stimulating more conscious decision-making processes. In the final analysis, talking about good practices only makes sense if one accepts that the goodness of a practice is not inherent in its structure, but in its capacity to activate contextual questions and actions within an open and collective learning-oriented logic.

On an operational level, the activities linked to the selection and analysis of good practices were developed according to a methodological design that reflects and concretises the theoretical-methodological framework outlined in the introduction. In particular, it was decided not to treat the practices as exportable or mechanically replicable models, but as situated experiences, to be analysed in their specificity, in the conditions that enabled their effectiveness, within the social relations that sustained them. This approach responds to the criticism expressed by Nicoletta Stame and Albert Hirschman towards any attempt at reductive simplification that aims to isolate determining variables or transform lessons learnt into generalisable formulas to be applied elsewhere. In line with this perspective, the idea of an evaluation functional only to the reporting of expected results was rejected, opting instead for an approach that also paid attention to unexpected, indirect effects and to the plurivocity of outcomes. For this reason, the project activities were geared towards the construction of generative knowledge, conceived as a form of situated knowledge capable of inspiring new possibilities, broadening the horizon of practices, and enhancing the experiential and contextual knowledge of the actors involved. Overall, the process of analysing good practices did not aim to establish "models of success", but to recognise collective learning experiences and value them as stimuli for action. Each practice was treated as a unique constellation of experiences and consequences, of direct and indirect effects (cf. Hirschman, 1967, in Stame, 2015, p. 186), whose distinctive elements offer insights, not formulae, and whose trajectories may suggest possibilities to be explored, rather than strategies to be imported. In the following chapters, the research phases for the identification, selection, and description of the selected good practices will be presented in detail, providing an in-depth analysis of the pathways and conditions that favour the socialisation and sustainable entrepreneurship of young women in disadvantaged conditions.

2 Empirical Framework and Research Phases for the Identification of Good Practices in Sustainable Entrepreneurship Socialisation

This chapter details the empirical implementation of the selection criteria and the individual phases in which research activities for the identification and analysis of good practices for the socialisation of young women, disadvantaged due to gender and generational factors, into sustainable entrepreneurship, included in the project INTERGEN, were organised.

As mentioned previously, the adopted approach focuses on identifying successful measures and analysing related learning opportunities that can foster critical reflection and creative adaptation, thereby informing the development of more effective solutions for addressing policy challenges in specific contexts.

The selection of practices was guided by qualitative criteria aimed at identifying effective interventions in fostering the socialisation of entrepreneurial values, skills, and experiences, with a particular focus on sustainability and women's empowerment. The selected initiatives include both support actions for the development of entrepreneurial skills and mindsets and direct support for the start-up of autonomous projects or activities. Moreover, the use of innovative teaching methodologies capable of activating meaningful learning processes in both formal (schools, universities, and training institutions) and informal (workshops, mentoring, and field experiences) contexts was considered central to the selection process.

A strong territorial focus constitutes a cornerstone of the adopted approach, with rural areas receiving particular research attention, acknowledging both their distinct cognitive characteristics and their transformative potential for the target group.

Despite rural areas often being portrayed as fragile spaces when compared to urban contexts, with limited employment opportunities, restricted access to services, and ongoing depopulation, an increasing number of good practices show how women are actively transforming rural areas. These practices respond directly to contemporary challenges facing rural and agricultural systems, such as the transition to sustainable food systems, the lack of generational renewal, and the need to reconnect agriculture with communities and consumers.

Analysing these experiences is crucial to move beyond deficit-focused narratives of rurality and gender inequality, and to emphasise women's tangible contributions to social innovation and local development. Moreover, the focus on good practices helps to make visible forms of innovation centred on small-scale, incremental, and care-oriented innovations—frequently led by women—which play a crucial role in addressing social and environmental fragilities and yet remain under-recognised.

After a first level of selection, the practices were further filtered according to selective criteria discussed and agreed upon with various stakeholders. The objective was to collect expert perspectives from institutions, research bodies, third-sector organisations and women's networks in order to ground the analytical framework in concrete experiences and policy-relevant insights.

Stakeholders' consultation phase provided a multi-level and multidisciplinary overview of existing approaches, challenges, and enabling factors necessary to refine the criteria for identifying good practices and to capture practical knowledge about implementation, target-group needs, evaluation problems, and policy design. As a result, good practice was defined as a learning opportunity that can foster critical reflection and creative adaptation but also as a tool for rethinking development models and strengthening the social, economic, and environmental resilience of rural areas. The final conclusions therefore emerge from the triangulation of documentary evidence, empirical mapping, stakeholder knowledge, and collective interpretation.

From an operational point of view, the activity was initiated through a systematic collection of practices implemented in Italy and across Europe concerning the target group, with a specific focus on those related to entrepreneurship support and rural development. This process represented the starting point for populating the matrix aimed at providing an initial overview of the practices to be mapped and their potential impact on the target group. The collection was carried out by consulting available sources and data such as good practice catalogues, studies, institutional repositories and databases, as well as research and independent evaluation reports.[1]

The stakeholder consultation phase aimed to build consensus on the meaning of "good practice" in order to prepare the subsequent phase of mapping, selection, and analysis. Seven interviews were conducted with a total of ten stakeholders, including representatives of the cooperative sector, trade associations, and international organisations, expert researchers, persons in charge of the implementation of European and national programmes, and heads of regional hubs for social innovation.

The integration of the mapping led to a total of 31 practices being mapped within an analytical matrix highlighting their main dimensions (see Chap. 3), which were then described individually through reconnaissance sheets. The aspects considered included: type of intervention, project title and implementation period, measures adopted, context and objectives, geographical area and level of implementation, target actors and funding bodies.

Within the framework of an online workshop—Workshop for the Definition of Good Practices—the matrix was submitted to a group of experts and practitioners. The workshop involved representatives of the cooperative sector, researchers with experience in good practice and projects transfer, experts in labour market insertion support, representatives with experience in Equal Opportunities Commissions, and members of the Council for Agricultural Research and Analysis of Agricultural Economics.

Based on the results of the workshops, a set of selection criteria and territorial and thematic areas were defined for the completion of the mapping and the final selection of good practices. The ten finally selected practices were then further analysed and assessed according to the axes of innovativeness, transferability potential, and long-term sustainability.

[1] Reference resources include the European Social Fund portal, the DG EMPL repository, the Social Innovation Database, the CEDEFOP portal, the European Anti-Poverty Network, the Financial Instruments Compass, the International Labour Organisation portal, the OECD portal, INAPP and European Social Fund Managing Authorities resources. To these are added the resources focused on Rural Development, such as: the National Rural Network - Innovarurale, the International Day of Rural Women platform, the FAO platform, the EIP Agri focus group, the European Network for Rural Development, the EU CAP Network, the Newbie H2020 project, the FLIARA (Female-Led Innovation in Agriculture and Rural Areas) H2020 project, the Ruralization H2020 project, the LIVERUR H2020 project.

In the final phase of the study, evidence-informed principles for policy design were developed based on the analysis of the selected good practices. These will be presented in the concluding Sect. 4.

3 The Results of Good Practice Mapping

The mapping activity identified and analysed 31 good practices aimed at promoting socialisation to sustainable entrepreneurship among young women, through actions aimed at developing entrepreneurial skills, facilitating access to the labour market and strengthening women's economic inclusion.

The analysis and systematisation of practices took place through an analytical matrix organised on key dimensions related to both socialisation and women's empowerment. This systematisation has highlighted four main categories of intervention, reflecting different but often complementary approaches to the socialisation of young women into sustainable entrepreneurship: (a) sustainable female entrepreneurship immaterial support (which includes both formal and informal education, as well as mentoring and processes of awareness raising), (b) entrepreneurship support services (business incubation support, social welfare services, creation of employment opportunities for fragile or struggling individuals), (c) networking and mutual support, and (d) integrated actions, that is complex actions comprising several types of interventions.

A more detailed explanation follows, aiming at explaining the meaning and content of each category.

3.1 Sustainable Female Entrepreneurship Immaterial Support

A first and most substantial group of practices identified through the mapping concerns what can be defined as *immaterial support* for sustainable female entrepreneurship. This category includes all interventions that, rather than providing direct financial or material resources, act on the development of capabilities, agency, and an entrepreneurial mindset. In line with the capability approach adopted in this study, these practices aim at expanding women's real opportunities to act as entrepreneurs, by strengthening knowledge, skills, and self-confidence.

One of the main stakeholders involved in the process of assessing the selection of good practices stated:

> A practice proves to be valid when it succeeds in intervening in the material conditions of young women—by offering tools, training, access—but also when it stimulates a change in social representations of their role in the economy and in leadership [...] The most effective practices are also part of a structured process, which starts with training, includes mentorship and is completed with economic-financial support tools.

Within this category, four main sub-dimensions have been identified (formal/informal education, mentoring, and awareness raising). A first distinction is related to the difference between formal and informal education. (1) Formal education refers to structured and institutionalised learning pathways, delivered by recognised organisations and characterised by pre-defined curricula, certification mechanisms, and clearly defined learning objectives. In the mapped practices, only a limited number of initiatives fall into this category. The *AIDDA* (Association of Women Entrepreneurs and Business Managers) case represents one of the few formal education practices identified, providing structured training pathways in collaboration with universities and institutional partners. It supports young women through scholarships and educational programmes that combine academic knowledge with entrepreneurial experience. By providing a structured online training and orientation pathway for women aiming to start a micro-enterprise, the project *"Con ME al Centro"* (*With ME at the Centre*) from Unicredit is another example of how formal learning modules can be combined with expert-led sessions on business planning, digital marketing, finance, and sustainability. (2) Informal education, instead, includes a wide range of learning processes that occur outside institutionalised settings and are often based on experiential, practice-oriented, and flexible approaches. These forms of education are particularly relevant in the field of entrepreneurship, where learning-by-doing, peer exchange, and situated knowledge play a crucial role. Examples include *Entrepreneur Coaching in Germany*, which provides customised training and coaching pathways centred on real-life entrepreneurial challenges. Similarly, initiatives such as *EnterprisinGirls* combine training activities with interactive and experiential methods aimed at stimulating entrepreneurial attitudes among younger women. These practices reflect a shift from knowledge transmission to competence activation, emphasising reflexivity, adaptability, and problem-solving. (3) A third key component of immaterial support is mentoring, understood as a relational and processual form of accompaniment in which a more experienced individual supports the personal and professional development of a less experienced participant. Rather than on the transfer of codified knowledge, mentoring is based on the co-construction of learning through dialogue, trust, and shared experience. Practices such as *Mentorship in Milan* exemplify this approach, offering personalised guidance that helps women navigate uncertainty, build self-confidence, and make strategic decisions. Finally, (4) a fourth dimension concerns awareness raising and promotion, which plays a crucial role in addressing cultural and symbolic barriers to women's entrepreneurship. These initiatives aim to challenge gender stereotypes, increase the visibility of female role models and foster a cultural environment more conducive to women's economic participation. Practices such as *Women in Digital* from Unioncamere, *Kvinnors etablering,* and *LiFE | Call 4 Startup* focus on promoting women's access to specific sectors or opportunities, while *EnterprisinGirls* and *Fidapa BPW* combine awareness-raising activities with empowerment pathways. These interventions are particularly relevant in contexts where social norms and expectations continue to limit women's aspirations and perceived legitimacy as entrepreneurs.

3.2 Entrepreneurship Support Services

A second group of practices is centred on direct support for entrepreneurial development and labour market inclusion. These initiatives provide concrete tools for business creation and consolidation, including incubation services, access to finance and specialised consultancy. For example, *Business Support Programme for Women* and *Support for Innovative Start-ups (Smart & Start Italy)* offer structured support mechanisms for start-up development, combining financial instruments with advisory services. Within this group are also considered initiatives focusing on start-up competitions (*ADA ASBL—Women Serving Other Women; Intellectual Property Award—Invitalia; Make it a Case—Italian Society of Management*).

Other practices address more vulnerable groups by integrating social and welfare services into entrepreneurial pathways. In this regard, *Strong in the Workplace—Migrant Mothers Get on Board* represents a significant example, as it supports labour market integration through tailored services that take into account care responsibilities and migration backgrounds. Similarly, *D.I.A.N.A. Project—Women and Active Inclusion in Alta Irpinia* combines training and social inclusion measures, highlighting the importance of addressing structural barriers to women's economic participation. *EQW&L Toolkit (Equality for Work and Life)* elaborates strategies, toolkits, and legal information (both for unemployed women and the companies) aimed at facilitating the work-life balance.

3.3 Networking and Mutual Support

A third relevant cluster of practices focuses on the creation and strengthening of networks among women, aimed at facilitating the exchange of knowledge, experiences, opportunities, and resources useful for personal, work, or business growth. Networking emerges as a key mechanism for empowerment, enabling women to access resources that are often difficult to obtain individually. Initiatives such as *Terziario donna (Woman Tertiary), Donne in Campo (Women in the Field)*, and *Fidapa BPW* promote communities of practice among women entrepreneurs, fostering peer learning and collective action. Similarly, *Women on Board* and *APID Women Entrepreneurship* focus on building professional networks that support women's leadership and access to decision-making positions. In rural contexts, *Coordinamento Donne di Montagna* (*Mountain Women Coordination*) represents a significant example of transnational networking, aimed at enhancing women's roles in sustainable development and territorial governance. These practices demonstrate how relational capital and mutual support can act as key enabling factors for entrepreneurial trajectories. One of the interviewed stakeholders stated:

> The value [of a practice] lies not only in the economic results, but in the social and cultural transformation that the practice manages to activate [...] Continuity is often guaranteed

not by rigid legal forms, but by stable relationships and the commitment of intermediary actors such as NGOs, foundations or local networks.

In some cases, networking among women entrepreneurs or aspiring entrepreneurs involved the creation of online platforms to facilitate the exchange of ideas and experiences among network members.

3.4 Integrated Actions

Finally, a significant number of practices are characterised by an integrated approach, combining different types of interventions within a single framework. These initiatives simultaneously address training, mentoring, networking and, in some cases, financial and welfare support, thus responding more effectively to the complex and multidimensional needs of young women. For instance, *Women on Board* integrates leadership training, mentoring and networking activities, while *With ME at the Centre* combines personalised support, coaching, and empowerment pathways. In rural contexts, *Rural Women* and *Grass Ceiling* exemplify integrated approaches that link capacity-building activities with networking, innovation ecosystems, and policy-oriented actions. Similarly, *FLIARA* (*Female-Led Innovation in Agriculture and Rural Areas*) promotes socio-ecological innovation through a combination of research, networking, and support to women-led initiatives in agriculture. These practices highlight how the integration of multiple tools within coherent support ecosystems enhances both the effectiveness and the sustainability of interventions.

3.5 Characteristics of the Analysed Good Practices

The practices were described according to the geographical area and level of implementation (local, national, international), the nature of the proposing (private; public/private; third sector; informal), financing entities, and the social and employment characteristics of the target audience.

Considering the level of territorial implementation, 5 good practices imply interventions at the local/regional level, 16 at the national level, and 10 have an international character. Among them, it is interesting to highlight the possibility of cross-border cooperation (*FEMeco—Professionals in Business and Networking, an* Interreg project proposed by the cooperative Cramars in the mountain areas of Italy and Austria). They are almost equally divided between Italy (the main area of research) and Europe. In two cases, the focus is on developing countries (*Rural Women*, managed by IFAD and *ADA ASBL—Women Serving Other Women*).

The nature of the financing actors reveals a greater involvement of the public sector (14 cases), compared to practices financed by private actors (12) and using both public and private resources (5). Considering public funding, the main role is played by the European Social Fund, followed by the EU Horizon and Erasmus programmes, National authorities—directly or by means of public agencies—Regions and Municipalities. Among the private and public/private resources, the importance of professional, entrepreneurial, and farmers' associations emerges both in directly funding projects and managing public resources. NGOs also play a relevant role, while associations or other informal networks operate mainly in rural areas.

The initiatives mapped are located in heterogeneous contexts, ranging from urban environments, to more peripheral and rural territories. In some cases, the context of reference is defined by the presence of economic transition dynamics, such as the strengthening of the digital economy or the promotion of more sustainable production models, which call for a growing demand for innovative entrepreneurial skills.

A large part of the initiatives aims to develop new technical and entrepreneurial skills, with a focus on the areas of technology, digital, and social innovation. Similarly, the promotion of women's economic autonomy, often linked to business start-ups, micro-activities, or self-employment paths, is central. Many projects also aim to support work-life balance, recognising the burden of care as a structural obstacle to women's full participation.

Focusing on rural areas, eight good practices have been selected which are geared towards highlighting, in the present, the ways forward to give recognition to the role of women, creating a space that is at the same time one of personal fulfilment, environmental protection, and development for communities and territories.

The areas of intervention are mainly focused on the agro-sylvo-pastoral context, which still represents the economic system of reference for rural areas and at the same time the area of greatest difficulty in affirming, also culturally, the identity and entrepreneurial/innovative role of women.

Consequently, the main target of the actions concerns women entrepreneurs in agriculture and animal husbandry, while in one case the good practice concerns women in leadership positions *(FemEco)* and in one case professionals, also outside the agricultural sector (*Coordinamento Donne di montagna*).

The tools used to address the socialisation of women into entrepreneurship in rural areas focus on mutual support through networking activities, co-creation of knowledge and innovation (living labs), and exchange of good practices (communities of practice), as well as empowerment through support actions such as training, financial aid, transfer of technical skills, and access to markets. One project (*V/Faktor*) focuses specifically on family-work reconciliation to counter the emigration of skilled female workers and/or young parents from rural areas to the cities.

The good practices analysed address several aspects that well represent the peculiarities and difficulties of rural areas such as the possibility of making these territories more attractive to skilled workers (*V/Faktor*); socio-ecological innovation and the creation of ecosystems to support women working in an innovative way (*FLIARA, Grass Ceiling*); the valorisation of Alpine women's cultures with a view to sustainable development and the creation of collaborative networks (*Coordinamento Donne di montagna*); the participation of women in the administrative management of collective goods (*WONDER Commonlands*); the pursuit of food sovereignty to increase resilience in rural areas, especially in developing countries (*Rural Women*).

An important role in these contexts is played by traditional ecological knowledge and its transmission. The socialisation of women's innovative entrepreneurial activities in rural areas is shaped, on the one hand, by the centrality of territorial and community dimensions, and on the other by the cross-cutting relevance of care practices at both relational and ecosystem levels. Together, these elements contribute to a form of development capable of reconnecting the diverse components of the rural world.

The effectiveness of practices is measured first and foremost in their capacity for active involvement, strengthening the sense of belonging and generating informal but solid support networks. The value lies not only in the economic results but also in the social and cultural transformation that the practice manages to activate. Innovation, therefore, comes to concern not only entrepreneurial activity per se but the redefinition of gender roles and participation in the governance of territories. A good practice becomes therefore a space for cultural change, undermining traditional models of women's work and proposing alternative visions based on autonomy, solidarity, and mutualism.

4 Policy Design Principles for Socialisation of Female Entrepreneurship

4.1 Methodological Approach to the Development of the Design Principles

The policy guidelines presented in this section are grounded in the empirical and interpretive work carried out within the INTERGEN project and should be understood as evidence-informed principles for policy design rather than as universally transferable prescriptions. This distinction is necessary. In the field of female entrepreneurship, policy debate often relies on the language of "good practices" as if effective interventions could simply be replicated across contexts. The evidence produced within INTERGEN suggests a more cautious and analytically robust conclusion: good practices are not fixed models, but situated configurations of actors, resources, governance arrangements, and cultural frames whose relevance depends on the interaction between policy design and context (Welter, 2011). The value of analysing them lies not in identifying recipes, but in extracting the enabling conditions and critical success factors that can orient more coherent and context-sensitive interventions. This interpretation is fully consistent with the project's theoretical and methodological framework, which treats entrepreneurship as a socialisation process linked to empowerment, capabilities, access to opportunities, and the reduction of structural inequalities (Sen, 1999).

The study was articulated in a mixed-method, multi-step process. This methodological choice is not secondary since it strengthens the validity of the herewith presented design principles in two ways. On one side, it reduces the risk of deriving recommendations from isolated cases or normative assumptions detached from implementation realities; on the other, it allows policy learning to be anchored in the analysis of mechanisms rather than outcomes alone. In other words, the objective is not merely to identify whether a practice worked, but to understand under which conditions it generated relevant effects, for which profiles of women, and through which combinations of support, recognition, relational infrastructures, and institutional coordination. This is especially important in the field of female entrepreneurship, where barriers are not only economic but also cultural, symbolic, and territorial (Brush et al., 2009). The resulting implications should therefore be read as *policy design principles* grounded in an intersectional, context-aware, and capability-oriented understanding of entrepreneurship support.

4.2 Main Lessons and Design Principles for Policy Design

The analysis carried out within the INTERGEN project, combining the review of practices, stakeholder interviews, and workshop discussion, makes it possible to identify a set of lessons that are directly relevant for policy design.

A first lesson concerns the limits of fragmented policy approaches. Across the evidence collected, support for women's entrepreneurship often appears divided into separate measures, such as training, financial support, or short-term empowerment initiatives, with limited coordination among them. This weakens policy effectiveness because it fails to address the multidimensional nature of women's entrepreneurial trajectories (Verloo, 2006). The most promising experiences identified by the project are those that combine multiple and mutually reinforcing components, including managerial training, mentoring, access to credit, financial literacy, work-life balance sensitivity, peer support, and networking opportunities. What matters is not simply the availability of services, but their articulation within a coherent support ecosystem. For policy design, this implies the need to move beyond isolated instruments and to build *integrated frameworks* linking education, mentoring, financial support, territorial services, business accompaniment, and empowerment measures. It also calls for *stronger* coordination among public institutions, training organisations, associations, incubators, and firms, as well as closer alignment between local interventions and broader regional or national strategies.

A second lesson concerns the cultural and symbolic dimension of entrepreneurship socialisation. The evidence shows that barriers to women's entrepreneurship are not only technical or procedural, but also cultural and structural. This point is crucial because women are still often addressed as a generic disadvantaged group, rather than as heterogeneous actors with diverse capabilities, aspirations, and support needs. Policies built around undifferentiated target groups tend to produce weak targeting and limited results (Ahl, 2006). By contrast, practices that contribute to changing representations, increasing women's self-legitimation, and expanding the social recognition of women as entrepreneurs appear more capable of generating durable effects. From a policy perspective, this means that campaigns, storytelling, mentoring, and empowerment strategies should not be treated as secondary tools, but as integral components of transformative interventions. It also means that good practices should be used not as templates to be copied, but as generative contexts for policy learning, from which the enabling conditions of effective action can be identified and adapted.

The research also pointed to the need for an *intersectional and context-sensitive perspective* (Crenshaw, 1989). The target group of young unemployed women cannot be treated as homogeneous, since entrepreneurial opportunities and constraints vary according to multiple factors, including territorial location, educational background, care responsibilities, access to services, digital opportunities, and local labour-market conditions. The practices analysed in the project are situated in highly heterogeneous contexts, ranging from urban areas with dense entrepreneurial infrastructures to peripheral and rural territories characterised by weaker access to opportunities and support services. Effective interventions therefore require a situated reading of needs, resources, and barriers, together with the capacity to adapt policy instruments to different profiles and local conditions. This suggests that territorial mapping, participatory needs analysis, and the continuous updating of knowledge about beneficiaries should be treated as preconditions for effective action. This point becomes particularly significant in relation to rural areas. The project highlights that women in these contexts are often exposed to overlapping forms of disadvantage linked to weaker service provision, limited professional opportunities, more persistent gender norms, and stronger dependence on local economic structures. At the same time, the analysis warns against framing rural women solely through a deficit lens as in rural settings women can also act as protagonists of social innovation, community resilience, and new entrepreneurial models. This has a direct implication for policy design: interventions in rural areas should not merely compensate for disadvantage but should actively invest in women's capacity to contribute to local development, while addressing the structural barriers that constrain their agency.

A further lesson concerns the relational nature of entrepreneurial socialisation. The interviews repeatedly emphasised the importance of women's networks, peer support, mentoring, vertical communities built around shared goals and competences, and spaces for intergenerational exchange (OECD, 2023). These dimensions are not ancillary. They are mechanisms through which confidence is built, tacit knowledge is transmitted, isolation is reduced, and entrepreneurial aspirations become credible. Policies centred exclusively on the individual beneficiary while neglecting the relational infrastructures that sustain entrepreneurial agency are therefore likely to remain limited in both reach and durability (Calás et al., 2009). For policy makers, this means that women's networks, peer communities, mentoring systems, intergenerational exchange, and co-design mechanisms involving beneficiaries and local actors should be treated as core elements of policy architecture rather than optional additions.

Finally, the project highlights the importance of evaluation. Stakeholders called for more reliable metrics capable of assessing the actual impact of entrepreneurship support measures and their consistency with empowerment and inclusion objectives. They also criticised the tendency to rely mainly on quantitative indicators, such as the number of participants or funded initiatives, which say little about whether an intervention has strengthened women's agency, improved access to networks, or generated viable entrepreneurial pathways (Henry et al., 2016). The evidence instead points towards evaluation as a continuous and participatory process, useful not only for accountability but also for institutional learning and responsible transferability. From a policy design perspective, this means moving beyond narrow output metrics and incorporating impact indicators, based on the theory of change, related to empowerment, continuity, network activation, business sustainability, and institutional learning. Evaluation should not be treated as an ex post administrative exercise, but embedded in intervention design from the outset, so that policy can adapt, learn, and improve over time.

4.3 Concluding Remarks

The evidence generated within the INTERGEN project leads to the conclusion that the socialisation of female entrepreneurship is facilitated when policy moves beyond narrow start-up support logic and adopts a broader perspective that combines gender equality, social inclusion, empowerment, territorial development, and institutional coordination. The issue is not simply to help women create businesses. The issue is to create the social, cultural and organisational conditions under which entrepreneurship becomes a credible, accessible and sustainable pathway of autonomy. Policies that ignore this complexity will continue to produce formal measures with limited transformative effect, instead of contributing to reducing structural inequalities while expanding women's real capabilities to act as economic and social innovators.

Acknowledgements Author contributions: Carola Continenza authored Sect. 1; Maria Saide Liperi authored Sect. 2 and co-authored Sect. 4; Emilio Chiodo and Rita Salvatore co-authored Sect. 3; Maria Laura Fornaci and Maria Saide Liperi co-authored Sect. 4. All authors contributed to the revision of this chapter and approved the final version.

References

Aggett, S., Dunn, A., & Vincent, R. (2012). *Engaging with impact: How do we know if we have made a difference?* WellcomeTrust.

Ahl, H. (2006). Why research on women entrepreneurs needs new directions. *Entrepreneurship Theory and Practice, 30*(5), 595–621.

Brush, C. G., de Bruin, A., & Welter, F. (2009). A gender-aware framework for women's entrepreneurship. *International Journal of Gender and Entrepreneurship, 1*(1), 8–24.

Calás, M. B., Smircich, L., & Bourne, K. A. (2009). Extending the boundaries: Reframing "entrepreneurship as social change" through feminist perspectives. *Academy of Management Review, 34*(3), 552–569.

Carrà, E. (2008). *Buone pratiche e capitale sociale. Servizi alla persona pubblici e di privato sociale a confronto*. LED Edizioni Universitarie.

Crenshaw, K. (1989). *Demarginalizing the intersection of race and sex* (pp. 139–167). University of Chicago Legal Forum.

Davies, A., & Kochhar, A. (2000). A framework for the selection of best practices. *International Journal of Operations and Production Management, 20*(10), 1203–1217. https://doi.org/10.1108/01443570010343744

Donati, P. (2013). *Sociologia relazionale. Come cambia la società*. Editrice La Scuola.

Henry, C., Foss, L., & Ahl, H. (2016). Gender and entrepreneurship research: A review of methodological approaches. *International Small Business Journal, 34*(3), 217–241.

Misino, M. N. (2003). Le "Buone Pratiche". In L. Sanicola & G. Trevisi (Eds.), *Il progetto: Metodi e strumenti per l'azione sociale*. Liguori.

OECD. (2023). *The missing entrepreneurs 2023: Policies for inclusive entrepreneurship and self-employment*. OECD Publishing.

Peters, M. T., & Heron, T. E. (1993). When the best is not good enough: An examination of best practice. *The Journal of Special Education, 26*(4), 371–385. https://doi.org/10.1177/002246699302600403

RUS. (2024). *Report 2023: Capacity building e best practice nelle università italiane*. https://www.unical.it/media/medias/2024/RUS_-_Rapporto_CBBP_2023_-_30_gennaio_2024.pdf

Sen, A. (1999). *Development as freedom*. Alfred Knopf.

Stame, N. (2015). Hirschman, il possibilismo e la valutazione. *RIV Rassegna Italiana di Valutazione, 62*, 103–119.

Verloo, M. (2006). Multiple inequalities, intersectionality and the European Union. *European Journal of Women's Studies, 13*(3), 211–228.

Welter, F. (2011). Contextualizing entrepreneurship: Conceptual challenges and ways forward. *Entrepreneurship Theory and Practice, 35*(1), 165–184.

Sustainability, Gender, and Generation: Findings Through the Delphi Technique on Young Women's Entrepreneurship for Inclusive Growth

Francesca Colella, Laura Falci, and Carola Continenza

Abstract In a context characterised by persistent gender inequalities and high youth unemployment rates, the INTERGEN project aimed to promote the social and economic inclusion of young women, framing entrepreneurship beyond the sole dimension of individual agency. Structural, cultural, and sectoral barriers continue to influence entrepreneurial choices, and female entrepreneurial activity remains lower than male activity. Many social inequalities originate within the labour market, where gender and culture interact dynamically. The Delphi findings show that female entrepreneurship is re-situated within a systemic configuration of constraints and opportunities, as policies fail to translate into tangible resources. Empowerment as a transformative process is a key driver of inclusive growth. Entrepreneurship among young women must be framed within a complex ecosystem of structural, cultural, and generational factors. It therefore becomes crucial to strengthen tools such as expert mentoring, sustainability-oriented training, and work-life balance infrastructures.

1 The INTERGEN Project and the Socialisation of Female Entrepreneurship: Tools and Challenges

In a context characterised by persistent gender inequalities and high youth unemployment rates, the *INTERGEN project—The Socialisation of Young Unemployed Women into Sustainable Entrepreneurship*—aimed to promote the social and economic inclusion of young women by developing a socio-economic investigation intended to understand the factors influencing the socialisation of young women into

F. Colella (✉) · L. Falci
Department of Humanities, University of L'Aquila, L'Aquila, Italy
e-mail: francesca.colella1@univaq.it; laura.falci@univaq.it

C. Continenza
Department of Education Sciences, University of Roma 3, Rome, Italy
e-mail: carola.continenza@uniroma3.it

R. Cellini et al. (eds.), *Cultural, Social, and Political Participation in the Internet Era*, Contributions to Economics, https://doi.org/10.1007/978-3-032-33072-7_16

entrepreneurship. Within the framework of the National Recovery and Resilience Plan (NRRP), the project aligns with its priorities of social justice, gender equality, and the reduction of inequalities. To this end, it implemented an integrated approach combining empirical research with a mixed-methods design and targeted engagement activities. In particular, this section presents the study conducted using the Delphi Technique, which involved experts to collect shared evaluations and perspectives in order to construct policymaking scenarios and define strategic guidelines aimed at fostering social inclusion and education for sustainable entrepreneurship among young women.

The project was carried out through a partnership among the University of L'Aquila (Coordinating Institution), Sapienza University of Rome, University of Teramo, and University of Chieti-Pescara. As mentioned, the general objective was pursued through a socio-economic study on the socialisation of disadvantaged individuals into sustainable entrepreneurship, with particular reference to young women aged 18–34, adopting an intersectional perspective. The specific objectives included: producing data and analyses on factors relevant to sustainable entrepreneurship, mapping best practices for inclusive entrepreneurial education, defining strategic guidelines to enhance socio-economic diversity, and constructing policymaking scenarios aimed at inclusion and social justice. The study was carried out using innovative methodological approaches, combining structured surveys, qualitative interviews within the best-practices mapping, and Delphi analysis with experts, to ensure a positive and sustainable impact on the target communities and on policies supporting female entrepreneurship.

It was considered that achieving the general objective could generate impacts at several interconnected levels. On the socio-economic level, entrepreneurial education initiatives can contribute to counteracting inequalities and promoting the inclusion of young women. On the scientific level, the transdisciplinary study allowed for the implementation of the theoretical-conceptual framework, while the results produced data through the Delphi technique with experts to construct policymaking scenarios aimed at social cohesion and inclusion. Furthermore, as previously mentioned, a mapping of best practices was conducted to facilitate entrepreneurial education and support the social inclusion of unemployed young women from an equity perspective. Key elements related to the processes of socialisation into sustainable entrepreneurship were identified, and strategic guidelines were produced for the design and planning of policies to provide more targeted and effective responses to specific challenges.

The project represents an innovative and original experiment within the Italian context, not only in terms of objectives, target group, and the transdisciplinary and intersectional approach of the intervention but also from a methodological standpoint. During the implementation of the socio-economic survey, significant challenges emerged regarding the engagement of the target group in the web survey, attributable to the fragmentation of communication channels with young unemployed women, the likely fragile trust in research and training initiatives, and well-known personal and socio-economic vulnerabilities that often limit their willingness to participate in activities not immediately perceived as useful for labour market access, in an empowerment perspective (Colella, 2025). These challenges were overcome through the involvement of a survey agency, which enabled the quantitative investigation via a web survey. In this way, the project directly gave voice to the target audience, involving 1000 young women online aged 18–34, who were neither students nor employed, residing across the national territory.

In parallel, within the project, a Delphi study was conducted with ten experts in female entrepreneurship from various professional sectors, to gather strategic indications on the structural conditions, opportunities, and barriers influencing the socialisation of young women into sustainable entrepreneurship. The third paragraph presents the distinctive features of the study and the results obtained.

This dual data collection method, combining the direct perspective of young women with the expert perspective of professionals, allows female entrepreneurship to be framed both in terms of the concrete needs of the target group and with respect to the structural and cultural conditions that influence its development. This integrated perspective provides a useful framework for understanding the specific challenges women face in the Italian labour market and justifies attention to the national socio-economic context.

In Italy, women enter the labour market later than in other countries, and their presence in the workforce and public life remains a key indicator of social functioning (Bianco, 1997). The COVID-19 pandemic exacerbated gender inequalities, hindering women's access, retention, and career progression, especially in sectors most exposed or affected by social distancing measures (INAPP, 2021). These conditions reinforce a structurally lower female employment rate compared to men, affecting job quality and growth opportunities, and making the role of economic autonomy and female entrepreneurship even more relevant as tools of empowerment and levers for the sustainability and competitiveness of the economic system.

Within this framework, as will be further discussed in the following paragraph, data from the Global Entrepreneurship Monitor (GEM) confirm that female entrepreneurial activity remains lower than male activity. Although the gender gap is slowly decreasing and women show greater attention to the social and environmental aspects of enterprises, structural, cultural, and sectoral barriers continue to influence entrepreneurial choices. These findings underscore the need for targeted policies to promote the inclusion and empowerment of female entrepreneurs, both globally and in Italy.

2 Female Entrepreneurship and Sustainability: Structural and Cultural Challenges Tackling Gender Inequalities

The GEM has periodically collected reports on established and emerging trends in entrepreneurship for over 25 years, gradually building the world's most extensive database of entrepreneurial activity (GEM, 2025a, p. 11). Overall, over the last 25 years, levels of global early-stage entrepreneurial activity have increased: for economies consistently participating in GEM research over time, 38 out of 74 have shown a significant increase since their first participation (GEM, 2024a, p. 25). As for female entrepreneurship, which will be explored in greater depth later on, the latest reports show that the gender gap in entrepreneurial activity is narrowing, albeit slowly. Furthermore, in 2023, only 5 economies out of 49 reached a satisfactory assessment in both social support for women entrepreneurs and resource access compared to men (GEM, 2024a, p. 19) and, in 2024, women's relative access to resources was scored as less than sufficient for 25 economies out of 51 (GEM, 2025a, p. 13).

Furthermore, women-led businesses globally demonstrate a stronger commitment to social and environmental sustainability, with female entrepreneurs being 5 percentage points more likely than men to prioritise sustainability over strictly financial goals (GEM, 2025b, p. 29).

Focusing on global female entrepreneurship (GEM, 2025b, p. 17), women's startup activity remained below men's in 47 out of 51 countries overall. Also, in most economies, men are more likely to start a business than women, and far more likely to own an established business, underscoring the ongoing structural and cultural barriers that women face across all contexts (GEM, 2025b, p. 13; 18).

Demographically, women entrepreneurs are slightly younger on average, with a higher proportion aged 18–35 (43.9%) than men (42.4%), while their male counterparts are slightly more often in the 35–54 range. Women entrepreneurs are also generally better educated than men, with higher shares of post-secondary (45.0% women vs. 43.0% men) and graduate (14.5% women vs. 14.0% men) levels of education (GEM, 2025b, p. 23).

However, gender differences in household income remain stark: more women are concentrated in the lower and middle thirds of income, while men show higher representation in the upper third; these patterns influence access to capital, social networks, and safety nets, impacting business startup and growth trajectories (GEM, 2025b, p. 24).

Significant gender specificities also emerge from entrepreneurial perception and the reasons for starting or closing a business. Risk aversion, also known as fear of failure and its consequences, is another area where gender disparities have historically been reported, and this is, unfortunately, an upward trend across most countries (GEM, 2024b, p. 44). This phenomenon remains a formidable obstacle to new startups: in 2023, at least two in five adults seeing good opportunities would not start a business for fear it might fail in 35 of the 45 participating economies, and for 37 of them the proportion of women was higher (GEM, 2024a, p. 19).

In addition, women are overrepresented in lower-growth, consumer-facing sectors like retail and hospitality and, as will be discussed in greater detail, this sectoral segregation often results from societal perceptions of "women-appropriate" fields. Despite this, opportunity recognition for women has strongly increased globally over the past two decades, suggesting women are paying more attention to new market and business opportunities (GEM, 2024b, p. 43).

In 2024, 71.1% of women reported "job scarcity" as their primary motivation for launching a business, reflecting structural economic pressures and self-employment as a necessary way to generate income (GEM, 2025b, p. 27). For a gender comparison, women cited as their three top reasons for business closure: "business not profitable" (29.4%), "family or personal reasons" (21.0%), and "problems getting finance" (16.2%), while men mentioned "family or personal reasons" (14.3%) as their fourth reason for business closure, representing the largest and most consistent gender gap in GEM data (W/M ratio 1.47). This reinforces the need for gender-responsive entrepreneurship policies that account for the unique burdens women face, as high exit rates often embed systemic inequities rather than simple personal choices (GEM, 2025b, p. 31).

As for female entrepreneurship in Italy, women-led businesses represent a significant component of the country's economy, mainly focused on services (72.6% compared to 60.1% of non-female businesses) (Unioncamere et al., 2025, pp. 27–28) and located predominantly in the South (Unioncamere et al., 2025, p. 4). From an organisational perspective, Italian female entrepreneurship is characterised by micro-enterprises, with 96.2% having fewer than 10 employees (Unioncamere et al., 2025, p. 25). More specifically, Italian women-led businesses account for more than a fifth of the national production system, totalling over 1.3 million units and representing 22.2% of all registered businesses (Unioncamere et al., 2025, p. 12). Only 10.3% of these businesses are led by women under 35, with a decrease of 24.5% over the last decade; anyway, this figure is comparable to that of non-female businesses (Unioncamere et al., 2025, p. 20) and, like global trends, Italian female entrepreneurs have higher average education levels than their male counterparts (25.1% have a university degree compared to 20.6%) (Unioncamere et al., 2025, pp. 55–56).

Importantly, they contribute decisively to increasing female employment rates, as women represent 54% of employees in female-led companies compared to 39% in non-female-led ones (Unioncamere et al., 2025, p. 15). However, these companies often show a lower incidence of employees with university degrees, permanent contracts, and full-time employment (Unioncamere et al., 2025, p. 16). Regarding corporate welfare policies (flexible working hours, voluntary part-time work, remote working), female-led businesses are more likely to adopt work-life balance policies than non-female-led businesses (28% compared to 21.6%), combining economic growth and social value (Unioncamere et al., 2025, p. 61).

Lastly, in terms of reasons to start a business, both Italian female and male entrepreneurs declare that it is not the need to generate income or the lack of job opportunities, but rather it is related to enhancing professional skills and interest in a specific project (Unioncamere et al., 2025, p. 49). However, there is also work to be done on their survival and consolidation: 5 years after startup, there is a 5% differential between female and male-owned businesses, which increases further after the first 5 years of activity (Unioncamere et al., 2025, p. 23).

The context of Italian and global female entrepreneurship data provides an opportunity to discuss gender inequality, particularly related to working conditions. In fact, many social inequalities originate precisely from and within the labour market, where social risks are unfairly distributed among different groups (Argentin, 2020). The link between work and inequality highlights the interconnections between the economic system and the social dimensions of markets and institutions, allowing us to observe how the various forms of inequality stem from the intertwining of economic and productive issues, welfare systems and social policies, socio-demographic composition and family models (Esping-Andersen, 1990; Ferrera, 1993). Nevertheless, gender inequality seems to be—historically and culturally—among the most pervasive and resistant, with gaps still existing today in almost all areas of social life: from employment rates to income, from the low presence of women in top positions to political under-representation, gender gaps remain very wide (cf. Salmieri, 2020).

Specifically referring to female entrepreneurial behaviour, reflecting on social norms and more or less explicit constraints imposed on women is essential to understanding how and why women and men perform and achieve different results in self-employment (Carranza et al., 2018). In fact, gender and culture interact dynamically and have an impact on female entrepreneurship, shaping gender role expectations and identities, and the economic and social environment in which women's entrepreneurship is embedded (Bullough et al., 2022). Many of these factors are widely recognised in sociological, economic, and business literature; therefore, they continue to be used today as key indicators for examining and measuring trends and developments in women's entrepreneurship.

With reference to gender role expectations and identities, women often experience bias and stereotypes stemming from expectations on female leadership styles and perceptions (Oakley, 2000; Prime et al., 2008), leading to discrimination when women are viewed less favourably than men as potential leaders because expected behaviours for their gender roles are inconsistent with attributions of leadership (Eagly & Karau, 2002); this may contribute significantly to greater gender obstacles in achieving entrepreneurial success and growth (Bullough et al., 2022).

It is also interesting to notice how unfavourable segregation in the labour market also leads to similar segregation and representation in their self-employment choices, as they tend to reflect women's segregation in the labour market (Bowden & Mummery, 2009; Halford & Leonard, 2006). This dynamic is accounted for by the labour market segmentation theory, which classifies the market into primary and secondary sectors based on several variables, including gender (Mora & Muro, 2015). Essentially, men tend to concentrate in primary sectors characterised by higher productivity and elevated wages, whereas women are more prevalent in secondary sectors, with low productivity, less profitable activities, and lower pay (cf. Mroczek-Dąbrowska & Gaweł, 2020). Furthermore, the prevalence of women in certain areas traditionally labelled as "female" is sometimes attributed to a self-perpetuating cycle that reflects and reinforces previous representation in those sectors (Damelang & Ebensperger, 2020); this perspective suggests occupational segregation as a direct consequence of gender socialisation processes (Karamessini & Ioakimoglou, 2007).

Another useful point for understanding the differences and gaps in male and female entrepreneurial behaviours is to consider the **reasons** for starting a business. According to the approach of Reynolds et al. (2005), these reasons can be listed as *opportunity* and *necessity* and refer, respectively, to the identification of a business opportunity or the compulsion to undertake an entrepreneurial activity because job alternatives are non-existent or unsatisfactory (cf. Mazzucchelli et al., 2024; cf. Wennekers et al., 2005). Previous studies refer to the *push-pull* factors, sometimes interdependent, that would orient people towards entrepreneurship: push factors describe dissatisfaction with the current condition, such as a job with no prospects for growth or limited flexibility; pull factors, on the other hand, consist of seizing and exploiting an opportunity, such as an entrepreneurial idea (Kuzilwa, 2005). In other words, push factors represent economic and employment needs, also seen as a second choice or an *exit strategy* when a first choice is not available (cf. Carranza et al., 2018), also including frustration, or the impossibility of pursuing a career, the need for flexibility to find a balance between work and family life, the need for inclusion in the labour market, and to increase income and financial independence (Manolova et al., 2008; Orhan & Scott, 2001).

All these factors may result in many economic, social, and cultural barriers women may encounter on their path to entrepreneurship: poor education or socialisation in entrepreneurship, limited mobility, lack of support, and difficulties in acquiring financial resources. From this perspective, examining contextual aspects, such as those related to the media or social policies, is essential to understanding certain impacts on entrepreneurial intention. For example, the imaginary and attractiveness of entrepreneurial careers depend on how entrepreneurs are portrayed in the media, which in turn is shaped by cultural norms and expectations (Laguía & Moriano, 2021). Furthermore, the presence of alternative job opportunities, high employment rates, and strong welfare systems are all factors that can limit the creation of new businesses (Meoli et al., 2020). Socialisation processes into entrepreneurship must come into play to prevent certain internal limitations such as low self-confidence and self-perception, risk aversion, reluctance to seek external financing, and lack of confidence in one's entrepreneurial abilities (Carranza et al., 2018; McCracken et al., 2015). In particular, representing entrepreneurship as gender-neutral and, above all, showcasing a greater number of women entrepreneurs as role models could be encouraged to deconstruct the stereotypical paradigm *think entrepreneur-think male* (Laguía et al., 2022) and improve women's conceptualisations of entrepreneurship, alleviating some of the cultural barriers in sectors with low female representation (Mazzucchelli et al., 2024).

Finally, an important element in analysing women's entrepreneurial behaviour is their work-life balance: these circumstances call for sociological reflection on the symbolic, cultural, personal, and social dimensions around the constructs of time and power, evocative *symbolic fields* in which gender inequalities are particularly evident as they highlight the structural and cultural disparities that determine an unequal presence and participation of men and women in both domestic and work environments (Monticelli & Falci, 2024).

In conclusion, the analysis of persistent gender inequalities in income, health, education, work, and entrepreneurial behaviour encourages a reflection on the close relationship between gender equality and social sustainability. Focusing on female entrepreneurship, these discussions are closely linked to women's empowerment, a multidimensional process that develops both at the individual level, through the strengthening of self-esteem, self-efficacy, critical awareness and decision-making skills, and at the collective level, addressing common challenges and promoting sustainable and participatory change, sense of belonging and shared responsibility (Colella, 2025). In this sense, empowerment is a transformative process oriented towards social justice and the redistribution of power to all individuals, especially those traditionally marginalised (Colella, 2025; Freire, 1970). When applied to gender equality, empowerment becomes an indispensable tool for promoting equal access to resources, opportunities, and rights, encouraging the active participation and autonomy of women across personal, social, political, and economic spheres (Colella, 2025). In the absence of gender equality, aspirations for social and economic justice remain unfulfilled; women's empowerment, therefore, plays a key role in achieving gender equality, understood as the absence of gender disparities in opportunities, resources, services, benefits, decision-making power, and influence. In this light, female entrepreneurship can be seen as a powerful response to women's *internalised subordination* (Malhotra et al., 2002), while women's empowerment acts as a catalyst for social innovation processes by promoting societal change and transformation.

To conclude, the literature reviewed highlights a wide range of factors influencing women's entrepreneurship, including structural inequalities, cultural norms, labour market segmentation, and socialisation processes. However, within different theoretical and disciplinary frameworks, these dimensions are often addressed separately, resulting in a fragmented understanding of the phenomenon, with little attention paid to how structural, cultural, and socialisation processes interact and reinforce each other in shaping women's entrepreneurial trajectories. Given these considerations, this study adopted an integrative approach to bring these dimensions together within a shared analytical perspective and, at the empirical level, employed the Delphi technique with a multidisciplinary and pluralistic panel of experts to move beyond a fragmented understanding of women's entrepreneurship and to explore how barriers, resources, and opportunities emerge through the interaction between institutional conditions, cultural expectations, and individual behaviour. In this way, the study has contributed to a broader systemic framework and understanding of women's entrepreneurship, moving beyond interpretations that treat its determinants as isolated or predominantly individual factors, integrating disciplines such as sociology and labour studies, economics and industrial relations, welfare policies, sustainable entrepreneurship, and entrepreneurship policy design.

3 The Socialisation into Sustainable Entrepreneurship: Insights from the INTERGEN Delphi Study

3.1 Methodological Aspects of the Delphi Study in the INTERGEN Project

Within the framework of the project INTERGEN, part of the empirical research was conducted using the Delphi technique, involving ten experts in female entrepreneurship from different professional sectors. The Delphi technique is configured as a structured process divided into several phases, in which, through the administration of a questionnaire for each phase, information relevant to the investigation is collected. In other words, drawing on Linstone and Turoff (1975), it can be defined as a method for structuring a group communication process which does not take place face to face, as it is mediated by the researcher. In this way, it is possible to preserve the opinions of the experts involved, overcoming the limitations of direct interaction and the potential for conflict of opinion among different groups of experts (Colella, 2011). It was decided to conduct two Delphi rounds, concluding the data collection at the second step after verifying that the data were exhaustive and useful in addressing the research objectives. During the first phase, a questionnaire consisting of 12 open-ended questions was administered in order to explore the experts' views on the following topics of interest:

- gender inequalities,
- socialisation into sustainable entrepreneurship and key competences,
- sustainable entrepreneurship.

The responses were processed into an anonymous synthesis by the research team and subsequently sent to the panel together with the second questionnaire, constituting the second step of the data collection. The results emerging from the first step of the Delphi investigation represented the knowledge base for the construction of the second data collection instrument, allowing for a more precise articulation of the scenarios outlined by the experts in relation to the key dimensions that progressively emerged during the analysis. The questionnaire of the second phase, consisting of 24 closed-ended questions, was structured into four sections:

- evaluation of existing measures mentioned by the experts,
- structural conditions for equity,
- emerging needs and future priorities for young women,
- future visions and scenarios focused on the construction of possible and/or desirable medium- to long-term scenarios, consistent with the values of the INTERGEN project.

Only at the end of the second data collection was the identity of the experts who constituted the panel disclosed. The composition of the panel remained unchanged between the first and second steps, ensuring continuity in the analytical process. The selection privileged profiles with recognised expertise in the themes under study, in order to ensure the presence of different disciplinary and professional perspectives. The panel consisted of ten experts drawn from academia, institutions, and the professional sector, with expertise in the sociology of work and organisations, economics and management, labour and welfare policies, industrial relations, female entrepreneurship, social inclusion, and entrepreneurship policy design. This plurality of perspectives made it possible to construct an articulated framework, allowing different disciplinary backgrounds to interact and contribute to the development of policy scenarios.

3.2 Sociological Insights from the Delphi Findings

Overall, the results of the Delphi consultation outline a framework in which female entrepreneurship is removed from an individualising interpretation and re-situated within a systemic configuration of constraints and opportunities. As reflected in the main findings summarised in Table 1, the emphasis on social infrastructures, social capital, and policies supporting work-life balance indicates that, for the experts involved, any potential expansion of female entrepreneurship cannot be entrusted solely to individual motivation or resilience; rather, it requires a transformation of the structural conditions that regulate both access to and permanence within entrepreneurial activity.

The analysis of the Delphi findings reveals how the panel of experts attributes a moderate level of effectiveness to public policies and existing institutional instruments, despite the formal recognition of their reference role. This critical assessment is sociologically significant insofar as it reveals the perceived distance between the declared intentions of policies and their actual capacity to affect the material conditions of potential women entrepreneurs. First, an institutional distance emerges concerning more generalist measures, particularly those of a fiscal or

Table 1 Selected results from the second Delphi round (INTERGEN project)

Dimension	Selected item	Experts' evaluation
Effectiveness of existing policies	Fondo Impresa Donna	Rated as moderately effective by 70% of experts
Sustainability policies	NRRP funding for sustainable projects	Rated as moderately effective by 80% of experts
Support measures	Continuous mentoring/tutoring	Ranked as the most effective option by 60% of experts
Structural conditions	Work-life balance infrastructures	Identified as the highest priority by 80% of experts
Policy approach	Systemic approach to policymaking	Preferred by 50% of experts

Source: Authors' elaboration on data from the second Delphi round of the INTERGEN project. Note: The table reports selected items corresponding to the options most frequently selected or highest rated by the panellists selective nature. Within the panel, instruments such as regional calls for female and youth entrepreneurship, tax credits, and funds supporting gender pay equality receive mixed and often unenthusiastic evaluations. These are measures which, although formally oriented towards economic support, fail to translate into tangible resources capable of neutralising structural barriers such as access to credit or the precariousness of socio-economic conditions. This tendency can be interpreted considering a classic distinction in the sociology of public policy between formal policy and real policy: that is, between what is declared in norms and what actually occurs in people's everyday lives.

The reflection proposed by Bertarini (2022) suggests a useful analytical key for interpreting these divergences: according to Bertarini, female entrepreneurship, although often portrayed as a practice of economic emancipation, remains closely connected to the definition of an effective legal and regulatory framework capable of transcending the rhetoric of formal equality in order to guarantee equal opportunities de facto. This implies that policies are evaluated not only in terms of their existence but, above all, in terms of their real accessibility. The widespread perception within the panel that measures such as the Fondo Impresa Donna or incentives for innovative startups are insufficient on their own to compensate for gender disadvantages indicates that these are seen as partially useful, yet insufficient in the absence of deeper and more interconnected structural conditions. From this perspective, it is not surprising that among the measures indicated, those receiving almost unanimous consensus in terms of effectiveness in reducing gender inequalities in the field of entrepreneurship and self-employment are those aimed at ensuring work-life balance, such as, for example, the strengthening of educational services (Table 1).

Regarding the evaluation of measures already in place aimed at supporting and incentivising entrepreneurial sustainability, the panellists' assessments are rather unenthusiastic; none of the measures already implemented is considered truly effective. Among the most appreciated measures, albeit moderately, are the NRRP funds allocated to entrepreneurial projects oriented towards environmental sustainability and the NRRP calls supporting the ecological conversion of production processes. By contrast, the Italian Green New Deal; the Nuova Sabatini Green (investments to purchase or lease machinery, equipment, plants, capital goods, Industry 4.0 and green technologies); the National Energy Efficiency Fund (aimed at promoting interventions designed to achieve national energy efficiency targets); and the FRI—Circular Economy (a fund promoting research and development projects for the reconversion of production processes within the circular economy) are generally evaluated as moderately or only slightly effective in encouraging the creation of sustainable enterprises (Table 1).

From this perspective, the panel's critique fits into a broader debate on the quality of institutions and their capacity to mitigate systemic inequalities. While the formal guarantee of gender equality represents an indispensable prerequisite for public action, it does not automatically translate into effective equity if institutions fail to produce a genuine "levelled playing field" in social, economic, and labour practices.

Another critical aspect concerns the delivery and usability of resources. Many panellists express reservations regarding the effectiveness of funding schemes and measures that require technical expertise, complex project-design capacities, or established relationships with institutional networks. This raises the issue of the gap between institutional capacity and individual capacity: measures requiring high levels of bureaucratic literacy tend to favour those who already possess cultural and social capital, leaving out the most disadvantaged potential women entrepreneurs. Bertarini implicitly highlights this tension, noting that the affirmation of female entrepreneurship cannot be considered exclusively from a normative standpoint but requires reflection on the effective implementation of a regulatory and institutional framework capable of making women non-marginal economic actors (cf. Bertarini, 2022).

Finally, the panel's critical evaluation of existing policies also raises the issue of the systemic coherence of public policies. Upon closer examination, measures, when taken individually, often appear fragmented and disconnected from other dimensions that influence access to female entrepreneurship: work-life balance, territorial welfare, access to credit, and mentoring and accompaniment pathways. This lack of integrated coherence reflects the difficulty institutions face in configuring a support ecosystem that is not merely a sum of isolated instruments but rather a network of policies that mutually reinforce one another to neutralise multiple barriers.

Accordingly, the panellists consider the most effective policymaking approach for promoting entrepreneurship to be precisely the "systemic approach" (Table 1), namely, an approach capable of integrating all the various levels transversally, from the regulatory to the educational. This indication appears consistent with the interpretation of policymaking developed in the public policy literature, which emphasises that policies cannot be understood or designed as isolated single interventions but rather as configurations of decisions and actions oriented towards the management of collective problems (cf. Anderson, 2003). From this perspective, the effectiveness of a policy depends on the capacity to coordinate different instruments and to embed them within broader institutional arrangements, in which actors, resources, and constraints combine dynamically (Bobbio et al., 2017; Regonini, 2001).

With regard to the priorities that public policies should pursue over the next 5 years, experts reiterate the urgency of intervention in the creation and strengthening of infrastructures capable of facilitating the balance between working life and family life. Within this macro-area, a range of policies and specific measures can be identified which, if adequately strengthened, could increase well-being both inside and outside the domestic sphere. As highlighted in sociological literature, work-life balance problems, far from being attributable to individual responsibility, should be interpreted as the effect of specific institutional, social, and welfare arrangements that generate an unequal distribution of responsibilities and care work between couples (Naldini & Saraceno, 2011).

Concerning support instruments specifically aimed at accompanying young women in the creation and development of sustainable enterprises, the panellists express no doubts: expert and continuous mentoring is considered the most effective instrument of all, followed by the creation of calls and structural funds dedicated to female entrepreneurship. This almost unanimous indication highlights how the relational and educational dimension plays a significant role and is considered a priority, even compared to economic resources and structural funds for business startups. Being able to rely on expert support and a constant presence may, in fact, represent a fundamental contribution, especially for the most vulnerable categories of aspiring women entrepreneurs, such as those entering the world of business for the first time and who cannot rely on already consolidated social or family networks. In Italy, in fact, as data on entrepreneurship show, those who inherit an already established business are more likely to remain active for a longer period of time.

A further indication useful for the reorientation of policies concerning sustainable female entrepreneurship emerges from the shared urgency, expressed by the panellists, of promoting, within public policies as well as within training programmes, an alternative vision to the current financial, economic, and productive system, one grounded in sustainability, equity, and collective well-being. The challenge, therefore, consists in counterbalancing dominant messages and redirecting them towards a paradigm oriented towards sustainability in all its dimensions. Such a vision finds clear expression in the conception of the enterprise proposed by Adriano Olivetti, a figure who in this context may be considered a paradigmatic role model. In a well-known interview with the sociologist Luciano Gallino, he stated that the enterprise must produce wealth, create employment, and disseminate throughout the territory, in communities and towns, the fruits of labour and the revenues deriving from success achieved on the market; and redistribute a large share of profits, allowing them to flow back to the surrounding community through different channels, not only in the form of higher wages but also by promoting economic development through various means (Gallino, 2009). In an economic context strongly oriented towards hyper-productivism and the unrestrained pursuit of profit, the urgency of reconsidering the foundations of economic action emerges clearly. Technical progress and unlimited economic growth cannot be regarded as morally obligatory, nor can they in themselves justify a primacy over the social and ethical purposes of the economy (Zamagni, 2019). It is therefore not merely a matter of requiring enterprises to produce goods and services that society requires for its proper functioning, but of demanding that such production be realised through economic strategies and everyday practices structured within a paradigm oriented towards social, environmental, and economic sustainability (Nocenzi, 2025).

Experts also call attention to the risk of the diffusion of phenomena such as greenwashing and pinkwashing, emphasising the need for public policies on sustainable female entrepreneurship to include adequate instruments to prevent them. From a theoretical standpoint, these indications are consistent with the literature that interprets greenwashing as a communicative practice aimed at maintaining unchanged economic and productive arrangements through misleading representations of environmental performance. From this perspective, greenwashing may be understood as a strategy that produces a disjunction between public declarations concerning sustainability and the actual practices of organisations, thereby enabling the reproduction of "business-as-usual" models through the construction of apparently virtuous environmental narratives (Roos, 2025). Within this interpretative framework, the problem concerns not only the truthfulness of individual environmental claims but, more broadly, the relationship between discursive representations and material practices. As highlighted by Roos, greenwashing is precisely based on the possibility of manipulating or confusing the relationship between what is declared (representations and public narratives) and the actual material and environmental conditions to which such declarations refer (Roos, 2025). Similarly, the reference to pinkwashing recalls the possibility that the theme of female entrepreneurship and gender equity may also be incorporated into communicative strategies that emphasise values of equity and sustainability without necessarily translating into structural transformations of organisational practices or conditions of access to resources. In this perspective, the experts' attention to verification and accountability instruments suggests the need for public policies capable not only of promoting sustainable entrepreneurship but also of preventing these categories from being reduced to rhetorical devices devoid of real transformative capacity. In this sense, the requests emerging from the panel, concerning the introduction of independent monitoring systems and the introduction of sanctions, can be interpreted as attempts to reconstruct a stronger link between the symbolic and the substantive dimensions of economic action.

In conclusion, the results of the Delphi consultation highlight how socialisation into sustainable female entrepreneurship cannot be reduced to the mere introduction of economic incentives or financial instruments. On the contrary, the indications emerging from the panel underline the need to intervene across a plurality of interconnected dimensions, including the strengthening of welfare infrastructures, the enhancement of support and mentoring networks, greater systemic coherence in public policies, and the introduction of instruments aimed at preventing and countering phenomena of greenwashing and pinkwashing. Taken together, these findings contribute to shifting attention from an individualising vision of entrepreneurship towards a broader and more structural interpretation, in which the emergence of sustainable entrepreneurial practices appears closely linked to the configuration of the institutional, social, and cultural conditions within which economic actors operate.

4 Concluding Remarks

The INTERGEN project highlights that female youth entrepreneurship in Italy cannot be interpreted as an exclusively individual phenomenon, but must be placed within a complex ecosystem of structural, cultural, and generational factors. In this sense, the study contributes to the literature on female entrepreneurship by adopting an integrated perspective that brings into dialogue different analytical approaches: individual-level interpretations (motivations, skills, agency), structural constraints (labour market conditions, welfare regimes, access to resources), and cultural dimensions (gender norms, stereotypes, and socialisation processes).

By integrating these perspectives, the findings challenge approaches that tend to consider these dimensions separately and instead highlight their interdependence. The persistence of gender inequalities and socio-economic barriers calls for interpretations that go beyond unidimensional explanations, showing how entrepreneurial trajectories are the result of the interaction between institutional arrangements, cultural expectations, and individual capabilities.

Consistent with the literature discussed, which highlights a plurality of factors influencing female entrepreneurship, this study adopts a perspective that explicitly addresses the tendency of existing research to treat structural, cultural, and individual dimensions separately. Instead, the present work is grounded in an approach that seeks to recompose these analytical levels, emphasising their interdependence in shaping women's entrepreneurial trajectories. In this sense, the Delphi findings contribute not only empirically but also theoretically, offering an integrated and systemic interpretation of how institutional conditions, cultural expectations, and individual behaviours interact in practice.

The results of the Delphi study show that existing institutional measures, although formally aimed at promoting equality and supporting female entrepreneurship, are often insufficient in practice. Their effectiveness is limited not only by structural constraints, such as access barriers and bureaucratic complexity but also by cultural and relational factors that affect the actual usability of these tools. In this sense, the findings contribute to the literature by highlighting the gap between the formal design of policies and their actual implementation. We further found that existing measures are often fragmented and poorly coordinated, resulting in a limited capacity to structurally address gender inequalities.

This evidence strengthens the contribution of the study to the existing literature, as it shows that the main limitation does not lie only in the inadequacy of individual policies, but in their systemic disconnection, confirming the need to overcome fragmented analytical and normative approaches in the study of female entrepreneurship. Within this framework, the expert panel identifies as priorities tools such as qualified mentoring, sustainability-oriented training, and the strengthening of work-life balance infrastructures, which simultaneously affect individual capabilities and the structural conditions of access to entrepreneurship.

A systemic policy approach emerges as essential, one capable of integrating economic, social, and educational measures while overcoming the fragmentation of current interventions. Such an approach is considered fundamental for building an ecosystem that supports not only the creation of women-led enterprises but also their continuity and development. The evidence collected also underscores the importance of a systemic vision of sustainable entrepreneurship, in which economic growth, social equity, and ethical values are integrated rather than in conflict. The involvement of experts from different disciplines made it possible to outline policy scenarios that go beyond encouraging new business creation and instead aim to build an enabling environment for their long-term sustainability, while counteracting phenomena such as sectoral segregation, greenwashing, and pinkwashing.

Finally, the INTERGEN project confirms that socialisation into female entrepreneurship is a multidimensional and transformative process that requires simultaneous action on human capital, social capital, and institutional conditions in order to promote inclusion, economic autonomy, and social innovation. Women's empowerment is therefore not an isolated objective, but a strategic component of inclusive and sustainable development, capable of generating positive effects at both the individual and collective levels.

Promoting female entrepreneurship thus means recognising and addressing the interconnections between gender, generation, and sustainability, adopting integrated and participatory approaches capable of transforming structural constraints into concrete opportunities for development and social cohesion.

From a future research perspective, further comparative analysis across different national contexts would be valuable in order to assess how the observed dynamics may take different forms under varying institutional arrangements and welfare models.

Acknowledgements Although the work is the result of a shared reflection, Francesca Colella (Project coordinator, Univ. of L'Aquila) wrote the first paragraph and the Concluding Remarks, Laura Falci (Research Fellow on this project) wrote the second paragraph, while Carola Continenza (Research Fellow on this project) wrote the third one.

References

Anderson, J. E. (2003). *Public policymaking: An introduction*. Houghton.

Argentin, G. (2020). Lavoro e disuguaglianze. In O. Giancola & L. Salmieri (Eds.), *Sociologia delle disuguaglianze. Teorie, metodi, ambiti* (pp. 151–162). Carocci.

Bertarini, B. (2022). *L'imprenditoria femminile. L'empowerment delle donne tra diritto e mercato*. Il Mulino.

Bianco, M. L. (1997). *Donne al lavoro. Cinque itinerari fra le diseguaglianze di genere*. Paravia.

Bobbio, L., Pomatto, G., & Ravazzi, S. (2017). *Le politiche pubbliche: Problemi, soluzioni, incertezze, conflitti*. Edizioni Bruno Mondadori.

Bowden, P., & Mummery, J. (2009). *Understanding movements in modern thought: Understanding feminism*. Acumen.

Bullough, A., Guelich, U., Manolova, T. S., & Schjoedt, L. (2022). Women's entrepreneurship and culture: Gender role expectations and identities, societal culture, and the entrepreneurial environment. *Small Business Economics, 58*, 985–996.

Carranza, E., Dhakal, C., & Love, I. (2018). *Female entrepreneurs: How and why are they different?* International Bank for Reconstruction and Development/The World Bank.

Colella, F. (2011). *Focus group. Ricerca sociale e strategie applicative*. FrancoAngeli.

Colella, F. (2025). *Oltre la tensione individuo-società. Il processo di empowerment come chiave di rigenerazione del legame sociale*. FrancoAngeli.

Damelang, A., & Ebensperger, S. (2020). Gender composition of occupations and occupational characteristics: Explaining their true relationship by using longitudinal data. *Social Science Research, 86*, 102394.

Eagly, A. H., & Karau, S. J. (2002). Role congruity theory of prejudice toward female leaders. *Psychological Review, 109*(3), 573–598.

Esping-Andersen, G. (1990). *The three worlds of welfare capitalism*. Polity Press.

Ferrera, M. (1993). *Modelli di solidarietà. Politica e riforme sociali nelle democrazie*. Il Mulino.
Freire, P. (1970). *Pedagogia degli oppressi*. Einaudi.
Gallino, L. (2009). *L'impresa irresponsabile*. Einaudi.
GEM (Global Entrepreneurship Monitor). (2024a). *GEM 2023/2024 global report: 25 years and growing*. https://www.gemconsortium.org/report/global-entrepreneurship-monitor-gem-20232024-global-report-25-years-and-growing
GEM (Global Entrepreneurship Monitor). (2024b). *GEM 2023/24 women's entrepreneurship report: Reshaping economies and communities*. https://www.gemconsortium.org/report/202324-womens-entrepreneurship-report-reshaping-economies-and-communities-2
GEM (Global Entrepreneurship Monitor). (2025a). *GEM 2024/2025 global report: entrepreneurship reality check*. https://gemconsortium.org/report/gem-20242025-global-report-entrepreneurship-reality-check-4
GEM (Global Entrepreneurship Monitor). (2025b). *GEM 2024/2025 women's entrepreneurship report navigating challenges, driving change*. https://gemconsortium.org/report/gem-20242025-womens-entrepreneurship-report-navigating-challenges-driving-change-2
Halford, S., & Leonard, P. (2006). Place, space and time: Contextualizing workplace subjectivities. *Organization Studies, 27*(5), 657–676.
INAPP Report. (2021). *Lavoro, formazione e società in Italia nel passaggio all'era post Covid-19*. https://www.inapp.gov.it/pubblicazioni/rapporto/edizioni-pubblicate/rapporto-inapp-2021
Karamessini, M., & Ioakimoglou, E. (2007). Wage determination and the gender pay gap: A feminist political economy analysis and decomposition. *Feminist Economics, 13*(1), 31–66.
Kuzilwa, J. A. (2005). The role of credit for small business: A study of the National Entrepreneurship Development Fund in Tanzania. *The Journal of Entrepreneurship, 14*(2), 131–161.
Laguía, A., & Moriano, J. A. (2021). Perceived representation of entrepreneurship in the mass media and entrepreneurial intention. *International Entrepreneurship and Management Journal, 17*, 401–421.
Laguía, A., Wach, D., Garcia-Ael, C., & Moriano, J. A. (2022). "Think entrepreneur-think male": The effect of reduced gender stereotype threat on women's entrepreneurial intention and opportunity motivation. *International Journal of Entrepreneurial Behavior and Research, 28*(4), 1001–1025.
Linstone, H., & Turoff, M. (1975). *The Delphi method: Techniques and applications*. Addison-Wesley Pub.
Malhotra, A., Schuler, S. R., & Boender, C. (2002). *Measuring women's empowerment as a variable in international development. Background paper prepared for the World Bank workshop on poverty and gender: New perspectives*. The World Bank.
Manolova, T. S., Brush, C. G., & Edelman, L. F. (2008). What do women entrepreneurs want? *Strategic Change, 17*(3–4), 69–82.
Mazzucchelli, S., Bosoni, M. L., & Medina, L. (2024). Analisi della letteratura sociologica. In S. Mazzucchelli (Ed.), *Imprenditorialità femminile. Cultura, relazioni, complessità e nuove prospettive nell'era post-pandemica* (pp. 70–96). FrancoAngeli.
McCracken, K., Marquez, S., Kwong, C., Stephan, U., Castagnoli, A., & Dlouhà, M. (2015). *Women's entrepreneurship: Closing the gender gap in access to financial and other services and in social entrepreneurship*. European Parliament, Policy Department C: Citizens' Rights and Constitutional Affairs.
Meoli, A., Fini, R., Sobrero, M., & Wiklund, J. (2020). How entrepreneurial intentions influence entrepreneurial career choices: The moderating influence of social context. *Journal of Business Venturing, 35*, 1059–1082.
Monticelli, A., & Falci, L. (2024). Tempo e potere nei principali indici gender-related. Riflessione sociologica, trend evolutivi e buone pratiche. *The Lab's Quarterly, XXVI*(4), 71–94.
Mora, J. J., & Muro, J. (2015). Labor market segmentation in a developing country. *The Indian Journal of Labour Economics, 58*(3), 477–486.
Mroczek-Dąbrowska, K., & Gaweł, A. (2020). Determinants of female entrepreneurship in male- and female-dominated sectors in selected European countries. *International Entrepreneurship Review, 6*(2), 55–68.

Naldini, M., & Saraceno, C. (2011). *Conciliare famiglia e lavoro. Vecchi e nuovi patti tra sessi e generazioni*. Il Mulino.
Nocenzi, M. (Ed.). (2025). *Sostenibilità e sviluppo sostenibile. Una lettura transdisciplinare*. UTET.
Oakley, J. G. (2000). Gender-based barriers to senior management positions: Understanding the scarcity of female CEOs. *Journal of Business Ethics, 27*(4), 321–324.
Orhan, M., & Scott, D. (2001). Why women enter into entrepreneurship: An explanatory model. *Women in Management Review, 16*(5), 232–247.
Prime, J., Jonsen, K., Carter, N., & Maznevski, M. L. (2008). Managers' perceptions of women and men leaders: A cross cultural comparison. *International Journal of Cross Cultural Management, 8*(2), 171–210.
Regonini, G. (2001). *Capire le politiche pubbliche*. Il Mulino.
Reynolds, P., Bosma, N., Autio, E., Hunt, S., De Bono, N., Servais, I., & Chin, N. (2005). Global entrepreneurship monitor: Data collection design and implementation 1998-2003. *Small Business Economics, 24*, 205–231.
Roos, A. (2025). Greenwashing: A critical realist approach to the study of false ecological claims. *Journal of Critical Realism, 24*(2), 176–197. https://doi.org/10.1080/14767430.2025.2503634
Salmieri, L. (2020). Genere e disuguaglianze. In O. Giancola & L. Salmieri (Eds.), *Sociologia delle disuguaglianze. Teorie, metodi, ambiti* (pp. 185–198). Carocci.
Unioncamere, Centro Studi Guglielmo Tagliacarne, & Si.Camera. (2025). *L'imprenditoria femminile in Italia, report*. https://www.unioncamere.gov.it/sites/default/files/articoli/2025-11/Imprenditoria%20femminile%20in%20Italia_def%20%281%29.pdf
Wennekers, S., Van Wennekers, A., Thurik, R., & Reynolds, P. (2005). Nascent entrepreneurship and the level of economic development. *Small Business Economics, 24*, 293–309.
Zamagni, S. (2019). *Responsabili. Come civilizzare il mercato*. Il Mulino.

Entrepreneurship Education in Action: Preventing the NEET Phenomenon. Lessons from La Paranza Case Study

Angelo Bonfanti, Rossella Canestrino, Vania Vigolo, Giovanna Bagnato, and Francesco Bonetti

Abstract The rise of young people not in employment, education, or training (NEET) is a major concern in Europe, particularly in disadvantaged areas. Entrepreneurship education is seen as a strategy to enhance inclusion and employability, though it remains underexplored outside formal schooling. This study examines La Paranza cooperative in Naples and identifies key drivers, including experiential learning, place-based approaches, mentorship, active participation, and stakeholder networks. These factors foster skills, self-esteem, and local identity, supporting pathways into employment. The findings show that entrepreneurship education can develop beyond schools, contributing to inclusive policies that address youth marginalization and reduce NEET conditions.

1 Introduction

Italy is one of the countries in the European Union that has one of the highest rates of young individuals aged 15–29 who are Not in Employment, Education, or Training, referred to as NEET youth. Precisely, Italy recorded a NEET rate of about 15.2% in 2024, significantly above the EU average of approximately 11% (Eurostat, European Commission). This socio-economic phenomenon has been further aggravated by the COVID-19 pandemic, which has exacerbated the gap between already disadvantaged regions, such as those in Southern Italy, where rates were already significantly above the national average: in 2024, the NEET rate reached about 26.2% in Calabria, 25.7% in Sicily, and 24.9% in Campania (ISTAT).

To address this pressing challenge, the Italian government has introduced a range of targeted youth-focused policies and investment strategies within the

A. Bonfanti (✉) · V. Vigolo · G. Bagnato
Department of Management, University of Verona, Verona, Italy
e-mail: angelo.bonfanti@univr.it; vania.vigolo@univr.it; giovanna.bagnato@univr.it

R. Canestrino · F. Bonetti
Department of Business and Quantitative Studies, Parthenope University of Naples, Naples, Italy
e-mail: rossella.canestrino@uniparthenope.it; francesco.bonetti@univr.it

R. Cellini et al. (eds.), *Cultural, Social, and Political Participation in the Internet Era*, Contributions to Economics, https://doi.org/10.1007/978-3-032-33072-7_17

National Recovery and Resilience Plan (PNRR). As part of this framework, several cascade funding calls have been launched and organized into thematic Spokes, each supporting the implementation of specific research and innovation projects with direct territorial impact. Conducted under Spoke 8 "Social Sustainability" of the extended partnership project "GRInS—Growing Resilient, Inclusive and Sustainable," funded under Mission 4 of the PNRR, this study was developed within the ENTREDU4NEET project, which investigates how entrepreneurial education can enhance the skilling and reskilling of NEET youth, enabling them to pursue new venture creation and fostering their cultural, economic, and social inclusion. By generating evidence-based insights, it aims to support policymakers in designing effective interventions to reduce youth disengagement and prevent the consolidation of the NEET phenomenon.

Although management scholars consider NEET youth to be a significant concern within the framework of European Union policies, they have so far paid very little attention to this part of the population from an entrepreneurial perspective. Building on the evidence that entrepreneurship can serve as a meaningful pathway to enhance employability and social participation among vulnerable youth (e.g., Ripamonti & Barberis, 2021; Zhartay et al., 2020), it becomes essential to examine entrepreneurship education as the structured educational counterpart of these entrepreneurial opportunities (e.g., Banha et al., 2022; Miço, & Cungu, 2023), because it can equip young people, including those at risk of becoming NEET, with the skills, mindset, and networks needed to construct sustainable and inclusive career trajectories that encourage labor market inclusion.

To fill the identified gap, this study considers the importance of investing in entrepreneurship education by examining how entrepreneurship education prevents the development of NEETs by answering the following two research questions:

RQ1. What factors enable the development of entrepreneurship education to reduce the NEET phenomenon?

RQ2. What benefits can young people who are involved in entrepreneurship education activities obtain?

This chapter presents one of the best practices identified within the ENTREDU4NEET project. It explores a significant entrepreneurial initiative that supports the cultural, economic, and social inclusion of NEET individuals in Southern Italy by facilitating their (re)skilling and engagement in new venture creation. Following a qualitative approach that was conducted through an in-depth case-study analysis, the research examined the empirical evidence of La Paranza, a social cooperative founded in 2006 with the aim of managing the "San Gennaro" Catacombs and other activities in the Rione Sanità district of Naples, which is aligned with the objective of promoting social innovation and the inclusion of disadvantaged youth through entrepreneurship education.

The contribution of this study is twofold. First, the findings contribute to the academic debate on the role of entrepreneurship education in preventing the NEET phenomenon, revealing that not only businesses but also social cooperatives are local actors involved in entrepreneurship education. Second, the study offers practitioners and policymakers suggestions for preventing the growth of the NEET population by implementing practices that promote entrepreneurship.

The chapter is organized as follows: after a literature review of entrepreneurship education and NEET youth, the methodology is described, and the case study results are discussed. Theoretical and practical implications are presented. Finally, the study concludes with a discussion of its limitations and provides further directions for future research.

2 Literature Review

2.1 The Development of Research About NEET Youth

The term NEET was coined in the United Kingdom in the mid-1990s to capture a new youth category that fell outside both the education system and the labor market. Previous research has proposed different classifications of NEET subgroups to better understand the heterogeneity of this part of the population. Among the most influential frameworks in the sociology literature, Yates and Payne (2006) distinguished three main categories. First, they identified the Transitional NEET, which refers to the young people who experience a temporary phase outside education, employment, or training due to personal or contextual circumstances, but who are generally able to reintegrate relatively quickly. A second category includes Young Parent NEET, which comprises individuals who consciously withdraw from education or the labor market to undertake caregiving responsibilities, typically associated with early parenthood. Finally, the Complicated NEET category is a group characterized by multiple and overlapping vulnerabilities, such as homelessness, involvement in criminal activities, mental health difficulties, or behavioral disorders, which place them at heightened risk of long-term marginalization. Young people in the latter category are more likely to experience social exclusion and what Ball et al. (2000) termed a "hazy future," as they often lack clear aspirations and are stigmatized as a "complex" social group. Furthermore, Eurofound's 2016 report "Exploring the diversity of NEETs" disaggregated the NEET population into seven sub-groups, such as re-entrants, short-term unemployed, long-term unemployed, unavailable due to family responsibilities, unavailable due to disability/illness, discouraged workers, and "other NEETs." These classifications emphasize that NEET status is not a homogeneous condition but rather reflects a high level of heterogeneity that entails diverse needs and support requirements, which must be recognized in the design of effective and targeted interventions.

The United Kingdom led the European scholarly interest in the topic, followed by Italy, and then Austria, France, and Germany. While the United Kingdom leads the field in terms of volume, Italy occupies a strategic position as the second-largest contributor, reflecting both the severity of the NEET challenge at the national level and the growing relevance of Italian scholarship in the international literature.

Considering the distribution of academic studies on NEET individuals by subject area, most publications belong to the field of Business, Management, and Accounting (43.6%), followed by the other disciplines of Social Sciences (27.9%). Together, these two areas account for more than 70% of the total output, highlighting how the NEET phenomenon is predominantly examined through economic, managerial, and social science perspectives.

The first studies on NEETs in management literature emerged in 2002, and their frequency increased significantly from 2016 onward. This trend suggests that the academic debate has progressively intensified its focus on NEET youth, particularly in the last decade, likely in response to broader structural challenges such as economic recessions, the development of the 2008 crisis, and the more recent disruptions caused by the COVID-19 pandemic.

Despite the recognition of NEET youth as a key priority in European Union policy agendas, management research has devoted far less attention to understanding this part of the population through the lens of entrepreneurship and entrepreneurial development.

2.2 *Studies on NEETs Through the Lens of Entrepreneurship and Entrepreneurship Education*

Past research directly linking entrepreneurship and the NEET condition remains strongly limited. For example, Zhartay et al. (2020) investigated the development of youth entrepreneurship in Kazakhstan as a response to the socio-economic vulnerability of young people, including the growing prevalence of NEETs, and a lever for national innovation and economic growth. They revealed how youth entrepreneurship initiatives serve as channels for employment, social inclusion, and self-realization, and underlined the potential of entrepreneurship as a preventive and strategic tool to re-engage NEET youth and prevent their long-term marginalization.

Ripamonti and Barberis (2021) highlighted that the risk of becoming NEET in Italy is strongly influenced by structural territorial resources. Economic capital emerges as the most direct protective factor against youth disengagement, particularly in disadvantaged Southern regions, while cultural capital exerts only an indirect influence through its contribution to economic development. These findings suggest that fostering youth participation in the labor market requires strengthening the socio-economic ecosystem at the local level. Thus, these scholars outlined the need for territorial investments and skill-enhancing strategies for supporting youth entrepreneurial pathways and preventing long-term marginalization.

Haug et al. (2023) proposed a systematic review that directly connects entrepreneurial initiatives and NEET inclusion. They identified entrepreneurship promotion as one of the emerging service innovations targeted at disengaged youth, with the potential to enhance agency, identity formation, and participation. However, existing efforts are described as fragmented, short-term, and poorly integrated into consistent educational frameworks. The study, therefore, calls for structured, long-term entrepreneurial education models that combine co-creation, flexible pedagogies, and ecosystem support to achieve sustainable social and economic inclusion.

From these studies, it emerged that entrepreneurship, although still fragmented in relation to youth inclusion, is recognized as a lever for reducing youth disengagement and NEET status. In this perspective, entrepreneurship education assumes a fundamental role.

Entrepreneurship education refers to the structured development of knowledge, skills, and attitudes that enable individuals to identify opportunities, mobilize resources, and create value through entrepreneurial action (Gibb, 2002). It emphasizes both the acquisition of entrepreneurial competencies and the development of a mindset oriented toward initiative, creativity, and proactive behavior, which are essential for participation in economic and social life. Through several factors—such as the entrepreneurial ecosystem surrounding students (Pittaway et al., 2011), family background (Hahn et al., 2020), the instructors involved in education (San-Martín et al., 2021), collaborations with entrepreneurs or existing businesses (Steira et al., 2024), experiential learning (Ramsgaard & Christensen, 2018), the availability of qualified lecturers, adequate facilities, effective teaching methods, sufficient funding, and government support (Amadi & Eze, 2019)—entrepreneurship education fosters both entrepreneurial intention and entrepreneurial orientation (e.g., Bolton & Lane, 2012; Gabbianelli et al., 2021). Precisely, entrepreneurial intention is understood as an expected behavior (Ajzen, 1991) reflecting a state of mind characterized by a conscious awareness and deliberate conviction to create a new business venture in the future (Liñán & Fayolle, 2015). In contrast, entrepreneurial orientation refers to proactivity, innovativeness, risk-taking, autonomy, and competitive aggressiveness (Lumpkin & Dess, 1996, 2001; Rauch et al., 2009). Entrepreneurial intention and entrepreneurial orientation together translate educational experiences into concrete behavioral tendencies, supporting youth employability. In this perspective, entrepreneurship education acts as the enabling mechanism through which both intention and orientation develop (Somjai & Sangperm, 2019), facilitating youth inclusion and reducing the risk of long-term disengagement, particularly among vulnerable groups such as NEET youth.

However, very few studies have investigated how structured entrepreneurial learning experiences may prevent school disengagement or support NEET reintegration. In this regard, Banha et al. (2022) highlighted that, although entrepreneurship education is widely recognized to equip young people with creativity, initiative, and employability skills, which are particularly relevant for reducing the risk of becoming NEET, the existing research has focused mainly on student outcomes. The authors revealed a critical gap: very little is known about how entrepreneurship education is adopted and sustained within school systems. They emphasize that effective implementation requires supportive infrastructures, teacher training, and alignment with educational policies.

Miço & Cungu (2023) showed that entrepreneurship education can only be effective if teachers themselves are adequately equipped with entrepreneurial competencies. Drawing on the EntreComp framework, the study demonstrated that teachers often lack the skills, training, and confidence needed to embed entrepreneurial learning into their practice. Since transversal competences such as initiative, resilience, and problem-solving are essential for preventing youth disengagement and promoting employability, this contribution highlights a crucial condition for NEET prevention: strengthening teachers' entrepreneurial competence as a prerequisite for ensuring that entrepreneurship education becomes a sustainable and impactful component of schooling.

This scarcity of research highlights the need to better understand how entrepreneurship education can be designed, implemented, and sustained to effectively address youth marginalization, fostering the skills, mindset, and opportunities required for active social and economic inclusion. Unfortunately, the entrepreneurial responses currently documented in the literature remain limited and often insufficiently integrated into broader educational and territorial development strategies.

This chapter presents the case study of La Paranza as one of the best practices to support the cultural, economic, and social inclusion of NEET youth, facilitating their (re)skilling and engagement in new venture creation.

3 Method

3.1 Research Design

To address the research questions and the exploratory nature of this study, as well as the limited existing knowledge on the topic, a qualitative approach was adopted through an in-depth case-study analysis. This approach offers a comprehensive way to investigate complex phenomena (Yin, 2003), allowing for an in-depth examination of a subject within its real-life context (Stake, 2005; Ridder, 2017). It also provides valuable insights into individuals' lived experiences and the contexts in which they are embedded (Lamnek, 2010). As Creswell and Poth (2016) point out, exploratory qualitative designs are particularly effective when dealing with emerging areas where existing theories or frameworks fail to offer complete explanations. This approach also allows us to elucidate "What factors foster the development of entrepreneurship education to mitigate the NEET phenomenon?" and "What benefits do young people gain from participating in entrepreneurship education initiatives?" penetrating the so-called black box, rendering an in-depth case study especially appropriate for investigating rare and underexplored phenomena (Fiss, 2009; Ridder, 2017; Yin, 2003). In this regard, the social cooperative La Paranza, located in the South of Italy, was chosen as a compelling case for its ability to shed light on the research themes and to provide transferable theoretical insights for initiatives fostering social innovation and youth inclusion through entrepreneurship education (Yin, 2003). This case is not new in the literature, given that it has already been examined with specific reference to other topics, such as social business models (Canestrino et al., 2019) and to governance and urban regeneration practices (Fiorentino et al., 2023). The extensive scholarly attention devoted to this case highlights its value as a unique and original empirical setting, which enables a deeper level of investigation—in this study on the entrepreneurship education topic—and offers inspiration for advancing theoretical developments (Siggelkow, 2007).

The data collection was carried out by combining both primary and secondary sources. As primary data, semi-structured in-depth interviews were conducted because they allow participants to narrate their experiences and reflections freely, encouraging open and thoughtful storytelling (Creswell & Creswell, 2018). Complementing the interviews, secondary data from the social cooperative's website and internal press releases were analyzed and included in the final dataset.

3.2 The Case Study Selected: La Paranza

In the heart of Naples, La Paranza was established in 2006 within the Sanità district, a neighborhood traditionally located outside of any productive or tourism system, mainly because of its reputation as a dangerous, violent, criminal place. Rione Sanità is an area of Naples marked by sharp social inequalities yet endowed with extraordinary human and artistic resources, which became the starting point for a remarkable journey of community self-development.

Born as a social cooperative, La Paranza was founded through the efforts of Father Antonio Loffredo, parish priest, who had an ambitious dream: to transform the local reality by fostering a new attitude toward work. That dream soon became the dream of many young people who, over the years, have sought to transform their neighborhood from within.

Since its establishment, La Paranza has recovered approximately 10,500 square meters of neglected cultural and artistic heritage, transforming previously inaccessible spaces into community assets. Over time, the cooperative has developed a wide range of cultural and tourism services, including hospitality, guided tours of the revitalized sites, thematic itineraries that showcase a lesser-known sacred side of Naples, and the restoration of historic frescoes and mosaics. The objective was not to leave the city, but to change it by putting local skills and energy into the service of the community itself.

Over time, La Paranza has emerged as a model of social and cultural regeneration, bringing together archeologists, restorers, art historians, craftspeople, and social workers, all united by a shared vision: to restore life and dignity to a once-neglected heritage. A central role is played by young residents of the district, often aged between 22 and 28, who take on direct responsibility for managing several historical sites, becoming the custodians of their own future.

3.3 Data Collection

To capture diverse perspectives, the primary data was collected through semi-structured interviews with the members of La Paranza, each fulfilling essential roles within the cooperative. Particularly, three organizational key informants were interviewed: the founder of La Paranza and currently marketing and communications manager; the human resource manager; and a tourist guide and staff member, mitigating the risk of single-source bias.

To further include the perspectives of direct beneficiaries of entrepreneurial education initiatives, namely NEET youth, five additional short semi-structured interviews were conducted with young members of La Paranza who had been involved in the cooperative for several years and had experienced its development over time, transforming their life condition from NEET to people in employment, education, or training (EET). They were asked to reflect on the educational, social, entrepreneurial, and employment-related benefits obtained through their participation in the project. This additional data source allowed the analysis to incorporate the voices of the young beneficiaries themselves, strengthening the empirical grounding of the findings on perceived outcomes.

Moreover, drawing from the literature on entrepreneurship education and social inclusion, the interview protocol covered the following three key themes: (a) history of the social cooperative and goal of preservation of NEET youth; (b) factors for development of entrepreneurship education to reduce the NEET phenomenon; and (c) benefits offered to young people by participating in entrepreneurship education initiatives. These themes were explored through open-ended questions designed to elicit a wide range of perspectives (Gioia et al., 2013). Before data collection began, three professors specializing in entrepreneurship development and social innovation reviewed the interview guide. Their insightful feedback helped fine-tune the wording and enhance both clarity and conceptual alignment in the final draft.

Prior to conducting the interviews, all participants were contacted via email and provided with detailed information about the research's purpose, objectives, and the main topics to be discussed. Participants were then asked for their consent to record the conversation for academic purposes. The collected data were securely stored in the university's database, with access strictly limited to authorized research staff to ensure confidentiality and data integrity (Sinkovics et al., 2008). Because all interviewees were based in Italy, all interviews were conducted in Italian and subsequently translated into English by the research team, ensuring the authenticity and interpretive reliability of the data. Each interview lasted between 60 and 90 min and was carried out between August 2025 and October 2025.

Finally, consistent with the research design, primary and secondary sources were used to corroborate each other, overcoming the most common problems related to individual bias and ensuring data triangulation and minimizing potential single-source bias (Jack & Raturi, 2006).

3.4 Data Analysis

After combining primary and secondary data into a unique dataset, NVivo software (version 14) was used to systematically interpret them. Next, the Gioia methodology was applied, which unfolded through four analytical stages: quotations, first-order categories, second-order themes, and aggregate dimensions (Magnani & Gioia, 2023). At the first stage, direct quotations captured participants' own words. These statements were then grouped into first-order categories reflecting their expressed views. The subsequent analysis identified second-order themes, which represented higher-level conceptual insights emerging from those categories. Finally, the aggregate dimensions integrated these themes into coherent theoretical constructs.

To this end, a blended approach was adopted, allowing the data to speak for themselves through the inductive identification of key themes. In practice, two researchers collaboratively conducted and transcribed the four stages of the Gioia process. A third researcher then reviewed and reconciled any inconsistencies. Finally, all researchers reached full agreement on the ultimate dimensions before finalizing the dataset.

4 Findings

In this section, the results are presented and discussed sequentially in relation to the two following aspects: (1) factors for the development of entrepreneurship education, and (2) benefits obtained by young people participating in entrepreneurship education initiatives.

4.1 Factors for the Development of Entrepreneurship Education

In the case of La Paranza, entrepreneurship education emerges through a nonformal, community-based learning process grounded in the cultural and social context of the Sanità district, which has long suffered from disinvestment, unemployment, and limited prospects for young people. Focusing specifically on NEET youth, La Paranza employs and trains those at risk of social exclusion, allowing them to gain skills, income, and attachment to place while improving safety and the reputation of the district. This approach embodies a community-driven model of entrepreneurship education, where youth learn through direct engagement in value creation for their own neighborhood.

The cooperative deals with the recovery, management, and public opening of the Catacombs of San Gennaro (and San Gaudioso), turning abandoned heritage into an economically viable and socially inclusive enterprise and transforming it into a leading cultural attraction and a generator of local jobs. In this sense, the cooperative's intervention can be defined as a "heritage-as-jobs platform." Youth are trained as guides, front-of-house staff, and operations assistants at the catacombs, and they run workshops for schools and visitors. Their professional development follows a "learning by doing" approach, where cultural heritage becomes both a training environment and a workplace. As one interviewee said:

> We want to enhance the artistic and cultural heritage of the district. Our mission is to reclaim cultural heritage to create work opportunities for youth, restore community pride, and stimulate local development, inviting young residents to take direct responsibility for managing cultural heritage sites, tourism services, and event organization.

Entrepreneurial learning is also fostered through co-creation and active participation of the young members of the cooperative who are involved in the design, governance, and implementation of all activities.

This experiential dimension is supported by strong, transformative educational leadership, driven by Father Antonio Loffredo, who encouraged local youth to believe in their abilities and take ownership of the future of their community. Especially in the initial phases when mistrust and low self-esteem prevailed, the Church and parish leadership were crucial in building trust and mobilizing youth, as an interviewee highlighted:

> Young people in the Sanità district rarely leave their neighborhood and are often unaware of their own skills and of the value of local resources. To inspire change, Father Antonio Loffredo engaged a small group of youths (aged 17–20) and took them to visit European cities such as Paris, London, and Amsterdam. These shared experiences strengthened trust, built a sense of community, and helped them recognize the potential of their neighborhood. As their confidence and collective vision grew, they decided to act, transforming their reality around a dream that had become their own.

Youth pathways are intentionally designed with NEET inclusion in mind. Recruitment occurs through parishes, schools, and community networks. Motivation, relational trust, and the willingness to take responsibility are valued as much as previous education, recalling Father Antonio Loffredo's early insight:

> Young people first need to believe in themselves and in the value of their own community.

Not only did the parish priest act as a facilitator of opportunities, a motivational guide, and a value-based role model, but the development of young participants is also supported by mentorship—crucial in fostering entrepreneurial growth—further provided by professionals and specialized educators, who equipped them with technical skills in hospitality, restoration, event management, and cultural storytelling, ensuring that competence building was directly aligned with real market and community needs. Training covers storytelling, languages, hospitality skills, teamwork, local ambassadorship, problem-solving abilities, and proactivity in real operational settings. Over time, youth progress from trainees to paid staff in tours, ticketing, events, communications, and coordination, or transition toward employment in the cultural and tourism sector citywide.

La Paranza offers a safe environment for experimentation, where errors are considered valuable opportunities for learning, contributing to the development of self-efficacy and responsible risk-taking. Moreover, the initiative is rooted in place-based learning, with the district itself serving as an entrepreneurial laboratory. Entrepreneurship education is embedded in local social and cultural identity, as one of the interviewees said with these words:

> We founded La Paranza to regenerate a neighborhood divided between contrasts and great resources.

The cooperative has gradually developed a wider cultural ecosystem with new theater initiatives, music events, publishing, and creative workshops. This enabled the multiplication of roles for young people and broadened the attractiveness of the area. Digital engagement and innovative tourism products further demonstrate the cooperative's entrepreneurial orientation toward innovation and opportunity recognition.

La Paranza operates within a rich stakeholder ecosystem. In addition to the Church, Fondazione "Con il Sud" and subsequent philanthropic and civic collaborations played a crucial role in unlocking heritage sites and establishing strong institutional partnerships. The cooperative has been widely recognized for excellence. The Catacombs of Naples were awarded "Best Onsite Experience in the World" (2020/2021), and La Paranza received the European Heritage Award/Europa Nostra for youth-led regeneration. These relationships and recognitions have enabled the La Paranza model to generate tangible territorial impact over time, as one interviewee noted:

> Visitors to the Catacombs have increased fivefold, and a social economy has developed, giving birth to a network of small cooperatives and artisans.

The cooperative also highlights the transferability of this approach, emphasizing that:

> The management model of the Catacombs was designed to be replicable in other historic-artistic sites.

All these factors highlight that La Paranza constitutes a significant and innovative example of entrepreneurship education in action, transforming vulnerable young people traditionally considered at risk of exclusion into active agents of cultural, economic, and social regeneration within their own community.

4.2 *Benefits Obtained by Young People Participating in Entrepreneurship Education Initiatives*

Young people from the Sanità district gain a wide range of professional, entrepreneurial, social, and employment benefits through their engagement in the entrepreneurial model implemented by La Paranza. In terms of professional benefits, they acquire valuable, market-oriented skills, including tour guiding, visitor services, hospitality, event management, cultural heritage restoration, storytelling, and digital communication, which enhance their employability across the heritage, tourism, and creative industries. This learning-by-doing approach ensures that training is not abstract but embedded in real enterprise activities, making the competencies gained immediately applicable to the regional labor market.

The additional interviews with young beneficiaries confirm that these benefits are not only organizationally observed but also directly experienced by participants. Several respondents described La Paranza as a formative environment in which they learned to assume responsibility, work in teams, coordinate people, interact with visitors from different countries, and manage cultural and relational activities. One young member explained that, at the beginning, they did not imagine creating "all this," but that participation in the cooperative taught them "to take responsibility, work in a group and build something that remains." Another respondent described La Paranza as "a school of life and enterprise," emphasizing the acquisition of organizational, administrative, and entrepreneurial competencies through daily practice.

In terms of entrepreneurial benefits, participants develop key entrepreneurial capacities such as initiative, problem-solving, adaptability, teamwork, and place-based leadership. Over time, they move from being passive recipients of support to active agents of change within their neighborhood, demonstrating stronger entrepreneurial intention and orientation: they recognize local opportunities and actively contribute to value creation in their community. This entrepreneurial transformation is reflected in the words of one respondent, who described La Paranza as "a school of life and entrepreneurship," where young people learned that "even in a difficult neighborhood, it is possible to create a sustainable economic model starting from culture." From the beneficiaries' perspective, entrepreneurial learning emerged through the concrete experience of transforming abandoned places into opportunities for work, culture, and community development. Participants reported that the cooperative changed the way they perceived themselves and their territory, helping them understand that they could have a real impact on their community. This reinforces the interpretation of La Paranza as a place-based entrepreneurial learning environment, where opportunity recognition, initiative, and value creation are developed through direct engagement with local heritage.

In terms of social benefits, through their involvement in La Paranza, many NEET youth experience meaningful social inclusion, community recognition, and identity enhancement. By taking responsibility for previously abandoned heritage sites, they become ambassadors of the Sanità district, challenging the negative stereotypes associated with their background and reinforcing their self-esteem. As one young participant explained: "Working at the Catacombs means feeling that you are doing something meaningful for the place where you live. It gives you dignity, economic autonomy, and pride. Today, I can imagine my future in Naples without feeling the need to leave."

As noted on the cooperative's website, the growth of visitors has stimulated a broader social economy, "giving birth to a network of small cooperatives and artisans," enabling young people to envision a future in their own neighborhood rather than seeking work opportunities elsewhere.

The interviews also reveal important personal and social outcomes. Young participants associated the cooperative with increased self-confidence, dignity, autonomy, pride, and a renewed sense of belonging to Naples and the Sanità district. One respondent stated that working at the Catacombs means feeling useful for the place where one lives, while another emphasized that the experience helped her overcome shyness and feel part of a project that matters for the city. Particularly relevant is the fact that some participants reported having resumed their studies, improved their educational qualifications, or reconsidered their future in Naples rather than feeling forced to leave.

In terms of employment, the partnership model and stakeholder ecosystem of La Paranza—including church leadership, philanthropic foundations, and professional educators—offer these young people structured pathways into employment: from recruitment and onboarding, through onsite training and coaching, to paid roles and progression into broader cultural and tourism employment across the city.

The tangible impact of this pathway is affirmed by external recognition, demonstrating that youth moving from NEET status to working in a world-class heritage enterprise is both possible and replicable.

Employment benefits are therefore intertwined with life-course stability. Respondents repeatedly underlined that La Paranza provided not only jobs but also the conditions to build families, plan the future, and remain in the neighborhood. The fact that the cooperative now employs more than 80 people, many of them under 35, was interpreted by beneficiaries as evidence that a sustainable economic model can be built even in a disadvantaged urban area by starting from culture, responsibility, and community care. Several respondents also connected employment stability with long-term life planning. As one participant noted:

> The greatest benefit has been seeing many young people choose to stay here instead of leaving. I myself was able to build a family thanks to this work.

In summary, the beneficiaries' voices show that La Paranza produces multidimensional benefits: professional skills, entrepreneurial competencies, renewed self-confidence, educational reengagement, social recognition, economic autonomy, and future stability. These accounts strengthen the interpretation of entrepreneurship education as a strategic asset for youth engagement and territorial regeneration, because the benefits are not merely inferred from organizational outcomes, but empirically anchored in the lived experiences of young participants.

5 Discussion

The findings of this study show that entrepreneurship education can emerge outside formal schooling or business-led initiatives through community-based experiential learning, particularly when targeted at NEET youth in deprived contexts. The case of

La Paranza demonstrates that social cooperatives and territorial networks can act as crucial educational agents, providing the conditions through which vulnerable youth can develop entrepreneurial intention, orientation, and employability. This aligns with studies emphasizing the importance of supportive learning environments and cooperative practices (Haug et al., 2023) but advances the debate by demonstrating how these conditions are constructed. In La Paranza, learning is embedded in real entrepreneurial activities—cultural heritage valorization, tourism services, event organization—which confirms that place-based and practice-oriented models generate more effective competence development than traditional instruction (Gibb, 2002).

Furthermore, this study reveals the centrality of mentorship, both relational and professional, in empowering young people and enabling entrepreneurial development. The combined role of Father Loffredo and specialized educators embodies a multilevel mentoring structure that builds the psychological readiness and practical capabilities required for entrepreneurial action, an aspect overlooked in previous management research on NEETs.

This research also highlights the importance of structural and relational conditions in preventing NEET pathways. While economic capital has been identified as a determinant of NEET rates in disadvantaged territories (Ripamonti & Barberis, 2021), the findings of this study highlight that investments in social capital, trust-building, and institutional partnerships are equally crucial in sustaining entrepreneurial learning and youth employability. The stakeholder ecosystem supporting La Paranza (church actors, philanthropic foundations, and civic and cultural organizations) ensures long-term scalability, reflecting recent calls for ecosystemic approaches to youth entrepreneurship (Haug et al., 2023).

6 Implications and Conclusions

This study contributes to filling the research gap identified in the literature regarding entrepreneurship education as a strategic tool to prevent the NEET phenomenon (Banha et al., 2022; Miço, & Cungu, 2023). While previous studies acknowledged both the heterogeneity of the NEET population (Yates & Payne, 2006) and the potential role of entrepreneurship in reducing youth marginalization (Zhartay et al., 2020; Haug et al., 2023), empirical evidence on concrete educational mechanisms and contexts that foster youth employability remains scarce. By examining La Paranza, a socially rooted entrepreneurial initiative operating in a highly disadvantaged urban area, this study advances theoretical, practical, and social understanding of how entrepreneurship education can be effectively designed, implemented, and sustained to support vulnerable youth. Indeed, unlike prior studies on the La Paranza case, which focus on governance systems for civic wealth creation (Fiorentino et al., 2023) and sustainable business models for social value creation (Canestrino et al., 2019), this study shifts the attention toward entrepreneurship education as a strategy for the social inclusion and employability of NEET youth. More specifically, the findings show how entrepreneurship education operates not only as a knowledge-transfer process but also as a transformative social change capable of triggering identity reconstruction, trust development, entrepreneurial intention, and employability among NEET youth in marginalized urban contexts.

In terms of theoretical implications, the results extend the conceptualization of entrepreneurship education as the main antecedent through which intention and orientation emerge and translate into employability outcomes (Somjai & Sangperm, 2019). This study empirically highlights this process: La Paranza fosters aspiration, risk-taking, opportunity recognition, and proactive behavior, transforming NEET youth from passive individuals into active contributors (EET) within their community. This supports and enriches prior conceptualizations of entrepreneurship intention (Ajzen, 1991; Liñán & Fayolle, 2015) and entrepreneurship orientation (Lumpkin & Dess, 1996, 2001) by illustrating their manifestation in early and nonformal entrepreneurial experiences. In addition, the findings underscore the importance of trust, identity building, and relational embeddedness as crucial dimensions of entrepreneurial learning, which remain underexplored in mainstream entrepreneurship education literature.

In terms of practical implications, the results provide actionable guidance for both policymakers and practitioners designing entrepreneurship education for at-risk youth. First, programs should adopt experiential learning models, ensuring that training is embedded in real entrepreneurial activities and connected to territorial opportunities. Second, the role of mentorship—both professional and relational—must be institutionalized to support confidence building, risk-taking, and progressive responsibility. Moreover, the case suggests multi-actor cooperation among schools, social enterprises, local institutions, and religious or civic organizations. Entrepreneurship education is more effective when delivered as a shared responsibility across the ecosystem rather than delegated to schools alone. Practitioners should also prioritize pathways that enable youth to transition from training to paid employment, ensuring long-term sustainability of inclusion outcomes.

In terms of social implications, this study highlights that entrepreneurship education can serve as a powerful lever for social inclusion, particularly in marginalized urban contexts that face a high risk of NEET status. By empowering young people to become protagonists of local regeneration, the model fosters community pride, challenges negative stereotypes, and cultivates a collective identity and sense of belonging. The transformation of abandoned cultural heritage into a source of employment and dignity illustrates how territorial assets can be mobilized to combat social and economic exclusion. Additionally, by improving neighborhood safety, strengthening social cohesion, and stimulating a local social economy, the initiative contributes to broader urban development goals and aligns with European strategies for youth empowerment and green-cultural transitions. These insights reinforce the importance of investing in community-rooted interventions that combine economic opportunities with cultural and civic inclusion.

This study is not without limitations. It is based on a single case study supported by interviews with three organizational key informants and five young beneficiaries.

While this approach enables an in-depth understanding of context-specific dynamics and offers valuable qualitative insights, it also limits the generalizability of the findings. Although the inclusion of young beneficiaries strengthens the empirical grounding of the findings, the perspectives gathered still reflect a restricted group of actors and may overlook alternative viewpoints within the broader community of beneficiaries and stakeholders.

Additionally, the absence of longitudinal data prevents us from fully capturing the long-term evolution of the initiative or the stability of its outcomes for NEET youth. Future studies should expand the sample of respondents, include multiple case studies, and adopt mixed methods to strengthen the robustness and external validity of the results.

References

Ajzen, I. (1991). The theory of planned behavior. *Organizational Behavior and Human Decision Processes, 50*, 179–211.

Amadi, E. A., & Eze, S. C. (2019). Factors influencing the implementation of entrepreneurship education in tertiary institutions in Rivers State. *International Journal of Innovative Social & Science Education Research, 7*, 22–36.

Ball, S. J., Maguire, M., & Macrae, S. (2000). Space, work and the 'new urban economies'. *Journal of Youth Studies, 3*(3), 279–300.

Banha, F., Coelho, L. S., & Flores, A. (2022). Entrepreneurship education: A systematic literature review and identification of an existing gap in the field. *Education Sciences, 12*(5), 336.

Bolton, D., & Lane, M. D. (2012). Individual entrepreneurial orientation: Development of a measurement instrument. *Education + Training, 54*, 219–233.

Canestrino, R., Ćwiklicki, M., Di Nauta, P., & Magliocca, P. (2019). Creating social value through entrepreneurship: The social business model of La Paranza. *Kybernetes, 48*(10), 2190–2216.

Creswell, J. W., & Creswell, J. D. (2018). *Research design: Qualitative, quantitative, and mixed methods approaches*. Sage.

Creswell, J. W., & Poth, C. N. (2016). *Qualitative inquiry and research design: Choosing among five approaches*. Sage.

Fiorentino, R., Landriani, L., Lardo, A., & Marciano, S. (2023). Governance systems for civic wealth creation through a new accessibility to cultural heritage: The case of "La Paranza". In M. Del Baldo, M. Piber, P. Demartini, & S. Aureli (Eds.), *Cultural heritage as a trigger for civic wealth creation and sustainable urban development* (pp. 33–56). RomaTrE-Press.

Fiss, P. C. (2009). Case studies and the configurational analysis of organizational phenomena. In D. S. Byrne & C. C. Ragin (Eds.), *The SAGE handbook of case-based methods*. Sage.

Gabbianelli, L., Bonfanti, A., Adaui, C. R. L., & Mion, G. (2021). An overview of students' entrepreneurial intention antecedents. *Piccola Impresa/Small Business, 1*, 48–77.

Gibb, A. (2002). In pursuit of a new "enterprise" and "entrepreneurship" paradigm for learning: Creative destruction, new values, new ways of doing things and new combinations of knowledge. *International Journal of Management Reviews, 4*, 233–269.

Gioia, D. A., Corley, K. G., & Hamilton, A. L. (2013). Seeking qualitative rigor in inductive research: Notes on the Gioia methodology. *Organizational Research Methods, 16*, 15–31.

Hahn, D., Minola, T., Bosio, G., & Cassia, L. (2020). The impact of entrepreneurship education on university students' entrepreneurial skills: A family embeddedness perspective. *Small Business Economics, 55*(1), 257–282.

Haug, S., Nylund, M., Samuelsen, H., Stokke, L., & Sønderskov, M. (2023). Service innovations targeting NEETs: A systematic review. *Journal of the Knowledge Economy*.

Jack, E. P., & Raturi, A. S. (2006). Lessons learned from methodological triangulation in management research. *Management Research News, 29*, 345–357.

Lamnek, S. (2010). *Qualitative Sozialforschung. Lehrbuch*. Beltz.

Liñán, F., & Fayolle, A. (2015). A systematic literature review on entrepreneurial intentions: Citation, thematic analyses, and research agenda. *International Entrepreneurship and Management Journal, 11*, 907–933.

Lumpkin, G. T., & Dess, G. G. (1996). Clarifying the entrepreneurial orientation construct and linking it to performance. *Academy of Management Review, 21*(1), 135–172.

Lumpkin, G. G., & Dess, G. G. (2001). Linking two dimensions of entrepreneurial orientation to firm performance: The moderating role of environment and industry life cycle. *Journal of Business Venturing, 16*, 429–451.

Magnani, G., & Gioia, D. (2023). Using the Gioia methodology in international business and entrepreneurship research. *International Business Review, 32*, 102097.

Miço H., & Cungu J. (2023). Entrepreneurship education, a challenging learning process towards entrepreneurial competence in education. *Administrative Sciences, 13*(1), 22.

Pittaway, L., Rodriguez-Falcon, E., Aiyegbayo, O., & King, A. (2011). The role of entrepreneurship clubs and societies in entrepreneurial learning. *International Small Business Journal, 29*, 37–57.

Ramsgaard, M. B., & Christensen, M. E. (2018). Interplay of entrepreneurial learning forms: A case study of experiential learning settings. *Innovations in Education and Teaching International, 55*, 55–64.

Rauch, A., Wiklund, J., Lumpkin, G. T., & Frese, M. (2009). Entrepreneurial orientation and business performance: An assessment of past research and suggestions for the future. *Entrepreneurship Theory and Practice, 33*, 761–787.

Ridder, H. G. (2017). The theory contribution of case study research designs. *Business Research, 10*, 281–305.

Ripamonti, E., & Barberis, S. (2021). The association of economic and cultural capital with the NEET rate: Differential geographical and temporal patterns. *Journal for Labour Market Research, 55*, 1–17.

San-Martín, P., Fernández-Laviada, A., Pérez, A., & Palazuelos, E. (2021). The teacher of entrepreneurship as a role model: Students' and teachers' perceptions. *The International Journal of Management Education, 19*, 100358.

Siggelkow, N. (2007). Persuasion with case studies. *Academy of Management Journal, 50*(1), 20–24.

Sinkovics, R. R., Penz, E., & Ghauri, P. N. (2008). Enhancing the trustworthiness of qualitative research in international business. *Management International Review, 48*, 689–714.

Somjai, S., & Sangperm, N. (2019). Exploring the nexus between entrepreneur orientation, entrepreneur education, entrepreneur self-efficacy and entrepreneur intention among university students in Thailand. *International Journal of Innovation, Creativity and Change, 6*, 319–338.

Stake, R. E. (2005). Qualitative case studies. In N. K. Denzin & Y. S. Lincoln (Eds.), *The SAGE handbook of qualitative research*. Sage.

Steira, I. M., Wigger, K., & Rasmussen, E. (2024). Variety of entrepreneurial skills measured in the entrepreneurship education literature. *Education + Training, 66*, 755–776.

Yates, S., & Payne, M. (2006). Not so NEET? A critique of the use of 'NEET' in setting targets for interventions with young people. *Journal of Youth Studies, 9*(3), 329–344.

Yin, R. K. (2003). *Designing case studies*. Sage.

Zhartay, Z., Khussainova, Z., & Yessengeldin, B. (2020). Development of the youth entrepreneurship: Example of Kazakhstan. *Entrepreneurship and Sustainability Issues, 8*, 1190–1208.

Preventing and Addressing the NEET Phenomenon Through Entrepreneurial Education: The Potential Role of Social Impact Bonds

Veronica De Crescenzo, Giorgio Mion, Pierpaolo Magliocca, and Irene Gottoli

Abstract Entrepreneurial education plays a vital role in preventing both school dropouts and the NEET phenomenon, making funding for entrepreneurial education essential. Adequate financial resources are needed to sustain and enhance educational programs, especially in underserved areas where dropout risks are highest. This chapter first explores grant programs focused on preventing and addressing the NEET phenomenon in Italy, particularly through entrepreneurship education initiatives, both during and after the COVID-19 pandemic. Additionally, the research examines Social Impact Bonds as potential strategic tools able to support these initiatives by engaging diverse stakeholders and the wider community, thereby fostering an inclusive development model. Through analysis of the Indigo Impact Bond Dataset, this chapter aims to highlight the scope and target populations of funded projects for NEETs in Europe, as well as to identify potential funding challenges for such projects. The analysis revealed two main issues with funding educational strategies aimed at NEETs. First, it is challenging to establish clear causal relationships between the implemented activities and the reduction of school dropouts. Second, preventive measures tend to be very costly, time-consuming, and require substantial human resources. Given the complexity of these preventive actions, and in line with the goals outlined in the United Nations Agenda 2030, funding programs should focus on prioritizing long-term perspectives to effectively address and reduce educational poverty and the NEET phenomenon.

V. De Crescenzo (✉) · G. Mion
Department of Management, University of Verona, Verona, Italy
e-mail: veronica.decrescenzo@univr.it; giorgio.mion@univr.it

P. Magliocca
Department of Social Sciences, University of Foggia, Foggia, Italy
e-mail: pierpaolo.magliocca@unifg.it

I. Gottoli
Department of Human Sciences, University of Verona, Verona, Italy
e-mail: irene.gottoli@univr.it

R. Cellini et al. (eds.), *Cultural, Social, and Political Participation in the Internet Era*, Contributions to Economics, https://doi.org/10.1007/978-3-032-33072-7_18

1 Understanding the NEET Phenomenon and the Role of Entrepreneurial Education

In accordance with an inclusive view of development (Pouw & Gupta, 2017), the United Nations Agenda 2030 highlighted the different aspects of poverty and the relevance of the social dimension in sustainable development. Gupta and Vegelin (2016) further suggest that the Sustainable Development Goals (SDGs) outlined in Agenda 2030 reflect a normative commitment to social justice and inclusive policies that are grounded in the relational aspects of development.

Education, equal access to essential services, health care, and inclusion are crucial dimensions of sustainable and fair development, as much as environmental and economic dimensions. With specific reference to the educational sphere, Agirreazkuenaga (2020) underscores the role of education as a critical instrument for realizing the SDGs and fostering inclusive development. Consequently, the struggle against poverty cannot be limited to filling the financial gaps between different areas of the world or social groups, but concerns the creation of an inclusive environment that enables each person's special capacities. That is, the idea of sustainable and inclusive development implies a holistic process of inclusion that allows all people—regardless of their physical, psychological, or cultural characteristics—to both benefit from educational, social, and healthcare services, and access the job market. Under this remit, financial policies would need to look beyond the traditional neoclassical vision of development as a natural consequence of economic and financial growth (Diesendorf et al., 2024).

These ideas, along with changing demographic dynamics and the progressive inability of the public sector to detect and solve social needs without wider systemic interventions in terms of generative welfare, meant that the need for a more inclusive environment for young people (especially if they demonstrate special needs) was recognized before the pandemic outbreak. Despite such aims, the pandemic crisis limited (and, in some cases, prohibited) social relations and access to services. Young people in particular have suffered the consequences of extended lockdowns and interruptions to such services as school support; physical, psychological, and spiritual therapies; educational programs; and extracurricular activities (e.g., Snape & Viner, 2020; Stavridou et al., 2020; Kauhanen et al., 2023). The start of work paths (including job training and apprenticeships) was also significantly slowed by the pandemic.

Further to these points, the education and training sector also suffered a contraction in resources for peripheral interventions and a progressive reduction in services offered by public actors. Consequently, even without evidence of economic poverty, new forms of educational and social poverty have developed, preventing many young people from being included in their communities.

One of the most tangible consequences of educational poverty is the so-called NEET (Not in Education, Employment, or Training) phenomenon (Mussida & Sciulli, 2023), which refers to young people aged 15–29 who are not engaged in education, employment, or training. This phenomenon, which was first diagnosed in the 1980s (Mascherini, 2019), has been recognized by the European Union as a critical area of policy intervention, particularly through the Europe 2020 flagship initiative Youth on the Move and the Youth Opportunities Initiative (2012–2013) (Eurofound, 2012).

The NEET phenomenon is the consequence of diverse factors that previous studies classified into two major groups: disadvantage and disaffection (Mascherini, 2019). The first group concerns social factors such as poverty, and family or school characteristics, whereas the second concerns students' school paths. As is easily predictable, the two groups are not independent of each other, with Coles et al. (2002) demonstrating that life experiences before becoming NEET are crucial to the abandonment of school, training, or a job. Above all, the economic and job conditions of parents, special education needs, and membership in an ethnic minority group are disadvantageous factors that promote disaffection and increase the likelihood of becoming NEET. Disaffection factors can also arise from the poor quality of the educational and training services offered or because of the conditions of entry into the world of work.

It is also important to recognize the diversity encompassed by the concept of NEET, which is a multi-layered construct that incorporates various situations encountered by young people while transitioning to employment (Serrière & Elder, 2025). The COVID-19 pandemic further exacerbated these issues (Eurofound, 2021), highlighting the urgent need for comprehensive prevention and support strategies at the European, national, and local levels.

Italy stands out among EU member states for its persistently high NEET rates. The Italian definition of NEET encompasses a broader age range (15–34 years) than the European standard. The share of NEET in Italy in 2020 reached 25.1%, 7.5 percentage points higher than the EU average of 17.6%, and has remained above 20% over the past 5 years, with a heightened effect for females (De Luca et al., 2025). In response to what former European Central Bank President Mario Draghi termed a "lost generation" during the presentation of the European Central Bank Annual Report on April 7, 2016, the Italian government adopted the NEET Plan in 2022. A policy framework formalized through a joint Youth–Labor Policy Decree, this plan aims to reduce the number of NEETs, which currently exceeds 3 million, most of whom are women (1.7 million).

In this context, entrepreneurial education is considered to play a crucial role in preventing school dropout and addressing the NEET phenomenon. By providing young people with skills and knowledge beyond standard academics, entrepreneurial education encourages adaptability, creativity, and resilience—key qualities for today's competitive labor market. Funding is crucial for supporting sustainable efforts in entrepreneurial education, however. Adequate and well-managed financial resources are necessary to sustain, grow, and enhance educational programs, especially in underserved areas where the risks of early school dropout and the NEET situation are most pronounced.

This chapter examines the financial policies used to prevent and address the NEET phenomenon, highlighting in particular those that support entrepreneurship education programs. Additionally, the research examines Social Impact Bonds as potential strategic tools to support these initiatives. As outlined, Social Impact Bonds engage diverse stakeholders and the wider community, thereby fostering an inclusive development model.

2 Financial Policies: An Analysis of the Italian Practices During and After the COVID-19 Pandemic

Governments have the responsibility of taking action to reduce NEET rates, a major challenge faced by many nations. Significant efforts have been made to increase social spending, providing benefits to meet basic needs and support engagement in education and employment opportunities (Eurofound, 2012; Carcillo et al., 2015). European countries have expanded preventive intervention policies and programs to integrate young people into the workforce and education systems, aiming to reduce the economic and social impacts associated with the NEET phenomenon. Policies regarding the labor market and education institutions play a vital role in enabling successful youth transition (Brzinsky-Fay, 2017). A recent study (Lauri et al., 2025) has highlighted how different alternative institutional routes can help alleviate youth vulnerabilities and NEET rates. For instance, social benefits and education policies are essential for reducing youth vulnerabilities, which can be complemented by active labor-market policies or support for youth homeownership.

Considering the diversity encompassed by the basic concept of NEET and the complex nature of NEET status, policy responses to the NEET issue need to be multidimensional (Serrière & Elder, 2025). Policymakers must recognize the significant heterogeneity within this group and tailor policies accordingly, avoiding a one-size-fits-all approach (Redmond & McFadden, 2023).

One of the main challenges in tackling and preventing the NEET issue is the availability of funding to sustain expensive, labor-intensive, and time-consuming programs (Kluve, 2014). This problem is fundamental in a context where public funding is decreasing, and more projects compete for limited financial support. For instance, public financing was reduced following the 2008 crisis, with staffing and budget levels recovering only gradually (European Commission, 2018). Strategies and programs for public policy implementation aimed at tackling NEET issues must, therefore, address budget constraints, which often limit interventions to specific groups within the broader population (Maguire, 2015).

Adequate and well-targeted financial resources are also necessary to ensure the continuity, scalability, and effectiveness of educational initiatives, particularly in disadvantaged regions where the risk of early school leaving and the NEET phenomenon are most pronounced (Carcillo et al., 2015; Badunenko et al., 2025). A recent European-focused study (Youn & Kang, 2023) shows that increased public social spending can effectively lower the risk of young people becoming NEET, primarily benefiting socially disadvantaged groups. Notably, public investments in school-to-work transition initiatives and the labor market are crucial because they significantly influence NEET rates among those with underprivileged backgrounds—such as young people with low educational attainment, parents with limited education, and females (Youn & Kang, 2023).

Different financial policies currently exist to prevent or mitigate school and work dropouts among young people. Analyzing financial policies at the national and regional levels is critical for understanding how financial instruments and targeted measures can help shape more inclusive and effective pathways for young people at risk of becoming NEETs.

An analysis of key European, national, and regional financial policies implemented in Italy from 2020 to 2025—that is, during and after the COVID-19 pandemic—and aimed at preventing or counteracting school and work dropouts among young people was conducted through desk research. Data were gathered through a systematic and targeted web-based search across official and institutional databases (Duffy, 2002), including the Italian Ministry of Education and Merit, the Department for Youth Policies in the Presidency of the Council, and "Italia Domani," the National Recovery and Resilience Plan. The search process employed predefined keywords ("NEET," "school dropouts") to ensure the relevance and comparability of the collected information. Only data from verified, publicly accessible sources were included in the analysis, and regional plans were considered only if they were presented in the national database.

The key insights regarding the Italian context are summarized in Table 1, providing a clear overview of the principal findings from the research. By highlighting the key features of the grant programs, Table 1 provides a detailed understanding of the measures used in Italy to finance NEET initiatives.

Over the years, policies addressing the issues of NEETs and early school leaving have significantly evolved. They have transitioned from isolated, fragmented measures to a more comprehensive, multidimensional approach. This change reflects an understanding that the challenges associated with NEETs and early school leaving are complex and influenced by a range of social and economic factors. As a result, integrated responses across different levels of governance are necessary to tackle these issues effectively.

Financial policies can be classified into two main categories, each with distinct characteristics and objectives. The first category includes grant programs aimed at preventing young people from becoming NEET. These programs—often in collaboration with schools—fund activities and projects that support youth throughout their educational paths, particularly during the compulsory schooling period. The second category consists of grant programs focused on reintegrating NEET individuals into education, employment, or training. These programs establish broader community partnerships, working together with businesses, employment offices, and educational agencies to facilitate reintegration.

The analyzed policies increasingly emphasize personalized interventions, structural investments, the integration of entrepreneurial and digital skills, and local actions. Facilitating customized interventions involves tailoring educational and professional pathways to meet the individual needs, skills, and aspirations of young people, rather than using a one-size-fits-all approach. The goal is to offer

Table 1 Italian practices for preventing and addressing NEET during and after the COVID-19 pandemic

Grant's name	Funding source	Target	Prevent/ address	Regional target
PNRR M4C1I1.4	Next Gen EU—Italia	12–18 years old students	P/A	X
Garanzia Giovani—Misura Antidispersione	FSE/Stato	NEET 15–18	A	X
YES I Start Up	ANPAL/Invitalia	NEET 18–29	A	
SELFIEmployment	Invitalia (Garanzia Giovani)	NEET, nonactive women, inactive, long-term unemployed	A	
Incentivo NEET 2023	FSE+/Ministero del Lavoro	NEET 15–29	A	
Crescere in Digitale 2.0	ANPAL	NEET	A	X
Resto al Sud	Invitalia	18–55	A	X
Percorsi IeFP (Veneto)	FSE+/Regione	14–18 years old students	P	X
Avviso Multimisura POC—Giovani Puglia	POC FSE—Regione Puglia	NEET 15–29	A	X
Programma GOL—Regione Puglia	PNRR/Regione Puglia	NEET < 30	A	X
Bonus Assunzioni NEET—Campania	POR FESR/Regione Campania	NEET < 30	A	X
Progetto EMPOWER-NEET—Campania	Regione Campania	NEET under 35	P/A	X
IN-JOBs 4 NEETs—Campania/Lombardia	J.P. Morgan + Mestieri	NEET	A	X

guidance, mentoring, and customized training opportunities to help reduce the risk of marginalization. Conversely, structural investments have been enabled by large-scale programs and financial instruments, such as the PNRR (National Plan for Recovery and Resilience) and the FSE+ (European Social Fund Plus). These initiatives have allocated significant resources to the support of long-term education, training, and youth employment reforms. The primary goal of these investments is not only to deliver immediate solutions but also to enhance the resilience and adaptability of educational and labor systems.

Furthermore, it is acknowledged that the future employability of young people increasingly relies on their abilities to adapt to technological changes and participate in innovative initiatives. These skills are essential for entering the labor market, fostering creativity, and enabling problem-solving and opportunities for self-employment. Lastly, prioritizing territorial needs and local actions is crucial, particularly for regions facing structural challenges, such as Southern Italy. It is essential to tailor interventions to the socio-economic characteristics of specific areas to ensure that policies effectively address local needs.

3 Innovative Financial Tools: Lessons Learned from the Implementation of Social Impact Bonds Across Europe

In addition to traditional public grants, which are commonly used to fund social initiatives, some European countries are exploring alternative financing methods. Investigating alternative financing options for social policies is especially important in an environment where public spending is decreasing (Maguire, 2015; Youn & Kang, 2023).

One such method is funding provided by nongovernmental partners. Such funds are usually project-based, however, which could pose a risk because outreach activities depend on future funding availability and changing funder priorities. Additionally, project-based funding often means outreach activities are time-bound, so some young people may "fall through" during breaks between funding rounds or until new funding is confirmed (European Commission, 2018, p. 25).

Despite these risks, engaging multiple stakeholders in the financing process to meet social needs is good practice. Indeed, it has been emphasized that engaging a diverse group of stakeholders in designing and implementing policies to reduce and address the NEET phenomenon is crucial for achieving better results, especially in employment initiatives (Eurofound, 2012). In England, for instance, the increasing involvement of the private sector in the design, leadership, and financing of NEET programs has sparked significant debate (Maguire, 2015; Economy et al., 2022).

Such initiatives can receive partial funding through Social Impact Bonds. A Social Impact Bond is a typical example of social impact investment that aims to introduce the private sector and other funders to the world of social impact (OECD, 2016; Broccardo et al., 2020). Impact investments are defined as investments made with the purpose of achieving positive, quantifiable social and environmental impacts, in addition to financial returns (Global Impact Investing Network, 2025). Because such investments are designed to address the challenges governments face in investing in prevention and early intervention initiatives, Social Impact Bonds are viewed as a potential solution to the ongoing and increasing constraints on public spending (Social Finance, 2011).

More specifically, a Social Impact Bond is a form of payment-by-results contract, also known as a pay-for-success contract. In such agreements, governments do not pay upfront for inputs; instead, they pay according to the results achieved either at the end or at various stages of the contract. This transition from focusing on outputs to emphasizing outcomes is significant because it shifts the payment model from funding activities to rewarding the achievement of policy goals as measured by outcome indicators (OECD, 2016). This also means that investor returns in

Social Impact Bonds are tied to social outcomes (Social Finance, 2011). Private investors fund social projects and are rewarded only if the specified social outcomes are achieved, with their returns dependent on the achievement of these outcomes (Economy et al., 2022). The Social Impact Bond effect, defined as the independent impact of financing, plays a crucial role in defining the contract by highlighting the "improvements in outcomes due to financing" (Hevenstone et al., 2023, p. 931). This effect is distinct from the program effect, which refers to the causal impact of the social intervention itself, rather than the impact of the financing.

Social Impact Bonds are also particularly interesting because they serve as financing tools that promote collaboration among private investors, public entities, and service providers. The partnership among private investors, public entities, and service providers—which can involve varying degrees of collaboration among actors (fully collaborative, low-collaborative, and partially collaborative)—aims to jointly implement social and labor-market programs (La Torre et al., 2019). Because of the focus on social performance, Social Impact Bonds also rely on an independent evaluator who measures the intervention's impact on the target population using pre-established impact evaluation methods (Jackson, 2013). The presence of an ecosystem comprising universities, accelerators, entrepreneurs, and private investors engaged in long-term relationships has also been shown to be critical for successful entrepreneurship education (Wright et al., 2017; Rusu et al., 2022; Saoula et al., 2024).

Research on Social Impact Bonds is gaining more attention (Broccardo et al., 2020; Dahbi et al., 2024). Prior research on Social Impact Bonds has identified both their potential benefits and the risks associated with such financing of social projects (Arena et al., 2016; Fraser et al., 2018). Attention has also been paid to evaluating whether Social Impact Bonds can facilitate private-sector capital injections into the production of social goods and foster social innovation (Olson et al., 2024). For instance, the viability of Social Impact Bonds has been analyzed with reference to Italy, focusing on the ideological, cultural, technical, and governance barriers and opportunities related to that specific context (Bengo & Calderini, 2016). In this context, it has been stated that the Italian "social economy" (made up of associations, foundations, social co-operatives, charities, and social enterprises) is highly dependent on public financing or grants/donations. In addition, public services in Italy are highly fragmented, both geographically and across different levels of government.

The analysis undertaken in this chapter uses the Indigo Impact Bond Dataset to clarify how Social Impact Bonds support initiatives and programs addressing the NEET phenomenon in Europe. As has been noted, this analysis aims to both highlight the scope and target populations of funded projects related to NEETs and identify potential funding challenges across various European countries. The Indigo Impact Bond Dataset is a co-created, open learning platform that describes a specific form of impact-focused cross-sector partnership adopted worldwide since 2010 (Carter et al., 2024).

Within the broader context of Social Impact Bonds, only two thematic areas were selected for this analysis due to their significance in addressing the NEET

Table 2 Geographical and temporal distribution of Social Impact Bonds related to NEETs

Start date	Country and type of program (E&T/E)
2023	France (E&T)
2022	France (E&T)
2019	Russia (E); Belgium (E&T); 2 Portugal (E); UK (E)
2018	France (E&T); Portugal (E); UK (E)
2017	2 Portugal (E&T)
2016	2 Netherlands (E&T); UK (E)
2015	Netherlands (E&T); 3 UK (E&T)
2013	Germany (E&T); Netherlands (E&T)
2012	10 UK (E&T)

phenomenon: "Employment and Training" and "Education." According to the database (https://golab.bsg.ox.ac.uk/), 101 Social Impact Bonds have been issued in Europe between 2012 and 2024 to fund projects in these two key areas. Interestingly, these innovative financial instruments are not uniformly distributed, with some countries at the forefront of this dynamic approach to social investment and others yet to embrace its potential. Taking into account the thematic areas considered, the United Kingdom leads the way in the use of this approach, with 40 of the 101 Social Impact Bonds implemented. Other countries that have utilized these tools—although in fewer numbers than the United Kingdom—include Portugal (19 issues), France (15), and the Netherlands (13). Italy does not appear among the countries that employ Social Impact Bonds to fund social projects.

A comprehensive analysis of European issues is an essential first step toward identifying effective financing best practices for NEET programs. This analysis was conducted according to specific criteria, including the starting date, the amount of funds raised (when available), the type of interventions, and the target populations served by these initiatives. Given information regarding the nature of the interventions and the populations served, the key characteristics of the Social Impact Bonds used in "Employment and Training" and "Education" programs across various European countries that specifically target NEETs have been analyzed. Out of 101 Social Impact Bonds, 31 specifically target NEETs or related groups. The following analysis highlights the approaches used to address the challenges faced by NEETs, with particular attention given to efforts to promote engagement and enhance opportunities for these individuals.

Table 2 presents the geographical and temporal distribution of the 31 Social Impact Bonds specifically aimed at NEETs. Even within this sub-sample, the United Kingdom has the most issues (16 out of 31). In terms of the number of issuances, other countries that are relevant are Portugal (five Social Impact Bonds) and the Netherlands (four Social Impact Bonds). Regarding the types of programs, there is a clear dominance of issues related to the "Employment and Training" (E&T) thematic area (24 out of 31), while the "Education" (E) area is less represented.

As far as the temporal distribution of Social Impact Bonds specifically associated with NEETs is concerned, most issues occurred before 2018 (21 out of 31) and there appears to be a decline in their use in recent years. Unsurprisingly, there is a significant concentration of cases in the United Kingdom, particularly in the early years of the observed period. In 2012, for instance, 10 issues explicitly addressed the NEET phenomenon, all of which were based in the United Kingdom.

Another interesting aspect to analyze is the type of intervention being financed through the Social Impact Bond, as well as the specific target population the proposed program aims to serve. Examining the target population and focusing on the leading country reveals a difference in the targeted age groups. Table 3 shows, for instance, that nearly half of the United Kingdom's issues are aimed at very young people (aged 14–15), with the other half targeting a broader group of young people aged 14–24.

Apart from the United Kingdom's issues, explicit reference to NEET appears in only two other Social Impact Bonds, those issued by Portugal in 2017 and Belgium in 2019. Although the remaining Social Impact Bonds refer to populations closely associated with the usual conditions of NEETs, they do not explicitly use the term.

As observed in public financial policies, Social Impact Bonds can also be classified into two main categories. Of these, one aims to prevent young people from becoming NEET by supporting them during their education; the other seeks to reintegrate NEET individuals into education, employment, or training opportunities. These two groups of Social Impact Bonds can be easily classified by their target populations. For prevention-focused projects, the target population is usually labeled as "Student." In this group, a significant case is the set of issues in Portugal in 2018–2019, where the type of intervention explicitly mentions the problem of school dropout.

For the second category of intervention, it is essential to highlight the Netherlands' choice in 2016, with Social Impact Bonds aiming to reintegrate NEET individuals into education, employment, or training opportunities. The planned intervention to address the problem is self-employment. In detail, the intervention description states that, with the program, unemployed young people can be helped to "discover their passion and work toward starting their own company."

4 Conclusions

With the NEET phenomenon gaining strength in Europe, particularly in Italy—during and after the COVID-19 pandemic—regional, national, and supranational authorities have sought to implement financial policies to address this dynamically evolving issue. The discontinuity created by the pandemic, as well as by social, economic, and technological evolution, has, however, demonstrated the obsolescence of some traditional educational tools and the need for creative solutions (Yuon & Kang, 2023; Olson et al., 2024). This exploratory study underlines the need for funding programs that tailor reskilling solutions for those in the NEET cohort, with a focus on empowering and re-motivating young people.

Table 3 Type of intervention and target population of Social Impact Bonds related to NEETs

Start date	Country	Type of intervention	Target population
2023	France	Provide support program for professional integration and prevention of discrimination by improving student employability.	Students in their final year of study.
2022	France	Provide long-term mentoring (5 years) to remove all obstacles to the chosen professional's integration.	Young people/students.
2019	Russia	Improve the quality of general education.	Schools.
2019	Belgium	Get the so-called NEETs into work.	Young people who are not in education, employment, or training.
2019	Portugal	Predict early school dropouts through the use of an educational tool.	Students.
2019	UK	Ensure innovative learning design.	Children and young people aged 11–16 who are disengaged from education.
2019	Portugal	Predict early school dropouts through the use of an educational tool.	Students.
2018	France	Provide professional assistance.	Youth aged 16–25 who are on social welfare, struggling to find a job, or in unstable employment positions, who are isolated from the job market.
2018	UK	Improve achievement and well-being.	Primary school children.
2018	Portugal	Use an educational tool to predict early school leaving.	Students.
2017	Portugal	Increase the employability and socio-occupational inclusion.	NEET.
2017	Portugal	Increase the employability of unemployed young people.	Unemployed young people.
2016	UK	Improve achievement and well-being.	Primary school children.
2016	Netherlands	Help young people discover their passions and work toward starting their own company.	Unemployed young people aged 18–30.
2016	Netherlands	Help young people discover their passions and work toward starting their own company.	Youth (aged 18–30) without qualifications/underqualified.

(continued)

Table 3 (continued)

Start date	Country	Type of intervention	Target population
2015	UK	Help disadvantaged young people to participate and succeed in education or training.	Young people aged 14–17, 70% of whom will be gang members, ex-offenders/at risk of offending, in care/care leavers, and those with high levels of school absence.
2015	UK	Help disadvantaged young people aged 14–17 to participate and succeed in education or training.	Young people with behavioral, mental health, or well-being issues aged 14–17.
2015	UK	Help disadvantaged young people to participate and succeed in education or training.	Young people aged 14–17 who have poor attendance at or have been excluded from school, who have experience in the youth justice system, are "looked after," have special educational needs or disability.
2015	Netherlands	Provide young adults with programs that combine learning and working toward a diploma and a job.	Young adults aged 17–35 who have no qualifications and have been unemployed for 6–24 months.
2013	Germany	Provide mentoring support during the application process.	Young people below 25 who are coming from vulnerable backgrounds.
2013	Netherlands	Reduce unemployment.	Youth (aged 17–27) without qualifications.
2012	UK	Prevent young people from becoming NEET, or support those already NEET to re-engage with education, training, and employment.	Young people (14–15 years old) at risk of not gaining a GCSE in English.
2012	UK	Prevent young people from becoming NEET, or support those already NEET to re-engage with education, training, and employment.	Young people (14–15 year olds) with offending histories, substance misusers, and/or involved in gang activity.
2012	UK	Prevent young people from becoming NEET, or support those already NEET to re-engage with education, training, and employment.	14–16 year olds identified as having poor behavior, underperforming at school, or having other complex issues, and at risk of becoming NEET
2012	UK	Prevent young people from becoming NEET, or support those already NEET to re-engage with education, training, and employment.	Young people (14–15 year olds) in schools in areas with high levels of gang involvement and high rates of being NEET.

(continued)

Table 3 (continued)

Start date	Country	Type of intervention	Target population
2012	UK	Prevent young people from becoming NEET, or support those already NEET to re-engage with education, training, and employment.	14–19 year olds, including the most vulnerable young people and those falling through gaps in mainstream provision.
2012	UK	Prevent young people from becoming NEET, or support those already NEET to re-engage with education, training, and employment.	Young people (14–24 year olds)—NEET or in school with behavior putting them at risk of becoming NEET.
2012	UK	Prevent young people from becoming NEET, or support those already NEET to re-engage with education, training, and employment.	The most at-risk young people (14–24 years of age).
2012	UK	Prevent young people from becoming NEET, or support those already NEET to re-engage with education, training, and employment.	Young people aged 14–24, who are NEET or at risk of becoming NEET.
2012	UK	Prevent young people from becoming NEET, or support those already NEET to re-engage with education, training, and employment.	NEET (14–24 years of age).
2012	UK	Prevent young people from becoming NEET, or support those already NEET to re-engage with education, training, and employment.	The 20% of school pupils in the area most at risk of becoming NEET.

Among the different solutions proposed by the funders, it emerged that entrepreneurial education is becoming a key strategy for fostering active citizenship, social inclusion, and economic participation. Entrepreneurial education is increasingly recognized not just as an optional opportunity for a select group of motivated individuals, but as something that should be available to all young people, particularly those at risk of becoming or remaining NEETs. By equipping youth with entrepreneurial skills, these initiatives aim to empower them to create sustainable career paths, contribute to their communities, and fully engage in the socio-economic development of their regions.

From the exploratory analysis, it also emerged that strategies targeting young people aged 15 and above are only part of the work to be done, as there is considerable scope for preventive measures. However, these programs, from a funding perspective, suffer from two fundamental problems. The first concerns the difficulty of identifying clear causal relationships between activities carried out and the reduction of school dropouts—an issue exacerbated by the need to address multiple antecedents (e.g., family and cultural context, disposable income for accessing individually tailored services). Second, preventive actions are very costly, time-consuming, and require significant human resources. The complexity of preventive actions requires funding programs that prioritize long-term perspectives to create a broader impact on reducing educational poverty—a goal in line with Agenda 2030.

A cultural shift is required to overcome narrow-view solutions. This cultural transformation requires a collaborative approach to the programs aimed at preventing and addressing the NEET phenomenon. Different stakeholders must be involved in systemically building an educational environment that engages, motivates, and reskills young people who have dropped out of school, training, or the labor market (Wright et al., 2017; Rusu et al., 2022; Saoula et al., 2024). Of these stakeholders, community involvement can be implemented at two levels: managerial and financial. If initial insights at the organizational level are identified in pioneering projects, such as entrepreneurial education projects, there is significant scope to develop community participation during the project financing phase.

This study has outlined some possible innovative solutions for financial support for projects aimed at combatting educational poverty and school dropout. Social Impact Bonds are a form of social impact investing that encourages collaboration among private investors, public entities, and service providers to address social issues (Social Finance, 2011; Hevenstone et al., 2023). Social Impact Bonds clearly represent one potential financial tool aligned with the necessary cultural shift to overcome narrow-view solutions. Furthermore, they are seen as beneficial to public spending because the public sector pays only for successful projects. That is, although projects can be carried out now, payments for successful ones will be made later, after the programs' outcomes are assessed.

The analysis clearly shows that the Social Impact Bonds have been adopted across Europe—although not in Italy, which has not so far pursued this path—and their capacity to prioritize the supporting and enhancing of education programs to prevent the NEET phenomenon. When examining the various financial policies implemented across Europe, it is, however, essential to acknowledge that Social Impact Bonds offer benefits but also entail risks. As already mentioned, educational strategies targeting young people face the challenge of establishing clear causal links between activities and reduced school dropout rates. This issue is crucial for pay-by-result contracts such as Social Impact Bonds. These programs are, therefore, carefully assessed to ensure investors receive their returns. Additionally, private investors awaiting outcomes often prefer to finance programs with a high chance of success, thus focusing their investments on the most promising opportunities.

The analysis proposed in this chapter presents some limitations. Providing a conceptual model of the potential relationships between actors is outside the scope of this research because of the chosen methodology. To develop such a model, future research should conduct interviews with the diverse actors involved in the funding ecosystem. Moreover, regarding the Social Impact Bonds analysis, we are aware that the outcomes of the financed initiatives were not examined. A systematic assessment of project outcomes would help identify which types of programs perform well and which do not, thereby informing future decisions.

Given the potential and risks associated with Social Impact Bonds—and given Italy's decision not to use them in the past—a proactive approach for Italy might be to set up small-scale, local pilot programs to test their effectiveness. This small-scale solution may help both identify significant social issues in the region and develop associated social programs to address them. Additionally, it might aim to identify private investors and service providers most appropriate for participation, thus enhancing the creation of an effective ecosystem characterized by a mix of educational, managerial, and financial competencies.

References

Agirreazkuenaga, L. (2020). Education for Agenda 2030: What direction do we want to take going forward? *Sustainability, 12*(5), 2035. https://doi.org/10.3390/su12052035

Arena, M., Bengo, I., Calderini, M., & Chiodo, V. (2016). Social impact bonds: Blockbuster or flash in a pan? *International Journal of Public Administration, 39*(12), 927–939. https://doi.org/10.1080/01900692.2015.1057852

Badunenko, O., Mazrekaj, D., Kumbhakar, S. C., & De Witte, K. (2025). The effect of funding for disadvantaged students on academic underachievement. *Humanities and Social Science Communications, 12*, 1386. https://doi.org/10.1057/s41599-025-05524-1

Bengo, I., & Calderini, M. (2016). New development: Are social impact bonds (SIBs) viable in Italy? A new roadmap. *Public Money & Management, 36*(4), 303–306. https://doi.org/10.1080/09540962.2016.1162999

Broccardo, E., Mazzuca, M., & Frigotto, M. L. (2020). Social impact bonds: The evolution of research and a review of the academic literature. *Corporate Social Responsibility and Environmental Management, 27*, 1316–1332. https://doi.org/10.1002/csr.1886

Brzinsky-Fay, C. (2017). The interplay of educational and labour market institutions and links to relative youth unemployment. *Journal of European Social Policy, 27*(4), 346–359. https://doi.org/10.1177/0958928717719198

Carcillo, S., Fernández, R., Königs, S., & Minea, A. (2015). *NEET youth in the aftermath of the crisis: Challenges and policies*. OECD Social, Employment and Migration Working Papers, No. 164. OECD Publishing. https://doi.org/10.1787/5js6363503f6-en.

Carter, E., Outes, V. J., Paul, O., Macdonald, J. R., & Airoldi, M. (2024). The impact bond dataset: A tool to investigate socially motivated cross-sector partnerships. *Research Data Journal for the Humanities and Social Sciences*, 1–14.

Coles, B., Hutton, S., Bradshaw, J., Craig, G., Godfrey, C., & Johnson, J. (2002). *Literature review of the costs of being 'not in education, employment or training' at age 16–18*. DfES Research Report 347. Her Majesty's Stationery Office.

Dahbi, F., Carrasco, I., & Petracci, B. (2024). A systematic literature review on social impact bonds. *Finance Research Letters, 62*(Part A), 105063. https://doi.org/10.1016/j.frl.2024.105063

De Luca, G., Rocca, A., Mazzocchi, P., Pizzolante, F., & Quintano, C. (2025). Italian NEETs in 2012–2021: Job search channels and labour market reforms. *International Journal of Manpower, 46*(10), 103–124. https://doi.org/10.1108/IJM-04-2024-0251

Diesendorf, M., Davies, G., Wiedmann, T., Spangenberg, J. H., & Hail, S. (2024). Sustainability scientists' critique of neoclassical economics. *Global Sustainability, 7*(e33). https://doi.org/10.1017/sus.2024.36

Duffy, M. E. (2002). Methodological issues in web-based research. *Journal of Nursing Scholarship, 34*(1), 83–88.

Economy, C., Carter, E., & Airoldi, M. (2022). Have we 'stretched' social impact bonds too far? An empirical analysis of SIB design in practice. *International Public Management Journal, 26*(3), 413–436. https://doi.org/10.1080/10967494.2022.2077867

Eurofound. (2012). *NEETs – Young people not in employment, education or training: Characteristics, costs and policy responses in Europe*. Publications Office of the European Union.

Eurofound. (2021). *Impact of COVID-19 on young people in the EU*. Publications Office of the European Union.

European Commission. (2018). *Effective outreach to NEETs. Experience from the ground.*

Fraser, A., Tan, S., Lagarde, M., & Mays, N. (2018). Narratives of promise, narratives of caution: A review of the literature on social impact bonds. *Social Policy & Administration, 52*, 4–28. https://doi.org/10.1111/spol.12260

Global Impact Investing Network – GIIN. (2025, January). *Impact investing. A guide to this dynamic market*.https://thegiin.org/publication/post/about-impact-investing/#what-is-impact-investing

Gupta, J., & Vegelin, C. (2016). Sustainable development goals and inclusive development. *International Environmental Agreements, 16*, 433–448. https://doi.org/10.1007/s10784-016-9323-z

Hevenstone, D., Fraser, A., Hobi, L., Przepiorka, W., & Geuke, G. G. M. (2023). The impact of social impact bond financing. *Public Administration Review., 83*(4), 930–946. https://doi.org/10.1111/puar.13631

Jackson, E. T. (2013). Evaluating social impact bonds: Questions, challenges, innovations, and possibilities in measuring outcomes in impact investing. *Community Development, 44*(5), 608–616. https://doi.org/10.1080/15575330.2013.854258

Kauhanen, L., Wan Mohd Yunus, W. M. A., Lempinen, L., Peltonen, K., Gyllenberg, D., Mishina, K., et al. (2023). A systematic review of the mental health changes of children and young people before and during the COVID-19 pandemic. *European child & adolescent psychiatry, 32*(6), 995–1013. https://doi.org/10.1007/s00787-022-02060-0

Kluve, J. (2014). *Youth labor market interventions comprehensive programs that focus on skills can reduce unemployment and upgrade skills in OECD countries*. IZA Word of Labor.

La Torre, M., Trotta, A., Chiappini, H., & Rizzello, A. (2019). Business Models for sustainable finance: The case study of social impact bonds. *Sustainability, 11*(7), 1887. https://doi.org/10.3390/su11071887

Lauri, T., Toots, A., Chevalier, T., Broka, A., & Hofäcker, D. (2025). Policy mixes and youth vulnerability in Europe: A qualitative comparative analysis of the NEET rate. *Journal of European Social Policy, 35*(2), 157–172. https://doi.org/10.1177/09589287241311159

Maguire, S. (2015). Young people not in education, employment or training (NEET): Recent policy initiatives in England and their effects. *Research in Comparative and International Education, 10*(4), 525–536. https://doi.org/10.1177/1745499915612186

Mascherini, M. (2019). *Origins and future of the concept of NEETs in the European policy agenda*. In J. O'Reilly et al. (Eds.), *Youth labor in transition: Inequalities, mobility, and policies in Europe*. Oxford Academic. https://doi.org/10.1093/oso/9780190864798.003.0017

Mussida, C., & Sciulli, D. (2023). Being poor and being NEET in Europe: Are these two sides of the same coin? *The Journal of Economic Inequality, 21*(2), 463–482. https://doi.org/10.1007/s10888-022-09561-7

OECD. (2016). *Social impact bond: State of play and lessons learned*. OECD Working Papers.

Olson, H., Painter, G., Albertson, K., Fox, C., & O'Leary, C. (2024). Are social impact bonds an innovation in finance or do they help finance social innovation? *Journal of Social Policy, 53*(2), 407–431. https://doi.org/10.1017/S0047279422000356

Pouw, N., & Gupta, J. (2017). Inclusive development: A multi-disciplinary approach. *Current Opinion in Environmental Sustainability, 24*, 104–108. https://doi.org/10.1016/j.cosust.2016.11.013

Redmond, P., & McFadden, C. (2023). Young people not in employment, education or training (NEET): Concepts, consequences and policy approaches. *Economic and Social Review, 54*(4), 285–327.

Rusu, V. D., Roman, A., & Brindusa, T. M. (2022). Determinants of entrepreneurial intentions of youth: The role of access to finance. *Engineering Economics, 33*(1), 86–102. https://doi.org/10.5755/j01.ee.33.1.28716

Saoula, O., Abid, M. F., Ahmad, M. J., & Shamim, A. (2024). What drives entrepreneurial intentions? Interplay between entrepreneurial education, financial support, role models and attitude towards entrepreneurship. *Asia Pacific Journal of Innovation and Entrepreneurship, 19*(2), 128–148. https://doi.org/10.1108/APJIE-10-2023-0189

Serrière, N., & Elder, S. (2025). *Handbook on policy areas to reduce youth in NEET status*. International Labour Organization. Employment, Labour Markets and Youth Branch. https://doi.org/10.54394/MMRV0675

Snape, M. D., & Viner, R. M. (2020). COVID-19 in children and young people. *Science, 370*(6514), 286–288.

Social Finance (2011). *A technical guide to commissioning social impact bonds*.

Stavridou, A., Stergiopoulou, A. A., Panagouli, E., Mesiris, G., Thirios, A., Mougiakos, T., et al. (2020). Psychosocial consequences of COVID-19 in children, adolescents and young adults: A systematic review. *Psychiatry and clinical neurosciences, 74*(11). https://doi.org/10.1111/pcn.13134

Wright, M., Siegel, D. S., & Mustar, P. (2017). An emerging ecosystem for student start-ups. *The Journal of Technology Transfer, 42*, 909–922. https://doi.org/10.1007/s10961-017-9558-z

Youn, M., & Kang, C. (2023). The role of the welfare state for NEETs: Exploring the association between public social spending and NEET in European countries. *Sage Open, 13*(3). https://doi.org/10.1177/21582440231193864

Foreign Entrepreneurship in the District of Municipalities of Catania and Messina: Preliminary Findings

Mohamed Rida Kheit, Massimo Mucciardi, Andrea Nucita, and Mariachiara Fichera

Abstract This chapter examines immigrant entrepreneurship in the metropolitan areas of Catania and Messina in Sicily, focusing on foreign-born business owners holding an Italian VAT number. Based on a quantitative survey of 83 cases, the study analyses entrepreneurial trajectories, business characteristics, startup resources, support networks, and relations with the institutional system. The findings show that migrant businesses are concentrated in retail trade, food services, and personal care and are mainly organized as microenterprises and sole proprietorships. Startup capital derives mostly from personal and family savings, while access to formal credit remains limited. Family and community networks play a crucial role in both business creation and daily management, whereas relations with formal support systems remain weak. Overall, immigrant entrepreneurship emerges as both a strategy of socio-economic stabilization and a resource for local development and social cohesion.

1 Introduction

The phenomenon of immigrant entrepreneurship, understood as the intersection between individuals' migratory journeys and the creation of an organized economic

M. R. Kheit · M. Fichera
Comunità di Sant'Egidio – Sicilia OdV ETS, Messina, Italy
e-mail: mohamedridakheit@gmail.com; mariachiara.fichera18@gmail.com

M. Mucciardi (✉)
Department of Cognitive, Psychological and Educational Sciences, and Cultural Studies, University of Messina, Messina, Italy
e-mail: massimo.mucciardi@unime.it

A. Nucita
Comunità di Sant'Egidio – Sicilia OdV ETS, Messina, Italy

Department of Cognitive, Psychological and Educational Sciences, and Cultural Studies, University of Messina, Messina, Italy
e-mail: andrea.nucita@unime.it

R. Cellini et al. (eds.), *Cultural, Social, and Political Participation in the Internet Era*, Contributions to Economics, https://doi.org/10.1007/978-3-032-33072-7_19

activity in the host country, has long demonstrated its relevance within the socio-economic fabric, becoming the subject of analysis in various branches of the social sciences.

It is first necessary to clarify what is meant by "immigrant enterprise": according to the definition commonly adopted by Italian Chambers of Commerce, immigrant enterprises are those in which the entrepreneur (in sole proprietorships) or the majority of partners or managing partners (in companies) were born abroad. In recent years, the presence of immigrant entrepreneurs in Italy has grown significantly. In particular, over the past decade, the Italian business landscape has been enriched by the migrant component, with an increase of about 40%. According to the Annual Report on the Economy of Immigration (Fondazione Leone Moressa, 2023), more than 600,000 immigrant-owned businesses operate in the country, accounting for around 10% of the total. This figure places Italy in line with other European countries—such as Germany, France, and the United Kingdom—where, for decades, migrant entrepreneurship has been a strategic pillar for local economic development and urban regeneration. In theoretical debate, migrant entrepreneurship is analysed from multiple perspectives (Entzinger, 2000; Entzinger & Biezeveld, 2003). A useful interpretative lens is also provided by the mixed embeddedness approach, which links migrant entrepreneurship to the interaction between individual resources, social networks, market opportunities, and institutional contexts (Kloosterman & Rath, 2001). This perspective also stresses that entrepreneurial outcomes depend on the matching between available resources and opportunity structures, a point that is particularly relevant for understanding migrant entrepreneurship in local urban economies (Kloosterman, 2010). The literature also distinguishes between a socio-economic inclusion perspective, which interprets business activity as a tool for integration into the local fabric and emancipation from a condition of subordination, and a necessity self-employment perspective, whereby the entrepreneurial choice often arises from difficulties in accessing regular waged employment, bureaucratic obstacles, discrimination, and structural constraints that prevent migrants from fully utilizing their skills in the official labour markets. However, as emphasized by recent Italian scholarship, the migrant entrepreneurial pathway is never linear: it may emerge as a response to urgent needs, but sometimes evolves into an opportunity for personal and family fulfilment, eventually generating virtuous dynamics of economic revitalization in marginalized neighbourhoods and territories.

Within this context, Sicily stands out as an emblematic case—a region historically characterized by emigration, which over recent decades has become a place of stable settlement for growing and diverse foreign communities. Sicily, the primary landing point in the Mediterranean for many migration flows, now hosts an increasingly significant immigrant entrepreneurial presence. According to the 2024 Immigration and Entrepreneurship Report published by Centro Studi e Ricerche IDOS (2024), as of December 31, 2023, the island counted 29,862 immigrant businesses, representing 6.3% of all regional businesses. This figure is particularly significant when considered against Sicily's unique socio-economic background, which has long been marked by one of the highest youth unemployment rates in Italy, widespread job insecurity, and a business environment mainly comprised of family-run micro-enterprises. Despite these structural weaknesses, immigrant entrepreneurship in Sicily has demonstrated above-average dynamism: in the same period, businesses run by foreigners grew by +9.3% (2018–2023), compared to an increase of only +1.5% for Italian-owned businesses. Data from Unioncamere-InfoCamere (2025) reveal that sole proprietorships led by foreign-born individuals are steadily expanding in Sicily, mirroring national trends. These businesses are particularly concentrated in retail trade—especially food-related activities—catering, crafts, and personal services, which represent core sectors of migrant entrepreneurship across the region.

Within the regional landscape, the metropolitan cities of Catania and Messina stand out as two major centres of economic settlement, hosting 18.5% and 14.9%, respectively, of all active immigrant businesses in Sicily. Catania represents the region's second-largest foreign entrepreneurial hub, preceded only by Palermo, while Messina also records a significant and steadily growing presence. These two urban realities thus constitute particularly interesting contexts in which to closely observe the contribution of migrant entrepreneurship to local development.

Despite the growing importance of this phenomenon, it should be noted that, until now, there have been no specific studies dedicated to analysing the development and operational characteristics of immigrant entrepreneurship in the individual metropolitan cities of Sicily. Academic research to date has, in fact, been limited to outlining an overview at the national or, at most, regional level, without delving into the local specificities. As a result, fundamental aspects, such as the concrete needs of foreign entrepreneurs in the area, the difficulties perceived in the local institutional context, and the strategies they adopt to adapt to the socio-economic environment, remain largely unexplored at the urban scale. Accordingly, the literature highlights several significant knowledge gaps (Unioncamere-InfoCamere, 2025). On the one hand, as mentioned above, there is a lack of empirical studies focused on specific urban contexts capable of providing an in-depth snapshot of immigrant entrepreneurship in the local realities and capturing their specific features. On the other hand, longitudinal analyses tracing the evolution of the phenomenon at the local level remain limited, as does scholarly attention to the support policies enacted by territorial institutions to foster immigrant entrepreneurship.

In response to these critical gaps, the municipalities of Catania and Messina were identified and selected as pilot areas for the present investigation, with the aim of advancing a more grounded understanding of immigrant entrepreneurial dynamics. This approach underscores the necessity of moving beyond national-level aggregates by integrating quantitative analysis with a localized perspective attentive to both medium- and long-term trajectories, as well as the (still underexplored) role of municipal and regional support mechanisms. This research attempts to fill, at least in part, these gaps through the collection of new field data and an in-depth analysis of the phenomenon at the micro-local level.

The research was guided by two main questions, formulated to direct the collection and analysis of empirical data:

Q1: What are the main difficulties migrants encounter when starting their businesses? Do these difficulties stem from relationships with the main institutional bodies (such as Chambers of Commerce)? If so, what possible solutions could be adopted to overcome these linguistic and bureaucratic obstacles?

Q2: In what way does entrepreneurship serve as a privileged means of preventing the economic vulnerability of migrants? And how does managing an organized economic activity become a tool for building ties and connections with the local socio-economic fabric?

These research questions reflect both an interest in the initial barriers that new immigrant entrepreneurs may face and a focus on the potentially protective and integrative role of business activity within the migration journey. The underlying hypotheses concern, on the one hand, the presence of specific criticalities in relationships with institutions (bureaucracy, regulations, language) and, on the other, the function of entrepreneurship as a factor in the socio-economic stabilization of immigrants (CESPI, 2019).

This chapter is structured as follows: the next section presents in detail the research design and methodology. Section 3 discusses the main findings of the empirical analysis. Finally, some concluding remarks close the article, reflecting on the implications of the results and future research directions.

2 Description of the Research

The study adopted a quantitative methodological approach, based on the collection of data through a standardized questionnaire. In total, 83 structured face-to-face questionnaires were administered to foreign-born entrepreneurs operating in the two cities under analysis, with 51 in the metropolitan area of Catania and 32 in Messina. The dual-city design should therefore be read as an exploratory comparison between two relevant Sicilian urban contexts rather than as a basis for inferential city-level estimates. Catania and Messina are analysed jointly because the aim is to identify common patterns of migrant entrepreneurship, while keeping visible the different numerical weight of the two local subsamples. The fieldwork was conducted between January and March 2025 using the non-probability "snowball" sampling technique. The administered questionnaire consisted of numerous multiple-choice and pre-set questions to be posed to the target population or a sample thereof, in order to guarantee the neutrality of the data collection instrument itself.

In quantitative research, the formulation of questions is a key element to ensure the validity and reliability of the data, as it must guarantee, firstly, the principle of stimulus invariance meaning that questions must be asked in the same way to all respondents, so as to have the same meaning for everyone (while minimizing interpretative discretion); and secondly, the uniformity of meaning for comparison purposes (Amaturo, 2012). The combination of these factors enables the precise measurement and analysis of the numerical data relating to the characteristics of immigrant entrepreneurial forms in the cities of Catania and Messina, with the aim of identifying objective and generalizable results.

The questionnaires were administered directly by the research operators through face-to-face interviews at the workplaces of the entrepreneurs. This face-to-face method was chosen to facilitate participation and overcome potential language barriers or reluctance, while also ensuring that each respondent correctly understood each question. Specifically, in order to profile the socio-demographic and entrepreneurial characteristics of the sample and highlight the most significant trends, descriptive data analysis techniques were used. Given the exploratory nature of the study and the relatively small sample size, no advanced inferential analyses were conducted; however, the descriptive analysis proved adequate for highlighting recurring patterns and points of interest, laying the groundwork for future investigations on a larger scale.

2.1 *Structure of the Questionnaire*

The questionnaire is structured into 59 multiple-choice questions, divided into specific sections: socio-demographic, closed, semi-closed, and semi-open questions that provide an initial overview of the context, migratory background, and social environment of the respondents.

A final section, containing the Likert scale, is used to observe a general concept (attitude) that cannot be directly observed; in this case, it allows us to measure the level of satisfaction of entrepreneurs regarding their lives and the services offered in the territories of Messina and Catania. The first section is dedicated to the statement on the protection of personal data (Regulation EU, 2016; Italian Legislative Decree, 2003, 2018). The second section is aimed at collecting information about the entrepreneur, the legal form of the business, and the economic activity carried out by entering the ATECO code (ISTAT, 2025). The third section focuses on the socio-demographic characteristics of the respondent, who is required to provide information about their household, a significant factor considering that the presence of a reference community is, in many cases, the only source of support for starting a business. The fourth section aims to reconstruct the migratory journey and the subsequent phase of Italian integration of the respondent. The fifth section consists of a series of questions focusing on entrepreneurial activity, in which the respondent is asked to discuss their business since its inception. In this section, numerous questions aim to uncover any access to public funding, loans, or other forms of assistance provided by credit institutions. The sixth section contains a series of questions intended to capture the company's structure. These elements are necessary to assess the degree of immigrant entrepreneurship. In this section, intermediary figures such as accountants or associations, often volunteer-based, to whom entrepreneurs commonly turn for major bureaucratic requirements, may also emerge, as these often represent one of the main difficulties in starting and developing the business. The seventh section is designed to assess the entrepreneurs' satisfaction with life and business activity in Italy. A final section is reserved for the interviewer's evaluation of the quality of the interview.[1]

2.2 *Expected Contribution of the Results*

Despite the limitations inherent to an exploratory study conducted on a local scale, the results obtained aim to provide useful insights to guide reflection and intervention in the field of immigrant entrepreneurship. In particular, the evidence collected could serve as a starting point for a shared rethinking of key solutions regarding the main issues identified. Four possible priority areas of intervention emerge:

I. Raising awareness among local institutions: Promoting greater awareness among key territorial institutional bodies of the growing presence of businesses run by foreigners and their role in the local economic fabric. This includes information and training initiatives aimed at public officials and administrators on the specific needs and potential of migrant entrepreneurship.
II. Rethinking information and support channels: Improving and adapting the communication channels through which information and support measures for entrepreneurship (calls for proposals, incentives, services) are disseminated. In particular, the linguistic and cultural accessibility of these tools should be assessed, ensuring that foreign entrepreneurs can fully understand and benefit from them.
III. Dialogue between key stakeholders and migrant communities: Establishing a permanent roundtable for dialogue among institutions, third sector organizations (trade associations, unions, NGOs), and representatives of entrepreneurial migrant communities. A structured dialogue would facilitate the prompt identification of challenges in the field and the co-design of appropriate solutions, creating an integrated support network.
IV. Promoting a model of socio-economic integration: Valuing the entrepreneurial initiative of immigrants as a factor of inclusion and development, recognizing its positive contribution. This may translate into the implementation of local policies that facilitate access to credit for non-native entrepreneurs, simplify bureaucratic procedures for starting businesses by foreigners, and create dedicated mentorship or entrepreneurial training programmes. An integration system based on supporting migrant entrepreneurship can generate reciprocal benefits for both migrant entrepreneurs and local communities.

[1] Thanks to Miriam Milici from the BRIDGES research project for supervising the IT implementation of the questionnaire.

3 Analysis of Results[2]

The overall significance of the phenomenon is far from marginal: as of 2023, there are 29,862 businesses run by immigrants in Sicily, accounting for 6.3% of all regional enterprises. Within this framework, Catania and Messina represent two major hubs of migrant economic activity, hosting 18.5% and 14.9%, respectively, of all businesses run by immigrants in the region (IDOS, 2024). The sample under examination, though numerically limited, is situated within an urban context where migrant entrepreneurship is well established and makes a significant contribution to the local socio-economic fabric. The analysed sample consists of 83 immigrant entrepreneurs operating in the cities of Catania and Messina.[3] More precisely, 61.4% of the interviews were collected in Catania and 38.6% in Messina. In 84.3% of cases, the respondent was the entrepreneur, manager, or owner, while in 15.7% of cases, the questionnaire was completed by a person delegated by the entrepreneur. The majority are men, 78.3%, while women constitute 21.7% of the sample. The underrepresentation of women only partially reflects the regional figure, since in Sicily, 29% of immigrant-led businesses are managed by women. The average profile is that of a settled adult entrepreneur with a family network in the area. A total of 78.3% are married, 66.3% have children, and 54.2% currently live with their family as a couple with children. From the perspective of human capital, there is also a certain degree of variety: 22.9% completed lower secondary school, 18.1% report a vocational qualification, 32.5% hold a secondary school diploma, and 16.9% have a university degree. These figures confirm the presence of a non-negligible stock of formal and vocational human capital within the sample, contradicting the stereotype that tends to associate migrant entrepreneurship exclusively with low-skilled and unqualified labour. Regarding the country in which educational qualifications were obtained, the sample presents considerable diversity. The most frequent countries are Bangladesh, 33.7%, Sri Lanka, 16.9%, Italy, 10.8%, China, 7.2%, Nigeria, 6.0%, and Senegal, 6.0%, alongside smaller presences from other countries. This pattern is broadly consistent with the internal diversity of immigrant entrepreneurship in Sicily, even though the survey is exploratory and not statistically representative.

[2] The reader is cautioned that, since the observed sample may not be representative of the entire population of foreign entrepreneurs operating in the two municipalities of Catania and Messina, all results should be regarded as indicative.

[3] For reasons of space, the tables and figures relating to the survey are not included in this chapter, but they are available from the authors upon request. All statistical analyses and data processing were carried out using STATA ver. 15.1.

3.1 Migratory Paths and Initial Labour Market Integration

The respondents exhibit medium to long-term migratory trajectories, characterized by progressive settlement in Italy. A total of 75.9% have been living in Catania or Messina for more than 10 years, including 41.0% who have resided there for between 10 and 20 years, 26.5% for between 20 and 30 years, and 8.4% for more than 30 years. Only 7.2% arrived between 1 and 5 years ago, while 16.9% have lived in the area for between 5 and 10 years. These data indicate a clear prevalence of consolidated settlement trajectories. Furthermore, 39.8% of respondents previously lived in other Italian municipalities before settling in their current city, whereas 60.2% report that they have always lived in Catania or Messina since their arrival in Italy. The entrepreneurial establishment in Sicily was therefore often preceded by other experiences of residence and work within Italy, suggesting internal mobility before local stabilization. The motivations that led these entrepreneurs to migrate to Italy are predominantly linked to work and family. The most frequent reason for arrival is a work permit, reported by 42.2% of the sample, followed by family reunification, 36.1%. Smaller shares arrived for study or tourist reasons, 6.0%, or for asylum-related reasons, 2.4%, while 12.0% indicated other personal trajectories. It should also be noted that 80.7% of respondents did not have a guaranteed job upon arrival, whereas only 19.3% did. This confirms that, for most of them, migration was initially marked by economic uncertainty and by the need to seek employment after arrival. In this respect, the limited recognition of migrant human capital and the concentration in lower segments of the labour market are fully consistent with the broader interpretative framework outlined by Sciortino (2015). Their first job in Italy was most often in unqualified occupations, 48.2%, followed by qualified occupations in commerce and services, 22.9%, and by craft, skilled manual, or agricultural work, 16.9%. By contrast, in the country of origin, the most common condition was inactivity or unemployment, 43.4%, followed by craft and skilled manual work, 20.5%. These figures suggest that entrepreneurship frequently developed after an initial phase of precarious or low-skilled labour market incorporation. In this sense, migration was often perceived as a means of upward mobility, aimed at overcoming limited opportunities in the country of origin and gradually building more stable socio-economic positions in Italy.

3.2 Starting a Business: Characteristics, Resources, and Motivations

The timing and modalities of business establishment vary within the sample, although some common patterns are evident. The year of business foundation ranges from 1993 to 2025. A clear concentration of new openings is observed in the most recent decade: 63.9% of businesses were founded from 2015 onwards, with particularly visible concentrations in 2015, 2021, and 2024. This trend confirms the recent dynamism of immigrant entrepreneurship in the two cities under analysis. From a legal standpoint, sole proprietorships and artisan firms overwhelmingly prevail, accounting for 89.2% of all cases. General partnerships represent 4.8%, while limited liability companies account for 6.0%. This distribution is coherent with a model of small-scale entrepreneurship based on relatively simple organizational forms, low entry thresholds, and strong dependence on individual or family initiative.

As for business sectors, retail trade is predominant, representing 54.2% of all cases, followed by food and beverage services, 25.3%, and personal services, 7.2%. Smaller shares are found in manufacturing, construction, transport, and other activities. The sample is therefore concentrated in sectors traditionally associated with immigrant entrepreneurship, especially those characterized by relatively easy entry, direct contact with local demand, and a strong reliance on self-employment and family labour mobilization. Business creation was most often an individual undertaking. A total of 61.4% of respondents started their business alone, while 20.5% did so with a relative or family member and 13.3% with a friend of the same nationality. Joint initiatives with Italians or with entrepreneurs of other nationalities are much less frequent. This confirms the centrality of close trust-based relations in the startup phase. The entrepreneurial choice reflects a combination of necessity and opportunity factors. The most frequent main reason given was the desire not to depend on an employer, 41.0%, followed by the wish to improve working conditions, 28.9%. Other respondents emphasized the search for stable income, 7.2%, the perception of having sufficient skills and abilities, 9.6%, or prior entrepreneurial experience in the country of origin. Some also referred to administrative or residence-related reasons. In this respect, the survey is coherent with observations advanced by Zupi (2025), who notes that regulatory and residence-related constraints may indirectly encourage self-employment strategies. More generally, the coexistence of constraint and aspiration confirms the interpretative perspective proposed by Shapero and Sokol (1982), according to which entrepreneurship often emerges from the interaction between external pressures and positive internal motivations.

As for the financial resources used to start up, the businesses in the sample rely predominantly on internal and informal channels. The most frequently reported primary source was savings accumulated through work in Italy, 51.8%. Savings from the country of origin account for 10.8%, family savings for 13.3%, and loans from relatives or friends for 13.3%. By contrast, bank loans represent only 4.8%. In addition, 84.3% did not prepare a business plan, 83.1% did not use financial services such as microcredit or loans, and 96.4% did not participate in public calls for grants. These figures indicate that business startup is overwhelmingly based on self-financing and informal trust networks, while formal channels of financial planning and institutional support remain marginal. The very limited use of public grants and financial services appears to reflect more than a simple lack of formal opportunities. It may also indicate limited awareness of available instruments, low trust in institutional procedures, and a perceived sufficiency of informal family and community channels in the startup phase. The linguistic dimension also deserves attention. At the time of startup, 77.1% reported knowing Italian, while smaller shares relied primarily on English, French, or their own language. This suggests that linguistic integration was uneven and that some businesses were initially established under conditions of partial distance from the surrounding institutional environment. Overall, the startup appears as a process rooted in personal initiative, family support, and gradual adaptation rather than in structured forms of external assistance. This pattern is consistent with the theory of mixed embeddedness advanced by Kloosterman and Rath (2001), according to which immigrant entrepreneurship develops through the interaction between social networks, opportunity structures, and institutional contexts.

3.3 Social Capital and Support Networks, Relationship with the Institutional System

The survey strongly highlights the central role of ethnic and family social capital in supporting immigrant entrepreneurs, both at the startup stage and during business development. A total of 74.7% of respondents report having friends or relatives who have already started an autonomous business, while 72.3% believe they could ask friends or relatives for help in case of difficulty. In addition, 78.3% state that family and friends think they made the right decision in becoming entrepreneurs, whereas only 4.8% report a negative judgement. This suggests that social capital operates not only as a practical resource but also as a source of moral legitimation. In this respect, the evidence is in line with the broader interpretation proposed by Greve and Salaff (2003), who stress the strategic importance of social networks in entrepreneurial action. When asked whether there are other entrepreneurs with whom they can discuss business-related difficulties, 55.4% answered yes and a further 9.6% answered perhaps. Among those who indicated the presence of such interlocutors, the most frequent reference is to entrepreneurs of the same nationality, while Italian entrepreneurs are mentioned less often. This pattern confirms that support networks are still strongly structured around co-ethnic ties. A similar result emerges at the startup stage. When deciding to open a business, 42.2% turned mainly to friends or relatives, while 25.3% turned to no one. Only 4.8% turned to the Chamber of Commerce and 4.8% to trade associations. The open answers show that accountants often function as the practical gateway to business creation and compliance, much more than formal institutional actors. This finding deserves particular attention because accountants do not simply provide technical assistance. In many cases, they appear to act as mediators between migrant entrepreneurs and the institutional environment, translating formal obligations into practical decisions and reducing uncertainty in dealing with administrative procedures. The internal organization of the businesses also reflects the centrality of community-based resources. A total of 31.3% of firms have no employees, while 48.2% have between one and three employees. Among firms with employees, 63.2% employ only workers from the entrepreneur's country of origin, 7.0% employ only Italians, 28.1% report a mixed workforce, and 1.8% employ only workers of other nationalities. These data point to a strong tendency to rely on family and co-ethnic labour, especially in the smallest firms. Relations with formal institutions remain weak. Only 36.1% report having relations with trade associations, and these relations mainly concern accounting, tax, and social security advice. Likewise, although 80.7% say they know the Chamber of Commerce, 57.8% never use its services and 39.8% use them only once or twice a year. Among the reasons for not using the Chamber, the most frequent open-ended answer is that the accountant takes care of everything. This confirms that institutional access is frequently mediated rather than direct. The same distance is visible in financial and crisis-related support. Only 16.9% report having used financial services such as microcredit or loans, whereas 83.1% did not. Periods of crisis were experienced by 63.9% of respondents. Yet, when asked to whom they turned in those periods, 34.9% answered no one, 21.7% indicated friends or relatives, and only a very small minority referred to trade associations or other formal actors. In addition, 42.2% report having adopted no specific strategy, while 19.3% adapted their business activity to market difficulties and only 4.8% acquired new entrepreneurial skills. This suggests a form of resilience based more on endurance and informal coping than on structured external support. Overall, the evidence points to a model of entrepreneurship in which autonomy and informal networks prevail, while formal support structures remain underused, weakly trusted, or poorly integrated into the everyday experience of foreign entrepreneurs. Relations with the institutional ecosystem therefore remain fragile, and this fragility may limit not only access to resources but also opportunities for broader economic integration and business growth.

4 Conclusions

The results of this research suggest that foreign entrepreneurship in the metropolitan areas of Catania and Messina constitutes not only a growing economic phenomenon but also a relevant channel of socio-economic stabilization, local integration, and long-term settlement. The evidence collected points to the capacity of many migrant entrepreneurs to invest in the territory, build economic and social networks, and gradually consolidate their presence within the local community, thus contributing to the vitality of the urban context. However, despite the positive elements observed, several persistent critical issues still require attention and intervention. Significant barriers remain in access to institutional and financial support systems, and these continue to represent a major obstacle to the full development of immigrant entrepreneurship. These limitations are not merely administrative or procedural but are also linked to cultural dimensions and to mutual perceptions between migrants and institutions.

The study aims not only to fill a knowledge gap but also to offer practical suggestions for improvement, so that these insights may inform local policymaking and encourage further quantitative and qualitative research on the role of foreign entrepreneurship in the socio-economic development of Italian urban areas. A particularly relevant issue concerns access to financial resources, which remains limited within the sample and calls for more inclusive and culturally aware approaches by institutions and financial actors. In this respect, future research should explore more thoroughly the economic, cultural, and informational barriers that may hinder the use of formal financial instruments among migrant entrepreneurs. Moreover, the research has shown that linguistic, bureaucratic, and informational barriers continue to limit the effective participation of immigrant entrepreneurs in the wider entrepreneurial and institutional ecosystem. The low level of interaction with local business associations, the Chamber of Commerce, and formal support channels testifies to a gap that must be addressed through targeted policies, the expansion of multilingual and intercultural services, and the strengthening of mediation and mentoring initiatives. From a policy perspective, these results suggest that support measures should not be limited to the formal availability of services, but should also improve their accessibility, intelligibility, and credibility among migrant entrepreneurs. Strengthening trusted mediation channels, while progressively connecting them with Chambers of Commerce, trade associations, and credit institutions, could help transform informal resilience into more stable pathways of inclusion and business development. Taken together, the findings answer the first research question by showing that the main difficulties faced by migrant entrepreneurs concern limited access to formal support channels, weak interaction with institutional actors, and strong dependence on informal networks. They also answer the second research question by suggesting that entrepreneurship may function as a pathway of socio-economic stabilization and local embeddedness, even though this relationship should be explored further through broader and more robust empirical designs. Ultimately, enhancing the contribution of foreign entrepreneurs does not benefit only the individuals and communities directly involved but may also generate broader advantages for the local context, from economic vitality to urban regeneration and intercultural dialogue. From a methodological point of view, this research should be regarded as a first step towards a deeper understanding of this complex phenomenon. The sample is limited and cannot be considered representative of the entire foreign entrepreneurial population in Catania and Messina. In this regard, it should be noted that many foreign entrepreneurs refused to answer the questionnaire due to a well-founded fear of being exposed to subsequent administrative or judicial inspections. Data collection was also influenced by time, logistical, and relational constraints, resulting in the possible underrepresentation of some categories of entrepreneurs. Moreover, the use of a directly administered survey instrument may introduce social desirability bias, as some respondents may have overstated their satisfaction or underestimated their difficulties for cultural or self-presentational reasons. Future developments should therefore expand the empirical base and improve the sampling strategy in order to strengthen the robustness and analytical scope of the results. Finally, it is hoped that the findings of this study will encourage policymakers, institutions, and local communities to adopt more open, forward-looking, and culturally sensitive strategies capable of valuing diversity as a resource for social and economic progress.

Acknowledgement The research was conducted within the BRIDGES project, coordinated by the Comunità di Sant'Egidio in collaboration with researchers from the COSPECS Department at the University of Messina. It aimed to investigate migrant and foreign entrepreneurship in the metropolitan areas of Messina and Catania, focusing on its key characteristics and its potential role in fostering inclusion through interactions with families, other businesses, institutions, and trade associations.

References

Amaturo, E. (2012). *Metodologia della ricerca sociale*. UTET.

Centro Studi e Ricerche IDOS. (2024). *Rapporto immigrazione e imprenditoria 2024*. IDOS Edizioni.

CESPI. (2019). *Common Home. Migrazione e sviluppo in Italia*. CeSPI.

Entzinger, H. (2000). The dynamics of integration policies: A multidimensional model. In J. Doomernik & H. Entzinger (Eds.), *Migration and integration: The dynamics of inclusion and exclusion* (pp. 97–118). Amsterdam University Press.

Entzinger, H., & Biezeveld, R. (2003). *Benchmarking in immigrant integration*. European Research Centre on Migration and Ethnic Relations, University of Utrecht.

Fondazione Leone Moressa. (2023). *Rapporto annuale sull'economia dell'immigrazione*. il Mulino.

Greve, A., & Salaff, J. W. (2003). Social networks and entrepreneurship. *Entrepreneurship Theory and Practice, 28*(1), 1–22.

ISTAT. (2025). *Classificazione delle attività economiche ATECO. Anno 2025*. ISTAT.

Italian Republic. (2003). *Legislative Decree No. 196 of 30 June 2003: Italian Personal Data Protection Code*.

Italian Republic. (2018). *Legislative Decree No. 101 of 10 August 2018: Provisions for the adaptation of national legislation to Regulation (EU) 2016/679*.

Kloosterman, R. C. (2010). Matching opportunities with resources: A framework for analysing (migrant) entrepreneurship from a mixed embeddedness perspective. *Entrepreneurship & Regional Development, 22*(1–2), 25–45.

Kloosterman, R., & Rath, J. (2001). Immigrant entrepreneurs in advanced economies: Mixed embeddedness further explored. *Journal of Ethnic and Migration Studies, 27*(2), 189–201.

Regulation (EU) 2016/679. (2016). General Data Protection Regulation. *Official Journal of the European Union*, L119, 1–88.

Sciortino, G. (2015). *È possibile misurare l'integrazione degli immigrati? Lo stato dell'arte*. In *Dipartimento di Sociologia e Ricerca Sociale, Quaderno 63*.

Shapero, A., & Sokol, L. (1982). The social dimensions of entrepreneurship. In C. A. Kent, D. L. Sexton, & K. H. Vesper (Eds.), *Encyclopedia of entrepreneurship* (pp. 72–90). Prentice-Hall.

Unioncamere, & Infocamere. (2025). *Imprese straniere: +140 mila in 10 anni, una su tre ha oltre un decennio*. Unioncamere and InfoCamere.

Zupi, M. (2025). *Focus Migrazioni Internazionali n. 52: Osservatorio Quadrimestrale n. 3, 2024, Settembre-Dicembre*. CESPI, Centro Studi di Politica Internazionale.

Practices and Social Relations in Foreign Entrepreneurship in Catania and Messina

Andrea Biagiotti, Alessandro Irrera Assanti, Giuliana Russo, and Tiziana Tarsia

Abstract This chapter investigates migrant entrepreneurship in the metropolitan contexts of Catania and Messina. Building on the growing economic and social relevance of migrant-owned businesses, the study explores their characteristics, relational dynamics, and key challenges, with particular attention to territorial embeddedness and interactions with the local ecosystem. The research adopts an integrated methodological approach combining quantitative and qualitative tools, with a primary focus on semi-structured interviews conducted with migrant entrepreneurs and key actors such as accountants, Chambers of Commerce, and trade associations. Findings show that migrant entrepreneurship is often a pathway to autonomy, evolving from necessity into a life project, with social networks playing a key role in business creation and consolidation. At the same time, significant challenges persist, including limited access to credit, language barriers, bureaucratic complexity, and weak institutional engagement. The study highlights implications for training interventions aimed at strengthening access to financial, informational, and relational resources.

1 Introduction

This contribution explores the phenomenon of foreign entrepreneurship in the metropolitan areas of Catania and Messina.[1] The study stems from the growing

[1] This study refers to a component of a broader research project, which, in addition to the interviews discussed in this contribution, also involved the statistical analysis of data collected through a questionnaire. Kheit et al., for further details on the quantitative analysis (infra).

A. Biagiotti · A. Irrera Assanti · T. Tarsia (✉)
Department of Cognitive, Psychological and Educational Sciences, and Cultural Studies, University of Messina, Messina, Italy
e-mail: andrea.biagiotti@unime.it; tarsia.tiziana@unime.it

G. Russo
Comunità di Sant'Egidio – Sicilia OdV ETS, Messina, Italy
e-mail: lagiulianarusso@gmail.com

R. Cellini et al. (eds.), *Cultural, Social, and Political Participation in the Internet Era*, Contributions to Economics, https://doi.org/10.1007/978-3-032-33072-7_20

awareness of the economic relevance of migrant entrepreneurship and from the lack of in-depth studies in recent scientific literature at the urban and regional scale in Sicily. The scientific interest of this research lies in its attempt to fill this gap by adopting a qualitative approach based on direct engagement with the actors involved in the phenomenon.

The study was conducted through semi-structured interviews[2] addressed not only to migrant entrepreneurs but also to key actors within the local economic ecosystem (such as accountants, representatives of Chambers of Commerce, and trade associations), with the aim of capturing the phenomenon from multiple perspectives. The most innovative aspect of the research lies precisely in its effort to intertwine different levels of analysis—subjective, relational, and institutional—and to examine the territorial dimension of migrant entrepreneurship, observing how it becomes embedded in specific urban contexts, generating forms of social capital, support networks, and micro-systems of cooperation that often remain invisible to statistical surveys.

The aim pursued is twofold: on the one hand, the study seeks to shed light on a constantly evolving phenomenon by analyzing the social, cultural, bureaucratic, and economic challenges that foreign entrepreneurs face on a daily basis; on the other hand, it aims to stimulate institutional reflection, with the goal of developing proposals to be addressed to institutional actors, in order to guide the design of effective organizational, procedural, and policy practices to respond to these challenges.

As the project employed both quantitative and qualitative research methods, the fieldwork was characterized by continuous comparison between the results emerging from the structured questionnaire and those from the interviews. In this chapter, particular attention is given to the findings derived from interviews with economic and institutional actors.

2 The "BRIDGES" Project: Research Design and Research Context

The project was coordinated by the Comunità di Sant'Egidio – Sicilia ODV ETS and carried out in collaboration with researchers from the COSPECS Department at the University of Messina. It aimed to investigate migrant and foreign entrepreneurship

[2] Twenty-two semi-structured interviews were conducted. Specifically: 11 were conducted with entrepreneurs in Messina (of which 6 focused on training aspects); 9 were conducted in Catania (of which 2 focused on training); 1 was conducted with a representative of the Messina Chamber of Commerce; 1 was conducted with a representative of the Catania Chamber of Commerce; and 1 was conducted with a representative of a trade association. The codes used in the interviews correspond to: CT_IMP (entrepreneur from Catania); ME_IMP (entrepreneur from Messina); ME_CCA (Chamber of Commerce of Messina); CT_CCA (Chamber of Commerce of Catania); ME_ASC (Trade Association of Messina).

in the metropolitan areas of Messina and Catania, with the objective of identifying the specific characteristics of the phenomenon in these contexts and exploring its potential role in fostering inclusion, particularly through entrepreneurs' interactions with family members, other business owners, institutions, and trade associations.

A necessary starting point was to define what is meant by foreign-owned enterprises. The phenomenon is defined as businesses in which control and ownership are entirely or predominantly held by individuals not born in Italy or with a migrant background (Unioncamere, InfoCamere, 2023). In practice, therefore, the necessary and sufficient condition for identifying these firms is the nationality of the owner, while the field of investigation remains the Italian context. These enterprises operate within the Italian regulatory framework and interact with local actors and institutions in the areas where they establish their activities.

Over the past decade, the Italian economic landscape has been significantly enriched by the presence of foreign entrepreneurship, which accounts for approximately 39.7% (Fondazione Leone Moressa, 2024). According to the Annual Report on the Economics of Immigration (ibid.), there are over 600,000 foreign-owned businesses in Italy, representing around 10% of the total.

In Sicily, in 2023, there were 29,862 migrant-owned businesses, accounting for 6.3% of the total number of enterprises in the region. Within this framework, Catania and Messina represent two major hubs of economic settlement, hosting 18.5% and 14.9%, respectively, of all foreign-owned businesses in the region.

Active participation in the economic system constitutes a relevant aspect of the broader process of social inclusion, as it creates opportunities for interaction and for acquiring a complex system of rules and conventions, including social ones (such as greater proficiency in the local language).

However, a well-established body of sociological literature invites us to reconsider the assumption that active participation in the economic system—such as engagement in entrepreneurial activity—automatically fosters social inclusion. Rather, these processes are contingent upon a set of social, institutional, and relational conditions that shape their outcomes. More critical perspectives have shown that participation in economic activity may, under certain conditions, fail to produce inclusion or may even reproduce existing inequalities. In contexts characterized by labor market flexibilization and economic insecurity, forms of self-employment and micro-entrepreneurship often overlap with a precarious financial state, where economic participation does not translate into stability or full social integration (Standing, 2011). In a similar way, a certain literature has highlighted how fragmented and unstable work trajectories can undermine long-term identity construction and social belonging, thereby limiting the integrative potential of economic engagement (Sennett, 1998). These dynamics have been further explored in recent studies showing how contemporary forms of entrepreneurship—for example and in particular necessity-driven or platform-based ones—may reproduce precarious conditions rather than alleviate them (Cieslik, 2015; Wood et al., 2019).

Furthermore, the broader institutional and territorial context plays a crucial role in mediating these dynamics. As argued in the literature on local development and industrial districts, entrepreneurial activity tends to foster inclusion when it is supported by cohesive local systems, strong institutions, and shared norms (Bagnasco, 1977; Trigilia, 2002). Conversely, in more fragmented or peripheral contexts, entrepreneurship may remain weakly embedded and less capable of generating inclusive effects. Beck's analysis of the individualization of risk further underscores how, in contemporary economies, the burdens associated with market participation are increasingly shifted onto individuals, making the outcomes of entrepreneurial engagement more uncertain and stratified (Beck, 2000). Recent empirical approaches also suggest that the inclusiveness of entrepreneurship is strongly linked to access to welfare provisions, institutional support, and opportunity structures, which remain unevenly distributed across social groups (Williams & Vorley, 2015; Ram et al., 2017).

In recent decades, in Western economies, access to financial services and their proper use have gradually become a prerequisite for participation in economic life. This requirement becomes even more crucial when migrants do not merely seek to participate in economic life through employment, but rather through engaging in entrepreneurial activities, which are inherently risk-laden.

Migrants often lack a financial and credit history in Italy, as well as consolidated assets; they tend to have a lower income capacity compared to the average of those entering the labor market and experience lower recognition and valuation of their skills (Istat, 2024; Ciciriello, 2012). The combination of these factors exposes migrant entrepreneurs to higher levels of economic and financial precariousness and an increased risk of social exclusion. Access to financial services and products represents an essential resource in the process of integration, and exclusion from such access therefore entails significantly higher social costs for migrants compared to local citizens (Ceschi, 2019).

Consequently, active participation in the country's economic and social life—resulting directly from financial inclusion—if supported and facilitated at the institutional level, can create opportunities for growth for both migrants and society, contributing to the reduction of social exclusion risks.

Despite the growing relevance of the phenomenon, recent literature lacks specific investigations into its development and functioning at the level of individual metropolitan areas, particularly in Sicily. Existing studies provide a general overview, relying primarily on aggregated data at the national or regional scale. There is a lack of empirical research based on a mixed-method approach—both quantitative and qualitative—capable of examining concrete needs, the subjective perceptions of challenges and opportunities, as well as the adaptation strategies developed by entrepreneurs within local urban contexts.

This research was therefore conducted with the aim of helping to shed light on this specific area of inquiry. Although exploratory in nature, the study represents a meaningful starting point, capable of guiding and supporting future, more extensive research, including from a comparative perspective across urban contexts.

3 Interviews with Entrepreneurs and Institutional Actors

Within the framework of the research, the qualitative investigation was conducted with the main actors involved in the phenomenon, starting with entrepreneurs and ultimately engaging with key representatives of the local economic ecosystem, such as accountants, Chambers of Commerce in the metropolitan areas under study, trade unions, and trade associations. These subjects were approached through semi-structured interviews.

When the research required the collection of interview data, the research team encountered the first major challenge of the study: reaching migrant entrepreneurs. Despite the significant presence of business owners with a migrant background in both areas under investigation, researchers often observed a general "reluctance" among participants to engage in this type of conversation. The reasons provided by the entrepreneurs themselves ranged from lack of interest, to heavy workloads, to outright refusal, or a more implicit "lack of trust."

To obtain the qualitative data needed for the study, the researchers conducted fieldwork in the streets of both cities, identifying areas that could be considered *hotspots* with a high concentration of businesses run by foreign nationals, in order to attempt a direct approach. Building on these initial contacts, the research then proceeded through what can be described as a "snowball sampling" strategy: participants who agreed to an initial interview acted as intermediaries, connecting the researchers with other migrant entrepreneurs within their networks (often family members or members of the same ethnic community). This approach facilitated greater trust and a sense of reassurance among subsequent interviewees, fostering a perceived "sense of protection" and security.

It was therefore decided to rely on the relational networks of these entrepreneurs. A substantial body of literature identifies relationships among individuals as the primary vehicle through which social capital is manifested and accumulated (Bourdieu, 1986 ed.it. 2001). This form of capital is structured within relationships and constitutes a collective resource that can support cooperation among different social actors (Coleman, 2016), based on both bonding ties of trust and reciprocity and bridging ties (Putnam, 2004).

The research team developed three different interview guides, each tailored to the three target groups identified for the study. As an initial step, it was decided to engage with the Chambers of Commerce of the two cities. An interview was designed to investigate the phenomenon of foreign entrepreneurship as perceived by local economic institutions, with questions also focusing on existing policies targeting this segment of entrepreneurs and on the strategies adopted by the Chambers of Commerce in their interactions with these professionals.

The aim of this interview was to identify the services provided to foreign entrepreneurs intending to start a business in the local area.

Already from these two interviews with institutional actors, as well as from the interview conducted with a trade association in Messina, several themes emerged that were later incorporated into the interview guide for entrepreneurs. The development of this guide also drew on findings from a preliminary analysis of the data collected through the questionnaires. Field notes and reflections from the research team were also particularly relevant. An interview guide was thus developed for foreign entrepreneurs, aimed at investigating aspects such as the individual's entrepreneurial background, the role of co-nationals in shaping entrepreneurial choices, any support received from institutional actors and organizations such as Chambers of Commerce or trade associations, and the coping strategies adopted during periods of difficulty.

Further methodological reflections emerged from the direct field experience of the researchers. Despite the undeniable differences that characterize the urban structures of Messina and Catania—differences that fall within the "anthropological rules" of territorial analysis—it is noteworthy that the attitudes and behaviors of entrepreneurs appear largely comparable. In both cities, the vast majority of interviews were conducted in the workplace and during working hours, often taking advantage of "break" moments familiar to the interviewees. Moreover, the most effective strategy proved to be an initial contact aimed at presenting the research and the research team, combined with a request to schedule a follow-up appointment on a subsequent day, agreed upon with the entrepreneur, in order to conduct the interview.

At the time of writing, the analysis presented in this contribution is based on interviews with nine foreign entrepreneurs, six of whom have their registered offices in Catania and three in Messina.

3.1 First Analysis of the Main Thematic Areas

The interviews were conducted between late 2024 and the summer of 2025.

With regard to the geographical origin of the migrant participants, the sample shows considerable diversity, reflecting the varied landscape of migrant entrepreneurship in Sicily. The interviewees come from South Asian countries (e.g., Bangladesh, Pakistan, Sri Lanka), as well as from Africa, China, and Eastern Europe. This sample reflects the distribution of migrant entrepreneurship across the island. According to data reported by IDOS, the top five nationalities among foreign entrepreneurs in Sicily are Moroccans, followed by individuals from Bangladesh and the Indian subcontinent, then Chinese, Tunisians, and—an interesting case for the region—EU citizens from Germany who have settled in Sicily (Lasagni, 2025).

The data analyzed below derive from the semi-structured interviews examined by the research team. In order to analyze these contents comparatively, the material was categorized using labels[3] designed to capture the underlying "concept" embedded in each statement. The following thematic labels were identified:

[3] The labels followed the central themes of the interview track.

1. Autonomy of choice
2. Support networks
3. Asset management
4. Constraints of doing business
5. Coping strategies
6. Relationships with Chambers of Commerce and trade associations
7. The key role of the accountant

3.2 Autonomy of Choice

The accounts of almost all interviewees reveal a strong desire to create an autonomous economic space, governed by freely chosen rules.

> I decided to become an entrepreneur because my husband and I wanted to start our own business. (. . .) It was a personal choice; I wanted it to be a family business. (08CT_IMP)

The most interesting finding concerns entrepreneurial choice as a response to labor constraints: many migrants become entrepreneurs out of necessity, but over time transform this condition into a life project. This phenomenon has been defined as "entrepreneurship out of necessity" (Fairlie & Robb, 2008), which can evolve into forms of "entrepreneurship by opportunity" when the local context provides the appropriate enabling conditions. The skills that many foreign entrepreneurs describe as having been developed over time and through effort, often linked to their cultural and biographical background, can be understood as forms of human capital (Arrighetti & Traù, 2013), acquired through practical experience and even informal apprenticeship pathways, both in their countries of origin and, in some cases, in Italy.

Although often not formally recognized through certifications or qualifications, such knowledge constitutes a fundamental resource in the development of autonomous entrepreneurial trajectories (Ambrosini, 2020; Dheer, 2018). The literature also confirms that migrant entrepreneurs frequently draw on skills acquired in "marginal" or informal work contexts, developing adaptive strategies grounded in practical experience, observation, and hands-on learning (Riss & Groen, 2020). These competencies represent a competitive advantage that enables them to overcome barriers to accessing formal markets, institutions, and economic opportunities, as widely documented in the international literature (Granovetter, 1985; Etemad, 2023).

3.3 Support Networks

One of the aspects that emerged from the outset is the value of the community, not only in terms of belonging but also in relation to the entrepreneurial community—a concept grounded in social science literature. Fortunato and Alter (2015) define it as a set of entrepreneurs rooted in a specific territory, or connected through sectoral similarities, whose relationships also influence economic development and mutual support. These ties, which are in part developed along lines of similarity in business models, may reinforce what has been discussed so far regarding the mobilization of forms of human and social capital that foreign entrepreneurs draw upon both in the initial stages of business creation and in its subsequent consolidation.

The value of the community emerged both in the phases related to business start-up—where it influences the choice of sector as well as bureaucratic procedures for formalizing entrepreneurial activity—and in the day-to-day practices involved in running a business.

> All my XX friends and contacts, once they arrived here, were doing this. They were all traders who had goods to take to weekly markets. They went to XX and other places. I already knew what I had to do. In the house where I lived, everyone was engaged in street trading. That's why I had the confidence to do it. (04_CT_IMP)

Thus, communities play a crucial role in the quality of life of foreign entrepreneurs. They constitute "support networks" for entrepreneurs.

3.4 Limits of Entrepreneurship and Coping Strategies

During the interviews, entrepreneurs described the main obstacles they face on a daily basis. The difficulties encountered range from dealing with the bureaucracy that characterizes public bodies responsible for business services, to accessing microcredit, and even to the mistrust of some consumers.

Among the first challenges faced by foreign entrepreneurs is the language barrier. Others also reported that access to microcredit or to public funds allocated for businesses often appears to be a real "utopia."

> Getting financing is a problem for foreign entrepreneurs. The bank asks for many things that you simply don't have. That's the problem. The bank asks for a lot. The loan is, for example, 6,000 euros . . . what do you need those 6,000 euros for? You spend 6,000 euros right away! But getting a loan of 23,000, 30,000, or 40,000 euros is not possible. That's why many have closed their businesses! (. . .) People don't have the required guarantees. (04_CT_IMP)

Almost all interviewees described a remarkable degree of resilience. The ability to cope with crises and sustain their economic activity clearly emerged from the accounts of several entrepreneurs, although many of them were ultimately unable to succeed.

> We try to get by . . . to close the stall and work depending on the season . . . with fruit picking. In the summer, we go to work at the seaside. Everyone does this. During the slow periods, we focus on fruit harvesting, the grape harvest, olives when they're pressed. In May, when they come back, they spend June, July, and August working at the seaside. (04CT_IMP).

If this is the fate of many smaller entrepreneurs—namely those who choose to operate as sole proprietors—more diverse and structured coping strategies are adopted by those organized in more complex business forms. The case of the following entrepreneur is particularly illustrative:

> So, we had a crisis after COVID. (...) How did I overcome it? Um... by making new investments, that (...) We received support from the State! There was a lot of help, like reductions in energy costs, in taxes. Reductions... and also money, yes, yes. They helped. (12ME_IMP)

It is reasonable to assume that there is a relationship between the legal form of a business and its ability to access support mechanisms. As the complexity of the legal structure increases—along with greater guarantees, particularly in terms of liability regimes—the opportunities to access microcredit or public funding also appear to increase.

Since the panel of interviewees consists predominantly of small entrepreneurs, mainly sole proprietors engaged in retail activities, the issue of asset management seems to intersect, to some extent, with challenges related to access to microcredit and the ability to cope with periods of crisis affecting business survival.

3.5 *The Key Role of the Accountant*

From the outset, the fundamental role of the accountant emerged clearly. This professional supports the entrepreneur from the very start of the business, accompanying them through its various stages and managing relations with the Chamber of Commerce. The interviews with entrepreneurs highlighted how the search for a professional suited to their needs is often long and complex; once the "right" accountant—considered competent and reliable—is found, they become a key point of reference.

Initial findings from interviews with professionals also point to the central importance of trust in the relationship established with the entrepreneur:

> Our work is a consulting activity, so the consultant—the accountant—has to be a person of trust. (...) Moreover, consider that this type of entrepreneur is different from, say, those who rely on a lawyer (...). In our case, if we take on these clients, we keep them for many years; unless something irreparable happens, clients rarely leave a firm once they have built a relationship of trust. (10CT_IMP)

If the accountant represents a key point of reference for Italian entrepreneurs, they become a true compass for migrant entrepreneurs, who—also due to obstacles such as language barriers and excessive bureaucratization—tend to delegate to professionals those activities that require a high level of technical expertise. It is precisely this trust-based relationship, which develops through the natural stages of running a business, that leads migrant entrepreneurs to prefer interacting with professionals rather than engaging directly with institutional channels such as Chambers of Commerce and trade associations.

3.6 Relationships with the Commerce Chamber and Trade Associations

As already indicated by the interviews, it emerged that foreign entrepreneurs only occasionally visit the Chamber of Commerce, preferring to delegate such interactions to their accountant whenever possible.

The situation is somewhat different with regard to trade associations. Most of the entrepreneurs interviewed reported that they were unfamiliar with them and had never come into contact with them. The only entrepreneurs who had direct experience with such associations were those engaged in activities requiring specific certifications.

With reference to the organization of training courses for migrant entrepreneurs, it emerged that Chambers of Commerce organize such initiatives only sporadically, often in partnership with trade associations. Regarding the types of training courses offered at the institutional level, the representative of Confesercenti Messina stated:

> So, the services we offer to foreign companies—let's say, in quotation marks, those owned by foreign nationals—are exactly the same as those we provide to our fellow citizens. At the moment, about 7–8% of our members in Confesercenti are non-EU nationals (. . .). What kind of services do they usually request? They often ask for training courses related to food and beverage service; for example, those opening Chinese restaurants or similar businesses, or Japanese ones, need to take the SAB course; so they need the certification, and there must be a designated responsible person. They don't ask for, for example, the course for commercial agents; there isn't even one. Or health certificates. (02ME_ASC)

While the services most frequently requested by foreign entrepreneurs continue to focus on training related to the activities they traditionally engage in, rather than on financial education, the importance of the latter appears to be recognized at the institutional level. For this reason, the Chamber of Commerce of Messina has recently introduced a dedicated service desk where all entrepreneurs—not only foreign ones—can access a proximity service providing guidance on new forms of business.

> So, we have services that we can offer which are innovative, in addition to the traditional ones provided by all Chambers of Commerce, and we have opened a service desk that is digital but also open three times a week. It is called 'SNI', the new entrepreneurship desk, which offers opportunities to anyone who wants to enter the world of entrepreneurship (. . .). Not only in terms of calls for proposals and funding, but also in terms of guidance and mentoring for entrepreneurial activity, all the way to the development of a business plan, and thus how to turn a business idea into an actual project. (03ME_CCA)

4 Navigating Training Planning

4.1 A "Stumbling Block" in the Fieldwork

The final part of the qualitative research focused on the training needs of foreign entrepreneurs. Before presenting an initial analysis of the results, it is useful to report a "stumbling block" (Merton & Barbour, 2008) encountered by the research team, which may offer some methodological insights relevant both for future research on the topic and for the planning of training interventions. As will be shown, the description of the process of engaging entrepreneurs highlights the need to address not only the content of training, but also its modes of delivery, as well as the spaces and timing in which it is provided.

The focus group, initially planned and partly organized, was ultimately transformed, out of necessity, into a series of individual interviews. Although at first it was considered both feasible and useful to organize a focus group, it proved impossible to engage entrepreneurs in either of the two cities. At the first signs of resistance, the research team attempted to adopt various coping strategies, but these did not yield any results.

Some constraints had already emerged from the analysis of the interviews and the ethnographic field notes. It became evident that foreign entrepreneurs are often directly involved in managing their own businesses; therefore, it was necessary to take into account that they worked both in the morning and in the afternoon and, in most cases, every day. This led to a key consideration: the individuals the research aimed to involve had very little time to devote to activities outside their daily work. The research team therefore reflected on scheduling, day of the week, and location.

Initially, the interviewers who had established direct contact with the entrepreneurs during the first phase of the research explored their availability, but without achieving sufficient convergence. An additional constraint concerned language. The pool from which participants could be selected was, in fact, narrower than originally anticipated. The need, in a focus group, to create a space for synchronous discussion in a setting outside the workplace also brought to light another previously identified limitation: language proficiency. For the focus group to function effectively, it would have been necessary to bring together entrepreneurs who were available on the same day and at the same time and who also had a sufficient command of the Italian language.

At an initial stage, it seemed possible to involve a larger number of participants in Catania, and it was therefore decided to organize the focus group in that city. The selected venue was centrally located and easily accessible to the entrepreneurs. It was also decided to offer a modest financial incentive, combined with reimbursement for travel expenses; indeed, some entrepreneurs from Messina had also expressed their willingness to travel to Catania.

Despite all these efforts, however, the focus group did not take place. In the end, the number of participants who had confirmed their attendance was too low (only two individuals). Consequently, it was decided not to attempt it again and instead to shift toward conducting semi-structured interviews with new entrepreneurs.

4.2 The Interviews

The thematic areas structuring the interview guide were the same as those initially designed for the focus group, but they were expanded and articulated differently. Following the analysis of previously collected data, it was decided to focus on the different stages of the business lifecycle and on some of the critical issues already identified. In addition, the interview guide was designed to elicit narratives of problematic experiences (Becker, 2007), in order to bring out coping strategies and to identify the actors (both individuals and institutions) involved in a situated manner and the roles they played. Furthermore, infographics were developed to support the comprehension of the questions.

Specifically, the interview guide addressed the start-up phase of the business, its development, the use of external funding (both public and private), and language-related issues. A total of eight interviews were conducted (with three men and five women) in Catania and Messina, and took place in person in October 2025. The participants came from diverse backgrounds: two women from Senegal, one from Sri Lanka, one from Romania, one from Palestine, one man from Albania, and two from Ghana. The interviewed entrepreneurs had already started their businesses and had therefore encountered, in their daily professional lives, the issues explored in the research.

For this reason, training was not conceived solely as instruction or education in entrepreneurship and "capacity building for entrepreneurship" (Costa, 2015, 587–588); rather, in line with the Futurae project (Ferrara & Noviello, 2025)—a significant collaboration between the Ministry of Labour and Unioncamere—entrepreneurs were considered as experts endowed with "contributory expertise" (Collins & Evans, 2015), capable of providing insights, based on their practical knowledge, into future needs and training demands.

For this reason, entrepreneurs were invited to reflect "aloud" on problematic situations they had encountered, on the decision-making processes used to address them, on the solutions adopted, and on possible areas for improvement grounded in their professional and social practices.

4.3 Preliminary Analysis

This analysis focuses on three thematic areas: language use, access to funding, and marketing practices.

Language use is a particularly relevant theme due to its pervasiveness and cross-cutting nature. The interviews clearly highlight two levels to be considered: the first concerns language as a communicative medium in interactions with customers and other social actors. One entrepreneur states, "studying to learn the language is essential for me, because an entrepreneur is in contact with the public" (21ME_IMP). The second level concerns language as knowledge and mastery of specialized, technical, and procedural terminology related to the regulatory framework in Italy: "If there are, of course, specific things that I do not understand, then I pass them on [meaning to the accountant or others who can understand them]" (15CT_IMP).

The issue of funding also emerges as a recurring theme throughout the lifecycle of the business. The responses suggest that initial financial support could be useful in the start-up phase, for instance, to cover rental costs. The choice of location becomes a strategic factor for business survival: "... I tried to find a place where I think there are people passing by" (16CT_IMP); and again: "... I have always tried to open in the center of Messina, where nightlife was and still is active" (19ME_IMP).

Moreover, the entrepreneurs interviewed emphasize that funding is also necessary to renew equipment, experiment with new materials, or continue purchasing materials of a certain quality: "funding for my business ... it is very small, I don't need much, but equipment, materials, also the IT part, computers. All of this is useful to me, it's a good thing" (22ME_IMP).

It is also highlighted that funding can be useful for expanding the customer base and promoting the business through digital technologies. In both cases—language and access to funding—relationships with professionals and informal networks of friends and family play a crucial role. In this regard, one entrepreneur states: "I was lucky once because a friend of mine found it and called me. But if she hadn't been there, I wouldn't even have known that this funding existed. I could have missed it, not applied, and that's what happened to many others" (22ME_IMP_). Another adds: "This year my accountant called me and said: 'Look, there is a funding call in Messina'" (20ME_IMP).

Finally, marketing activities are essential for promoting products and attracting new customers: "I created small flyers, shared them online, on Facebook, and circulated them" (18ME_IMP); and again: "we created a page, my husband took care of it on Facebook, without any cost, that is, for free" (15CT_IMP).

5 Discussion of the Results and Future Perspectives

The data analyzed provide, through the privileged perspective of the social actors involved in the phenomenon, an initial snapshot of migrant entrepreneurship in the metropolitan areas of Catania and Messina.

A preliminary analysis shows that foreign entrepreneurs carefully choose the economic activity they undertake, based on their training and experience, and devote most of their time to it. They tend to delegate to a specific professional figure—the accountant—all those activities and bureaucratic requirements that involve even a minimal level of technical expertise. With regard to the strategies adopted to cope with periods of crisis, it should be noted that entrepreneurs typically seek support from the individuals who constitute their network of "social capital." It has also been observed that only businesses organized in more complex legal forms and with consolidated experience over time are able to manage crises effectively, including through access to microcredit.

While the accountant represents a key point of reference for entrepreneurs in general, this role appears indispensable in the organized management of economic activity for migrant entrepreneurs, who face additional obstacles compared to native entrepreneurs.

Among the main difficulties encountered by migrant entrepreneurs are language barriers and the bureaucratic complexity of procedures and authorizations related to their business activities. These challenges are particularly evident in interactions with Chambers of Commerce and trade associations, whose services are often overlooked or avoided by migrant entrepreneurs.

In conclusion, some brief recommendations can be outlined in terms of planning training interventions. For those who have already started a business, it may be useful to provide content related to the use of new digital tools and social networks for promoting their activities and to create a physical and virtual bulletin board or platform for accessing and exchanging operational information, for example, on the costs of materials, equipment, and rental spaces. Such an environment could be conceived as a space for knowledge co-production (Nonaka et al., 2000). Likewise, it would be potentially useful to establish accessible spaces offering immediate guidance and support for accessing public calls and funding opportunities.

Acknowledgment Data analysis was carried out by the entire research team of the "BRIDGES" project. Thanks to Myriam Milici and Carmela Lo Presti. Sincere thanks also go to all the entrepreneurs and institutional representatives involved in the interviews.

References

Ambrosini, M. (2020). *Immigrazione irregolare e inclusione inattesa*. Il Mulino.

Arrighetti, A., & Traù, F. (2013). *Nuove strategie delle imprese italiane*. Donzelli.

Bagnasco, A. (1977). *Tre Italie: La problematica territoriale dello sviluppo italiano*. Il Mulino.

Beck, U. (2000). *The brave new world of work*. Polity Press.

Becker, H. (2007). *I trucchi del mestiere. Come fare ricerca sociale*. Il Mulino.

Bourdieu, P. (2001). Le forme del capitale. In L. Calabrò (Ed.), *Sociologia e cultura* (pp. 241–258). FrancoAngeli.

Ceschi, S. (Ed.). (2019). *Common Home, Migrazione e sviluppo in Italia*. Caritas Italiana.

Cicirello, L. (2012). L'economia degli imprenditori stranieri in provincia di Milano. *Geotema, 43–45*, 195–200.

Cieslik, J. (2015). Entrepreneurship in emerging economies: Enhancing its contribution to socio-economic development. *International Journal of Social Economics, 42*(4), 340–358.

Coleman, J. S. (2016). In E. Cattaneo (Ed.), *Il capitale sociale. Costruzione e uso*. Erickson.

Collins, H., & Evans, R. (2015). Expertise revisited, Part I—Interactional expertise. *Studies in History and Philosophy of Science Part A, 54*, 13–123.

Costa, M. (2015). Capacità all'imprenditorialità come leva per una migrazione inclusive. In M. Tomarchio, S. Ulivieri (Eds.), *Pedagogia militante, diritti, culture, territori* (pp. 578–589). Atti del 29° convegno nazionale SIPED.

Dheer, R. J. S. (2018). Entrepreneurship by immigrants: A review of existing literature and directions for future research. *International Entrepreneurship and Management Journal, 14*(3), 555–614. https://doi.org/10.1007/s11365-018-0506-7

Etemad, H. (2023). Migrant entrepreneurship in Europe: A systematic literature review. *Journal of International Entrepreneurship, 21*(1), 1–25. https://doi.org/10.1007/s10843-023-00317-

Fairlie, R. W., & Robb, A. M. (2008). *Race and entrepreneurial success*. The MIT Press.
Ferrara, M., & Noviello, G. (2025). Dal modello familiare all'impresa integrata: il ruolo del Progetto Futurae nell'imprenditoria immigrate. *Economia Aziendale Online, 16*(4), 1233–1249.
Fondazione Moressa. (2024). *Rapporto annuale 2024 sull'economia dell'immigrazione*. https://integrazionemigranti.gov.it/it-it/Ricerca-news/Dettaglio-news/id/4002/Dai-lavoratori-immigrati-l88%2D%2Ddel-PIL-italiano
Fortunato, M. W.-P., & Alter, T. R. (2015). Community entrepreneurship development: An introduction. *Community Development, 46*(5), 1–12. https://doi.org/10.1080/15575330.2015.1080742
Granovetter, M. (1985). Economic action and social structure: The problem of embeddedness. *American Journal of Sociology, 91*(3), 481–510. https://doi.org/10.1086/228311
Istat. (2024). *Condizioni di vita e reddito delle famiglie. Anni 2023-2024*. Roma.
Lasagni, A. (2025). *Rapporto Immigrazione e Imprenditoria 2024*. Edizioni Idos.
Merton, R. K., & Barber, E. G. (2008). *Viaggi e avventure della Serendipity*. Il Mulino.
Nonaka, I., Toyama, R., & Konno, N. (2000). SECI, Ba and leadership: A unified model of dynamic knowledge creation. *Long Range Planning, 33*(1), 5–34.
Putnam, R. D. (2004). *Capitale sociale e individualismo. Crisi e rinascita della cultura civica in America*. Il Mulino.
Ram, M., Jones, T., & Villares-Varela, M. (2017). Migrant entrepreneurship: Reflections on research and practice. *International Small Business Journal, 35*(1), 3–18.
Riss, C., & Groen, A. (2020). Migrant entrepreneurs and the role of embeddedness in entrepreneurial opportunities. *Journal of Small Business & Entrepreneurship, 32*(6), 585–603. https://doi.org/10.1080/08276331.2020.1804714
Sennett, R. (1998). *The corrosion of character: The personal consequences of work in the new capitalism*. W. W. Norton.
Standing, G. (2011). *The precariat: The new dangerous class*. Bloomsbury Academic.
Trigilia, C. (2002). *Sviluppo locale: Un progetto per l'Italia*. Laterza.
Unioncamere, InfoCamere. (2023). *Futurae. Programma imprese migranti. Report II Semstre 2023*. Accessed March 31, 2026, from https://www.integrazionemigranti.gov.it/AnteprimaPDF.aspx?id=6073
Williams, C. C., & Vorley, T. (2015). Institutional asymmetry: How formal and informal institutions affect entrepreneurship in Bulgaria. *International Small Business Journal, 33*(8), 840–861.
Wood, A. J., Graham, M., Lehdonvirta, V., & Hjorth, I. (2019). Good gig, bad gig: Autonomy and algorithmic control in the global gig economy. *Work, Employment and Society, 33*(1), 56–75.

Mapping Migrant Entrepreneurship and Integration in Italy: A Descriptive Analysis

Giulia Contu, Carla Massidda, Marco Ortu, and Silvio Tunis

Abstract This chapter analyses migrant entrepreneurship and migrant integration in Italy, examining their interaction across provinces between 2013 and 2022. Using an original dataset covering 102 provinces and 24 economic sectors, the study reconstructs the evolution, sectoral structure, and territorial distribution of foreign individual-owned firms (self-employment), alongside two composite integration indicators: the Social Integration Index and the Occupational Integration Index. Results show a steady growth of migrant entrepreneurship. Moreover, while integration indicators generally improve, particularly in labour market participation, structural differences persist across provinces. Multivariate analyses indicate that higher entrepreneurial intensity and sectoral diversification tend to be associated with stronger local integration outcomes.

1 Introduction

This chapter aims to provide a joint descriptive assessment of migrant entrepreneurship and migrant integration in Italy, highlighting how these two dimensions interact across territories.[1] The analysis is descriptive in scope and does not aim to identify

[1] The relationship between integration and immigrant entrepreneurship is gaining increasing international scholarly attention (Brzozowski, 2019; Massidda et al., 2024, 2026). Within this strand, the Mixed Embeddedness Theory (Kloosterman et al., 1999) has emerged as a key interpretative framework, highlighting the interplay between migrants' resources and local opportunity structures, and can be read in conjunction with other approaches such as Human Capital Theory

G. Contu · C. Massidda (✉) · M. Ortu
Department of Economics and Business Sciences, University of Cagliari, Cagliari, Italy
e-mail: giulia.contu@unica.it; massidda@unica.it; marco.ortu@unica.it

S. Tunis
Department of Economics and Business Administration, University of Cagliari, Cagliari, Italy

R. Cellini et al. (eds.), *Cultural, Social, and Political Participation in the Internet Era*, Contributions to Economics, https://doi.org/10.1007/978-3-032-33072-7_21

causal relationships between these dimensions, but rather to document patterns of co-evolution and territorial co-occurrence.

The analysis draws on an original provincial-level dataset developed by the IDOS Study Center, which harmonizes multiple administrative and statistical sources for 102 provinces and 24 economic sectors over the period 2013–2022. This dataset is structured around two complementary components: the first traces the evolution and structural characteristics of foreign entrepreneurship, measured through the number of both foreign firms and business owners; the second captures migrant integration through a composite framework of social and occupational indicators.

2 General Overview at the National Level

This section examines migrant entrepreneurship at the national level, focusing on migrant individual business owners (self-employed). The analysis adopts a multi-dimensional perspective, incorporating sectoral distribution, gender, and country of origin to provide a comprehensive overview of migrant entrepreneurial activity in Italy.

In 2022, a total of 6,019,276 companies were operating in Italy, of which 647,797 (nearly 11%) are classified as foreign firms.[2] Compared to just 10 years earlier (497,080), this number has increased by more than 30%. By contrast, Italian firms have experienced a persistent decline over the period. Out of a total of approximately 6 million firms, a little more than half (3,058,986) are individual business owners, of which 480,102 (about 15.7%) have foreign proprietorship. As with total firms, this number has been increasing since 2013 (400,587 at that time), despite the slight decline between 2021 and 2022. Conversely, Italian business owners have followed a persistent downward trend. As a consequence, the share of foreign owners among total owners has increased from about 12.26% to slightly under 16%, albeit with a generally declining growth rate. The smallest annual increase was recorded in 2022 (+0.87% compared to 2021), while the largest occurred in 2014 (+6.02% compared to 2013). This positive dynamic cannot be attributed solely to demographic growth in the immigrant population. Instead, it reflects rising entrepreneurial propensity among foreign residents, as evidenced by the growth in the share of self-employed individuals relative to the average number of employed foreign adults. Over the period from 2013 to 2022, this indicator has increased from 15.27% to 18.59%. The sharpest annual increase occurred in 2015, when the share rose by 1.14% from the previous year. By contrast, minor contractions are observed in 2017 (−0.04%)

(Becker, 1962), Blocked Mobility Theory (Kim et al., 1989), and (Segmented) Assimilation Theory (Gordon, 1964).

[2] Foreign firms and foreign business owners are defined in accordance with InfoCamere's classification.

and in 2019 (−0.29%). The latest available data for 2022 indicates a modest 0.33% increase over the previous year, suggesting gradual stabilization.

This overall pattern is further informed by examining key structural dimensions of migrant self-employment. From a gender perspective, the share of female foreign business owners among total foreign business owners has increased steadily over the considered period, rising from 22.68% in 2013 to 24.21% in 2022. Except for a temporary decline in 2020, the trend exhibits a largely consistent year-on-year increase, pointing to a gradual yet persistent expansion of female participation in foreign entrepreneurship in Italy.

A complementary perspective emerges when considering sectoral specialization. Foreign business owners are predominantly concentrated in Wholesale and Retail Trade, which accounts for 35.94% of entrepreneurial activity, followed by Construction (26.19%) and Manufacturing (7.43%). A broadly similar distribution characterizes Italian business owners, who also exhibit a strong concentration in Wholesale and Retail Trade, albeit at a lower share (26.98%), followed by Agriculture (22.93%) and Construction (12.99%).

Finally, heterogeneity in migrant entrepreneurship is evident by country of origin. The largest groups of foreign entrepreneurs originate from Morocco (12.44%), Romania (10.84%), and China (10.74%), followed by Albania (7.92%), Bangladesh (6.37%), Pakistan (4.29%), Egypt (4.14%), Nigeria (3.74%), Senegal (3.53%), and Switzerland (3.15%).

3 The Scenario at the Provincial Level

We now turn to the provincial-level analysis. To this end, we propose using maps that classify provinces into quartiles to illustrate the spatial distribution and facilitate a comparison of the provincial landscape between 2013 and 2022. The figures illustrate the situation in 2013 and 2022, along with the change observed between these 2 years.

3.1 Total Foreign Business Owners

Figure 1 shows that the number of foreign business owners increases in nearly all provinces between 2013 and 2022, with particularly notable growth in Napoli, Milano, and Roma. In general, major urban areas such as Roma, Milano, and Torino record the highest numbers of foreign business owners in both 2013 and 2022. By contrast, smaller southern provinces such as Oristano, Isernia, and Enna remain at the lower end of the distribution, despite experiencing modest growth over the period.

As the number of Italian business owners declines across all provinces between 2013 and 2022, the share of foreign business owners among total business owners

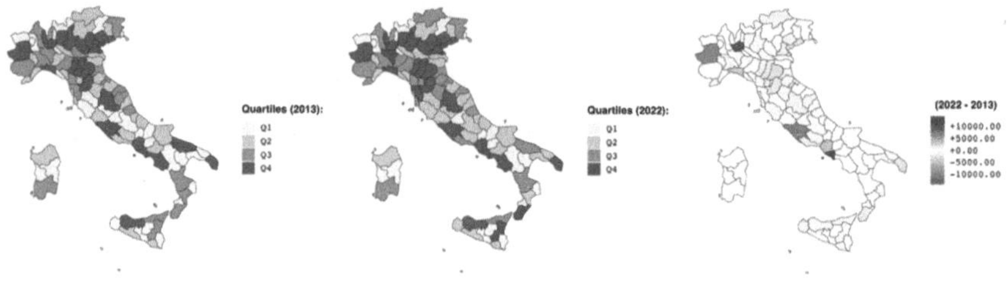

Fig. 1 Total foreign business owners. Source: Author's calculations based on IDOS Study Center data

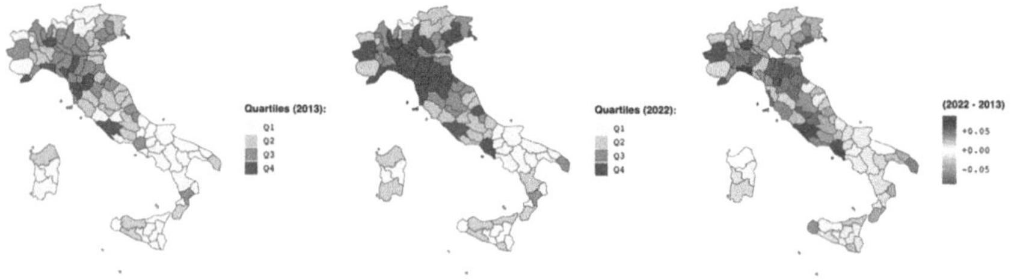

Fig. 2 Share of foreign business owners over total owners. Source: Author's calculations based on IDOS Study Center data

increases in almost all provinces during this period. As shown in Fig. 2, provinces such as Prato, Firenze, Milano, and Roma record the highest share in both years, while southern provinces, including Taranto, Potenza, and Oristano, remain at the bottom, despite modest overall increases.

Hence, as highlighted in the national overview, the provincial-level evidence further confirms a higher self-employment propensity of foreign nationals. This is confirmed by Fig. 3, which shows that, between 2013 and 2022, the share of foreign business owners relative to the average number of employed foreign adults increases in all provinces, with particularly strong growth in several southern provinces, including Napoli, Trapani, Caserta, and Lecce. Southern provinces such as Catanzaro, Caserta, and Lecce consistently display the highest values of this indicator in both 2013 and 2022, whereas northern provinces, including Bolzano, Trento, and Aosta, remain at the lower end of the distribution.

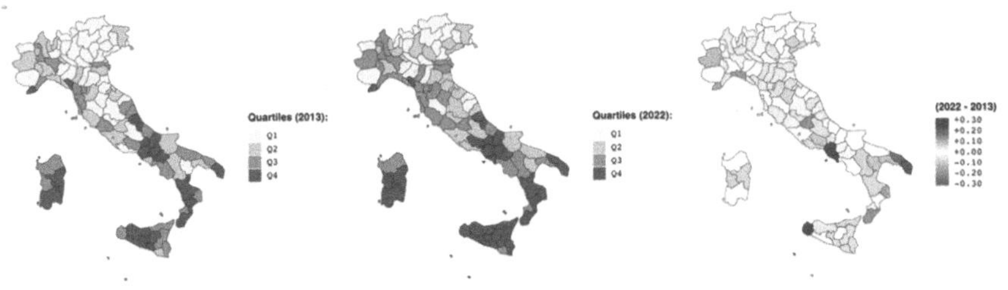

Fig. 3 Share of foreign business owners over foreign adults employed. Source: Author's calculations based on IDOS Study Center data

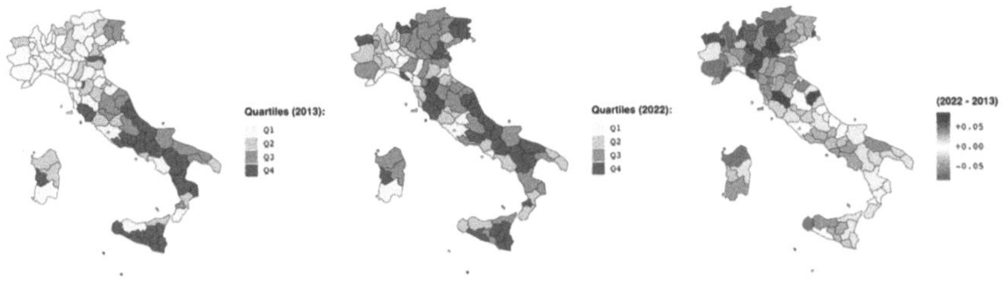

Fig. 4 Share of female foreign business owners over total foreign owners. Source: Author's calculations based on IDOS Study Center data

3.2 A Gender Perspective

Adopting a gender perspective reveals a distinctive pattern of change over time. Figure 4 shows that, between 2013 and 2022, the share of female foreign business owners relative to total foreign owners increases substantially in northern and several central provinces, while some southern provinces, such as Trapani and Napoli, experience the largest declines. Across the observed period, although the highest shares of female owners in 2022 remain concentrated in the South and Centre (e.g., Avellino, Benevento, and Potenza), some provinces, such as Enna and Napoli, decline in rank or record a reduction in their share. By contrast, several northern and central provinces, including Lodi and Prato, registered increases, reflecting the broader regional shift highlighted in the figure.

3.3 Owners by Sector and Country of Origin

Providing a concise provincial-level description of migrant firms by sector and country of origin for the entire period from 2013 to 2022 is challenging, given the volume of data involved. To address this complexity, we rely on the approach proposed by Bettin et al. (2026), which introduces two original indicators.

The first captures the degree of sectoral concentration among all foreign firms. To adapt this indicator to the scope of this chapter, we recalculate the sectoral concentration indicator only for migrant business owners (SEC_F_{it}) as follows:

$$SEC F_{it} = \sum_{s=1}^{S} (q f_{sit} * 100)^2$$

where $q f_{sit} = \frac{f_{sit}}{\sum_{s=1}^{S} f_{sit}}$ is the share of firm owners in sector s in the overall number of foreign owners in province i in year t, and S is the number of sectors. Notice that SEC_F_{it} is always positive and ranges from nearly 0 to 10,000: 0 is the minimum level of sectoral concentration, while 10,000 represents the maximum, namely the limit case of full concentration where a single sector captures all foreign business owners.

As highlighted by Bettin et al. (2026) for total foreign firms, we confirm here that the indicator calculated for only foreign business owners is higher in the South and the Islands. This reflects the more limited diversification of economic activities in these areas, where migrant entrepreneurship is often concentrated in a few traditional or lower-entry-barrier sectors, such as retail trade, construction, and hospitality. This pattern is consistent with broader structural characteristics of the Italian economy, in which southern regions typically have a narrower productive base and fewer opportunities for sectoral diversification than the Centre-North. Furthermore, Fig. 5 (Panel (a)) shows that SEC_F_{it} declines in nearly all provinces between 2013 and 2022, pointing to a broad shift towards greater diversification.

The second indicator proposed by Bettin et al. (2026) measures the extent of ethnic concentration among foreign business owners and is calculated as follows:

$$ETH F_{it} = \sum_{j=1}^{N} \left(q f_{jit} * 100\right)^2$$

where $q f_{jit} = \frac{f_{jit}}{\sum_{j=1}^{N} f_{jit}}$ is the share of firms established by foreigners of country j, in province i in year t, and N is the number of foreign nationalities in each province. In this case, as Bettin et al. (2026) argue, no clearly defined geographic pattern emerges. However, as shown in Fig. 5 (Panel (b)), ETH_F_{it} decreases in most provinces between 2013 and 2022, particularly in those in the South, indicating greater ethnic diversity. Changes are more pronounced in southern provinces.

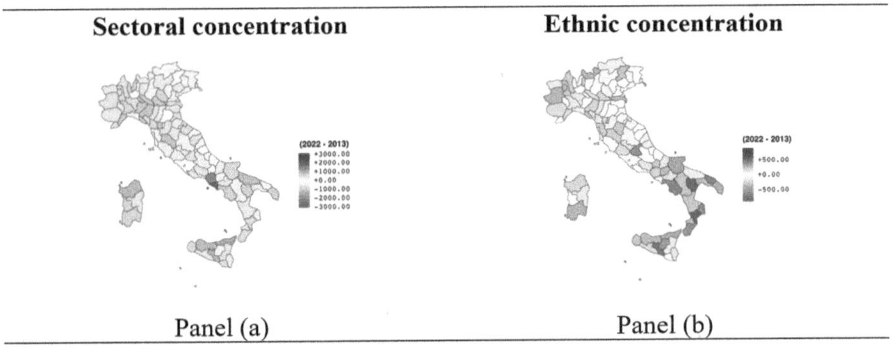

Fig. 5 Variations in sectoral and ethnic concentration. (**a**) Sectoral concentration; (**b**) Ethnic concentration. Source: Author's calculations based on IDOS Study Center data

The simultaneous decline in both sectoral and ethnic concentration among foreign business owners points to a progressive diversification of migrant self-employment at the provincial level. This pattern may reflect both within-province diversification, as existing groups expand into a wider range of activities, and compositional changes in the population of foreign entrepreneurs, including the entry of new national groups active in different sectors. While the present analysis does not allow us to disentangle these mechanisms, the joint reduction in the two indices is consistent with increasing heterogeneity in entrepreneurial profiles within provinces.

4 Migrant Integration in Italy at the Provincial Level

4.1 Conceptual Background

The analysis of integration dynamics is based on indicators developed by the IDOS Research Centre for the period 2013–2022. This framework builds on a research tradition that began in 2001, when IDOS started collaborating with CNEL (Consiglio Nazionale dell'Economia e del Lavoro) to produce reports on immigrant integration in Italy. Initially conceived as a regional Index of Territorial Integration, the framework evolved in 2006 into a provincial Composite Index of Immigrant Integration structured around two dimensions: social stability and labour market integration.

As outlined by Massidda (2026), In 2009, the index was revised and renamed Integration Potential Index (*IPI*), composed of two sub-indices: the Social Integration Index (*SII*) and the Occupational Integration Index (*OII*). This structure remained in use until the end of the IDOS–CNEL collaboration. In 2020, IDOS, in

IPI Integration Potential							
SII Social Integration Index				*OII* Occupational Integration Index			
IND_NAT	*IND_SS*	*IND_RAD*	*IND_IL*	*IND_CMO*	*IND_AIL*	*IND_PNUE*	*IND_IMP*
Naturalisation Indicator	*Stable Residence Indicator*	*Settlement Indicator*	*High School Enrolment Indicator*	*Labour Market Participation Indicator*	*Employment Intensity Indicator*	*Non-EU Labour Market Participation Indicator*	*Entrepreneurship Indicator*

Fig. 6 Outline of *IPI* composition (indices and indicators)

partnership with the NIHMP (National Institute for Health, Migration and Poverty), updated the indicators based on 2016 data (IDOS, 2020).

Over time, the composite index and its components experienced several methodological changes. Although the overall structure stabilized after 2009, the specific indicators continued to evolve, limiting strict intertemporal comparability.

To overcome this issue, IDOS developed a harmonized provincial time series for 2013–2022, based on the 2009 framework and incorporating selected updates from the latest revisions. This process resulted in a coherent composite *IPI* and its two sub-indices (namely *SII* and *OII*), each derived from four constituent elements, as illustrated in Fig. 6.

The following sub-sections outline the structure of these composite indices.

4.2 Social Integration Index

According to the IDOS definition (IDOS, 2020), the Social Integration Index (*SII*) "*measures the degree of accessibility, for foreigners, to certain domains that are essential for their non-subordinate social inclusion, as well as their level of integration within the social fabric through the attainment of specific legal statuses that guarantee and/or confirm a stable and mature integration into the host society*" (IDOS, 2020). Coherently with this definition, the *SII* comprises the following four indicators (definitions from IDOS, 2020):

IND_NAT: Average number of citizenship acquisitions per 1000 foreign residents (IDOS elaboration based on Istat data).

IND_SS: Percentage of long-term Non-EU residence permits relative to the total number of Non-EU valid residence permits (IDOS elaboration based on data from Istat and the Ministry of the Interior).

IND_RAD: Percentage of residence permits issued for family reasons relative to the total number of short-term residence permits (IDOS elaboration based on data from Istat and the Ministry of the Interior).

Table 1 *SII* by macro-area: 2013 vs 2022

Macroarea	2013	2022
North-East	100.0	100.0
North-West	72.6	94.5
Centre	40.3	80.1
Islands	14.0	79.1
South	1.0	1.0

Source: Author's calculations based on IDOS Study Center data

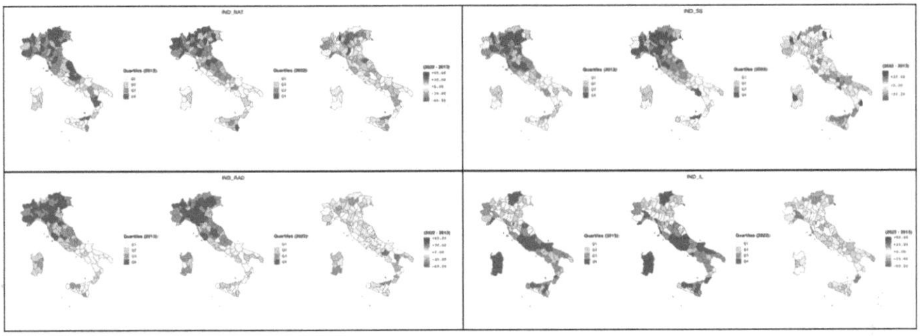

Fig. 7 The four indicators of *SII* (2013–2022). Source: Author's calculations based on IDOS Study Center data

IND_IL: Percentage of foreign students enrolled in academic upper-secondary schools (classical, scientific, linguistic, artistic, and socio-psycho-pedagogical tracks) out of the total number of foreign students enrolled in upper-secondary education (IDOS elaboration based on data from the Ministry of Education).

The evolution of *SII* over time is thoroughly documented in Bettin et al. (2026) and Massidda (2026). Drawing on their analysis, the highest index values are shown to cluster in central and northern provinces in both 2013 and 2022. Moreover, although some areas experience setbacks, the overall pattern emerging from these contributions indicates a general improvement of the *SII* across most of the country (cf. Table 1).

To gain a deeper understanding of the factors shaping the dynamics captured by the *SII* index, we examine the trajectories of the four standardized indicators that compose the index. Figure 7 shows that *IND_NAT*, *IND_SS*, and *IND_RAD* exhibit higher values in the central and northern provinces, whereas *IND_IL* records comparatively higher levels in the South and the Islands. Moreover, while *IND_SS* and *IND_IL* display predominantly positive changes over the period, the patterns associated with *IND_NAT* and *IND_RAD* are markedly more heterogeneous.

The deterioration of *IND_RAD* and *IND_NAT*, contrasted with the improvements in *IND_SS* and *IND_IL*, points to an asymmetry in integration pathways. On the one hand, the growth in long-term residence permits and enrolment in general high schools signals progress in structural integration, as migrants achieve greater legal stability and their children access educational tracks conducive to upward mobility. On the other hand, weaker performance in settlement and naturalization may reflect regulatory constraints or socio-economic barriers limiting family reunification and citizenship acquisition. This divergence suggests that while legal and educational inclusion is advancing, deeper forms of civic integration and long-term community anchoring remain more difficult to attain, revealing persistent structural bottlenecks.

4.3 Occupational Integration Index

According to the IDOS definition (IDOS, 2020), the Occupational Integration Index (*OII*) "*measures the degree and quality of immigrants' participation in the local labour market, taking into account both strictly quantitative factors and factors indicative of the nature and stability of immigrants' employment*" (IDOS, 2020). Coherently with this definition, *OII* is composed of the following four indicators:

IND_CMO: Percentage of foreign employed relative to the total foreign resident population (IDOS elaboration based on data from INPS and Istat).

IND_AIL: Average annual number of employed foreign workers relative to the total number of foreign-born workers employed during the year, multiplied by 100 (IDOS elaboration based on data from INPS).

IND_PNUE: Percentage of Non-EU nationals among the total foreign-born employed population during the year (IDOS elaboration based on data from INPS).

IND_IMP: Percentage of foreign entrepreneurs (owners) relative to the adult foreign resident population (IDOS elaboration based on data from Istat and InfoCamere/Fondazione G. Tagliacarne).

Analogously to *SII*, the evolution of *OII* over time is discussed in Bettin et al. (2026) and Massidda (2026). According to their overview, the provincial landscape has undergone notable shifts over the 2013–2022 period. In 2013, the highest values were observed in the North and on the Islands. By 2022, the index shows an upward trend in the Centre and in the North-West, as well as in the South. In contrast, a pattern of decline is observed in the North-East and in the Islands (cf. Table 2).

As above, to gain a deeper understanding of *OII* dynamics, Fig. 8 reports the trajectories of the four standardized indicators that compose the index. As shown, *IND_AIL* and *IND_PNUE* exhibit higher values in the Centre–North, whereas the other two indicators display a more dispersed spatial distribution.

Moreover, improvements in *IND_AIL* and *IND_PNUE* are more evident in several central and southern areas, though not uniformly. *IND_IMP* shows a broadly consistent upward trend nationwide, highlighting the growing role of migrant entrepreneurship, whereas *IND_CMO* follows a more irregular, territorially differentiated pattern. Overall, the evidence points to differentiated dynamics in labour market integration. Stronger improvements in *IND_AIL* and *IND_PNUE*

Table 2 *OII* by macro-area: 2013 vs 2022

Macroarea	2013	2022
North-East	100.0	87.6
North-West	95.7	100.0
Islands	82.4	1.0
Centre	52.8	61.1
South	1.0	34.2

Source: Author's calculations based on IDOS Study Center data

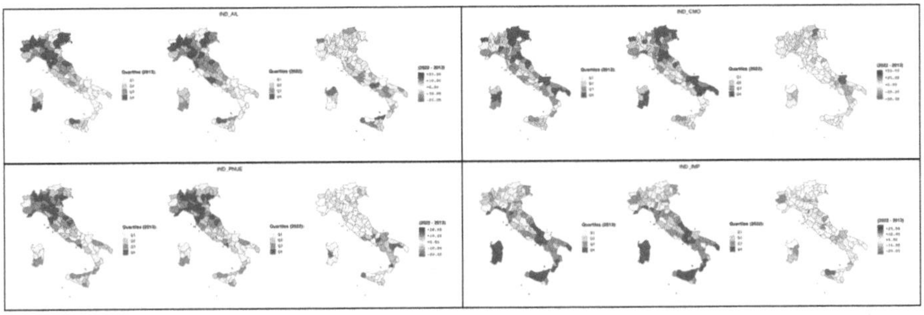

Fig. 8 The four indicators of O*II* (2013–2022)

in several central and southern provinces indicate rising employment intensity and greater participation of non-EU nationals, suggesting increasing stabilization of migrant employment. *IND_IMP* shows a consistent nationwide upward trend, confirming the expanding role of migrant entrepreneurship. By contrast, the mixed pattern of *IND_CMO* reflects labour market participation rates that remain sensitive to territorial and sectoral differences.

5 Entrepreneurship and Integration: A Combined View

To complement the previous descriptive evidence, this section develops a joint perspective on migrant entrepreneurship and migrant integration by combining the provincial distribution of foreign business owners by sector with the two synthetic indexes of integration, namely the *SII* and *OII*.

5.1 Cluster Analysis

The clustering approach is used to identify groups of provinces sharing similar combinations of migrant entrepreneurship and integration outcomes. Analytically, this allows moving beyond the isolated reading of single indicators and detecting broader territorial profiles in which entrepreneurial structure and integration conditions tend to co-occur. From a policy perspective, identifying these joint entrepreneurship–integration regimes helps distinguish contexts with different strengths and vulnerabilities, thereby providing a more informative basis for place-based, context-specific interventions.

The analysis relies on provincial-level information for 102 Italian provinces and 24 economic sectors over 2013–2022. For the entrepreneurship component, we compute time-averaged sectoral counts of foreign business owners for each province–sector pair to capture persistent structural characteristics rather than short-run fluctuations. *SII* and *OII* are considered at the provincial level over the same reference period and included as additional dimensions of the feature space. The resulting province-by-variable matrix (24 sectoral firm-count variables plus *SII* and *OII*) is standardized prior to analysis to ensure that differences reflect relative profiles rather than measurement scales.

Clustering is performed using k-means on standardized variables (Euclidean distance). A five-cluster solution (K=5) is selected as a parsimonious balance between within-cluster homogeneity and between-cluster separation (Rousseeuw, 1987), based on standard diagnostics (e.g., elbow and silhouette criteria). Since the full sample clustering (Fig. 9) is strongly influenced by three metropolitan outliers (Milano, Roma, and Torino), we therefore repeat the analysis after excluding these outliers.

The reduced-sample clustering again yields five clusters. This specification reveals a more internally differentiated structure among non-metropolitan provinces, with groups that differ systematically in entrepreneurial intensity and sectoral composition, as well as in their integration profiles, as captured by *SII* and *OII*. The cluster profiles suggest a gradient of economic organization and integration context.

Cluster 0 mainly includes southern and peripheral provinces with low foreign-owned firm density and a predominance of traditional activities, often paired with comparatively weaker integration scores. Cluster 1 corresponds to an intermediate and relatively diversified configuration, with mid-range *SII* and *OII*. Cluster 2 captures localized growth poles with comparatively stronger industrial and commercial intensity and more favourable occupational inclusion. Cluster 3 is represented by Napoli, which emerges as a distinct large urban economy within Southern Italy, with a specific combination of entrepreneurial scale and integration outcomes. Cluster 4 comprises larger northern and central cities with high entrepreneurial intensity and diversified productive structures, generally associated with higher *SII* and *OII*. Overall, the results indicate that heterogeneity is not solely determined by the largest metropolitan systems but also by meaningful structural differences in entrepreneurship and integration across the broader set of provinces.

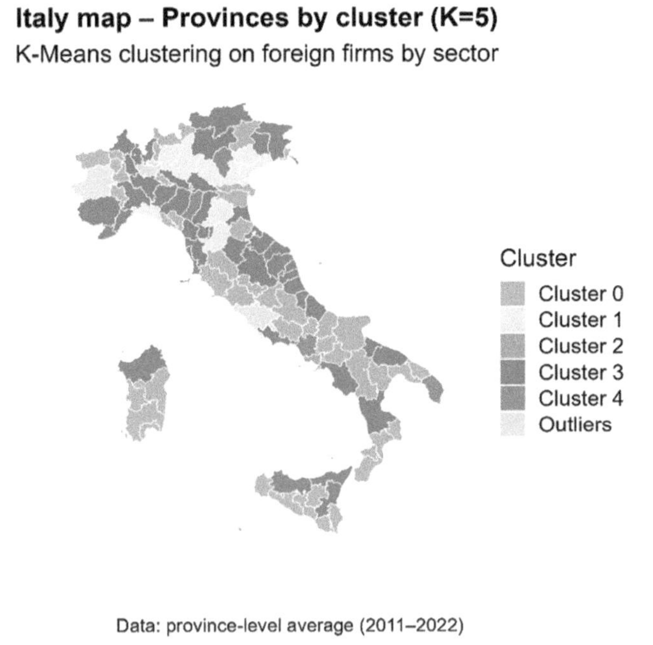

Fig. 9 Spatial distribution of clusters (full sample). Note: Data province-level average

5.2 *Principal Component Analysis*

We conduct a principal component analysis (PCA) as a complementary diagnostic to support the interpretation of the clustering results. PCA provides a low-dimensional representation of the standardized variables used for clustering (sectoral firm counts, SII, and OII) by transforming correlated variables into orthogonal components explaining most of the variance. Rather than replacing clustering, PCA helps visualize how clusters differentiate along the main latent dimensions and highlights which sectors and integration indicators contribute most to these gradients, offering an interpretable two-dimensional representation of provincial similarities.

5.2.1 Projection of Clusters on the First Two Principal Components

Figure 10 reports the provinces in the plane spanned by the first two principal components, with colours indicating the k-means partition. The first component (PC1, explaining 44.8% of the variance) summarizes the dominant gradient in the data and can be interpreted as a broad axis of entrepreneurial intensity and structural diversification: provinces located towards one side of the axis exhibit higher and

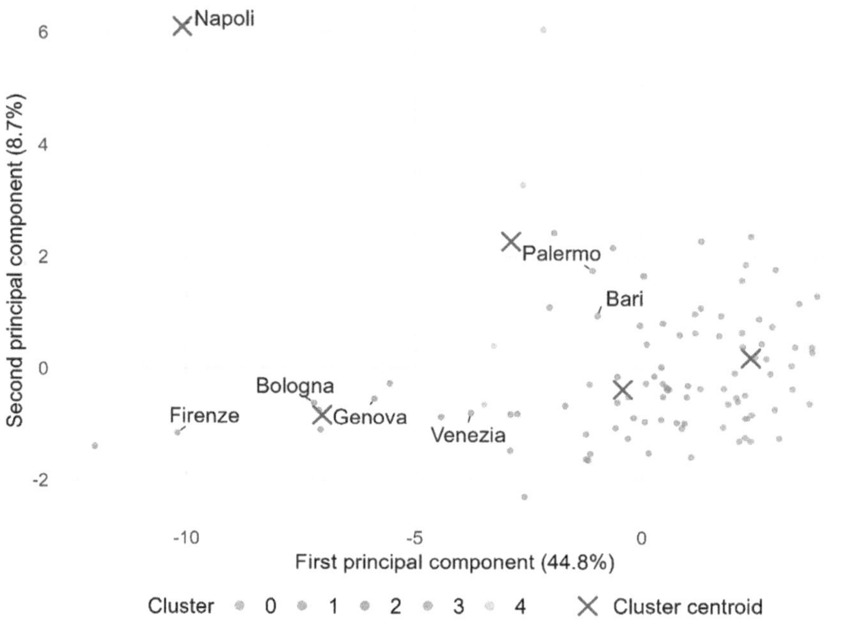

Fig. 10 PCA: projection of provinces on the first two components. Source: Author's calculations based on IDOS Study Center data

more widespread sectoral concentrations of foreign-owned firms, while provinces on the opposite side display lower firm density and a more limited sectoral presence. The sign of the axis is conventional in *PCA*; interpretation therefore concerns relative positioning along the component rather than "positive" versus "negative" values.

The second component (PC2; 8.7% of explained variance) captures a secondary contrast that is primarily compositional. In the reduced-sample setting (excluding the largest metropolitan outliers), the cloud of provinces in Fig. 10 becomes more dispersed, indicating that the representation is no longer dominated by pure scale effects. Several provinces emerge as reference points because they occupy extreme or distinctive positions in the *PC* space, consistent with their role as structurally salient territories within their macro-areas. Overall, Fig. 10 corroborates that the clusters reflect not only differences in the magnitude of migrant entrepreneurship but also meaningful variation in sectoral orientation coupled with systematic differences in *SII* and *OII*. This provides the appropriate bridge to the interpretation of the clustering map in terms of joint "entrepreneurship–integration" provincial regimes.

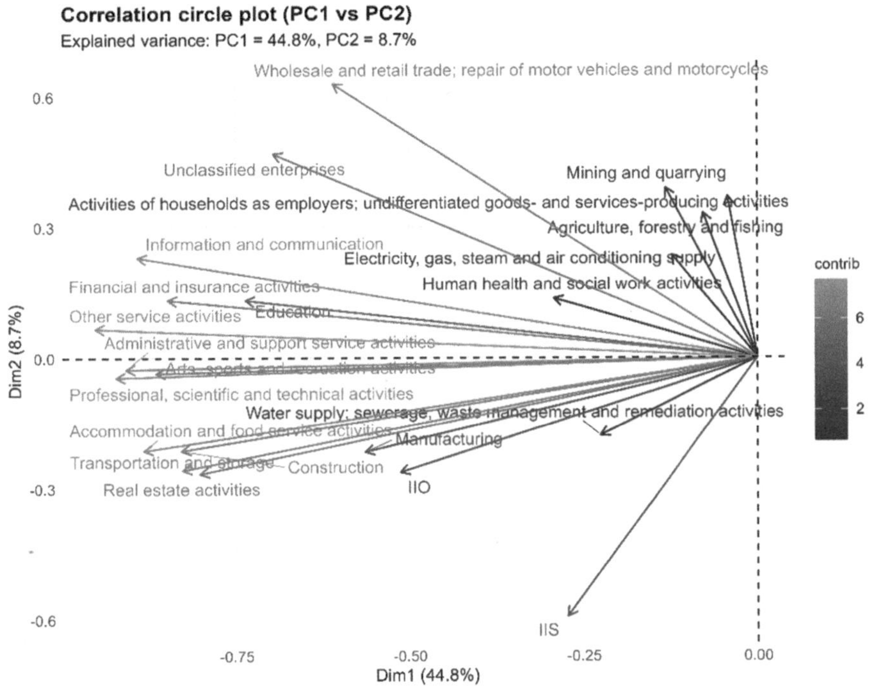

Fig. 11 Correlation circle plot for the first two principal components. Source: Author's calculations based on IDOS Study Center data

5.2.2 Correlation Circle and Interpretation of Loadings

To substantiate the interpretation of the *PCA* axes, Fig. 11 reports the correlation circle (also known as the variable factor map) for *PC1* and *PC2* (Husson et al., 2017). Each arrow corresponds to one original variable (sectoral firm counts, *SII*, *OII*). The arrow indicates the direction of increasing values of the variable in the *PC* space; the angle between two arrows approximates their correlation (small angles imply positive correlation; opposite directions imply negative correlation; near-orthogonality implies weak association). The arrow length reflects the quality of the variable's representation on the first two components (i.e., the magnitude of its correlations with *PC1* and *PC2*): longer arrows indicate variables that contribute more to the structure observed in the *PC1*–*PC2* plane.

Figure 11 shows that *PC1* is primarily driven by a broad set of sectors that act as markers of entrepreneurial intensity and diversification, most notably trade, construction, manufacturing, transport and storage, accommodation and food services, and real estate, whose arrows align along the main axis. In addition, *SII* and *OII* load on the same side of the first component, indicating that provinces with higher levels and broader sectoral articulation of foreign-owned firms tend to be associated with systematically different (typically higher) integration profiles in the reduced two-dimensional representation. *PC2* captures a more compositional contrast: variables related to traditional and resource-based activities (e.g., agriculture and extractive sectors) align on one side of the second axis, whereas several production- and service-oriented activities align on the opposite side, marking provinces characterized by a more urban, tertiary–industrial profile of migrant entrepreneurship. Within this dimension, the positions of *SII* and *OII* clarify whether the compositional shift is accompanied by differences in social versus occupational inclusion, helping interpret the separation of clusters in Fig. 10 as reflecting not only the intensity of entrepreneurship but also the type of sectoral specialization associated with the local integration context. This *PCA*-based reading strengthens the substantive interpretation of the clustering solution: clusters can be understood as groupings emerging from the joint configuration of sector-specific foreign-owned firm counts and the two integration indicators, rather than from entrepreneurship alone.

6 Conclusions

Over the period 2013–2022, migrant entrepreneurship in Italy has exhibited sustained and structurally significant growth, in clear contrast to the declining trend observed among Italian-owned firms. At the national level, both the number and the share of foreign-owned businesses increased steadily, reflecting not only demographic expansion but also a rising entrepreneurial propensity among foreign residents. This expansion has been accompanied by a gradual process of sectoral diversification and a decline in ethnic concentration, particularly in Southern provinces, although major metropolitan areas, such as Milano, Roma, and Napoli, remain key entrepreneurial hubs. From an integration perspective, both the social and the occupational dimensions show overall improvement, with labour market dynamics playing a particularly prominent role. Indicators related to employment intensity and entrepreneurship suggest that self-employment has become an increasingly stable and widespread channel of economic inclusion. At the same time, more heterogeneous trends in naturalization and family settlement highlight persistent barriers to deeper civic and long-term social integration. The joint cluster and *PCA* analyses reinforce the interpretation of entrepreneurship and integration as interconnected phenomena: provinces characterized by higher entrepreneurial intensity and broader sectoral diversification tend to display stronger integration profiles, revealing differentiated territorial regimes in which productive structure and integration processes evolve jointly. While these results point to systematic associations between the two dimensions, they should be interpreted with caution, as the analysis remains descriptive and does not establish causal relationships. Rather, the evidence provides a basis for future research aimed at identifying the underlying causal mechanisms.

Acknowledgement We thank Romano Piras and Anna Giulia Testa for their valuable and fruitful collaboration, and an anonymous Referee for helpful comments. The views and opinions expressed are solely those of the authors.

References

Bettin, G., Massidda, C., & Piras, R. (2026). *Foreign entrepreneurship and migrant integration: The role of ethnic and sectoral concentration in Italy*. Mimeo.

Becker, G. S. (1962). Investment in human capital: A theoretical analysis. *Journal of Political Economy, 70*(5, Part 2), 9–49.

Brzozowski, J. (2019). Entrepreneurship and economic integration of immigrants: A critical review of literature. *International Journal of Entrepreneurship and Innovation Management, 23*(6), 584–604.

Gordon, M. M. (1964). *Assimilation in American life: The role of race, religion, and national origins*. Oxford University Press.

Husson, F., Lê, S., & Pagès, J. (2017). *Exploratory multivariate analysis by example using R* (2nd ed.). Chapman and Hall/CRC.

IDOS. (2020). *Indici di inserimento sociale, occupazionale e sanitario degli immigrati in Italia. Il potenziale di integrazione dei contesti territoriali*. ISBN: 9788898544233.

Kim, K. C., Hurth, W. H., & Fernandez, M. (1989). Intra-group differences in business participation: Three Asian immigrant groups. *International Migration Review, 23*(1), 73–95.

Kloosterman, R., Van Der Leun, J., & Rath, J. (1999). Mixed embeddedness: (In)formal economic activities and immigrant businesses in the Netherlands. *International Journal of Urban and Regional Research, 23*(2), 252–266.

Massidda, C. (2026). *Social and occupational integration in migrant tourism entrepreneurship in Italy*. Mimeo.

Massidda, C., Piras, R., & Tunis, S. (2024). Migrant integration and Entrepreneurship: A systematic literature review through the lens of bibliometrics. *Rivista Internazionale di Scienze Sociali, 4*, 401–427. (First published online March 2025).

Massidda, C., Piras, R., & Tunis, S. (2026). Integration, ethnic concentration and migrant self-employment in EU countries. *REGION, 13*(1), 115–152.

Rousseeuw, P. J. (1987). Silhouettes: A graphical aid to the interpretation and validation of cluster analysis. *Journal of Computational and Applied Mathematics, 20*, 53–65.

FSC
www.fsc.org
MIX
Papier | Fördert gute Waldnutzung
FSC® C083411

Kolibri 360 GmbH
Ferdinand-Jühlke-Straße 7
99095 Erfurt, Deutschland
produktsicherheit@kolibri360.de